SELECTED POEMS OF ... SCHOOL,
WINTHROP MACKWORTH PRAED
AND THOMAS LOVELL BEDDOES

Selected Poems of

THOMAS HOOD,

WINTHROP MACKWORTH PRAED

and

THOMAS LOVELL BEDDOES

Edited by SUSAN J. WOLFSON
and PETER J. MANNING

UNIVERSITY OF PITTSBURGH PRESS

Published by the University of Pittsburgh Press, Pittsburgh, Pa. 15261

"A Lake" and "An Unfinished Draft" reproduced by the kind permission of the publishers Routledge & Kegan Paul © 1950, in *Plays and Poems of Thomas Lovell Beddoes*, ed. H. W. Donner.

Manufactured in the United States of America

Printed on acid-free paper

10 9 8 7 6 5 4 3 2 1

ISBN 0-8229-5760-4

CONTENTS

ACKNOWLEDGEMENTS   xi
TABLE OF DATES   xii
FURTHER READING   xxvi

THOMAS HOOD   1

PREFACE   3
*The Ballad of 'Sally Brown, and Ben the Carpenter' (Faithless
    Sally Brown)*   9
Fair Ines   11
Ode: Autumn   13
Sonnet. – Silence   15
Sonnet Written in Keats's Endymion   15
Sonnet: – Death   16
The Death-Bed   16
A Friendly *Epistle to Mrs Fry in Newgate*   17
Stanzas (I remember, I remember)   22
Autumn   23
Faithless Nelly Gray   23
The Last Man   26
Mary's Ghost   33
Ruth   35
Song (The stars are with the voyager)   35
Death in the Kitchen   36
The Dream of Eugene Aram, the Murderer   38
Domestic Asides; or, Truth in Parentheses   47
Ode to Mr Malthus   48
*Sally Simpkin's Lament; or, John Jones's
    Kit-Cat-Apostrophe*   52
A Waterloo Ballad   53
*A Parental Ode to My Son, Aged Three Years and Five
    Months*   56
I'm going to Bombay   58

*Ode To the Advocates for the Removal of Smithfield
        Market*   61
The Lament of Toby, the Learned Pig   64
Miss Kilmansegg and Her Precious Leg   67

HER PEDIGREE   67
HER BIRTH   69
HER CHRISTENING   75
HER CHILDHOOD   79
HER EDUCATION   81
HER ACCIDENT   85
HER PRECIOUS LEG   90
HER FAME   93
HER FIRST STEP   95
HER FANCY BALL   96
HER DREAM   105
HER COURTSHIP   110
HER MARRIAGE   114
HER HONEYMOON   122
HER MISERY   130
HER LAST WILL   134
HER DEATH   136
HER MORAL   140

Lear   141
The Song of the Shirt   141
The Workhouse Clock   144
The Bridge of Sighs   147
Stanzas (Farewell, Life!)   150

WINTHROP MACKWORTH PRAED   153

PREFACE   155
* * *
from *THE ETONIAN*   159
Laura   159
To Julia   166
The Bachelor   172
* * *
from *THE BRAZEN HEAD*   180
Chaunt I   180
Chaunt II   183

* * *

from *THE NEW MONTHLY MAGAZINE*   186
Time's Song   186
Good-Night to the Season   186
My Partner   190
The Fancy Ball   193
A Letter of Advice   197

* * *

Twenty-eight and Twenty-nine   201

* * *

from *LONDON MAGAZINE*   204
Arrivals at a Watering-Place   204
You'll Come to Our Ball (Our Ball)   208
School and Schoolfellows   211

* * *

from *THE CASKET*   214
Childhood and His Visitors   214
Beauty and Her Visitors   216

* * *

Anticipation   218
Lines Written for a Blank Page of 'The Keepsake'   219

* * *

from *THE LITERARY SOUVENIR*   221
The Legend of the Haunted Tree   221
Waterloo   235
The Belle of the Ball-Room, An Every-day Character   237
Stanzas Written in Lady Myrtle's Boccaccio   240

* * *

The Talented Man   243
One More Quadrille (The Last Quadrille)   245

* * *

from *THE MORNING POST*   247
Stanzas To the Speaker Asleep   247

THOMAS LOVELL BEDDOES   249

PREFACE   251
Alfarabi   257

* * *

from *THE IMPROVISATORE, in three Fyttes, with
    Other Poems* 262
To Night 262
To a Bunch of Grapes 262

*   *   *

THE BRIDES' TRAGEDY 264
    FROM ACT I.I: LINES, ' 'Twas on a fragrant bank I laid me
        down' with *Song* (Poor old pilgrim Misery) 264
    FROM ACT II.I with *Song* (A ho! A ho!) 266
    OPENING OF ACT III.II: Floribel's soliloquy, 'And must I
        wake again? Oh come to me' 268

*   *   *

from *THE ATHENAEUM* 269
Lines Written by the Author of 'The Bride's [sic] *Tragedy', in
    the blank-leaf of the 'Prometheus Unbound'* 269

*   *   *

fragments from *THE LAST MAN* 270
A Crocodile 270
Sweet to Die (*Death Sweet*) 270
Midnight Hymn 271
A Lake 271
Dream of Dying 271

*   *   *

from *OUTIDANA or effusions, amorous, pathetic and
    fantastical* 273
Lines Written at Geneva; July, 1824 273
A Dirge (To-day is a thought) 274
Sonnet: To Tartar, a Terrier Beauty 274
Pygmalion 275

*   *   *

fragment from *LOVE'S ARROW
    POISONED* 282
Humble Beginnings 282

*   *   *

from *TORRISMOND* 283
    FROM ACT I.III: Veronica's quatorzain (Come then, a song; a
        winding, gentle song) and *Song* (How many times do I
        love thee, dear?) 283
    FROM ACT I.IV (O father, father! must I have no father) 284

* * *

from *THE SECOND BROTHER*   285

FROM ACT I.I, with *Song* (Strew not earth with empty stars)   285

FROM ACT I.II, with *Song* (Will you sleep these dark hours, maiden)   286

FROM ACT II.I, a simile   286

* * *

songs from *DEATH'S JEST-BOOK*   287

OPENING OF ACT II.I: *Dirge* (If thou wilt ease thine heart)   287

FROM ACT III.III, with *Song by Isbrand* (Squats on a toad-stool under a tree)   288

FROM ACT IV.III, with *Songs* (We have bathed, where none have seen us; We have crowned thee queen of women; Lady, was it fair of thee; A cypress-bough, and a rose-wreath sweet)   290

FROM ACT V.IV, with *Songs* (My goblet's golden lips are dry; Old Adam, the carrion crow) and *Dirge* (We do lie beneath the grass)   294

* * *

Another Letter to the Same [Bryan Waller Procter]   297

The Ghosts' Moonshine   299

Lines written in the album of one who had watched the progress of the American and French revolutions   301

* * *

from *THE IVORY GATE*   303

Silenus in Proteus   303

Lord Alcohol   304

Dream-Pedlary   305

Love-in-Idleness   307

Dirge (Let dew the flowers fill)   308

An Unfinished Draft (A thousand buds are breaking)   309

Song of the Stygian Naiades   310

Thanatos to Kenelm   311

The Phantom-Wooer   312

Threnody (Far away)   313

* * *

songs and fragments from the revisions of *D E A T H ' S JEST-BOOK*   314

    FROM ACT I.I: *Song from the Ship* (To sea, to sea!)   314
    FROM ACT I.II: *A Beautiful Night*   315
    FROM ACT I.IV: *A Voice From the Waters* (The swallow leaves her nest); *A Subterranean City* (I followed once a fleet and mighty serpent)   316
    FROM ACT V.I: *The Slight and Degenerate Nature of Man* (Pitiful post-diluvians)   316

NOTES   317
INDEX OF TITLES AND FIRST LINES   382

ACKNOWLEDGEMENTS

The editors are grateful for the careful and encouraging supervision of Christopher Ricks, the resourceful and persevering research assistance of Andrew Krull of Princeton University, the savvy advice of Erik Gray of Princeton University, the assistance of the staff at the University's Firestone Library, the support for research and material expenses from the Princeton University Council on the Humanities, and the sharp-eyed review of Monica Schmoller.

TABLE OF DATES

Chronology of the poets' lives and writings, with contextual information about the social, historical and political events that affected them, as well as the literary culture of most relevance to their works as poets.

1798 *Lyrical Ballads* (anonymous; Wordsworth and Coleridge); Joanna Baillie, *Plays on the Passions*.

1799 Thomas Hood born in London. Thomas Forbes Kelsall (Beddoes's friend and, later, editor) born on a slave-owning plantation in the West Indies. Napoleon returns to France and becomes first consul.

1800 Second edition of *Lyrical Ballads* (volume signed by Wordsworth, with a new Preface). Union of England and Ireland.

1801 Thomas Moore, *Poems of Thomas Little*.

1802 Winthrop Mackworth Praed born in London. L.E.L. [Landon] born.

1803 Thomas Lovell Beddoes born at Clifton, Bristol; son of Anna Edgeworth (sister of novelist Maria Edgeworth) and Thomas Beddoes, a distinguished physician, friend of Coleridge, the Wordsworths and abolitionist Thomas Clarkson. Bulwer-Lytton born.

1804 Disraeli born.

1805 Scott, *Lay of the Last Minstrel*. Battle of Trafalgar; death of Nelson.

1806 Lady Morgan, *Wild Irish Girl*. William Pitt dies; Elizabeth Barrett born.

1807 Abolition of the slave trade. Wordsworth, *Poems, in Two Volumes*; Moore, *Irish Melodies*; Byron, *Hours of Idleness*.

1808 Death of Beddoes's father, Christmas Eve. Scott, *Marmion*.

1809 Byron, *English Bards and Scotch Reviewers*; Edgeworth, *Tales of Fashionable Life*. Tennyson, Poe, Edward FitzGerald and Charles Darwin born.

1810   Praed's mother dies; his eldest sister becomes a kind of foster-mother to him and his adored younger sister. Scott, *Lady of the Lake*.

1810–14 Praed at Langley Broom School, near Colnbrook, reading Plutarch and Shakespeare and becoming a good chess player.

1811   Hood's father and brother die; family in financial straits. Beddoes visits Ireland. P. B. Shelley and T. J. Hogg expelled from Oxford for *The Necessity of Atheism*. Prince of Wales becomes Regent, after George III deemed incompetent. Luddite riots against the weaving frames. National Society for the Education of the Poor founded. Austen, *Sense and Sensibility*. Thackeray born.

1812   Edgeworth, *The Absentee*; Byron, *Childe Harold's Pilgrimage* (Cantos I and II), an overnight sensation. Browning and Dickens born.

1813   Hood leaves school to work as a clerk in London to support his family. Byron, *Bride of Abydos* and *The Giaour*; Austen, *Pride and Prejudice*; Shelley, *Queen Mab*. Wordsworth gets a government patronage position; Napoleon defeated at Leipzig.

1814   Hood takes up engraving and publishes his first writings in the *Dundee Advertiser*. Beddoes's family moves to Bath, where he enters Bath Grammar School. Wordsworth, *The Excursion*; 10,000 copies of Byron's *Corsair* sell on the day of publication; Scott, *Waverley*; Austen, *Mansfield Park*. Napoleon abdicates.

1814–21 Praed at Eton (Shelley's school, 1804–10), where his poetry wins several prizes.

1815   Hood's health forces him to leave London for Dundee; begins the satirical rhymes of *The Dundee Guide*. Wordsworth's collected poems; 4-volume edition of Byron's poems. Napoleon escapes from Elba; battle of Waterloo; Napoleon exiled; restoration of the French monarchy. Corn Bill passed, with enormous benefits to landlords. Resumption of agitation for Parliamentary reform.

1816   Byron, *Childe Harold* (Canto III); Shelley, *Alastor*; Coleridge, *Christabel* and *Kubla Khan*; Austen, *Emma*. Byron leaves England amidst scandal. Elgin Marbles displayed; prosecution of William Hone (tried in 1817); Spa Field Riots. Charlotte Brontë born.

1817   Hood returns to London, apprenticed as engraver, eventually
        working on his own. Byron, *Manfred*; Moore, *Lalla Rookh*;
        Coleridge, *Biographia Literaria* and *Sibylline Leaves*; Keats's
        first volume, *Poems*. *Blackwood's Edinburgh Magazine*
        founded. Suspension of habeas corpus. Death of Austen;
        Princess Charlotte dies from complications in the birth of a
        stillborn child.

1817–20 Beddoes at Charterhouse school. Z.'s attacks on the 'Cock-
        ney School' in *Blackwood's*, targeting Hunt, Keats, and eventu-
        ally P. B. Shelley.

1818   Beddoes wins a prize for Latin essay and writes some fiction.
        Byron, *Childe Harold* (IV); Keats, *Endymion*; M. W. Shelley,
        Frankenstein. P. B. Shelley leaves England for ever. Emily
        Brontë born. European Alliance; habeas corpus restored in
        England.

1819   Beddoes's first publication, *The Comet*, in *The Morning Post*,
        6 July (signed 'E. D. Bodes'); writes *Alfarabi* and begins *The
        Improvisatore*. Praed's first publications appear in two Eton
        school periodicals. Hood, busy as an engraver in London,
        joins a literary society comprised chiefly of young ladies.
        Byron, *Don Juan* (Cantos I–II); P. B. Shelley, *The Cenci*;
        Scott, *Ivanhoe*. Reynolds's satire of Wordsworth's *Peter Bell*
        appears in advance of the poem itself. 'Peterloo Massacre' in
        August; Six Acts (abridging freedom of assembly, speech and
        print) passed in December. Birth of Queen Victoria.

1820   Praed founds and coedits *The Etonian*, a monthly from October
        to the next July, to which he contributes several poems, and
        joins debating society (generally taking the radical side on
        political issues). Beddoes wins prizes for Latin and Greek
        essays, travels to London, enters Pembroke College, Oxford
        in May. P. B. Shelley, *Prometheus Unbound and Other Poems*;
        Clare, *Poems Descriptive of Rural Life*; Hazlitt, *Lectures on the
        Dramatic Literature of the Age of Elizabeth*; Keats's last lifetime
        volume, *Lamia &c*. *London Magazine* and *John Bull* founded.
        Death of George III; accession of George IV; Queen Caroline
        tried for adultery. Dissolution of Parliament; Cato Street
        conspiracy. Royalist reactions throughout Europe; revolutions
        in Spain and Portugal.

1820–22 Lamb, *Essays of Elia* in *London Magazine*.

1820–23 Beddoes at Oxford. He is reading Praed's *Etonian* poems (Kelsall's Memoir, p. xxxix).

1821 The first editor of *London Magazine*, John Scott, waging a war of words with *Blackwood's* over its relentless abuse of the 'Cockneys' (Hazlitt, Hunt and Keats), sufficiently insults one of *Blackwood's* most acerbic writers, John Lockhart, to provoke a duel, which takes place in February, with Lockhart's deputy killing Scott. Hood joins *London Magazine* in the summer, and becomes a 'sort of sub-editor' (until 1823) and contributes 'Lion's Head' column, as well as poems, beginning in July with *To Hope* and in November *Ode to Dr Kitchener*. His mother dies, and he is left with the care of his four sisters. In the *London Magazine* circle he meets John Hamilton Reynolds (friend of Keats and soon to be Hood's brother-in-law), Lamb, De Quincey, Clare, Hazlitt, Bryan Waller Procter ('Barry Cornwall') and Allan Cunningham. Praed enters Trinity College Cambridge (Byron's college, 1805–7); continues to earn prizes for poetry not only in English (*Athens*, *Australasia*) but also in Greek (odes and epigrams), and reads classics with Macaulay. His first year at Oxford, Beddoes publishes *The Improvisatore*. Byron, *Don Juan* (III–V) and *Cain*; De Quincey, *Confessions of an English Opium Eater* (in *London Magazine*); Pierce Egan, *Life in London*; Procter, *Mirandola, A Tragedy*; Reynolds, *The Garden of Florence*; P. B. Shelley, *Epipsychidion* and *Adonais*. Keats and Napoleon die.

1822 Hood engaged to Reynolds's sister, Jane. Praed helps Charles Knight launch *Knight's Quarterly Magazine* and is a chief contributor. Learning of Shelley's death, he remarks, 'I have no reason to lament his death in any point of view' (Hudson, *A Poet in Parliament*, p. 76). Beddoes writes lines in praise of Shelley in a blank leaf of *Prometheus Unbound*; *The Brides' Tragedy* published in November. *The Poetical Works of Barry Cornwall*. Suicide of Castlereagh; Robert Peel becomes Home Secretary.

1823 Hood leaves *London Magazine*. Praed publishes *Australasia*. Enthusiastic reviews of *The Brides' Tragedy*, one by 'Barry Cornwall'; Beddoes publishes *The Romance of the Lilly* in *The Album*, meets Kelsall, spends the summer with him in Southampton, where he begins *The Second Brother*, *Love's*

Arrow Poisoned, *The Last Man* and *Torrismond*. He, Kelsall and Nicholas Waller Procter (Bryan's brother) sponsor the publication of 250 copies of Shelley's *Posthumous Poems*, John Hunt assuming the cost of another 250. Lamb, *Essays of Elia*; Campbell, *The Last Man*; Byron, *Don Juan* (VI–XIV); English translation of Grimms' *Tales*. Rudolph Ackermann introduces the gift-book annual, *Forget Me Not*. Jeremy Bentham and James Mill found *The Westminster Review*, a forum for philosophical radicals.

1824   Praed nearly fights a duel with a fellow student over the date of the Battle of Bunker's Hill (it was in 1775). Beddoes in London, 'turning over old plays in the Brit: Museum'; he reads Hood's 'Fairy Tale' in Spenserian stanzas, *The Two Swans*, in *New Monthly* (February), returns briefly to Oxford for exams, interrupting them to leave for Florence to see his dying mother, but, having stopped first in Milan and Paris, arrives too late; in Italy he meets W. S. Landor; continues with the plays; spends time in Bristol and London, where he visits Mary Shelley, a widow living in semi-seclusion. Beddoes is 'a very great admirer of our S.', she tells Leigh Hunt. *Posthumous Poems of Percy Bysshe Shelley* published and suppressed immediately by Shelley's father. Byron, *Don Juan* (XV–XVI); L.E.L., *The Improvisatrice*; the gift-book/annual craze begins with Alaric Watts's *The Literary Souvenir*. Death of Byron.

1825   Hood marries Jane Reynolds and with J. H. Reynolds publishes *Odes and Addresses to Great People* – a commercial success, three editions within a year. Praed graduates BA from Cambridge. Beddoes is chiefly in London, where he meets 'Political Justice' (Godwin, M. Shelley's father), Darley, and Procter who becomes a close friend; returns to Oxford in May to complete his BA; writes *Pygmalion* and begins *Death's Jest-Book*; publishes his translation of Schiller's *Philosophic Letters* in *Oxford Quarterly Magazine*; suddenly deciding on a career in medicine, he gives Kelsall all his MSS, and leaves England in June, matriculates at Göttingen University in July (staying until 1829); by December he knows he will never resume life in England. Panic in the financial markets. Founding of London University.

1825–7 Praed tutoring at Eton, a situation, Beddoes sneers to
Kelsall, that 'has chagrined all his poetical friends exceedingly'
(Donner, *Complete Works*, p. 601).

1825–9 Beddoes in Göttingen, studying medicine.

1826 Hood becomes drama critic of the *Atlas* and publishes his
poem *The Last Man* and *Whims and Oddities*, the latter volume,
an immediate success; *Blackwood's* (1827) quotes the Preface
and praises the designs as much as the poetry; Hood is 'a
most admirable fellow . . . with a warm heart – a sound head
– a disposition amiable and facetious'. Praed edits *The Brazen
Head*, a short-lived weekly paper, and begins to contribute to
The New Monthly Magazine (edited by Thomas Campbell);
he tries unsuccessfully for a Trinity Fellowship at Cambridge.
Beddoes finishes *Death's Jest-Book* 'in the rough'. M. W.
Shelley's novel, *The Last Man*. End of Lord Liverpool's
ministry. Smith and Elder introduce *Friendship's Offering*,
another gift-book annual, in which Hood will publish.

1827 Hood's daughter (his first child) dies, commemorated by
Charles Lamb's *On an Infant Dying as soon as Born*. Hood
publishes second series of *Whims and Oddities*, dedicated to
Scott (a great success), *The Plea of the Midsummer Fairies
. . . and Other Poems* and *National Tales* (the last two not
successful). Praed leaves Eton when he is elected as fellow of
Trinity College, Cambridge, and he begins to contribute to
such fashionable gift-book annuals as *The Literary Souvenir*
and *Friendship's Offering*; after Canning's death he is unsettled
by the reformers' democratic tendencies, and his politics
become more conservative. Beddoes decides to assimilate the
fragments of his unfinished play, *The Last Man*, into *Death's
Jest-Book*. Death of Blake; Scott acknowledges authorship of
Waverley novels; De Quincey, *On Murder Considered as One
of the Fine Arts* (*Blackwood's*); Poe, *Tamerlane*; Tennyson (and
two of his brothers), *Poems by Two Brothers*.

1828 Hood in Brighton, recovering from a severe attack of rheumatic
fever; edits *The Gem* (a Christmas annual), in which he pub-
lishes, and gets Lamb and Scott, among others, to contribute
to. Praed enters society, attends balls, the theatre, joins the
Athenaeum Club and continues to read law; he tours northern
Europe in the summer and dines with Wordsworth and S. T.

Coleridge at Antwerp. Beddoes visits England in the spring
to take his MA at Oxford, and again in the summer; returns
to Göttingen, receives his MD and completes *Death's Jest-
Book*; Procter gets Leigh Hunt to publish his 'Letter from
Cassel' (unsigned) in *The Companion* (April). *The Athenaeum*
and *The Spectator* founded; University College opens in
London. Society for the Diffusion of Useful Knowledge
founded.

1829 Hood publishes *Eugene Aram* (in *The Gem*) and *The Epping
Hunt*, with illustrations by Cruikshank; becomes one of the
proprietors of *The Athenaeum*; is pressed by his creditors.
Praed called to the Bar, 29 May. Beddoes sends *Death's
Jest-Book* to Procter, who, unable to interest any publisher,
urges substantial revisions; deeply depressed, Beddoes
attempts suicide, then indulges in a bout of heavy drinking
and extravagant behaviour and is dismissed from Göttingen;
moves to Würzburg and matriculates at the university (there
until 1833). *London Magazine* ceases publication. Poe's *Al
Aaraaf* and *Tamerlane and Other Poems*. Catholic Emanci-
pation Act (full civil and political rights for Roman Catholics)
passes with reluctant support from Wellington and Peel;
Praed, a Whig until this year, always favoured the measure,
and its passage enabled his alignment with the Tories.

1830 Hood publishes *Comic Melodies*, begins *Comic Annual*; daugh-
ter Frances born. Praed pays £1000 for a two-year seat in
Parliament and enters as a Conservative; earning a reputation
as a skilled debater and businessman, he is returned in 1830 and
1831; he tends his beloved elder sister, dying of consumption.
Beddoes writes *Dream-Pedlary*. Macaulay (Praed's Cambridge
classmate) enters Parliament as a Whig. Reform agitation;
death of George IV and accession of William IV; collapse of
Wellington's ministry. July Revolution in France; Charles X
deposed. Death of Hazlitt. Tennyson, *Poems, Chiefly Lyrical*;
Byron's Letters and Journals, with Life by Thomas Moore;
Cobbett, *Rural Rides*; Lyell's *Principles of Geology*.

1830–42 Hood edits *Comic Annual* and contributes most of the
literary pieces.

1831 Hood publishes *The Dream of Eugene Aram* with designs by
W. Harvey, and ends his connection with *The Athenaeum*.

Beddoes receives MD, joins the student political organization Germania Burschenschaft (dedicated to the unification of Germany under a constitutional monarchy), writes political articles for *Volksblatt* supporting the Reform Bill, attacking the English aristocracy and praising Brougham. First Reform Bill; dissolution of Parliament; general election; second Reform Bill rejected by the House of Lords; Bristol riots; 'Captain Swing' farmworkers' riots; final Reform Bill introduced. Praed opposes the Bill in speeches in the House of Commons and with political verses in the conservative newspapers, especially *The Morning Post*.

1831–3 Cholera epidemic in Europe and England.

1832 Hood moves to a country house in Essex, the maintenance of which he cannot afford. William IV pledges to create sixty new peers (Whig Lords) to secure passage of the Reform Bill; following reforms in districts of representation, Praed loses election to Parliament and returns to legal practice; his contributions to *The Morning Post* over the next two years help establish it as the leading conservative newspaper. Procter places two poems by Beddoes in *The Athenaeum*. Beddoes's political activities get him deported from Würzburg; he flees to Strasburg. Tennyson, *Poems* ['1833']; Lamb, *Last Essays of Elia*; Bulwer-Lytton, *Eugene Aram*; P. B. Shelley, *Mask of Anarchy*. Deaths of Crabbe, Scott and Goethe.

1832–40 Beddoes flees Germany for Switzerland, where he practises medicine.

1833 Hood, in financial straits and poor health, writes his three-volume novel *Tylney Hall*. In *The Morning Post* Praed defends Wellington (with materials furnished by him) from attacks in *The Times*, and publishes anonymously 'Trash dedicated without respect to James Halse, esq., MP', his rival in 1832. Impressed by his pieces in the *Post*, John Murray, publisher of the leading conservative review *The Quarterly*, asks Praed for contributions. Kelsall is unsuccessful in his attempt to get *Blackwood's* to publish the first scene of Beddoes's *The Second Brother*. Beddoes in Zurich, matriculates at the university in July; Kelsall places his poem on Shelley in *The Athenaeum*. Browning, *Pauline*; Carlyle, *Sartor Resartus*. Abolition of colonial slavery.

1833–5 Dickens's *Sketches by Boz*, the first serialized in the *Monthly Magazine*.

1834 With the dismissal of the Whig ministry and new elections, Praed returned to Parliament and appointed Secretary to the Board of Control in Peel's administration (1834–5). Hood publishes *Tylney Hall*, suffers serious financial losses after a break with his publisher of several years (Charles Tilt) and the failure of an engraving firm with which he was associated; Cunningham's *History of British Literature*, with notice of Hood, published. Hood deeply saddened by Lamb's death; death of Coleridge. Poor Law Amendment Act, ending subsidies, and forcing husbands, wives and children into separate workhouses.

1835 Hood's son Tom born and wife Jane nearly dies; financial crises; he leaves for Germany to avoid creditors, live more economically and work to pay off his debts. Praed's father dies; he marries Helen Bogle (the 'Helen' of his poems), wealthy daughter of a West Indian sugar-merchant, with whom he has two daughters; collects his political verses for private circulation. *Metropolitan Magazine* abusively rejects Kelsall's submission of the scene from Beddoes's *Second Brother*; Beddoes's nomination for chair of anatomy at the University of Zurich is refused by the board of education because of his political activities and lack of medical publications; visits Brussels; returns to England for a brief visit. Browning, *Paracelsus*.

1836–7 Dickens ('Boz'), *The Pickwick Papers*. Flu epidemic sweeps London in the winter.

1836 In poor health, Hood is frequently bedridden for long periods of time; he supports Talfourd's efforts to reform copyright law with a series of letters to *The Athenaeum*, 'Copyright and Copywrong'. Praed falls ill with influenza on Christmas Day.

1837 Hood moves to Ostend, Belgium, where his health worsens (spitting blood); publishes pieces in *The Athenaeum* including his satire on hypocrisy, *Ode to Rae Wilson, Esquire*. Praed returned to Parliament; appointed Deputy High Steward of Cambridge University; spends time revising his verse-tales, but his health is poor. Beddoes plans a volume of prose and poetry to be called *The Ivory Gate*. Carlyle, *The French Revolution*. Accession of Queen Victoria in June.

1837–9 Dickens, *Oliver Twist*.

1838 *Hood's Own; or, Laughter from Year to Year*, a monthly, appears and is a success. Praed, insulted by Bulwer-Lytton's taunts in the House of Commons, challenges him to a duel, but it is aborted; with Eton school friend Derwent Coleridge and others, he develops a proposal for educating working-class children; stricken with tuberculosis, his health worsens. In Zurich, Beddoes rents a theatre and plays Hotspur in *1 Henry IV*. Anti-Corn Law League founded.

1839 Hood visits England, staying with Charles Dilke, friend of Keats and editor of *The Athenaeum*. Praed returns to Parliament in February, visits Cambridge in May, dies on 15 July, at the age of thirty-seven. In Zurich, 8 September, a mob of 6000 peasants, instigated by conservatives, forces the resignation of the Radical government in which Beddoes had many friends; a close friend is murdered in the riot. Dickens, *Nicholas Nickleby*. Chartist riots after Parliament rejects petition.

1840 Hood returns to London, publishes his autobiographical *Up the Rhine* (first edition of 1500 sells out in two weeks) but the income is tied up in litigation with his publisher; reviews Dickens's *Master Humphrey's Clock*. Hood's *Miss Kilmansegg and Her Precious Leg* (serially in *New Monthly*) is a great success. Kelsall attempts unsuccessfully to interest John Wilson (*Blackwood's* 'Christopher North' and Professor of Moral Philosophy at the University of Edinburgh) in Beddoes's work. Beddoes flees Zurich in April, and lectures on drama at the Polytechnic Institution in London in June; travels to Berlin and enters the university in July. Thackeray, *Paris Sketch Book*; Dickens, *The Old Curiosity Shop* and *Barnaby Rudge*; Poe, *Tales*; Browning, *Sordello*. Queen Victoria marries her first cousin, Prince Albert of Saxe-Coburg-Gotha.

1841 *Punch* founded. Hood gets a grant from the Royal Literary Fund. Beddoes is in Berlin, attending lectures at the university.

1841–3 Hood continues to write for and edits *New Monthly*.

1841–9 Beddoes wandering through Germany, England and Switzerland.

1842 Hood's *Miss Kilmansegg* republished in *Comic Annual* with illustrations by John Leech; his friendship with Dickens begins. Beddoes in Berlin; visits London. Tennyson, *Poems*. Ashley's Act outlaws women and children in the mines; Chartist riots.

1842–59 Thackeray on the staff of *Punch*.

1843 Hood quarrels with the publisher of *New Monthly* and resigns as editor. Inspired by a report in *The Times* in October, his *The Song of the Shirt*, about the horrible oppression of female seamstresses, is published unsigned in the Christmas issue of *Punch*, an immediate sensation; also publishes *Whimsicalities: A Periodical Gathering, With Illustrations by Leech* (dated 1844). Beddoes in Baden en Suisse, returns to Zurich. Wordsworth succeeds Southey as Poet Laureate. Dickens, *A Christmas Carol*. Factory safety regulations; second cholera epidemic.

1844 Beddoes in Zurich, Baden, Basle, Strasburg, Mannheim, Frankfurt, Giessen, Berlin; publishes anti-Jesuit poems in the *Republikaner*, 'Lines written in Switzerland', and revises some of *Death's Jest-Book*. Hood has a severe attack of influenza. Founds *Hood's Magazine and Comic Miscellany*, priced 2 shillings and 6 pence, promising contributions from Browning and Dickens, ' "Mirth for the Millions", and light thoughts, to a Public sorely oppressed', and no 'Politics' – the last promise soon belied by *The Workhouse Clock* (April) and *The Bridge of Sighs* (May), the last, inspired by another story in *The Times*, winning great praise. November: On the petitioning of his friends, Hood receives a civil pension from Prime Minister Peel, an admirer of his writings; onset of his last illness. The first edition of Praed's poems, edited by R. W. Griswold, published in New York. Factory Act. Death of Thomas Campbell.

1844–5 Confined to his room, Hood continues to edit '*Mag*', which fails to turn a profit.

1845 1 March, readers of '*Mag*' are informed of Hood's 'dangerous illness': 'his physical strength has completely given way'; on 1 April 'of his approaching death'. 3 May: death of Hood, age forty-six, in Hampstead. Beddoes at Frankfurt, Zurich, and Baden, where he is fined for disturbing the peace with too much noise in his hotel room. Dickens, *Hard Times*. Irish famine.

1846   Death of Jane Hood; Hood's 2-volume *Poems* published. Beddoes at Frankfurt; returns to England for the last time, visits London; spends ten months chiefly in eccentric reclusion, visiting relatives. Thackeray, *Book of Snobs*; Lear, *A Book of Nonsense*. Corn Laws repealed. Civil war in Switzerland.

1847   Beddoes in England, sees Kelsall for the first time in twenty years; arrested in May for trying to set fire to Drury Lane Theatre; returns to Frankfurt in June, living until spring 1848 with a handsome nineteen-year-old man, Degen, a baker and would-be actor; during an autopsy, he cuts himself and becomes poisoned by a virus. Hood, *Poems of Wit and Humour*. C. Brontë, *Jane Eyre*; Tennyson, *The Princess*.

1848   May–June, Beddoes and Degen leave Frankfurt and tour Germany and Switzerland; they break up in July. Beddoes attempts suicide by slashing an artery in his leg, is admitted to a hospital and tended by Dr Frey, a friend from earlier days; the wound does not heal and the leg has to be amputated below the knee. Degen returns; Beddoes makes his will. Revolutions in western Europe; second French Republic. Emily Brontë, *Wuthering Heights*; Thackeray, *Vanity Fair*.

1849   January 26: Beddoes commits suicide in Basel, bequeathing his manuscripts to Kelsall. Arnold, *The Strayed Reveller*. Deaths of Maria Edgeworth and Poe.

1850   500 copies of Beddoes's *Death's Jest-Book, or The Fool's Tragedy*, edited by Kelsall, published anonymously; small sales but favourable reviews. Wordsworth's death. *The Prelude* published; Tennyson publishes *In Memoriam* and becomes Poet Laureate; Dickens, *David Copperfield* and the weekly journal *Household Words*; Browning, *Poems*.

1851   *Poems of Thomas Lovell Beddoes*, edited with a memoir by Kelsall (a rebinding of the remaindered *Death's Jest-Book* with *The Brides' Tragedy* comprise vol. 2); slow sales, but again favourable reviews, as well as the admiration of Tennyson (noted in Gosse, *Poetical Works*, Introduction, p. xxxv) and the Brownings (Robert and Elizabeth Barrett).

1854   Monument erected in Hood's memory, with a eulogy by

Richard Monckton Milnes (editor and author of Keats's *Life, Letters, and Literary Remains*, 1848). At Hood's request, the engraving beneath his bust reads 'He sang the Song of the Shirt'.

1855   Beddoes's remaindered 1851 *Poems* sold at auction; Beddoes is out of print until 1890.

1860   *Memorials of Thomas Hood* (by his son Tom and daughter Frances).

1861   *Fairy Land: By the late Thomas and Jane Hood, their Son and Daughter*.

1862   *The Works of Thomas Hood, Comic and Serious*, ed. Thomas Hood, jun.

1863   Helen Praed dies.

1864   The authorized edition of Praed's *Poems*, edited by Derwent Coleridge.

1867   Procter arranges for Kelsall to meet Browning, an admirer of Beddoes.

1868   May: Browning writes an enthusiastic letter to Kelsall about *Death's Jest-Book*.

1869   Kelsall decides to bequeath at his death all the 'Beddoes MSS, & papers' to Browning.

1872   Kelsall publishes a substantial essay on Beddoes in *Fortnightly Review* (a 'dying throw for Beddoes') that proves instrumental in renewing interest.

1873   Mrs Kelsall tells Browning about Beddoes's suicide. Receiving Kelsall's papers in a tin box, Browning fears what he would discover and does not open it for ten years.

1877   Procter's brief memoir of Beddoes appears in *An Autobiographical Fragment*.

1883   Browning invites Edmund Gosse to read the contents of 'that dismal Box' with him.

1885   Gosse writes an article on Beddoes for the *Dictionary of National Biography*.

1886   Dykes Campbell meticulously transcribes the Beddoes MSS in Browning's possession.

1888   *Political and Occasional Poems of Winthrop Mackworth Praed*, edited by Sir George Young.

1889   At Browning's death, the 'Box' documents are transferred to his eldest son Pen, with many of them lost in the confusion following his own sudden death in Italy; Campbell's transcriptions thus become the only MSS sources for most of the works.

1890   Gosse's edition of *The Poetical Works of Thomas Lovell Beddoes*.

1894   Gosse's edition of *The Letters of Thomas Lovell Beddoes*.

1896   Gosse republishes his 1890 'Memoir' in *Critical Kit-Kats*, drawing more readers to Beddoes.

FURTHER READING

HOOD

Editions

The Works of Thomas Hood, Comic and Serious, in Prose and Verse, edited with notes by his son, Thomas Hood jun. (7 vols., 1862; 10-volume edition with illustrations, London: Moxon, 1869–73); edited by his son and daughter, Frances Freeling Broderip (11 vols., 1882–4).

W. M. Rossetti (ed.), *The Poetical Works*, illustrated by G. Doré (London: Moxon, 1871–5). The Preface concludes, famously, by pronouncing Hood 'the finest English poet between the generation of Shelley and the generation of Tennyson' (p. xxxi).

Walter Jerrold (ed. with notes), *The Complete Poetical Works of Thomas Hood* (London: Oxford University Press, 1906).

John Clubbe (ed. with notes), *Selected Poems of Thomas Hood* (Cambridge: Harvard University Press, 1970). Numerous illustrations for the poems, by Hood and others; generous notes.

Letters and Biography

Memorials of Thomas Hood: Collected, Arranged, and Edited by his Daughter [Frances]: *With a Preface and Notes by his Son* [Thomas] (2 vols.; London: Moxon, 1860). Includes some anecdotes and much correspondence.

John Clubbe, *Victorian Forerunner: The Later Career of Hood* (Durham, NC: Duke University Press, 1968). The best critical study.

W. Jerrold, *Thomas Hood: His Life and Times* (New York: John Lane, 1909). The first standard biography, with letters and reminiscences.

Leslie Marchand (ed.), *Letters of Thomas Hood from the Dilke Papers in the British Museum* (New Brunswick, NJ: Rutgers University Press, 1945). Sixteen letters (mostly from Germany) and some miscellaneous poetry and prose.

Peter F. Morgan (ed.), *The Letters of Thomas Hood* (Toronto: University of Toronto Press, 1973). The standard edition.

John C. Reid, *Thomas Hood* (London: Routledge & Kegan Paul, 1963).

Criticism

Laurence Brander, *Thomas Hood* (London: Longmans, Green, 1963). Surveys life and works.

J. M. Cohen, 'Hood: The Language of Poetry', *Times Literary Supplement* (19 September 1952), pp. 605–6.

Roger B. Henkle, 'Comedy as Commodity: Thomas Hood's Poetry of Class Desire', *Victorian Poetry* 26 (Autumn 1988), pp. 301–18.

D. L. Hobman, 'Thomas Hood', *Contemporary Review* 187 (June 1955), pp. 397–401.

William Henry Hudson, 'Thomas Hood: the Man, the Wit, and the Poet', *A Quiet Corner in a Library* (Chicago: Rand McNally, 1915).

David Masson, 'Thomas Hood', *Macmillan's Magazine* (August 1860), pp. 315–24.

Paul Elmore More, *Shelburne Essays* (7th series, 1910). An appreciation of Hood's puns.

William Makepeace Thackeray, 'On a Joke I once heard from the late Thomas Hood', *Roundabout Papers* (1863; reprinted in *The Works of William Makepeace Thackeray*, 12 vols., 1878; X.66–75). An affectionate appreciation.

John Wilson, 'Hood's Whims and Oddities', *Blackwood's Edinburgh Magazine* 21 (January 1827), pp. 45–60. An influential enthusiastic appreciation.

'Hood: The Poet Behind the Jester's Mask', *Times Literary Supplement* (5 May 1945), p. 210.

PRAED

Editions

Derwent Coleridge (ed.), *Poems*, the 'authorized' edition, with the assistance of Praed's sister and nephew (2 volumes in one, 1864; reprinted in New York, 1885). A selection, omitting most of the later political poetry; marred by silent editorial emendations, substantive as well as accidental.

George Young (ed.), *Political and Occasional Poems* (London, 1888). Includes publications in *The Morning Chronicle* and *The Times* up to 1831, and *The Morning Post*, 1832–4; dates and original publication carefully established; some silent emendations, mostly of accidentals. The Introduction gives a careful account of Praed's shift from the radical political sympathies of his Eton days to his affiliation with the Tories in the Reform era; it also identifies a number of poems wrongly attributed to Praed in other editions.

Kenneth Allott (ed.), *Selected Poems of Winthrop Mackworth Praed* (Cambridge, Mass., Harvard University Press, 1953). Annotated, but also with silent emendations, mostly of accidentals.

Biography and Criticism

H. G. Hewlett, 'Poets of Society', *Contemporary Review* 20 (1872), pp. 238–68.

Derek Hudson, *A Poet in Parliament: A Life of Winthrop Mackworth Praed* (London: John Murray, 1939).

George Sainsbury, *Essays in English Literature, 1780–1860* (London: Percival, 1890).

BEDDOES

Editions

The Brides' Tragedy (London: Rivington, 1822); facsimile reprint with an Introduction by Jonathan Wordsworth (Banbury: Woodstock Books, 1993).

Thomas Forbes Kelsall (ed.), *The Poems, Posthumous and Collected, of Thomas Lovell Beddoes* (2 vols.; London: William Pickering, 1851). The Memoir by Kelsall includes the first publication of many of Beddoes's lively, wry, engaging letters.

Edmund Gosse (ed.), *The Poetical Works of Thomas Lovell Beddoes* (2 vols.; London: Dent, 1890). The Memoir by Gosse reveals Beddoes's suicide; includes poems not collected in 1851.

Edmund Gosse (ed.), *The Letters of Thomas Lovell Beddoes* (London: Elkin Mathews and John Lane, 1894).

Ramsay Colles (ed.), *The Poems of Thomas Lovell Beddoes* (London: George Routledge & Sons, 1906).

Edmund Gosse (ed.), *The Complete Works of Thomas Lovell Beddoes* (2 vols.; London: Franfrolico Press, 1928). A handsome limited edition; includes letters.

F. L. Lucas (ed.), *Thomas Lovell Beddoes: An Anthology* (Cambridge: Cambridge University Press, 1932). Includes letters.

H. W. Donner (ed.), *The Browning Box: Or, the Life and Works of Thomas Lovell Beddoes as Reflected in Letters by His Friends and Admirers* (Oxford: Oxford University Press, 1935). Especially interesting are Charles Bevan's recollections of Beddoes as a student at Charterhouse and Oxford, letters relevant to Kelsall's persistent though mostly unsuccessful efforts in the 1830s and 40s to interest publishers in Beddoes's work, and his later correspondence with Robert Browning, 'an enthusiastic admirer'.

H. W. Donner (ed.), *The Complete Works of Thomas Lovell Beddoes* (Oxford: Oxford University Press, 1935). The standard modern text; an exhaustively scholarly edition, including Beddoes's letters and political essays, with notes, detailed discussion of MSS and a comprehensive bibliography (including reviews) up to 1935.

H. W. Donner (ed.), *Plays and Poems of Thomas Lovell Beddoes* (London: Routledge & Kegan Paul, 1950). Includes a sampler of critical comments, and the first presentation of the 'early' (1824–8) version of *Death's Jest-Book* in its integrity.

Judith Higgins and Michael Bradshaw (eds), *Thomas Lovell Beddoes, Selected Poems* (Manchester: Carcanet Press, 1999).

Biography and Criticism (in addition to the Prefaces and Memoirs in the editions)

John Ashbery, 'Thomas Beddoes', *Poets on Poetry*, (eds.) Nick Rennison and Michael Schmidt (Manchester: Carcanet Press, 1997), pp. 10–11.

Harold Bloom, 'Thomas Lovell Beddoes: Dance of Death', *The Visionary Company: A Reading of English Romantic Poetry* (second edition; Ithaca, NY: Cornell University Press, 1971), pp. 439–44.

Fredrick Burwick, 'Death's Fool: Beddoes and Büchner', *The Haunted Eye: Perception and the Grotesque in English and German Romanticism* (Heidelberg: Carl Winter Universitäts-verlag, 1987), pp. 274–300.

Douglas Bush, 'Thomas Lovell Beddoes', *Mythology and the Romantic Tradition in English Poetry* (New York: W. W. Norton, 1963), pp. 192–6. Mostly on *Pygmalion*.

Louis O. Coxe, 'Beddoes: The Mask of Parody', *Hudson Review* 6 (1953), pp. 252–65. On the tone of 'mockery and excess' in *Death's Jest-Book*.

H. W. Donner, *Thomas Lovell Beddoes: The Making of a Poet* (Oxford: Basil Blackwell, 1935). Biography, scholarship and criticism.

Northrop Frye, 'Yorick: The Romantic Macabre', *A Study of English Romanticism* (Chicago: University of Chicago Press, 1968), pp. 51–85. On *Death's Jest-Book*.

Marilyn Gaull, 'Thomas Lovell Beddoes', *English Romanticism, The Human Context* (New York: W. W. Norton, 1988), pp. 105–8. Includes comments on *Death's Jest-Book*.

John Heath-Stubbs, 'The Defeat of Romanticism', *The Darkling Plain: A Study of the Later Fortunes of Romanticism in English Poetry from George Darley to W. B. Yeats* (London: Eyre & Spottiswoode, 1950), pp. 37–48. With comments on Beddoes's grotesques.

Ezra Pound, 'Beddoes and Chronology', *The Future* (September 1913); reprinted in *Selected Prose, 1909–1965*, (ed.) William Cookson (New York: New Directions, 1973), pp. 378–83.

Alan Richardson, '*Death's Jest-Book*: "Shadows of Words"', *A Mental Theater: Poetic Drama and Consciousness in the Romantic*

Age (Philadelphia: University of Pennsylvania Press, 1988), pp. 154–73. On the poetics of 'mental theater'.

Christopher Ricks, 'Thomas Lovell Beddoes: "A dying start"', *The Force of Poetry* (Oxford: Oxford University Press, 1984), pp. 135–62. Close readings of conceptual forces and their poetic effects.

Royall H. Snow, *Thomas Lovell Beddoes: Eccentric and Poet* (New York: Covici & Friede, 1928). In a biography contextualized with political events on the Continent, Snow questions the suicide; attention to the tone of the poems.

Lytton Strachey, 'The Last Elizabethan', *The New Quarterly* (1907); reprinted in *Books and Characters: French and English* (New York: Harcourt, Brace, 1922), pp. 237–65. The oft-repeated and influential categorization.

Arthur Symons, 'Thomas Lovell Beddoes', *The Academy* (1891); reprinted in *Figures of Several Centuries* (London: Constable, 1916), pp. 123–9. A representative appreciation of Beddoes's 'essentially lyrical' genius.

James R. Thompson, *Thomas Lovell Beddoes* (Boston: Twayne, 1985). Concise biography, with assessments of Beddoes's poetics in Romantic contexts and mid-twentieth-century critical theory.

Eleanor Wilner, *Gathering the Winds: Visionary Imagination and Radical Transformation of Self and Society* (Baltimore: Johns Hopkins University Press, 1975), pp. 73–106. Psychological tensions and existential contradictions, with an extended discussion of *Death's Jest-Book*.

SELECTED POEMS OF THOMAS HOOD,
WINTHROP MACKWORTH PRAED
AND THOMAS LOVELL BEDDOES

THOMAS HOOD

1799–1845

Thomas Hood was born in London. The writer of much satirical and humorous verse, he worked throughout his life on journals and magazines, at first as a sub-editor, critic and occasional writer, and later as an editor, founder and primary contributor. Many of his poems were first published in these publications, which included the *London Magazine*, *Punch* and *Hood's Magazine*. Though he became a successful and well-known journalistic and literary figure, Hood was plagued by financial trouble; in 1835 he left England for Germany in an attempt to avoid his creditors. He returned in 1840, and in 1844 received a civil pension. His health had been fragile for some time and he died the following year.

Hood displayed his ingenuity and unpredictable imagination through outrageous punning and grotesquerie; notable among his works are *The Dream of Eugene Aram* (1831), *The Song of the Shirt* (1843) and *The Bridge of Sighs* (1844). He also published a novel, *Tylney Hall* (1834), autobiographical writings and other prose.

PREFACE

Thomas Hood's fame as the leading English comic poet of the 1830s and 40s was not predicted by his first ventures, a poetry of belated Keatsian romanticism, with homages to Keats's recognizable genres, subjects and themes. But even in this phase, Hood was discovering a talent for comic ballads punctuated by outrageous puns and wordplay. The punning that would become his hallmark presses forward in the midst of early romantic devotions. One of the most controversial events sounds near the end of a long *Ode to Melancholy* (1827):

> Even the bright extremes of joy
> Bring on conclusions of disgust,
> Like the sweet blossoms of the May,
> Whose fragrance ends in must. (113–16)

Depending on temperament, critics may admire the extra senses of *May* and *must* or express disgust at the tonal rupture – the random grammatical jest of punning nouns into verbs as a way of enforcing the grimly deterministic wit. Whatever the judgement, it is clear that Hood's imagination would work more and more through, and often discover itself in, the twists and turns of such wordplay.

As the occasion of *Melancholy* suggests, Hood's wit is frequently animated by a sense of the inevitability and the pervasiveness of death. Most of his immediate family had died of consumption by the time he was twenty-one, and throughout his life his health was at best precarious, frequently quite poor. (His son Tom later said that as a boy he thought one of the advantages of being an adult was that one could spit blood.) Living longer than most consumptives in his day, Hood died just before his forty-seventh birthday. Across his first poems the shadow of death falls with a melancholy intensity, and his comic verse is typically sharpened by a vivid imagination of death and a mordant wit about its ghastly events. His cartoon illustrations for his verses (which we regret this edition cannot supply) are rendered in a similar spirit. Not just embellishments, they are often perverse textual supplements and visual puns.[1]

Thackeray gives a telling portrait. He recalled seeing Hood 'once as a young man, at a dinner . . . I quite remember his pale face; he was thin and deaf, and very silent; he scarcely opened his lips during the dinner, and he made one pun'.[2] That a pun is the sole issue of this near death-in-life aptly indicates a body of work that might, as much as Beddoes's, be called 'Death's Jest-Book'. Though other fine poets are (in)famous punsters (Shakespeare) and other fine punsters are sometimes poets (Lear, Carroll, Gilbert), Hood's imagination is distinct in its devotion to the impulse, especially its morbid events. The word becomes double, splitting in two, often as the poetry describes a body dismembered, becoming a dispensable or marketable inventory of parts ('a cannon-ball took off his legs,/ So he laid down his arms!'). A 'pun', Hood remarks in an 'Address' that he added to the second edition of *Whims and Oddities* (1827), 'is an accommodating word, like a farmer's horse, – with a pillion for an extra sense to ride behind; – it will carry single, however, if required. The Dennises are merely a sect, and I had no design to please, exclusively, those verbal Unitarians' (x); (neoclassical critic John Dennis had objected to Pope's punning). In the Preface to the second series of *Whims and Oddities* (1827) he elaborated his defence, with an implicit apology for an admittedly acquired taste: a pun 'is somewhat like a cherry: though there may be a slight outward indication of partition – of duplicity of meaning – yet no gentleman need make two bites at it against his own pleasure'. But he was not about to recall the offer: 'A double meaning shows double sense,' he insists (*Miss Kilmansegg and Her Precious Leg*). Deploying such verbal shifts and densities, Hood's comic verse often treats his early romantic themes to farce or morbid humour or, as in his epic extravaganza *Miss Kilmansegg*, infuses potentially serious subjects with mocking jeremiad.

Such effects may jar critical sensibility, even one as receptive to wordplay as William Empson's. 'It is difficult to see why a man like Hood, who wrote with energy when he was roused, should have produced so much verse of a trivial and undirected verbal ingenuity,' he complains regretfully, explaining that he says 'trivial', because

Hood 'uses puns to back away from the echoes and implications of words, to distract your attention by insisting on his ingenuity so that you can escape from sinking into meaning'.[3] Poe, for whom *Fair Ines* and *The Bridge of Sighs* mark Hood's highest achievement, hated the sinking into puns: 'they leave upon us a painful impression; for evidently they are the hypochondriac's struggle at mirth – the grinnings of the death's head.' The 'peculiar genius . . . of vivid *Fancy* impelled by Hypochondriasis' was betrayed by puns, Poe insisted, for Hood's 'true province was a very rare and ethereal *humor*, in which the mere pun was left out of sight, or took the character of the richest *grotesquerie*; impressing the imaginative reader with remarkable force, as if by a new phase of the ideal'.[4] Poe's concession to puns of '*glowing* grotesquerie' means to define a categorical difference, but for Hood it was all connected. It is utterly characteristic of the man who believed 'I have to be a lively Hood for a livelihood' that his poignant deathbed stanzas, *Farewell, Life!* – with their delicate and dramatic shift of the referent of 'Life' from this world to the next – are matched in the lore of Hood's deathbed by a remark to a friend that he was dying really 'to please the undertaker, who wished to urn a lively Hood'.[5] G. K. Chesterton grasped the other end of the stick with more sympathy: 'The tragic necessity of puns tautened and hardened Hood's genius.'[6]

As Chesterton recognizes, Hood's motivation for punning arose from the same sensibility that could abandon puns to tune a music of haunting moods, whether of supernatural possession, elegy or social anger. Hood 'was deeply engaged in pleading the case, in comedy and pathos, for the victimized lower classes, the seamstresses, displaced craftsmen, and the impoverished, over whom the fast-rising Victorian economy was running roughshod'.[7] Towards the end of his career he was writing influential poems of passion and protest on behalf of these socially oppressed classes. 'When he laid down his puns and pranks, put the motley off, and spoke out of his heart, all England and America listened with tears and wonder!' said Thackeray.[8] Hood evoked these tears with subjects already in the public domain, ripe for his sharp voicing. His inspirations, indeed motivations, came from newspaper accounts and actual events: *The Dream of Eugene Aram* (1829) draws on a famous historical anecdote, and the powerful protest poems of the 1840s – *The Song of the Shirt*,

The Lay of the Labourer, *The Workhouse Clock* – were sparked by reports of workers' plights in *The London Times*, as was the tragic elegy *The Bridge of Sighs*.

With the exception of Jerrold, most editors parse Hood's work into genres (romantic, comic, narrative, social protest). Like Jerrold, we prefer a chronological arrangement, to show the trajectory of Hood's career, as well as its various, often incongruous, commitments, even in phases dominated by a particular mode. Our base-texts are eclectic, ranging from the magazines and gift-book annuals in which Hood first reached wide audiences (the early *London Magazine* ballads, the annuals such as *Friendship's Offering*, *Forget Me Not*, Hood's *Comic Annual*) to later periodicals (*Punch*, *Hood's Magazine*) – to Hood's own volumes of poetry. Our notes give the text, with lifetime publication history and significant substantive variants, along with other contextual information. Our glosses are often indebted to the editions of Jerrold and Clubbe. Our few silent emendations involve correcting obvious printers' errata, modernizing certain conventions of punctuation or omitting stanza numbers (as we add line numbers).

Notes

1. The 'composite art' of Blake's plates is something of a precedent. Christopher Ricks remarks that Stevie Smith's illustrations of her poems ('something like doodling', she said) have a similar force.
2. William Makepeace Thackeray, 'On a Joke I once heard from the late Thomas Hood', *Works of Thackeray*, X.69.
3. William Empson, *Seven Types of Ambiguity* (1930; 3rd edn, Cleveland: Meridian Press, 1955), p. 125.
4. Edgar Allan Poe, *Marginalia*, in *The Complete Works of Edgar Allan Poe*, ed. James A. Harrison (NY: AMS Press, 1965), XVI.177–8.
5. The first remark is quoted by John C. Reid, *Thomas Hood*, p. 7; the second is reported by William Henry Hudson, *A Quiet Corner*, p. 25.
6. G. K. Chesterton, *The Victorian Age in Literature* (1913; London: Oxford University Press, 1955), who cites 'Sewing at once with a double thread a shroud as well as a shirt'; 'We thought her dying when she slept and sleeping when she died'; 'Oh God, that bread should be so dear and flesh

and blood so cheap'; and 'A cannon-ball took off his legs, so he laid down his arms' (pp. 18–19).

7. Roger Henkle, 'Comedy as Commodity', p. 301.
8. Thackeray, p. 70.

The Ballad of 'Sally Brown, and Ben the Carpenter' (Faithless Sally Brown)

An Old Ballad

Young Ben he was a nice young man,
    A carpenter by trade;
And he fell in love with Sally Brown,
    That was a lady's maid.

But as they fetch'd a walk one day,
    They met a press-gang crew;
And Sally she did faint away,
    While Ben he was brought to.

The Boatswain swore with wicked words,
10   Enough to shock a saint,
That though she did seem in a fit,
    'Twas nothing but a feint.

'Come, girl,' said he, 'hold up your head,
    He'll be as good as me;
For when your swain is in our boat,
    A boatswain he will be.'

So when they'd made their game of her,
    And taken off her elf,
She roused, and found she only was
20   A coming to herself.

'And is he gone, and is he gone?'
    She cried, and wept outright:
'Then I will to the water side,
    And see him out of sight.'

A waterman came up to her, –
    'Now, young woman,' said he,
'If you weep on so, you will make
    Eye-water in the sea.'

'Alas! they've taken my beau, Ben,
30   To sail with old Benbow';
And her woe began to run afresh,
     As if she had said Gee woe!

Says he, 'they've only taken him
     To the Tender ship, you see'; –
'The Tender-ship,' cried Sally Brown,
     'What a hard-ship that must be!

O! would I were a mermaid now,
     For then I'd follow him;
But, Oh! I'm not a fish-woman,
40   And so I cannot swim.

Alas! I was not born beneath
     The virgin and the scales,
So I must curse my cruel stars,
     And walk about in Wales.'

Now Ben had sail'd to many a place
     That's underneath the world;
But in two years the ship came home
     And all her sails were furl'd.

But when he call'd on Sally Brown,
50   To see how she went on,
He found she'd got another Ben,
     Whose Christian-name was John.

'O Sally Brown, O Sally Brown,
     How could you serve me so?
I've met with many a breeze before,
     But never such a blow!'

Then reading on his 'bacco box,
     He heaved a heavy sigh,
And then began to eye his pipe,
60   And then to pipe his eye.*

And then he tried to sing 'All's Well',
    But could not, though he tried;
His head was turn'd, and so he chew'd
    His pigtail till he died.

His death, which happen'd in his birth,
    At forty-odd befell:
They went and told the sexton, and
    The sexton toll'd the bell.

*Catullus has imitated this:
Ad dominam solam usque pipi-abat, – *Printer's Devil* [T.H.]

Fair Ines

O saw ye not fair Ines?
She's gone into the West,
To dazzle when the sun is down,
And rob the world of rest:
She took our daylight with her,
The smiles that we love best,
With morning blushes on her cheek,
And pearls upon her breast.

O turn again, fair Ines,
10   Before the fall of night,
For fear the Moon should shine alone,
And stars unrivall'd bright;
And blessed will the lover be
That walks beneath their light,
And breathes the love against thy cheek
I dare not even write!

Would I had been, fair Ines,
That gallant cavalier,
Who rode so gaily by thy side,
20   And whisper'd thee so near! –

Were there no bonny dames at home
Or no true lovers here,
That he should cross the seas to win
The dearest of the dear?

I saw thee, lovely Ines,
Descend along the shore,
With bands of noble gentlemen,
And banners wav'd before;
And gentle youth and maidens gay,
30   And snowy plumes they were; –
It would have been a beauteous dream,
– If it had been no more!

Alas, alas, fair Ines,
She went away with song,
With Music waiting on her steps,
And shoutings of the throng;
But some were sad, and felt no mirth,
But only Music's wrong,
In sounds that sang Farewell, Farewell,
40   To her you've loved so long.

Farewell, farewell, fair Ines,
That vessel never bore
So fair a lady on its deck,
Nor danc'd so light before, –
Alas for pleasure on the sea,
And sorrow on the shore!
The smile that blest one lover's heart
Has broken many more!

Ode: Autumn

I

I saw old Autumn in the misty morn
    Stand shadowless, like Silence listening
    To silence, – for no lonely bird would sing
Into his hollow ear from woods forlorn;
Nor lowly hedge, nor solitary thorn, –
Shaking his languid locks all dewy bright,
With tangled gossamer that fell by night,
    Pearling his coronet of golden corn.
Where are the songs of day-light? In the sun,
10   Oping the dusky eyelids of the South,
Till shade and silence waken up as one,
    And Morning sings with a warm odorous mouth:
Where are the merry birds? Away, away,
    On panting wings through the inclement skies,
        Lest owls should prey,
        Undazzled at noon day,
    And tear with horny beak their lustrous eyes.

II

Where are the blooms of Summer? In the West,
    Blushing their last to the last sunny hours,
20 When the mild Eve by sudden Night is prest,
        Like tearful Proserpine – snatch'd among flow'rs
        To a most gloomy breast:
Where is the pride of Summer – the green prime –
    The many, many leaves wind-wanton? – Three
On the moss'd elm – three on the naked lime
    Trembling – and one upon the old oak tree!
Where is the Dryad's immortality?
    Gone into mournful cypress and dark yew,
    Or wearing the long gloomy winter through
30 In the smooth holly's green eternity.

III

The squirrel gloats on his accomplish'd hoard;
　　The ants have brimm'd their garners with ripe grain,
　　　　And honey bees have stored
　　The sweets of Summer in their luscious cells;
The swallows all have wing'd across the main; –
　　But here the Autumn Melancholy dwells,
　　And sighs her tearful spells
Amongst the sunless shadows of the plain.
Alone – alone – upon a mossy stone,
40　　Until her drowsy feet forgotten be,
She sits and reckons up the dead and gone,
　　With the last leaves for a love-rosary;
　　Whilst the all-wither'd world spreads drearily,
Like a dim picture of the drowned past,
　　In the hush'd mind's mysterious far-away,
Doubtful what ghostly thing will steal the last
　　Into that distance – grey upon the grey.

IV

Aye, go and sit with her, and be o'ershaded
　　Under the languid downfal of her hair;
50　　She wears a coronal of flowers faded
　　Upon her forehead, like a constant care; –
　　There is enough of wither'd every where
To make her bower, and eternal gloom; –
　　There is enough of sadness to invite,
If only for the rose that died, whose doom
Is Beauty's, – she that with the exquisite bloom
　　Of conscious cheeks most beautifies the light: –
　　There is enough of sorrowing – and quite
Enough of bitter fruits this world doth bear,
60　　Enough of chilly droppings, for her bowl, –
Enough of fear, and shadowy despair,
　　To frame her cloudy prison for the soul.

Sonnet. – Silence

There is a silence where hath been no sound,
  There is a silence where no sound may be,
  In the cold grave – under the deep deep sea,
Or in wide desart where no life is found,
Which hath been mute, and still must sleep profound;
  No voice is hush'd, – no life treads silently,
  But clouds and cloudy shadows wander free,
That never spoke – over the idle ground:
But in green ruins, in the desolate walls
10   Of antique palaces, where Man hath been,
Though the dun fox, or wild hyena, calls,
    And owls, that flit continually between,
Shriek to the echo, and the low winds moan,
There the true Silence is, self-conscious and alone.

Sonnet
Written in Keats's Endymion

I saw pale Dian, sitting by the brink
  Of silver falls, the overflow of fountains
From cloudy steeps; and I grew sad to think
  Endymion's foot was silent on those mountains,
And he but a hush'd name, that Silence keeps
  In dear remembrance, – lonely, and forlorn,
Singing it to herself until she weeps
  Tears that perchance still glisten in the morn; –
And as I mused, in dull imaginings,
10   There came a flash of garments, and I knew
The awful Muse by her harmonious wings
    Charming the air to music as she flew –
Anon there rose an echo through the vale
Gave back Endymion in a dream-like tale.

Sonnet: – Death

It is not death, that some time in a sigh
   This eloquent breath shall take its speechless flight;
That some time the live stars, which now reply
   In sunlight to the sun, shall set in night;
   That this warm conscious flesh shall perish quite,
And all life's ruddy springs forget to flow; –
   That verse shall cease, and the immortal spright
Be lapp'd in alien clay, and laid below: –
It is not death to know this, but to know
10   That pious thoughts, which visit at new graves,
In tender pilgrimage will cease to go
   So duly and so oft; and when grass waves
Over the past-away, there may be then
No resurrections in the minds of men!

The Death-Bed

We watch'd her breathing thro' the night,
Her breathing soft and low,
As in her breast the wave of life
Kept heaving to and fro!

So silently we seemed to speak –
So slowly moved about!
As we had lent her half our powers
To eke her living out!

Our very hopes belied our fears
10 Our fears our hopes belied –
We thought her dying when she slept,
And sleeping when she died!

For when the morn came dim and sad –
And chill with early showers,
Her quiet eyelids closed – she had
Another morn than ours!

A Friendly *Epistle to Mrs Fry* in *Newgate*

'Sermons in stones' – *As You Like it*
'Out! out! damned spot' – *Macbeth*

I like you, Mrs Fry! I like your name!
It speaks the very warmth you feel in pressing
In daily act round Charity's great flame –
I like the crisp Browne way you have of dressing,
Good Mrs Fry! I like the placid claim
You make to Christianity, – professing
Love, and good *works* – of course you buy of Barton,
Beside the young *fry's* bookseller, Friend Darton!

I like, good Mrs Fry, your brethren mute –
10 Those serious, solemn gentlemen that sport –
I should have said, that *wear*, the sober suit
Shap'd like a court dress – but for heaven's court.
I like your sisters too, – sweet Rachel's fruit –
Protestant nuns! I like their stiff support
Of virtue – and I like to see them clad
With such a difference – just like good from bad!

I like the sober colours – not the wet;
Those gaudy manufactures of the rainbow –
Green, orange, crimson, purple, violet –
20 In which the fair, the flirting, and the vain, go –
The others are a chaste, severer set,
In which the good, the pious, and the plain, go –
They're moral *standards*, to know Christians by –
In short, they are your *colours*, Mrs Fry!

As for the naughty tinges of the prism –
Crimson's the cruel uniform of war –
Blue – hue of brimstone! minds no catechism;
And green is young and gay – not noted for
Goodness, or gravity, or quietism,
30   Till it is sadden'd down to tea-green, or
Olive – and purple's giv'n to wine, I guess;
And yellow is a convict by its dress!

They're all the devil's liveries, that men
And women wear in servitude to sin –
But how will they come off, poor motleys, when
Sin's wages are paid down, and they stand in
The Evil presence? You and I know, then
How all the party colours will begin
To part – the *Pittite* hues will sadden there,
40   Whereas the *Foxite* shades will all show fair!

Witness their goodly labours one by one!
Russet makes garments for the needy poor –
Dove-colour preaches love to all – and *dun*
Calls every day at Charity's street-door –
Brown studies scripture, and bids woman shun
All gaudy furnishing – *olive* doth pour
Oil into wounds: and *drab* and *slate* supply
Scholar and book in Newgate, Mrs Fry!

Well! Heaven forbid that I should discommend
50   The gratis, charitable, jail-endeavour!
When all persuasions in your praises blend –
The Methodist's creed and cry are, *Fry* for ever!
No – I will be your friend – and, like a friend,
Point out your very worst defect – Nay, never
Start at that word! – But I *must* ask you why
You keep your school *in* Newgate, Mrs Fry?

Too well I know the price our mother Eve
Paid for *her* schooling: but must all her daughters
Commit a petty larceny, and thieve –
60   Pay down a crime for '*entrance*' to your '*quarters*'?
Your classes may increase, but I must grieve
Over your pupils at their bread and waters!
Oh, tho' it cost you rent – (and rooms run high!)
Keep your school *out* of Newgate, Mrs Fry!

O save the vulgar soul before it's spoil'd!
Set up your mounted sign *without* the gate –
And there inform the mind before 'tis soil'd!
'Tis sorry writing on a greasy slate!
Nay, if you would not have your labours foil'd,
70   Take it *inclining* tow'rds a virtuous state,
Not prostrate and laid flat – else, woman meek!
The *upright* pencil will but hop and shriek!

Ah, who can tell how hard it is to drain
The evil spirit from the heart it preys in, –
To bring sobriety to life again,
Chok'd with the vile Anacreontic raisin, –
To wash Black Betty when her black's ingrain, –
To stick a moral lacquer on Moll Brazen,
Of Suky Tawdry's habits to deprive her;
80   To tame the wild-fowl-ways of Jenny Diver!

Ah, who can tell how hard it is to teach
Miss Nancy Dawson on her bed of straw –
To make Long Sal sew up the endless breach
She made in manners – to write heaven's own law
On hearts of granite. – Nay, how hard to preach,
In cells, that are not memory's – to draw
The moral thread, thro' the immoral eye
Of blunt Whitechapel natures, Mrs Fry!

In vain you teach them baby-work within:
90   'Tis but a clumsy botchery of crime;
'Tis but a tedious darning of old sin –
Come out yourself, and stitch up souls in time –
It is too late for scouring to begin
When virtue's ravell'd out, when all the prime
Is worn away, and nothing sound remains;
You'll fret the fabric out before the stains!

I like your chocolate, good Mistress Fry!
I like your cookery in every way;
I like your shrove-tide service and supply;
100   I like to hear your sweet *Pandeans* play;
I like the pity in your full-brimm'd eye;
I like your carriage and your silken grey,
Your dove-like habits, and your silent preaching;
But I don't like your Newgatory teaching.

Come out of Newgate, Mrs Fry! Repair
Abroad, and find your pupils in the streets.
O, come abroad into the wholesome air,
And take your moral place, before Sin seats
Her wicked self in the Professor's chair.
110   Suppose some morals raw! the true receipt's
To dress them in the pan, but do not try
To cook them in the fire, good Mrs Fry!

Put on your decent bonnet, and come out!
Good lack! the ancients did not set up schools
In jail – but at the *Porch!* hinting, no doubt,
That Vice should have a lesson in the rules
Before 'twas whipt by law. – O come about,
Good Mrs Fry! and set up forms and stools
All down the Old Bailey, and thro' Newgate-street,
120   But not in Mr Wontner's proper seat!

Teach Lady Barrymore, if, teaching, you
That peerless Peeress can absolve from dolour;
Teach her it is not virtue to pursue
Ruin of blue, or any other colour;
Teach her it is not Virtue's crown to rue,
Month after month, the unpaid drunken dollar;
Teach her that 'flooring Charleys' is a game
Unworthy one that bears a Christian name.

O come and teach our children – that ar'n't *ours* –
130 That heaven's straight pathway is a narrow way,
Not Broad St Giles's, where fierce Sin devours
Children, like Time – or rather they both prey
On youth together – meanwhile Newgate low'rs
Ev'n like a black cloud at the close of day,
To shut them out from any more blue sky:
Think of these hopeless wretches, Mrs Fry!

You are not nice – go into their retreats,
And make them Quakers, if you will. – 'Twere best
They wore straight collars, and their shirts sans *pleats*;
140 That they had hats *with* brims, – that they were drest
In garbs without *lappels* – than shame the streets
With so much raggedness. – You may invest
Much cash this way – but it will cost its price,
To give a good, round, real *cheque* to Vice!

In brief, – Oh teach the child its moral rote,
Not *in* the way from which it won't depart, –
But *out* – out – out! Oh, bid it walk remote!
And if the skies are clos'd against the smart,
Ev'n let him wear the single-breasted coat,
150 For that ensureth singleness of heart. –
Do what you will, his every want supply,
Keep him – but *out* of Newgate, Mrs Fry!

Stanzas (I remember, I remember)

I remember, I remember
The house where I was born,
The little window, where the sun
Came peeping in, at morn;
He never came a wink too soon,
Nor brought too long a day;
But now, I often wish the night
Had borne my breath away!

I remember, I remember
10   The roses, red and white,
The violets, and the lily cups –
Those flowers made of light;
The lilacs, where the robin built,
And where my brother set
The laburnum, on his birth-day, –
The tree is living yet!

I remember, I remember
Where I was used to swing,
And thought the air would rush as fresh
20   To swallows on the wing;
– My spirit flew in feathers, then,
That is so heavy, now;
And summer pools could hardly cool
The fever on my brow!

I remember, I remember
The fir trees dark and high;
I used to think their slender spires
Were close against the sky;
It was a childish ignorance, –
30   But now 'tis little joy
To know I'm further off from heaven,
Than when I was a boy!

Autumn

The autumn is old,
The sear leaves are flying; –
He hath gathered up gold,
And now he is dying; –
Old age, begin sighing!

The vintage is ripe,
The harvest is heaping, –
But some that have sowed
Have no riches for reaping;
10   Poor wretch, fall a weeping!

The year's in the wane,
There is nothing adorning,
The night hath no eve,
And the day hath no morning; –
Cold winter gives warning.

The rivers run chill,
The red sun is sinking;
And I am grown old,
And life is fast shrinking; –
20   Here's enow for sad thinking!

Faithless Nelly Gray

A Pathetic Ballad

Ben Battle was a soldier bold,
    And used to war's alarms;
But a cannon-ball took off his legs,
    So he laid down his arms!

Now as they bore him off the field,
    Said he, 'Let others shoot,
For here I leave my second leg,
    And the Forty-second Foot!'

The army-surgeons made him limbs:
10   Said he, – 'They're only pegs:
But there's as wooden members quite,
    As represent my legs!'

Now Ben he loved a pretty maid,
    Her name was Nelly Gray;
So he went to pay her his devours,
    When he'd devour'd his pay!

But when he called on Nelly Gray,
    She made him quite a scoff;
And when she saw his wooden legs,
20   Began to take them off!

'O, Nelly Gray! O, Nelly Gray!
    Is this your love so warm?
The love that loves a scarlet coat,
    Should be more uniform!'

Said she, 'I loved a soldier once,
    For he was blythe and brave;
But I will never have a man
    With both legs in the grave!

Before you had those timber toes,
30   Your love I did allow,
But then, you know, you stand upon
    Another footing now!'

'O, Nelly Gray! O, Nelly Gray!
    For all your jeering speeches,
At duty's call, I left my legs
    In Badajos's *breaches!*'

'Why, then,' said she, 'you've lost the feet
    Of legs in war's alarms,
And now you cannot wear your shoes
40   Upon your feats of arms!'

'O, false and fickle Nelly Gray!
    I know why you refuse: –
Though I've no feet – some other man
    Is standing in my shoes!

I wish I ne'er had seen your face;
    But, now, a long farewell!
For you will be my death: – alas!
    You will not be my *Nell!*'

Now when he went from Nelly Gray,
50   His heart so heavy got –
And life was such a burthen grown,
    It made him take a knot!

So round his melancholy neck,
    A rope he did entwine,
And, for his second time in life,
    Enlisted in the Line!

One end he tied around a beam,
    And then removed his pegs,
And, as his legs were off, – of course,
60   He soon was off his legs!

And there he hung, till he was dead
    As any nail in town, –
For though distress had cut him up,
    It could not cut him down!

A dozen men sat on his corpse,
    To find out why he died –
And they buried Ben in four cross-roads
    With a *stake* in his inside!

The Last Man

'Twas in the year two thousand and one,
A pleasant morning of May,
I sat on the gallows-tree, all alone,
A chaunting a merry lay, –
To think how the pest had spared my life,
To sing with the larks that day!

When up the heath came a jolly knave,
Like a scarecrow, all in rags:
It made me crow to see his old duds
10   All abroad in the wind, like flags; –
So up he came to the timbers' foot
And pitch'd down his greasy bags. –

Good Lord! how blithe the old beggar was!
At pulling out his scraps, –
The very sight of his broken orts
Made a work in his wrinkled chaps:
'Come down,' says he, 'you Newgate-bird,
And have a taste of my snaps!' –

Then down the rope, like a tar from the mast,
20   I slided, and by him stood;
But I wish'd myself on the gallows again
When I smelt that beggar's food, –
A foul beef-bone and a mouldy crust; –
'Oh!' quoth he, 'the heavens are good!'

Then after this grace he cast him down:
Says I, 'You'll get sweeter air
A pace or two off, on the windward side' –
For the felons' bones lay there –
But he only laugh'd at the empty skulls,
30   And offer'd them part of his fare.

'I never harm'd *them*, and they won't harm me:
Let the proud and the rich be cravens!'
I did not like that strange beggar man,
He look'd so up at the heavens –
Anon he shook out his empty old poke; –
'There's the crums,' saith he, 'for the ravens!'

It made me angry to see his face,
It had such a jesting look;
But while I made up my mind to speak,
40   A small case-bottle he took:
Quoth he, 'though I gather the green water-cress,
My drink is not of the brook!'

Full manners-like he tender'd the dram;
Oh, it came of a dainty cask!
But, whenever it came to his turn to pull,
'Your leave, good sir, I must ask;
But I always wipe the brim with my sleeve,
When a hangman sups at my flask!'

And then he laugh'd so loudly and long,
50   The churl was quite out of breath;
I thought the very Old One was come
To mock me before my death,
And wish'd I had buried the dead men's bones
That were lying about the heath!

But the beggar gave me a jolly clap –
'Come, let us pledge each other,
For all the wide world is dead beside,
And we are brother and brother –
I've a yearning for thee in my heart,
60   As if we had come of one mother.

I've a yearning for thee in my heart
That almost makes me weep,
For as I pass'd from town to town
The folks were all stone-asleep, –
But when I saw thee sitting aloft,
It made me both laugh and leap!'

Now a curse (I thought) be on his love,
And a curse upon his mirth, –
An' it were not for that beggar man
70   I'd be the King of the earth, –
But I promis'd myself, an hour should come
To make him rue his birth! –

So down we sat and bous'd again
Till the sun was in mid-sky,
When, just as the gentle west-wind came,
We hearken'd a dismal cry:
'Up, up, on the tree,' quoth the beggar man
'Till these horrible dogs go by!'

And, lo! from the forest's far-off skirts,
80   They came all yelling for gore,
A hundred hounds pursuing at once,
And a panting hart before,
Till he sunk adown at the gallows' foot
And there his haunches they tore!

His haunches they tore, without a horn
To tell when the chase was done;
And there was not a single scarlet coat
To flaunt it in the sun! –
I turn'd, and look'd at the beggar man,
90   And his tears dropt one by one!

And with curses sore he chid at the hounds
Till the last dropt out of sight,
Anon saith he, 'let's down again,
And ramble for our delight,
For the world's all free, and we may choose
A right cozie barn for to-night!'

With that, he set up his staff on end,
And it fell with the point due West;
So we far'd that way to a city great,
100 Where the folks had died of the pest –
It was fine to enter in house and hall,
Wherever it liked me best! –

For the porters all were stiff and cold,
And could not lift their heads;
And when we came where their masters lay
The rats leapt out of the beds: –
The grandest palaces in the land
Were as free as workhouse sheds.

But the beggar man made a mumping face,
110 And knocked at every gate:
It made me curse to hear how he whined,
So our fellowship turn'd to hate,
And I bade him walk the world by himself,
For I scorn'd so humble a mate!

So *he* turn'd right and *I* turn'd left,
As if we had never met;
And I chose a fair stone house for myself,
For the city was all to let;
And for three brave holydays drank my fill
120 Of the choicest that I could get.

And because my jerkin was coarse and worn,
I got me a properer vest;
It was purple velvet, stitch'd o'er with gold,
And a shining star at the breast! –
'Twas enough to fetch old Joan from her grave
To see me so purely drest! –

But Joan was dead and under the mould,
And every buxom lass;
In vain I watch'd, at the window pane,
130   For a Christian soul to pass; –
But sheep and kine wander'd up the street,
And browz'd on the new-come grass. –

When lo! I spied the old beggar man,
And lustily he did sing! –
His rags were lapp'd in a scarlet cloak,
And a crown he had like a King;
So he stept right up before my gate
And danc'd me a saucy fling!

Heaven mend us all! – but, within my mind,
140   I had kill'd him then and there;
To see him lording so braggart-like
That was born to his beggar's fare;
And how he had stolen the royal crown
His betters were meant to wear.

But God forbid that a thief should die
Without his share of the laws!
So I nimbly whipt my tackle out,
And soon tied up his claws, –
I was judge, myself, and jury, and all,
150   And solemnly tried the cause.

But the beggar man would not plead, but cried
Like a babe without its corals,
For he knew how hard it is apt to go
When the law and a thief have quarrels, –
There was not a Christian soul alive
To speak a word for his morals.

Oh, how gaily I doff'd my costly gear,
And put on my work–day clothes; –
I was tired of such a long Sunday life,
160   And never was one of the sloths;
But the beggar man grumbled a weary deal,
And made many crooked mouths.

So I haul'd him off to the gallows' foot,
And blinded him in his bags;
'Twas a weary job to heave him up,
For a doom'd man always lags;
But by ten of the clock he was off his legs
In the wind and airing his rags!

So there he hung, and there I stood
170   The LAST MAN left alive,
To have my own will of all the earth:
Quoth I, now I shall thrive!
But when was ever honey made
With one bee in a hive!

My conscience began to gnaw my heart
Before the day was done,
For other men's lives had all gone out,
Like candles in the sun! –
But it seem'd as if I had broke, at last,
180   A thousand necks in one!

So I went and cut his body down
To bury it decentlie; –
God send there were any good soul alive
To do the like by me!
But the wild dogs came with terrible speed,
And bay'd me up the tree!

My sight was like a drunkard's sight,
And my head began to swim,
To see their jaws all white with foam,
190   Like the ravenous ocean brim; –
But when the wild dogs trotted away
Their jaws were bloody and grim!

Their jaws were bloody and grim, good Lord!
But the beggar man, where was he? –
There was nought of him but some ribbons of rags
Below the gallows' tree! –
I know the Devil, when I am dead,
Will send his hounds for me! –

I've buried my babies one by one,
200   And dug the deep hole for Joan,
And cover'd the faces of kith and kin,
And felt the old churchyard stone
Go cold to my heart, full many a time,
But I never felt so lone!

For the lion and Adam were company,
And the tiger him beguil'd;
But the simple kine are foes to my life,
And the household brutes are wild.
If the veriest cur would lick my hand,
210   I could love it like a child!

And the beggar man's ghost besets my dream,
At night, to make me madder, –
And my wretched conscience, within my breast,
Is like a stinging adder; –
I sigh when I pass the gallows' foot,
And look at the rope and ladder! –

For hanging looks sweet, – but, alas! in vain,
My desperate fancy begs, –
I must turn my cup of sorrows quite up,
220   And drink it to the dregs, –
For there is not another man alive,
In the world, to pull my legs!

Mary's Ghost

A Pathetic Ballad

'Twas in the middle of the night,
    To sleep young William tried,
When Mary's ghost came stealing in,
    And stood at his bed-side.

O William dear! O William dear!
    My rest eternal ceases;
Alas! my everlasting peace
    Is broken into pieces.

I thought the last of all my cares
10   Would end with my last minute;
But tho' I went to my long home,
    I didn't stay long in it.

The body-snatchers they have come,
    And made a snatch at me;
It's very hard them kind of men
    Won't let a body be!

You thought that I was buried deep,
    Quite decent like and chary,
But from her grave in Mary-bone
20   They've come and bon'd your Mary.

The arm that used to take your arm
    Is took to Dr Vyse;
And both my legs are gone to walk
    The hospital at Guy's.

I vow'd that you should have my hand,
    But fate gives us denial;
You'll find it there, at Doctor Bell's,
    In spirits and a phial.

As for my feet, the little feet
30   You used to call so pretty,
There's one, I know, in Bedford Row,
    The t'other's in the city.

I can't tell where my head is gone,
    But Doctor Carpue can:
As for my trunk, it's all pack'd up
    To go by Pickford's van.

I wish you'd go to Mr P.
    And save me such a ride;
I don't half like the outside place,
40   They've took for my inside.

The cock it crows – I must begone!
    My William we must part!
But I'll be your's in death, altho'
    Sir Astley has my heart.

Don't go to weep upon my grave,
    And think that there I be,
They haven't left an atom there,
    Of my anatomie.

Ruth

She stood breast-high amid the corn,
Clasp'd by the golden light of morn;
Like the sweetheart of the sun,
Who many a burning kiss had won.

On her cheek an autumn flush
Deeply ripen'd – such a blush
In the midst of brown was born,
Like red poppies grown with corn.

Round her eyes her tresses fell –
Which were darkest none could tell;
But long lashes veil'd a light
That had else been all too bright;

And her hat with shady brim
Made her forehead darkly dim:
Thus she stood amid the stooks,
Praising God with her sweetest looks.

Sure, I said, Heav'n did not mean
Where I reap thou shouldst but glean:
Lay thy sheaf adown, and come
Share my harvest and my home.

Song (The stars are with the voyager)

The stars are with the voyager
   Wherever he may sail;
The moon is constant to her time;
   The sun will never fail;

But follow, follow round the world,
    The green earth and the sea;
So love is with the lover's heart,
    Wherever he may be.

Wherever he may be, the stars
10   Must daily lose their light;
The moon will veil her in the shade;
    The sun will set at night.
The sun may set, but constant love
    Will shine when he's away;
So that dull night is never night,
    And day is brighter day.

Death in the Kitchen

'Are we not here now?' – continued the corporal (striking the end
of his stick perpendicularly on the floor, so as to give an idea of
health and stability) – 'and are we not' (dropping his hat upon the
ground) 'gone! – in a moment?' – *Tristram Shandy*

Trim, thou art right! – 'Tis sure that I,
And all who hear thee, are to die.
    The stoutest lad and wench
Must lose their places at the will
Of Death, and go at last to fill
    The sexton's gloomy trench!

The dreary grave! – Oh, when I think
How close ye stand upon its brink,
    My inward spirit groans!
10 My eyes are fill'd with dismal dreams
Of coffins, and this kitchen seems
    A charnel full of bones!

Yes, jovial butler, thou must fail,
As sinks the froth on thine own ale;
   Thy days will soon be done!
Alas! the common hours that strike
Are knells; for life keeps wasting, like
   A cask upon the run.

Ay, hapless scullion! 'tis thy case:
Life travels at a scouring pace,
   Far swifter than thy hand.
The fast decaying frame of man
Is but a kettle, or a pan,
   Time wears away – with sand!

Thou needst not, mistress cook! be told,
The meat to-morrow will be cold
   That now is fresh and hot:
E'en thus our flesh will, by the by,
Be cold as stone: – Cook, thou must die!
   There's death within the pot!

Susannah, too, my lady's maid!
Thy pretty person once must aid
   To swell the buried swarm!
The 'glass of fashion' thou wilt hold
No more, but grovel in the mould
   That's not the 'mould of form'!

Yes, Jonathan, that drives the coach,
He too will feel the fiend's approach –
   The grave will pluck him down:
He must in dust and ashes lie,
And wear the churchyard livery,
   Grass-green, turn'd up with brown.

How frail is our uncertain breath!
The laundress seems full hale, but Death
    Shall her 'last linen' bring.
The groom will die, like all his kind;
And e'en the stable-boy will find
    His life no stable thing.

Nay, see the household dog – e'en *that*
50 The earth shall take! – The very cat
    Will share the common fall;
Although she hold (the proverb saith)
A ninefold life, one single death
    Suffices for them all!

Cook, butler, Susan, Jonathan,
The girl that scours the pot and pan,
    And those that tend the steeds –
All, all shall have another sort
Of service after this – in short,
60   The one the parson reads!

The dreary grave! – Oh, when I think
How close ye stand upon its brink,
    My inward spirit groans!
My eyes are fill'd with dismal dreams
Of coffins, and this kitchen seems
    A charnel full of bones.

The Dream of Eugene Aram, the Murderer

PREFACE [1831]

The remarkable name of Eugene Aram, belonging to a man
of unusual talents and acquirements, is unhappily associated
with a deed of blood as extraordinary in its details as any
recorded in our calendar of crime. In the year 1745, being
then an Usher, and deeply engaged in the study of Chaldee,

Hebrew, Arabic, and the Celtic dialects, for the formation of a Lexicon, he abruptly turned over a still darker page in human knowledge, and the brow that learning might have made illustrious, was stamped ignominious for ever with the brand of Cain. To obtain a trifling property, he concerted with an accomplice, and with his own hand effected, the violent death of one Daniel Clarke, a shoemaker of Knaresborough, in Yorkshire. For fourteen years nearly the secret slept with the victim in the earth of St Robert's Cave, and the manner of its discovery would appear a striking example of the Divine Justice, even amongst those marvels narrated in that curious old volume, alluded to in *The Fortunes of Nigel* [a novel by Sir Walter Scott, published in 1822], under its quaint title of 'God's Revenge against Murther'.

The accidental digging up of a skeleton, and the unwary and emphatic declaration of Aram's accomplice, that it could not be that of Clarke, betraying a guilty knowledge of the true bones, he was wrought to a confession of their deposit. The learned homicide was seized and arraigned; and a trial of uncommon interest was wound up by a defence as memorable as the tragedy itself for eloquence and ingenuity; – too ingenious for innocence, and eloquent enough to do credit even to that long premeditation which the interval between the deed and its discovery had afforded. That this dreary period had not passed without paroxysms of remorse, may be inferred from a fact of affecting interest. The late Admiral Burney was a scholar, at the school at Lynn in Norfolk, where Aram was an Usher, subsequent to his crime. The Admiral stated that Aram was beloved by the boys, and that he used to discourse to them of Murder, not occasionally, as I have written elsewhere, but constantly, and in somewhat of the spirit ascribed to him in the Poem.

For the more imaginative part of the version I must refer back to one of those unaccountable visions, which come upon us like frightful monsters thrown up by storms from the great black deeps of slumber. A lifeless body, in love and relationship the nearest and dearest, was imposed upon my back, with an overwhelming sense of obligation – not of filial piety merely, but some awful responsibility equally vague and intense, and involving, as it seemed, inexpiable sin, horrors unutterable, torments intolerable, – to bury my dead, like Abraham, out of my sight. In vain I attempted, again and again, to obey the mysterious mandate – by some dreadful process the burthen was replaced with a more stupendous weight of injunction, and an appalling conviction of the impossibility of its fulfilment. My mental anguish was indescribable; – the mighty agonies of souls tortured on the supernatural racks of sleep are not to be penned – and if in sketching those that belong to blood-guiltiness I have been at all successful, I owe it mainly to the uninvoked inspiration of that terrible dream.

T. H.

'Twas in the prime of summer time,
    An evening calm and cool,
And four-and-twenty happy boys
    Came bounding out of school:
There were some that ran and some that leapt,
    Like troutlets in a pool.

Away they sped with gamesome minds,
    And souls untouched by sin;
To a level mead they came, and there
10   They drave the wickets in:
Pleasantly shone the setting sun
    Over the town of Lynn.

Like sportive deer they coursed about,
    And shouted as they ran, –
Turning to mirth all things of earth,
    As only boyhood can;
But the Usher sat remote from all
    A melancholy man!

His hat was off, his vest apart,
20   To catch heaven's blessed breeze;
For a burning thought was in his brow,
     And his bosom ill at ease:
So he lean'd his head on his hands, and read
     The book between his knees!

Leaf after leaf he turn'd it o'er,
     Nor ever glanc'd aside,
For the peace of his soul he read that book
     In the golden eventide:
Much study had made him very lean,
30   And pale, and leaden-ey'd.

At last he shut the ponderous tome,
     With a fast and fervent grasp
He strain'd the dusky covers close,
     And fix'd the brazen hasp:
'Oh, God! could I so close my mind,
     And clasp it with a clasp!'

Then leaping on his feet upright,
     Some moody turns he took, –
Now up the mead, then down the mead,
40   And past a shady nook, –
And, lo! he saw a little boy
     That pored upon a book!

'My gentle lad, what is't you read –
     Romance or fairy fable?
Or is it some historic page,
     Of kings and crowns unstable?'
The young boy gave an upward glance, –
     'It is "The Death of Abel".'

The Usher took six hasty strides,
50   As smit with sudden pain, –
Six hasty strides beyond the place,
    Then slowly back again;
And down he sat beside the lad,
    And talk'd with him of Cain;

And, long since then, of bloody men,
    Whose deeds tradition saves;
Of lonely folk cut off unseen,
    And hid in sudden graves;
Of horrid stabs, in groves forlorn,
60   And murders done in caves;

And how the sprites of injur'd men
    Shriek upward from the sod, –
Aye, how the ghostly hand will point
    To show the burial clod;
And unknown facts of guilty acts
    Are seen in dreams from God!

He told how murderers walk the earth
    Beneath the curse of Cain, –
With crimson clouds before their eyes,
70   And flames about their brain:
For blood has left upon their souls
    Its everlasting stain!

'And well,' quoth he, 'I know, for truth,
    Their pangs must be extreme, –
Woe, woe, unutterable woe, –
    Who spill life's sacred stream!
For why? Methought, last night, I wrought
    A murder, in my dream!

One that had never done me wrong –
80   A feeble man, and old;
I led him to a lonely field, –
    The moon shone clear and cold:
Now here, said I, this man shall die,
    And I will have his gold!

Two sudden blows with a ragged stick,
    And one with a heavy stone,
One hurried gash with a hasty knife, –
    And then the deed was done:
There was nothing lying at my foot
90   But lifeless flesh and bone!

Nothing but lifeless flesh and bone,
    That could not do me ill;
And yet I fear'd him all the more,
    For lying there so still:
There was a manhood in his look,
    That murder could not kill!

And, lo! the universal air
    Seem'd lit with ghastly flame; –
Ten thousand thousand dreadful eyes
100   Were looking down in blame:
I took the dead man by his hand,
    And call'd upon his name!

Oh, God! it made me quake to see
    Such sense within the slain!
But when I touch'd the lifeless clay,
    The blood gushed out amain!
For every clot, a burning spot
    Was scorching in my brain!

My head was like an ardent coal,
110   My heart as solid ice;
My wretched, wretched soul, I knew,
    Was at the Devil's price:
A dozen times I groan'd; the dead
    Had never groan'd but twice!

And now, from forth the frowning sky,
    From the Heaven's topmost height,
I heard a voice – the awful voice
    Of the blood–avenging sprite: –
"Thou guilty man! take up thy dead
120   And hide it from my sight!"

I took the dreary body up,
    And cast it in a stream, –
A sluggish water, black as ink,
    The depth was so extreme: –
My gentle Boy, remember this
    Is nothing but a dream!

Down went the corse with a hollow plunge,
    And vanish'd in the pool;
Anon I cleans'd my bloody hands,
130   And wash'd my forehead cool,
And sat among the urchins young,
    That evening in the school.

Oh, Heaven! to think of their white souls,
    And mine so black and grim!
I could not share in childish prayer,
    Nor join in Evening Hymn:
Like a Devil of the Pit I seem'd,
    'Mid holy Cherubim!

And Peace went with them, one and all,
140   And each calm pillow spread;
But Guilt was my grim Chamberlain
    That lighted me to bed;
And drew my midnight curtains round,
    With fingers bloody red!

All night I lay in agony,
    In anguish dark and deep;
My fever'd eyes I dared not close,
    But stared aghast at Sleep:
For Sin had render'd unto her
150   The keys of Hell to keep!

All night I lay in agony,
    From weary chime to chime,
With one besetting horrid hint,
    That rack'd me all the time;
A mighty yearning, like the first
    Fierce impulse unto crime!

One stern tyrannic thought, that made
    All other thoughts its slave;
Stronger and stronger every pulse
160   Did that temptation crave, –
Still urging me to go and see
    The Dead Man in his grave!

Heavily I rose up, as soon
    As light was in the sky,
And sought the black accursed pool
    With a wild misgiving eye;
And I saw the Dead in the river bed,
    For the faithless stream was dry!

Merrily rose the lark, and shook
170   The dew-drop from its wing;
But I never mark'd its morning flight,
    I never heard it sing:
For I was stooping once again
    Under the horrid thing.

With breathless speed, like a soul in chase,
    I took him up and ran; –
There was no time to dig a grave
    Before the day began:
In a lonesome wood, with heaps of leaves,
180   I hid the murder'd man!

And all that day I read in school,
    But my thought was other where;
As soon as the mid-day task was done,
    In secret I was there:
And a mighty wind had swept the leaves,
    And still the corse was bare!

Then down I cast me on my face,
    And first began to weep,
For I knew my secret then was one
190   That earth refused to keep:
Or land or sea, though he should be
    Ten thousand fathoms deep.

So wills the fierce avenging Sprite,
    Till blood for blood atones!
Ay, though he's buried in a cave,
    And trodden down with stones,
And years have rotted off his flesh, –
    The world shall see his bones!

Oh, God! that horrid, horrid dream
200   Besets me now awake!
Again – again, with dizzy brain,
    The human life I take;
And my red right hand grows raging hot,
    Like Cranmer's at the stake.

And still no peace for the restless clay,
    Will wave or mould allow;
The horrid thing pursues my soul, –
    It stands before me now!'
The fearful Boy look'd up and saw
210   Huge drops upon his brow.

That very night, while gentle sleep
    The urchin eyelids kiss'd,
Two stern-faced men set out from Lynn,
    Through the cold and heavy mist;
And Eugene Aram walked between,
    With gyves upon his wrist.

Domestic Asides; or, Truth in Parentheses

'I really take it very kind,
This visit, Mrs Skinner!
I have not seen you such an age –
(The wretch has come to dinner!)

Your daughters, too, what loves of girls –
What heads for painters' easels!
Come here and kiss the infant, dears, –
(And give it p'rhaps the measles!)

Your charming boys I see are home
10   From Reverend Mr Russel's;
'Twas very kind to bring them both, –
(What boots for my new Brussels!)

What! little Clara left at home?
Well now I call that shabby:
I should have lov'd to kiss her so, –
(A flabby, dabby, babby!)

And Mr S., I hope he's well,
Ah! though he lives so handy,
He never now drops in to sup, –
20   (The better for our brandy!)

Come, take a seat – I long to hear
About Matilda's marriage;
You're come, of course, to spend the day! –
(Thank Heav'n, I hear the carriage!)

What! must you go? next time I hope
You'll give me longer measure;
Nay – I shall see you down the stairs –
(With most uncommon pleasure!)

Good-bye! good-bye! remember all,
30   Next time you'll take your dinners!
(Now, David, mind I'm not at home
In future to the Skinners!)'

Ode to Mr Malthus

My dear, do pull the bell,
    And pull it well,
And send those noisy children all up stairs,
    Now playing here like bears –
You George, and William, go into the grounds,
    Charles, James, and Bob are there, – and take your string,
        Drive horses, or fly kites, or any thing,
You're quite enough to play at hare and hounds, –
    You little May, and Caroline, and Poll,
10   Take each your doll,

And go, my dears, into the two-back pair,
    Your sister Margaret's there –
Harriet and Grace, thank God, are both at school,
    At far off Ponty Pool –
I want to read, but really can't get on –
Let the four twins, Mark, Matthew, Luke, and John,
    Go – to their nursery – go – I never can
    Enjoy my Malthus among such a clan!

    Oh Mr Malthus, I agree
20   In every thing I read with thee!
    The world's too full, there is no doubt,
    And wants a deal of thinning out, –
    It's plain – as plain as Harrow's Steeple –
    And I agree with some thus far,
    Who say the Queen's too popular,
    That is, – she has too many people.

    There are too many of all trades,
        Too many bakers,
        Too many every-thing makers,
30   But not too many undertakers. –
        Too many boys, –
        Too many hobby-de-hoys, –
Too many girls, men, widows, wives, and maids, –
There is a dreadful surplus to demolish,
        And yet some Wrongheads,
        With thick not long heads,
        Poor metaphysicians!
        Sign petitions
Capital punishment to abolish;
40   And in the face of censuses such vast ones
        New hospitals contrive,
        For keeping life alive,
Laying first stones, the dolts! instead of last ones! –
Others, again, in the same contrariety,
Deem that of all Humane Society

> They really deserve thanks,
> Because the two banks of the Serpentine,
> By their design,
> Are Saving Banks.

50   Oh! were it given but to me to weed,
>   The human breed,
> And root out here and there some cumbering elf,
>   I think I could go through it,
>   And really do it
> With profit to the world and to myself, –
> For instance, the unkind among the Editors,
>   My debtors, those I mean to say
>   Who cannot or who will not pay,
>   And all my creditors.
60   These, for my own sake, I'd destroy;
> But for the world's, and every one's,
> I'd hoe up Mrs G—'s two sons,
> And Mrs B—'s big little boy,
> Call'd only by herself an 'only joy'.
> As Mr Irving's chapel's not too full,
>   Himself alone I'd pull –
> But for the peace of years that have to run,
> I'd make the Lord Mayor's a perpetual station,
>   And put a period to rotation,
70   By rooting up all Aldermen but one, –
> These are but hints what good might thus be done!

> But ah! I fear the public good
>   Is little by the public understood, –
> For instance – if with flint, and steel, and tinder,
> Great Swing, for once a philanthropic man,
> Proposed to throw a light upon thy plan,
> No doubt some busy fool would hinder
> His burning all the Foundling to a cinder.

> Or, if the Lord Mayor, on an Easter Monday,
80   That wine and bun-day,
> Proposed to poison all the little Blue-coats,

Before they died by bit or sup,
Some meddling Marplot would blow up,
   Just at the moment critical,
   The economy political
Of saving their fresh yellow plush and new coats.

   Equally 'twould be undone,
   Suppose the Bishop of London,
      On that great day
90   In June or May,
When all the large small family of charity,
   Brown, black, or carrotty,
Walk in their dusty parish shoes,
In too, too many two–and–twos,
To sing together till they scare the walls
      Of old St Paul's,
Sitting in red, grey, green, blue, drab, and white,
   Some say a gratifying sight,
     Tho' I think sad – but that's a schism –
100   To witness so much pauperism –
Suppose, I say, the Bishop then, to make
In this poor overcrowded world more room,
     Proposed to shake
Down that immense extinguisher, the dome –
Some humane Martin in the charity *Gal*-way
   I fear would come and interfere,
   Save beadle, brat, and overseer,
   To walk back in their parish shoes,
   In too, too many two–and–twos,
110 Islington – Wapping – or Pall Mall way!

Thus, people hatch'd from goose's egg,
Foolishly think a pest, a plague,
And in its face their doors all shut,
On hinges oil'd with cajeput –
Drugging themselves with drams well spiced and cloven,
   And turning pale as linen rags
   At hoisting up of yellow flags,
While you and I are crying 'Orange Boven!'

Why should we let precautions so absorb us,
120   Or trouble shipping with a quarantine –
When if I understand the thing you mean,
We ought to *import* the Cholera Morbus!

Sally Simpkin's Lament;

or, John Jones's Kit-Cat-Astrophe

'He left his body to the sea,
And made a shark his legatee' – *Bryan and Pereene*

'Oh! what is that comes gliding in,
    And quite in middling haste?
It is the picture of my Jones,
    And painted to the waist.

It is not painted to the life,
    For where's the trowsers blue?
Oh Jones, my dear! – Oh dear! my Jones,
    What is become of you?'

'Oh! Sally dear, it is too true, –
10   The half that you remark
Is come to say my other half
    Is bit off by a shark!

Oh! Sally, sharks do things by halves,
    Yet most completely do!
A bite in one place seems enough,
    But I've been bit in two.

You know I once was all your own,
    But now a shark must share!
But let that pass – for now, to you
20   I'm neither here nor there.

Alas! death has a strange divorce
　　Effected in the sea,
It has divided me from you,
　　And even me from me!

Don't fear my ghost will walk o'nights
　　To haunt, as people say;
My ghost *can't* walk, for, oh! my legs
　　Are many leagues away!

Lord! think when I am swimming round,
30　　And looking where the boat is,
A shark just snaps away a *half*,
　　Without "a *quarter's* notice".

One half is here, the other half
　　Is near Columbia placed;
Oh! Sally, I have got the whole
　　Atlantic for my waist.

But now, adieu – a long adieu!
　　I've solved death's awful riddle,
And would say more, but I am doomed
40　　To break off in the middle!'

A Waterloo Ballad

To Waterloo, with sad ado,
　　And many a sigh and groan,
Amongst the dead, came Patty Head,
　　To look for Peter Stone.

'O prithee tell, good sentinel,
　　If I shall find him here?
I'm come to weep upon his corse,
　　My Ninety-Second dear!

Into our town a serjeant came,
10   With ribands all so fine,
A-flaunting in his cap – alas!
      His bow enlisted mine!

They taught him how to turn his toes,
      And stand as stiff as starch;
I thought that it was love and May,
      But it was love and March!

A sorry March indeed to leave
      The friends he might have kep', –
No March of Intellect it was,
20   But quite a foolish step.

O prithee tell, good sentinel,
      If hereabout he lies?
I want a corpse with reddish hair,
      And very sweet blue eyes.'

Her sorrow on the sentinel
      Appear'd to deeply strike: –
'Walk in,' he said, 'among the dead,
      And pick out which you like.'

And soon she picked out Peter Stone,
30   Half turned a corse;
A cannon was his bolster, and
      His mattrass was a horse.

'O Peter Stone, O Peter Stone,
      Lord here has been a skrimmage!
What have they done to your poor breast
      That used to hold my image?'

'O Patty Head, O Patty Head,
      You're come to my last kissing;
Before I'm set in the Gazette
40   As wounded, dead, and missing!

Alas! a splinter of a shell
   Right in my stomach sticks;
French mortars don't agree so well
   With stomachs as French bricks.

This very night a merry dance
   At Brussels was to be; –
Instead of opening a ball,
   A ball has opened me.

Its billet every bullet has,
50   And well it does fulfil it; –
I wish mine hadn't come so straight,
   But been a "crooked billet".

And then there came a cuirassier
   And cut me on the chest; –
He had no pity in his heart,
   For he had *steel'd his breast*.

Next thing a lancer, with his lance,
   Began to thrust away;
I call'd for quarter, but, alas!
60   It was not Quarter-day.

He ran his spear right through my arm,
   Just here above the joint; –
O Patty dear, it was no joke,
   Although it had a point.

With loss of blood I fainted off,
   As dead as women do –
But soon by charging over me,
   The *Coldstream* brought me to.

With kicks and cuts, and balls and blows,
70   I throb and ache all over;
I'm quite convinc'd the field of Mars
   Is not a field of clover!

O why did I a soldier turn
    For any royal Guelph?
I might have been a Butcher, and
    In business for myself!

O why did I the bounty take
    (And here he gasp'd for breath)
My shillingsworth of 'list is nail'd
80   Upon the door of death!

Without a coffin I shall lie
    And sleep my sleep eternal:
Not ev'n a *shell* – my only chance
    Of being made a *Kernel!*

O Patty dear, our wedding bells
    With never ring at Chester!
Here I must lie in Honour's bed,
    That isn't worth a *tester!*

Farewell, my regimental mates,
90   With whom I used to dress!
My corps is changed, and I am now,
    In quite another mess.

Farewell, my Patty dear, I have
    No dying consolations,
Except, when I am dead, you'll go
    And see th' Illuminations.'

A Parental Ode to My Son, Aged Three Years and Five Months

        Thou happy, happy elf!
(But stop, – first let me kiss away that tear) –
        Thou tiny image of myself!
(My love, he's poking peas into his ear!)

Thou merry, laughing sprite!
With spirits feather-light,
Untouch'd by sorrow, and unsoil'd by sin –
(Good heav'ns! the child is swallowing a pin!)

Thou little tricksy Puck!
With antic toys so funnily bestuck,
Light as the singing bird that wings the air –
(The door! the door! he'll tumble down the stair!)
Thou darling of thy sire!
(Why, Jane, he'll set his pinafore a-fire!)
Thou imp of mirth and joy!
In love's dear chain so strong and bright a link,
Thou idol of thy parents – (Drat the boy!
There goes my ink!)

Thou cherub – but of earth;
Fit playfellow for Fays, by moonlight pale,
In harmless sport and mirth,
(That dog will bite him if he pulls its tail!)
Thou human humming-bee, extracting honey
From ev'ry blossom in the world that blows,
Singing in Youth's Elysium ever sunny,
(Another tumble! – that's his precious nose!)

Thy father's pride and hope!
(He'll break the mirror with that skipping-rope!)
With pure heart newly stamp'd from Nature's mint –
(Where *did* he learn that squint?)
Thou young domestic dove!
(He'll have that jug off, with another shove!)
Dear nursling of the hymeneal nest!
(Are those torn clothes his best?)
Little epitome of man!
(He'll climb upon the table, that's his plan!)
Touch'd with the beauteous tints of dawning life –
(He's got a knife!)

Thou enviable being!
40 No storms, no clouds, in thy blue sky foreseeing,
        Play on, play on,
        My elfin John!
Toss the light ball – bestride the stick –
(I knew so many cakes would make him sick!)
With fancies buoyant as the thistle-down,
Prompting the face grotesque, and antic brisk,
        With many a lamb-like frisk,
(He's got the scissors, snipping at your gown!)

        Thou pretty opening rose!
50 (Go to your mother, child, and wipe your nose!)
Balmy, and breathing music like the South,
(He really brings my heart into my mouth!)
Fresh as the morn, and brilliant as its star, –
(I wish that window had an iron bar!)
Bold as the hawk, yet gentle as the dove, –
        (I'll tell you what, my love,
I cannot write, unless he's sent above!)

I'm going to Bombay

'Nothing venture, nothing have' – Old Proverb
'Every Indiaman has at least two mates' – *Falconer's Marine Guide*

My hair is brown, my eyes are blue,
And reckon'd rather bright;
I'm shapely, if they tell me true,
And just the proper height;
My skin has been admired in verse,
And called as fair as day –
If I *am* fair, so much the worse,
I'm going to Bombay!

At school I passed with some éclat;
10 I learn'd my French in France;
De Wint gave lessons how to draw,
And D'Egville how to dance; –
Crevelli taught me how to sing,
And Cramer how to play –
It really is the strangest thing –
I'm going to Bombay!

I've been to Bath and Cheltenham Wells,
But not their springs to sip –
To Ramsgate – not to pick up shells, –
20 To Brighton – not to dip.
I've tour'd the Lakes, and scour'd the coast
From Scarboro' to Torquay –
But tho' of time I've made the most,
I'm going to Bombay!

By Pa and Ma I'm daily told
To marry now's my time,
For though I'm very far from old,
I'm rather in my prime.
They say while we have any sun
30 We ought to make our hay –
And India has so hot an one,
I'm going to Bombay!

My cousin writes from Hyderapot
My only chance to snatch,
And says the climate is so hot,
It's sure to light a match. –
She's married to a son of Mars,
With very handsome pay,
And swears I ought to thank my stars
40 I'm going to Bombay!

She says that I shall much delight
To taste their Indian treats,
But what she likes may turn me quite,
Their strange outlandish meats. –
If I can eat rupees, who knows?
Or dine, the Indian way,
On doolies, and on bungalows –
I'm going to Bombay!

She says that I shall much enjoy, –
50   I don't know what she means, –
To take the air and buy some toy,
In my own palankeens, –
I like to drive my pony-chair,
Or ride our dapple grey –
But elephants are horses there –
I'm going to Bombay!

Farewell, farewell, my parents dear,
My friends, farewell to them!
And oh, what costs a sadder tear
60   Good-bye, to Mr M.! –
If I should find an Indian vault,
Or fall a tiger's prey,
Or steep in salt, it's all *his* fault,
I'm going to Bombay!

That fine new teak-built ship, the Fox,
A. I. – Commander Bird,
Now lying in the London Docks,
Will sail on May the Third;
Apply for passage or for freight,
70   To Nichol, Scott, and Gray –
Pa has applied and seal'd my fate –
I'm going to Bombay!

My heart is full – my trunks as well;
My mind and caps made up,
My corsets, shap'd by Mrs Bell,
Are promised ere I sup;
With boots and shoes, Rivarta's best,
And dresses by Ducé,
And a special licence in my chest –
80   I'm going to Bombay!

Ode

To the Advocates for the Removal of Smithfield Market

'Sweeping our flocks and herds' – *Douglas*

O PHILANTHROPIC men! –
For this address I need not make apology –
Who aim at clearing out the Smithfield pen,
And planting further off its vile Zoology –
Permit me thus to tell,
I like your efforts well,
For routing that great nest of Hornithology!

Be not dismay'd, although repulsed at first,
And driven from their Horse, and Pig, and Lamb parts,
10   Charge on! – you shall upon their hornworks burst,
And carry all their *Bull*-warks and their *Ram*-parts.

Go on, ye wholesale drovers!
And drive away the Smithfield flocks and herds!
As wild as Tartar-Curds,
That come so fat, and kicking, from their clovers,
Off with them all! – those restive brutes, that vex
Our streets, and plunge, and lunge, and butt, and battle;
And save the female sex
From being cow'd – like Iö – by the cattle!

20   Fancy, – when droves appear on
The hill of Holborn, roaring from its top, –
Your ladies – ready, as they own, to drop,
Taking themselves to Thomson's with a *Fear-on!*

        Or, in St Martin's Lane,
Scared by a Bullock, in a frisky vein, –
Fancy the terror of your timid daughters,
        While rushing souse
        Into a coffee-house,
        To find it – Slaughter's!

30   Or fancy this: –
Walking along the street, some stranger Miss,
Her head with no such thought of danger laden
When suddenly 'tis 'Aries Taurus Virgo!' –
You don't know Latin, I translate it ergo,
Into your Areas a Bull throws the Maiden!

        Think of some poor old crone
Treated, just like a penny, with a toss!
        At that vile spot now grown
        So generally known
40 For making a Cow Cross!

Nay, fancy your own selves far off from stall,
Or shed, or shop – and that an Ox infuriate
        Just pins you to the wall,
Giving you a strong dose of *Oxy-Muriate!*

Methinks I hear the neighbours that live round
        The Market-ground
Thus make appeal unto their civic fellows –
' 'Tis well for you that live apart – unable
        To hear this brutal Babel,
50 But our *firesides* are troubled with their *bellows.*

Folks that too freely sup
Must e'en put up
With their own troubles if they can't digest;
But we must needs regard
The case as hard
That *others'* victuals should disturb our rest,
That from our sleep *your* food should start and jump us!
We like, ourselves, a steak,
But, Sirs, for pity's sake!
60   We don't want oxen at our doors to *rump-us!*

If we *do* doze – it really is too bad!
We constantly are roar'd awake or rung,
Through bullocks mad
That run in all the "Night Thoughts" of our Young!'

Such are the woes of sleepers – now let's take
The woes of those that wish to keep *a Wake!*
Oh think! when Wombwell gives his annual feasts,
Think of these 'Bulls of Basan', far from mild ones;
Such fierce tame beasts,
70   That nobody much cares to see the Wild ones!

Think of the Show woman, 'what shows a Dwarf',
Seeing a red Cow come
To swallow her Tom Thumb,
And forc'd with broom of birch to keep her off!

Think, too, of Messrs Richardson and Co.,
When looking at their public private boxes,
To see in the back row
Three live sheeps' heads, a porker's, and an Ox's!
Think of their Orchestra, when two horns come
80   Through, to accompany the double drum!
Or, in the midst of murder and remorses,
Just when the Ghost is certain,
A great rent in the curtain,
And enter two tall skeletons – of Horses!

Great Philanthropics! pray urge these topics!
Upon the Solemn Councils of the Nation,
Get a Bill soon, and give, some noon,
The Bulls, a Bull of Excommunication!
Let the old Fair have fair-play as its right,
90   And to each show and sight
Ye shall be treated with a Free List latitude;
        To Richardson's Stage Dramas,
        Dio – and Cosmo – ramas,
        Giants and Indians wild,
        Dwarf, Sea Bear, and Fat Child,
And that most rare of Shows – a Show of Gratitude!

The Lament of Toby, the Learned Pig

'A little learning is a dangerous thing' – Pope

O heavy day! oh day of woe!
    To misery a poster,
Why was I ever farrow'd – why
    Not spitted for a roaster?

In this world, pigs, as well as men,
    Must dance to fortune's fiddlings,
But must I give the classics up,
    For barley-meal and middlings?

Of what avail that I could spell
10   And read, just like my betters,
If I must come to this at last,
    To litters, not to letters?

O, why are pigs made scholars of?
    It baffles my discerning,
What griskins, fry, and chitterlings,
    Can have to do with learning.

Alas! my learning once drew cash,
   But public fame's unstable,
So I must turn a pig again,
20   And fatten for the table.

To leave my literary line
   My eyes get red and leaky;
But Giblett doesn't want me *blue*,
   But red and white, and streaky.

Old Mullins used to cultivate
   My learning like a gard'ner;
But Giblett only thinks of lard,
   And not of Doctor Lardner!

He does not care about my brain
30   The value of two coppers,
All that he thinks about my head
   Is, how I'm off for choppers.

Of all my literary kin
   A farewell must be taken,
Good bye to the poetic Hogg!
   The philosophic Bacon!

Day after day my lessons fade,
   My intellect gets muddy;
A trough I have, and not a desk,
40   A sty – and not a study!

Another little month, and then
   My progress ends, like Bunyan's;
The seven sages that I loved
   Will be chopp'd up with onions!

Then over head and ears in brine
   They'll souse me, like a salmon,
My mathematics turn'd to brawn,
   My logic into gammon.

My Hebrew will all retrograde,
    Now I'm put up to fatten;
My Greek, it will all go to grease;
    The Dogs will have my Latin!

Farewell to Oxford! – and to Bliss!
    To Milman, Crowe, and Glossop, –
I now must be content with chats,
    Instead of learned gossip!

Farewell to 'Town'! farewell to 'Gown'!
    I've quite outgrown the latter, –
Instead of Trencher-cap my head
    Will soon be in a platter!

O why did I at Brazen-Nose
    Rout up the roots of knowledge?
A butcher that can't read will kill
    A pig that's been to college!

For sorrow I could stick myself,
    But conscience is a clasher;
A thing that would be rash in man,
    In me would be a rasher!

One thing I ask – when I am dead,
    And past the Stygian ditches –
And that is, let my schoolmaster
    Have one of my two flitches:

'Twas he who taught my letters so
    I ne'er mistook or miss'd 'em,
Simply by *ringing* at the nose,
    According to *Bell's* system.

Miss Kilmansegg and Her Precious Leg
A Golden Legend

'What is here?
Gold? yellow, glittering, precious gold?' – *Timon of Athens*

HER PEDIGREE

To trace the Kilmansegg pedigree,
To the very roots of the family tree,
   Were a task as rash as ridiculous:
Through antediluvian mists as thick
As London fog such a line to pick
Were enough, in truth, to puzzle Old Nick,
   Not to name Sir Harris Nicolas.

It wouldn't require much verbal strain
To trace the Kill-man, perchance, to Cain;
10   But waving all such digressions,
Suffice it, according to family lore,
A Patriarch Kilmansegg lived of yore,
   Who was famed for his great possessions.

Tradition said he feather'd his nest
Through an Agricultural Interest
   In the Golden Age of Farming;
When golden eggs were laid by the geese,
And Colchian sheep wore a golden fleece,
And golden pippins – the sterling kind
20 Of Hesperus – now so hard to find –
   Made Horticulture quite charming!

A Lord of Land, on his own estate,
He lived at a very lively rate,
   But his income would bear carousing;

Such acres he had of pasture and heath,
With herbage so rich from the ore beneath,
The very ewe's and lambkin's teeth
    Were turn'd into gold by browsing.

He gave, without any extra thrift,
30   A flock of sheep for a birthday gift
    To each son of his loins, or daughter:
And his debts – if debts he had – at will
He liquidated by giving each bill
    A dip in Pactolian water.

'Twas said that even his pigs of lead,
By crossing with some by Midas bred,
    Made a perfect mine of his piggery.
And as for cattle, one yearling bull
Was worth all Smithfield-market full
40   Of the Golden Bulls of Pope Gregory.

The high-bred horses within his stud,
Like human creatures of birth and blood,
    Had their Golden Cups and flagons:
And as for the common husbandry nags,
Their noses were tied in money-bags,
    When they stopp'd with the carts and waggons.

Moreover, he had a Golden Ass,
Sometimes at stall, and sometimes at grass,
    That was worth his own weight in money –
50   And a golden hive, on a Golden Bank,
Where golden bees, by alchemical prank,
    Gather'd gold instead of honey.

Gold! and gold! and gold without end!
He had gold to lay by, and gold to spend,
Gold to give, and gold to lend,
    And reversions of gold *in futuro*.

In wealth the family revell'd and roll'd,
Himself and wife and sons so bold; –
And his daughters sang to their harps of gold
60   'O bella eta del' oro!'

Such was the tale of the Kilmansegg Kin,
In golden text on a vellum skin,
Though certain people would wink and grin,
    And declare the whole story a parable –
That the Ancestor rich was one Jacob Ghrimes,
Who held a long lease, in prosperous times,
    Of acres, pasture and arable.

That as money makes money, his golden bees
Were the five per cents, or which you please,
70   When his cash was more than plenty –
That the golden cups were racing affairs;
And his daughters, who sang Italian airs,
    Had their golden harps of Clementi.

That the Golden Ass, or Golden Bull,
Was English John, with his pockets full,
    Then at war by land and water:
While beef, and mutton, and other meat,
Were almost as dear as money to eat,
And Farmers reaped Golden Harvests of wheat
80   At the Lord knows what per quarter!

HER BIRTH

What different dooms our birthdays bring!
For instance, one little manikin thing
    Survives to wear many a wrinkle;
While Death forbids another to wake,
And a son that it took nine moons to make
    Expires without even a twinkle!

Into this world we come like ships,
Launch'd from the docks, and stocks, and slips,
　　For fortune fair or fatal;
90　And one little craft is cast away
In its very first trip in Babbicome Bay,
　　While another rides safe at Port Natal.

What different lots our stars accord!
This babe to be hail'd and woo'd as a Lord!
　　And that to be shunn'd like a leper!
One, to the world's wine, honey, and corn,
Another, like Colchester native, born
　　To its vinegar, oil, and pepper.

One is litter'd under a roof
100　Neither wind nor water proof, –
　　That's the prose of Love in a Cottage, –
A puny, naked, shivering wretch,
The whole of whose birthright would not fetch,
Though Robins himself drew up the sketch,
　　The bid of 'a mess of pottage'.

Born of Fortunatus's kin,
Another comes tenderly usher'd in
　　To a prospect all bright and burnish'd:
No tenant he for life's back slums –
110　He comes to the world as a gentleman comes
　　To a lodging ready furnish'd.

And the other sex – the tender – the fair –
What wide reverses of fate are there!
Whilst Margaret, charm'd by the Bulbul rare,
　　In a garden of Gul reposes –
Poor Peggy hawks nosegays from street to street,
Till – think of that, who find life so sweet! –
　　She hates the smell of roses!

Not so with the infant Kilmansegg!
120   She was not born to steal or beg,
      Or gather cresses in ditches;
   To plait the straw, or bind the shoe,
   Or sit all day to hem and sew,
   As females must, and not a few –
      To fill their insides with stitches!

   She was not doom'd, for bread to eat,
   To be put to her hands as well as her feet –
      To carry home linen from mangles –
   Or heavy-hearted, and weary-limb'd,
130   To dance on a rope in a jacket trimm'd
      With as many blows as spangles.

   She was one of those who by Fortune's boon
   Are born, as they say, with a silver spoon
      In her mouth, not a wooden ladle:
   To speak according to poet's wont,
   Plutus as sponsor stood at her font,
      And Midas rock'd the cradle.

   At her first *début* she found her head
   On a pillow of down, in a downy bed,
140   With a damask canopy over.
   For although by the vulgar popular saw
   All mothers are said to be 'in the straw',
      Some children are born in clover.

   Her very first draught of vital air
   It was not the common chamelion fare
      Of plebeian lungs and noses, –
         No – her earliest sniff
         Of this world was a whiff
   Of the genuine Otto of Roses!

150 When she saw the light – it was no mere ray
Of that light so common – so everyday –
    That the sun each morning launches –
But six wax tapers dazzled her eyes,
From a thing – a gooseberry bush for size –
    With a golden stem and branches.

She was born exactly at half-past two,
As witness'd a timepiece in or-molu
    That stood on a marble table –
Shewing at once the time of day,
160 And a team of *Gildings* running away
    As fast as they were able,
With a golden God, with a golden Star,
And a golden Spear, in a golden Car,
    According to Grecian fable.

Like other babes, at her birth she cried;
Which made a sensation far and wide,
    Ay, for twenty miles around her;
For though to the ear 'twas nothing more
Than an infant's squall, it was really the roar
170 Of a Fifty-thousand Pounder!
        It shook the next heir
        In his library chair
And made him cry, 'Confound her!'

Of signs and omens there was no dearth,
Any more than at Owen Glendower's birth,
    Or the advent of other great people:
        Two bullocks dropp'd dead,
        As if knock'd on the head,
        And barrels of stout
180   And ale ran about,
        And the village-bells such a peal rang out,
    That they crack'd the village-steeple.

In no time at all, like mushroom spawn,
Tables sprang up all over the lawn;
Not furnish'd scantly or shabbily,
     But on scale as vast
     As that huge repast,
     With its loads and cargoes
     Of drink and botargoes,
190 At the Birth of the Babe in Rabelais.

Hundreds of men were turn'd into beasts,
Like the guests at Circe's horrible feasts,
     By the magic of ale and cider:
And each country lass, and each country lad,
Began to caper and dance like mad,
And even some old ones appear'd to have had
     A bite from the Naples Spider.

     Then as night came on,
     It had scared King John,
200 Who considered such signs not risible,
     To have seen the maroons,
     And the whirling moons,
     And the serpents of flame,
     And wheels of the same,
That according to some were 'whizzable'.

Oh, happy Hope of the Kilmanseggs!
Thrice happy in head, and body, and legs
     That her parents had such full pockets!
For had she been born of Want and Thrift,
210 For care and nursing all adrift,
It's ten to one she had had to make shift
     With rickets instead of rockets!

And how was the precious Baby drest?
In a robe of the East, with lace of the West,
Like one of Croesus's issue –
   Her best bibs were made
   Of rich gold brocade,
And the others of silver tissue.

And when the Baby inclined to nap
220 She was lull'd on a Gros de Naples lap,
By a nurse in a modish Paris cap,
   Of notions so exalted,
She drank nothing lower than Curaçoa,
Maraschino, or pink Noyau,
   And on principle never malted.

From a golden boat, with a golden spoon,
The babe was fed night, morning, and noon;
   And altho' the tale seems fabulous,
'Tis said her tops and bottoms were gilt,
230 Like the oats in that Stable-yard Palace built
   For the horse of Heliogabalus.

And when she took to squall and kick –
For pain will wring and pins will prick
   E'en the wealthiest nabob's daughter –
They gave her no vulgar Dalby or gin,
But a liquor with leaf of gold therein,
   Videlicet, – Dantzic Water.

In short, she was born, and bred, and nurst,
And drest in the best from the very first,
240   To please the genteelest censor –
And then, as soon as strength would allow,
Was vaccinated, as babes are now,
With virus ta'en from the best-bred cow
   Of Lord Althorp's – now Earl Spencer.

HER CHRISTENING

Though Shakspeare asks us, 'What's in a name?'
(As if cognomens were much the same),
    There's really a very great scope in it.
A name? – why, wasn't there Doctor Dodd,
That servant at once of Mammon and God,
250   Who found four thousand pounds and odd,
    A prison – a cart – and a rope in it?

A name? – if the party had a voice,
What mortal would be a Bugg by choice?
As a Hogg, a Grubb, or a Chubb rejoice?
    Or any such nauseous blazon?
Not to mention many a vulgar name,
That would make a doorplate blush for shame,
    If doorplates were not so brazen!

A name? – it has more than nominal worth,
260   And belongs to good or bad luck at birth –
    As dames of a certain degree know,
In spite of his Page's hat and hose,
His Page's jacket, and buttons in rows,
Bob only sounds like a page of prose
    Till turn'd into Rupertino.

Now to christen the infant Kilmansegg,
For days and days it was quite a plague,
    To hunt the list in the Lexicon:
And scores were tried, like coin, by the ring,
270   Ere names were found just the proper thing
    For a minor rich as a Mexican.

Then cards were sent, the presence to beg
Of all the kin of Kilmansegg,
    White, yellow, and brown relations:
Brothers, Wardens of City Halls,
And Uncles – rich as three Golden Balls
    From taking pledges of nations.

Nephews, whom Fortune seem'd to bewitch,
   Rising in life like rockets –
280 Nieces whose doweries knew no hitch –
Aunts as certain of dying rich
   As candles in golden sockets –
Cousins German, and cousin's sons,
All thriving and opulent – some had tons
   Of Kentish hops in their pockets!

For money had stuck to the race through life
(As it did to the bushel when cash so rife
Pozed Ali Baba's brother's wife) –
   And down to the Cousins and Coz-lings,
290 The fortunate brood of the Kilmanseggs,
As if they had come out of golden eggs,
   Were all as wealthy as 'Goslings'.

It would fill a Court Gazette to name
What East and West End people came
   To the rite of Christianity:
The lofty Lord, and the titled Dame,
   All di'monds, plumes, and urbanity:
His Lordship the May'r with his golden chain,
And two Gold Sticks, and the Sheriffs twain,
300 Nine foreign Counts, and other great men
With their orders and stars, to help M or N
   To renounce all pomp and vanity.

To paint the maternal Kilmansegg
The pen of an Eastern Poet would beg,
   And need an elaborate sonnet;
How she sparkled with gems whenever she stirr'd,
And her head niddle-noddled at every word,
And seem'd so happy, a Paradise Bird
   Had nidificated upon it.

310   And Sir Jacob the Father strutted and bow'd,
And smiled to himself, and laugh'd aloud,
   To think of his heiress and daughter –
And then in his pockets he made a grope,
And then, in the fulness of joy and hope,
Seem'd washing his hands with invisible soap,
   In imperceptible water.

He had roll'd in money like pigs in mud,
Till it seem'd to have enter'd into his blood
   By some occult projection:
320   And his cheeks, instead of a healthy hue,
As yellow as any guinea grew,
Making the common phrase seem true
   About a rich complexion.

And now came the nurse, and during a pause,
Her dead–leaf satin would fitly cause
   A very autumnal rustle –
So full of figure, so full of fuss,
As she carried about the babe to buss,
   She seem'd to be nothing but bustle.

330   A wealthy Nabob was Godpapa,
And an Indian Begum was Godmamma,
   Whose jewels a Queen might covet –
And the Priest was a Vicar, and Dean withal
Of that Temple we see with a Golden Ball,
   And a Golden Cross above it.

The Font was a bowl of American gold,
Won by Raleigh in days of old,
   In spite of Spanish bravado;
And the Book of Pray'r was so overrun
340   With gilt devices, it shone in the sun
Like a copy – a presentation one –
   Of Humboldt's 'El Dorado'.

Gold! and gold! and nothing but gold!
The same auriferous shine behold
   Wherever the eye could settle!
On the walls – the sideboard – the ceiling-sky –
On the gorgeous footmen standing by,
In coats to delight a miner's eye
   With seams of precious metal.

350   Gold! and gold! and besides the gold,
The very robe of the infant told
A tale of wealth in every fold,
   It lapp'd her like a vapour!
So fine! so thin! the mind at a loss
Could compare it to nothing except a cross
   Of cobweb with bank-note paper.

Then her pearls – 'twas a perfect sight, forsooth,
To see them, like 'the dew of her youth',
   In such a plentiful sprinkle.
360   Meanwhile, the Vicar read through the form,
And gave her another, not overwarm,
   That made her little eyes twinkle.

Then the babe was cross'd and bless'd amain;
But instead of the Kate, or Ann, or Jane,
   Which the humbler female endorses –
Instead of one name, as some people prefix,
Kilmansegg went at the tails of six,
   Like a carriage of state with its horses.

Oh, then the kisses she got and hugs!
370   The golden mugs and the golden jugs
   That lent fresh rays to the midges!
The golden knives, and the golden spoons,
The gems that sparkled like fairy boons,
It was one of the Kilmansegg's own saloons,
   But look'd like Rundell and Bridge's!

Gold! and gold! the new and the old!
The company ate and drank from gold,
　　They revell'd, they sang, and were merry;
And one of the Gold Sticks rose from his chair,
380　And toasted 'the Lass with the golden hair'
　　In a bumper of golden Sherry.

Gold! still gold! it rain'd on the nurse,
Who, unlike Danaë, was none the worse;
There was nothing but guineas glistening!
　　Fifty were given to Doctor James,
　　For calling the little Baby names,
　　　And for saying, Amen!
　　　The Clerk had ten,
And that was the end of the Christening.

HER CHILDHOOD

390　Our youth! our childhood! that spring of springs!
'Tis surely one of the blessedest things
　　That nature ever invented!
When the rich are wealthy beyond their wealth,
And the poor are rich in spirits and health,
　　And all with their lots contented!

There's little Phelim, he sings like a thrush,
In the selfsame pair of patchwork plush,
　　With the selfsame empty pockets,
That tempted his daddy so often to cut
400　His throat, or jump in the water-butt –
But what cares Phelim? an empty nut
　　Would sooner bring tears to their sockets.

　　Give him a collar without a skirt,
　　That's the Irish linen for shirt,
And a slice of bread, with a taste of dirt,

That's Poverty's Irish butter,
And what does he lack to make him blest?
Some oyster-shells, or a sparrow's nest,
    A candle-end and a gutter.

410   But to leave the happy Phelim alone,
Gnawing, perchance, a marrowless bone,
    For which no dog would quarrel –
Turn we to little Miss Kilmansegg,
Cutting her first little toothy-peg
With a fifty guinea coral –
    A peg upon which
    About poor and rich
Reflection might hang a moral.

Born in wealth, and wealthily nursed,
420   Capp'd, papp'd, napp'd and lapp'd from the first
    On the knees of Prodigality,
Her childhood was one eternal round
Of the game of going on Tickler's ground
    Picking up gold – in reality.

With extempore carts she never play'd,
Or the odds and ends of a Tinker's trade,
Or little dirt pies and puddings made,
    Like children happy and squalid;
The very puppet she had to pet,
430   Like a bait for the 'Nix my Dolly' set,
    Was a Dolly of gold – and solid!

Gold! and gold! 'twas the burden still!
To gain the Heiress's early goodwill
There was much corruption and bribery –
    The yearly cost of her golden toys
Would have given half London's Charity Boys
And Charity Girls the annual joys
    Of a holiday dinner at Highbury.

Bon-bons she ate from the gilt cornet;
440   And gilded queens on St Bartlemy's day;
    Till her fancy was tinged by her presents –
And first a goldfinch excited her wish,
Then a spherical bowl with its Golden fish,
    And then two Golden Pheasants.

Nay, once she squall'd and scream'd like wild –
And it shews how the bias we give to a child
    Is a thing most weighty and solemn: –
But whence was wonder or blame to spring
If little Miss K., – after such a swing –
450   Made a dust for the flaming gilded thing
    On the top of the Fish Street column?

HER EDUCATION

According to metaphysical creed,
To the earliest books that children read
    For much good or much bad they are debtors –
But before with their A B C they start,
There are things in morals, as well as art,
That play a very important part –
    'Impressions before the letters'.

Dame Education begins the pile,
460   Mayhap in the graceful Corinthian style,
    But alas for the elevation!
If the Lady's maid or Gossip the Nurse
With a load of rubbish, or something worse,
    Have made a rotten foundation.

Even thus with little Miss Kilmansegg,
Before she learnt her E for egg,
    Ere her Governess came, or her Masters –
Teachers of quite a different kind
    Had 'cramm'd' her beforehand, and put her mind
470   In a go-cart on golden castors.

Long before her A B and C.
They had taught her by heart her L. S. D.
　　And as how she was born a great Heiress;
And as sure as London is built of bricks,
My Lord would ask her the day to fix,
To ride in a fine gilt coach and six,
　　Like Her Worship the Lady May'ress.

Instead of stories from Edgeworth's page,
The true golden lore for our golden age,
480　　Or lessons from Barbauld and Trimmer,
Teaching the worth of Virtue and Health,
All that she knew was the Virtue of Wealth,
Provided by vulgar nursery stealth
　　With a Book of Leaf Gold for a Primer.

The very metal of merit they told,
And praised her for being as 'good as gold!'
　　Till she grew as a peacock haughty;
Of money they talk'd the whole day round,
And weigh'd desert like grapes by the pound,
490　　Till she had an idea from the very sound
　　That people with nought were naughty.

They praised – poor children with nothing at all!
Lord! how you twaddle and waddle and squall
　　Like common-bred geese and ganders!
What sad little bad little figures you make
To the rich Miss K, whose plainest seed-cake
　　Was stuff'd with corianders!

They praised her falls, as well as her walk,
Flatterers make cream cheese of chalk,
500　　They praised – how they praised – her very small talk,
　　As if it fell from a Solon;
Or the girl who at each pretty phrase let drop
A ruby comma, or pearl full-stop,
　　Or an emerald semi-colon.

They praised her spirit, and now and then,
The Nurse brought her own little 'nevy' Ben,
    To play with the future May'ress,
And when he got raps, and taps, and slaps,
Scratches, and pinches, snips, and snaps,
510   As if from a Tigress or Bearess,
They told him how Lords would court that hand,
And always gave him to understand,
        While he rubb'd, poor soul,
        His carroty poll,
    That his hair had been pull'd by 'a *Hairess*'.

Such were the lessons from maid and nurse,
A Governess help'd to make still worse,
Giving an appetite so perverse
    Fresh diet whereon to batten –
520 Beginning with A. B. C. to hold
Like a royal playbill printed in gold
    On a square of pearl-white satin.

The books to teach the verbs and nouns,
And those about countries, cities, and towns,
Instead of their sober drabs and browns,
    Were in crimson silk, with gilt edges; –
Her Butler, and Enfield, and Entick – in short
Her 'Early Lessons' of every sort,
    Look'd like Souvenirs, Keepsakes, and Pledges.

530 Old Johnson shone out in as fine array
As he did one night when he went to the play;
Chambaud like a beau of King Charles's day –
    Lindley Murray in like conditions –
Each weary, unwelcome, irksome task,
Appear'd in a fancy dress and a mask –
If you wish for similar copies ask
    For Howell and James's Editions.

Novels she read to amuse her mind,
But always the affluent match-making kind
540   That ends with Promessi Sposi,
And a father-in-law so wealthy and grand,
He could give cheque-mate to Coutts in the Strand;
      So, along with a ring and posy,
He endows the Bride with Golconda off hand,
      And gives the Groom Potosi.

Plays she perused – but she liked the best
Those comedy gentlefolks always possess'd
      Of fortunes so truly romantic –
Of money so ready that right or wrong
550 It always is ready to go for a song,
Throwing it, going it, pitching it strong –
They ought to have purses as green and long
      As the cucumber called the Gigantic.

Then Eastern Tales she loved for the sake
Of the Purse of Oriental make,
      And the thousand pieces they put in it –
But Pastoral scenes on her heart fell cold,
For Nature with her had lost its hold,
No field but the Field of the Cloth of Gold
560   Would ever have caught her foot in it.

What more? She learnt to sing, and dance,
To sit on a horse, although he should prance,
And to speak a French not spoken in France
      Any more than at Babel's building –
And she painted shells, and flowers, and Turks,
But her great delight was in Fancy Works
      That are done with gold or gilding.

Gold! still gold! – the bright and the dead,
With golden beads, and gold lace, and gold thread
570 She work'd in gold, as if for her bread;

The metal had so undermined her,
Gold ran in her thoughts and fill'd her brain,
She was golden-headed as Peter's cane
    With which he walk'd behind her.

HER ACCIDENT

The horse that carried Miss Kilmansegg,
And a better never lifted leg,
    Was a very rich bay, called Banker –
A horse of a breed and a mettle so rare, –
By Bullion out of an Ingot mare, –
580 That for action, the best of figures, and air,
    It made many good judges hanker.

And when she took a ride in the Park,
Equestrian Lord, or pedestrian Clerk,
    Was thrown in an amorous fever,
To see the Heiress how well she sat,
With her groom behind her, Bob or Nat,
In green, half smother'd with gold, and a hat
    With more gold lace than beaver.

And then when Banker obtain'd a pat,
590 To see how he arch'd his neck at that!
    He snorted with pride and pleasure!
Like the Steed in the fable so lofty and grand,
Who gave the poor Ass to understand,
That *he* didn't carry a bag of sand,
    But a burden of golden treasure.

A load of treasure? – alas! alas!
Had her horse but been fed upon English grass,
    And sheltered in Yorkshire spinneys,
Had he scour'd the sand with the Desart Ass,
600   Or where the American whinnies –

But a hunter from Erin's turf and gorse,
A regular thorough-bred Irish horse,
Why, he ran away, as a matter of course,
    With a girl worth her weight in guineas!

Mayhap 'tis the trick of such pamper'd nags
To shy at the sight of a beggar in rags,
    But away, like the bolt of a rabbit,
Away went the horse in the madness of fright,
And away went the horsewoman mocking the sight –
610 Was yonder blue flash a flash of blue light,
    Or only the skirt of her habit?

Away she flies, with the groom behind, –
It looks like a race of the Calmuck kind,
    When Hymen himself is the starter:
And the Maid rides first in the fourfooted strife,
Riding, striding, as if for her life,
While the Lover rides after to catch him a wife,
    Although it's catching a Tartar.

But the Groom has lost his glittering hat!
620 Though he does not sigh and pull up for that –
Alas! his horse is a tit for Tatt
    To sell to a very low bidder –
His wind is ruin'd, his shoulder is sprung,
Things, though a horse be handsome and young,
    A purchaser *will* consider.

But still flies the Heiress through stones and dust,
Oh, for a fall, if fall she must,
    On the gentle lap of Flora!
But still, thank Heaven! she clings to her seat –
630 Away! away! she could ride a dead heat
With the Dead who ride so fast and fleet,
    In the Ballad of Leonora!

Away she gallops! – it's awful work!
It's faster than Turpin's ride to York,
   On Bess that notable clipper!
She has circled the Ring! – she crosses the Park!
Mazeppa, although he was stripp'd so stark,
   Mazeppa couldn't outstrip her!

The fields seem running away with the folks!
640   The Elms are having a race for the Oaks!
   At a pace that all Jockeys disparages!
All, all is racing! the Serpentine
Seems rushing past like the 'arrowy Rhine',
The houses have got on a railway line,
   And are off like the first-class carriages!

She'll lose her life! she is losing her breath!
A cruel chase, she is chasing Death,
   As female shriekings forewarn her:
And now – as gratis as blood of Guelph –
650   She clears that gate, which has clear'd itself
   Since then, at Hyde Park Corner!

Alas! for the hope of the Kilmanseggs!
For her head, her brains, her body, and legs,
   Her life's not worth a copper!
         Willy-nilly,
         In Piccadilly,
A hundred hearts turn sick and chilly,
   A hundred voices cry, 'Stop her!'
And one old gentleman stares and stands,
660   Shakes his head and lifts his hands,
   And says, 'How very improper!'

On and on! – what a perilous run!
The iron rails seem all mingling in one,
   To shut out the Green Park scenery!

And now the Cellar its dangers reveals,
She shudders – she shrieks – she's doom'd, she feels,
To be torn by powers of horses and wheels,
    Like a spinner by steam machinery!

Sick with horror she shuts her eyes,
670 But the very stones seem uttering cries,
    As they did to that Persian daughter,
When she climb'd up the steep vociferous hill,
Her little silver flagon to fill
    With the magical Golden Water!

'Batter her! shatter her!
Throw and scatter her!'
Shouts each stony-hearted chatterer –
    'Dash at the heavy Dover!
Spill her! kill her! tear and tatter her!
680 Smash her! crash her!' (the stones didn't flatter her!)
'Kick her brains out! let her blood spatter her!
    Roll on her over and over!'

For so she gather'd the awful sense
Of the street in its past unmacadamized tense,
    As the wild horse overran it, –
His four heels making the clatter of six,
Like a Devil's tattoo, played with iron sticks
    On a kettle-drum of granite!

On! still on! she's dazzled with hints
690 Of oranges, ribbons, and colour'd prints,
A Kaleidoscope jumble of shapes and tints,
    And human faces all flashing,
Bright and brief as the sparks from the flints,
    That the desperate hoof keeps dashing!

On and on! still frightfully fast!
Dover-street, Bond-street, all are past!
But – yes – no – yes! – they're down at last!

The Furies and Fates have found them!
Down they go with a sparkle and crash,
700   Like a Bark that's struck by the lightning flash –
There's a shriek – and a sob –
And the dense dark mob
Like a billow closes around them!

    *   *   *   *   *

      *   *   *   *

'She breathes!'
'She don't!'
'She'll recover!'
'She won't!'
'She's stirring! she's living, by Nemesis!'
Gold, still gold! on counter and shelf!
710   Golden dishes as plenty as delf!
Miss Kilmansegg's coming again to herself
On an opulent Goldsmith's premises!

Gold! fine gold! – both yellow and red,
Beaten, and molten – polish'd, and dead –
To see the gold with profusion spread
In all forms of its manufacture!
But what avails gold to Miss Kilmansegg,
When the femoral bone of her dexter leg
Has met with a compound fracture?

720   God may sooth Adversity's smart;
Nay, help to bind up a broken heart;
But to try it on any other part
Were as certain a disappointment,
As if one should rub the dish and plate,
Taken out of a Staffordshire crate –
In the hope of a Golden Service of State –
With Singleton's 'Golden Ointment'.

HER PRECIOUS LEG

'As the twig is bent, the tree's inclined',
Is an adage often recall'd to mind,
730   Referring to juvenile bias:
And never so well is the verity seen,
As when to the weak, warp'd side we lean,
    While Life's tempests and hurricanes try us.

Even thus with Miss K. and her broken limb,
By a very, very remarkable whim,
    She shew'd her early tuition:
While the buds of character came into blow
With a certain tinge that served to show
The nursery culture long ago,
740   As the graft is known by fruition!

For the King's Physician, who nursed the case,
His verdict gave with an awful face,
    And three others concurr'd to egg it;
That the Patient to give old Death the slip,
Like the Pope, instead of a personal trip,
    Must send her Leg as a Legate.

The limb was doom'd – it couldn't be saved!
And like other people the patient behaved,
Nay, bravely that cruel parting braved,
750   Which makes some persons so falter,
They rather would part, without a groan,
With the flesh of their flesh, and bone of their bone,
    They obtain'd at St George's altar.

But when it came to fitting the stump
With a proxy limb – then flatly and plump
    She spoke, in the spirit olden;
She couldn't – she shouldn't – she wouldn't have wood!
Nor a leg of cork, if she never stood,
And she swore an oath, or something as good,
760   The proxy limb should be golden!

A wooden leg! what, a sort of peg,
   For your common Jockeys and Jennies!
No, no, her mother might worry and plague –
Weep, go down on her knees, and beg,
But nothing would move Miss Kilmansegg!
She could – she would have a Golden Leg,
   If it cost ten thousand guineas!

Wood indeed, in Forest or Park,
With its sylvan honours and feudal bark,
770   Is an aristocratical article:
But split and sawn, and hack'd about town,
Serving all needs of pauper or clown,
Trod on! stagger'd on! Wood cut down
   Is vulgar – fibre and particle!

And Cork! – when the noble Cork Tree shades
A lovely group of Castilian maids,
   'Tis a thing for a song or sonnet! –
But cork, as it stops the bottle of gin,
Or bungs the beer – the *small* beer – in,
780   It pierced her heart like a corking-pin,
   To think of standing upon it!

A Leg of Gold – solid gold throughout,
Nothing else, whether slim or stout,
   Should ever support her, God willing!
She must – she could – she would have her whim,
Her father, she turn'd a deaf ear to him –
   He might kill her – she didn't mind killing!
He was welcome to cut off her other limb –
   He might cut her all off with a shilling!

790   All other promised gifts were in vain,
Golden Girdle, or Golden Chain,
She writhed with impatience more than pain,

And utter'd 'pshaws!' and 'pishes!'
But a Leg of Gold! as she lay in bed,
It danced before her – it ran in her head!
It jump'd with her dearest wishes!

'Gold – gold – gold! Oh, let it be gold!'
Asleep or awake that tale she told,
And when she grew delirious:
800   Till her parents resolved to grant her wish,
If they melted down plate, and goblet, and dish,
The case was getting so serious.

So a Leg was made in a comely mould,
Of Gold, fine virgin glittering gold,
As solid as man could make it –
Solid in foot, and calf, and shank,
A prodigious sum of money it sank;
In fact 'twas a Branch of the family Bank,
And no easy matter to break it.

810   All sterling metal – not half-and-half,
The Goldsmith's mark was stamp'd on the calf –
'Twas pure as from Mexican barter!
And to make it more costly, just over the knee,
Where another ligature used to be,
Was a circle of jewels, worth shillings to see,
A new-fangled Badge of the Garter!

'Twas a splendid, brilliant, beautiful Leg,
Fit for the Court of Scander-Beg,
That Precious Leg of Miss Kilmansegg!
820   For, thanks to parental bounty,
Secure from Mortification's touch,
She stood on a member that cost as much
As a Member for all the County!

HER FAME

To gratify stern ambition's whims,
With hundreds and thousands of precious limbs
     On a field of battle we scatter!
Sever'd by sword, or bullet, or saw,
Off they go, all bleeding and raw, –
But the public seems to get the lock–jaw,
830   So little is said on the matter!

Legs, the tightest that ever were seen,
The tightest, the lightest, that danced on the green,
     Cutting capers to sweet Kitty Clover;
Shatter'd, scatter'd, cut, and bowl'd down,
Off they go, worse off for renown,
A line in the *Times*, or a talk about town,
     Than the leg that a fly runs over!

But the Precious Leg of Miss Kilmansegg,
That gowden, goolden, golden leg,
840   Was the theme of all conversation!
Had it been a Pillar of Church and State,
Or a prop to support the whole Dead Weight,
It could not have furnish'd more debate
     To the heads and tails of the nation!

East and west, and north and south,
Though useless for either hunger or drouth, –
The Leg was in every body's mouth,
     To use a poetical figure;
Rumour, in taking her ravenous swim,
850 Saw, and seized on the tempting limb,
     Like a shark on the leg of a nigger.

Wilful murder fell very dead;
Debates in the House were hardly read;
In vain the Police Reports were fed

With Irish riots and *rumpuses* –
The Leg! the Leg! was the great event,
Through every circle of life it went,
    Like the leg of a pair of compasses.

The last new Novel seem'd tame and flat,
860   The Leg, a novelty newer than that,
    Had tripp'd up the heels of Fiction!
It Burked the very essays of Burke,
And, alas! how Wealth over Wit plays the Turk!
As a regular piece of goldsmith's work,
    Got the better of Goldsmith's diction.

'A leg of gold! what of solid gold?'
Cried rich and poor, and young and old, –
    And Master and Miss and Madam –
'Twas the talk of 'Change – the Alley – the Bank –
870   And with men of scientific rank,
It made as much stir as the fossil shank
    Of a Lizard coeval with Adam!

Of course with Greenwich and Chelsea elves,
Men who had lost a limb themselves,
    Its interest did not dwindle –
But Bill, and Ben, and Jack, and Tom,
Could hardly have spun more yarns therefrom,
    If the leg had been a spindle.

Meanwhile the story went to and fro,
880   Till, gathering like the ball of snow,
By the time it got to Stratford-le-Bow,
    Through Exaggeration's touches,
The Heiress and Hope of the Kilmanseggs
Was propp'd on *two* fine Golden Legs,
    And a pair of Golden Crutches!

Never had Leg so great a run!
'Twas the 'go' and the 'Kick' thrown into one!
The mode – the new thing under the sun,

The rage – the fancy – the passion!
890 Bonnets were named, and hats were worn,
A la Golden Leg instead of Leghorn,
And stockings and shoes,
Of golden hues,
Took the lead in the walks of fashion!

The Golden Leg had a vast career,
It was sung and danced – and to show how near
Low Folly to lofty approaches,
Down to society's very dregs,
The Belles of Wapping wore 'Kilmanseggs',
900 And St Giles's Beaux sported Golden Legs
In their pinchbeck pins and brooches!

HER FIRST STEP

Supposing the Trunk and Limbs of Man
Shared, on the allegorical plan,
By the Passions that mark Humanity,
Whichever might claim the head, or heart,
The stomach, or any other part,
The Legs would be seized by Vanity.

There's Bardus, a six-foot column of fop,
A lighthouse without any light atop,
910 Whose height would attract beholders,
If he had not lost some inches clear
By looking down at his kerseymere,
Ogling the limbs he holds so dear,
Till he got a stoop in his shoulders.

Talk of Art, of Science, or Books,
And down go the everlasting looks,
To his crural beauties so wedded!
Try him, wherever you will, you find
His mind in his legs, and his legs in his mind,
920 All prongs and folly – in short a kind
Of Fork – that is Fiddle-headed.

What wonder, then, if Miss Kilmansegg,
With a splendid, brilliant, beautiful leg,
Fit for the court of Scander Beg,
Disdain'd to hide it like Joan or Meg,
    In petticoats stuff'd or quilted?
Not she! 'twas her convalescent whim
To dazzle the world with her precious limb, –
    Nay, to go a little high-kilted.

930   So cards were sent for that sort of mob
Where Tartars and Africans hob-and-nob,
And the Cherokee talks of his cab and cob
    To Polish or Lapland lovers –
Cards like that hieroglyphical call
To a geographical Fancy Ball
    On the recent Post-Office covers.

For if Lion-hunters – and great ones too –
Would mob a savage from Latakoo,
Or squeeze for a glimpse of Prince Le Boo,
940   That unfortunate Sandwich scion –
Hundreds of first-rate people, no doubt,
Would gladly, madly, rush to a rout,
    That promised a Golden Lion!

HER FANCY BALL

Of all the spirits of evil fame
That hurt the soul, or injure the frame,
    And poison what's honest and hearty,
There's none more needs a Mathew to preach
A cooling, antiphlogistic speech,
        To praise and enforce
950   A temperate course,
    Than the Evil Spirit of Party.

Go to the House of Commons, or Lords,
And they seem to be busy with simple words
   In their popular sense or pedantic –
But, alas! with their cheers, and sneers, and jeers,
They're really busy, whatever appears,
Putting peas in each other's ears,
   To drive their enemies frantic!

Thus Tories love to worry the Whigs,
960 Who treat them in turn like Schwalbach pigs,
Giving them lashes, thrashes, and digs,
   With their writhing and pain delighted –
But after all that's said, and more,
The malice and spite of Party are poor
To the malice and spite of a party next door,
   To a party not invited.

On with the cap and out with the light,
Weariness bids the world good night,
   At least for the usual season;
970 But hark! a clatter of horses' heels;
And Sleep and Silence are broken on wheels,
   Like Wilful Murder and Treason!

Another crash – and the carriage goes –
Again poor Weariness seeks the repose
   That Nature demands imperious;
But Echo takes up the burden now,
With a rattling chorus of row-de-dow-dow,
Till Silence herself seems making a row,
   Like a Quaker gone delirious!

980 'Tis night – a winter night – and the stars
Are shining like winkin' – Venus and Mars
Are rolling along in their golden cars
   Through the sky's serene expansion –
But vainly the stars dispense their rays,
Venus and Mars are lost in the blaze
   Of the Kilmanseggs' luminous mansion!

Up jumps Fear in a terrible fright!
His bedchamber windows look so bright,
    With light all the Square is glutted!
990 Up he jumps, like a sole from the pan,
And a tremor sickens his inward man,
For he feels as only a gentleman can,
    Who thinks he's being 'gutted'.

Again Fear settles, all snug and warm;
But only to dream of a dreadful storm
From Autumn's sulphurous locker;
    But the only electric body that falls,
Wears a negative coat, and positive smalls,
And draws the peal that so appals
1000   From the Kilmansegg's brazen knocker!

'Tis Curiosity's Benefit night –
And perchance 'tis the English Second-Sight,
    But whatever it be, so be it –
As the friends and guests of Miss Kilmansegg
Crowd in to look at her Golden Leg,
        As many more
        Mob round the door,
    To see them going to see it!

In they go – in jackets, and cloaks,
1010 Plumes, and bonnets, turbans, and toques,
    As if to a Congress of Nations:
Greeks and Malays, with daggers and dirks,
Spaniards, Jews, Chinese, and Turks –
Some like original foreign works,
    But mostly like bad translations.

In they go, and to work like a pack,
Juan, Moses, and Shacabac,
    Tom, and Jerry, and Springheel'd Jack,

For some of low Fancy are lovers –
1020 Skirting, zigzagging, casting about,
Here and there, and in and out,
With a crush, and a rush, for a full-bodied rout
   Is one of the stiffest of covers.

In they went, and hunted about,
Open mouth'd like chub and trout,
And some with the upper lip thrust out,
   Like that fish for routing, a barbel –
While Sir Jacob stood to welcome the crowd,
And rubb'd his hands, and smiled aloud,
1030 And bow'd, and bow'd, and bow'd, and bow'd,
   Like a man who is sawing marble.

For Princes were there, and Noble Peers;
Dukes descended from Norman spears;
Earls that dated from early years;
   And Lords in vast variety –
Besides the Gentry both new and old –
For people who stand on legs of gold,
   Are sure to stand well with society.

'But where – where – where?' with one accord
1040 Cried Moses and Mufti, Jack and my Lord,
   Wang-Fong and Il Bondocani –
When slow, and heavy, and dead as a dump,
They heard a foot begin to stump,
      Thump! lump!
      Lump! thump!
Like the Spectre in 'Don Giovanni'!

And lo! the Heiress, Miss Kilmansegg,
With her splendid, brilliant, beautiful leg,
   In the garb of a Goddess olden –
1050 Like chaste Diana going to hunt,
With a golden spear – which of course was blunt,
And a tunic loop'd up to a gem in front,
   To shew the Leg that was Golden!

Gold! still gold! her Crescent behold,
That should be silver, but would be gold;
    And her robe's auriferous spangles!
Her golden stomacher – how she would melt!
Her golden quiver, and golden belt,
    Where a golden bugle dangles!

1060   And her jewell'd Garter? Oh, Sin! Oh, Shame!
Let Pride and Vanity bear the blame,
That bring such blots on female fame!
    But to be a true recorder,
Besides its thin transparent stuff,
The tunic was loop'd quite high enough
    To give a glimpse of the Order!

But what have sin or shame to do
With a Golden Leg – and a stout one too?
    Away with all Prudery's panics!
1070   That the precious metal, by thick and thin,
Will cover square acres of land or sin,
            Is a fact made plain
            Again and again,
    In Morals as well as Mechanics.

A few, indeed, of her proper sex,
Who seem'd to feel her foot on their necks,
And fear'd their charms would meet with checks
    From so rare and splendid a blazon –
A few cried 'fie!' – and 'forward' – and 'bold!'
1080   And said of the Leg it might be gold,
    But to them it looked like brazen!

'Twas hard they hinted for flesh and blood,
Virtue, and Beauty, and all that's good,
    To strike to mere dross their topgallants –
But what were Beauty, or Virtue, or Worth,
Gentle manners, or gentle birth,
Nay, what the most talented head on earth
    To a Leg worth fifty Talents!

But the men sang quite another hymn
1090 Of glory and praise to the precious Limb –
Age, sordid Age, admired the whim,
      And its indecorum pardon'd –
While half of the young – ay, more than half –
Bow'd down and worshipp'd the Golden Calf,
      Like the Jews when their hearts were harden'd.

A Golden Leg! what fancies it fired!
What golden wishes and hopes inspired!
      To give but a mere abridgement –
What a leg to leg-bail Embarrassment's serf!
1100 What a leg for a Leg to take on the turf!
      What a leg for a marching regiment!

A Golden Leg! – whatever Love sings,
'Twas worth a bushel of 'Plain Gold Rings'
      With which the Romantic wheedles.
'Twas worth all the legs in stockings and socks –
'Twas a leg that might be put in the Stocks,
      N.B. – Not the parish beadle's!

And Lady K. nid-nodded her head,
Lapp'd in a turban fancy-bred,
1110 Just like a love-apple, huge and red,
      Some Mussul-womanish mystery;
            But whatever she meant
                  To represent,
      She talk'd like the Muse of History.

She told how the filial leg was lost;
And then how much the gold one cost;
      With its weight to a Trojan fraction:
And how it took off, and how it put on;
And call'd on Devil, Duke, and Don,
1120 Mahomet, Moses, and Prester John,
      To notice its beautiful action.

And then of the Leg she went in quest;
And led it where the light was best;
And made it lay itself up to rest
    In postures for painters' studies:
It cost more tricks and trouble by half,
Than it takes to exhibit a Six-Legg'd Calf
To a boothful of country Cuddies.

Nor yet did the Heiress herself omit
1130   The arts that help to make a hit,
    And preserve a prominent station.
She talk'd and laugh'd far more than her share;
And took a part in 'Rich and Rare
Were the gems she wore' – and the gems were there,
    Like a Song with an Illustration.

She even stood up with a Count of France
To dance – alas! the measures we dance
    When Vanity plays the Piper!
Vanity, Vanity, apt to betray,
1140   And lead all sorts of legs astray,
Wood, or metal, or human clay, –
    Since Satan first play'd the Viper!

But first she doff'd her hunting gear,
And favour'd Tom Tug with her golden spear,
    To row with down the river –
A Bonze had her golden bow to hold;
A Hermit her belt and bugle of gold;
    And an Abbot her golden quiver.

And then a space was clear'd on the floor,
1150   And she walk'd the Minuet de la Cour,
With all the pomp of a Pompadour,
    But although she began *andante*,
Conceive the faces of all the Rout,
When she finish'd off with a whirligig bout,
And the Precious Leg stuck stiffly out
    Like the leg of a *Figuranté!*

So the courtly dance was goldenly done,
And golden opinions, of course, it won
   From all different sorts of people –
1160 Chiming, ding-dong, with flattering phrase,
In one vociferous peal of praise,
Like the peal that rings on Royal days
   From Loyalty's parish-steeple.

And yet, had the leg been one of those
That dance for bread in flesh-colour'd hose,
   With Rosina's pastoral bevy,
The jeers it had met, – the shouts! the scoff!
The cutting advice to 'take itself off',
   For sounding but half so heavy.

1170 Had it been a leg like those, perchance,
That teach little girls and boys to dance,
To set, poussette, recede, and advance,
   With the steps and figures most proper, –
Had it hopp'd for a weekly or quarterly sum,
How little of praise or grist would have come
   To a mill with such a hopper!

But the Leg was none of those limbs forlorn –
Bartering capers and hops for corn –
That meet with public hisses and scorn,
1180   Or the morning journal denounces –
Had it pleas'd to caper from morn till dusk,
There was all the music of 'Money Musk'
   In its ponderous bangs and bounces.

But hark! – as slow as the strokes of a pump,
      Lump, thump!
      Thump, lump!
As the Giant of Castle Otranto might stump

To a lower room from an upper –
Down she goes with a noisy dint,
1190　For taking the crimson turban's hint,
A noble Lord at the Head of the Mint
　　Is leading the Leg to supper!

But the supper, alas! must rest untold,
With its blaze of light and its glitter of gold,
　　For to paint that scene of glamour,
It would need the Great Enchanter's charm,
Who waves over Palace, and Cot, and Farm,
An arm like the Goldbeater's Golden Arm
　　That wields a Golden Hammer.

1200　He – only HE – could fitly state
THE MASSIVE SERVICE OF GOLDEN PLATE,
　　With the proper phrase and expansion –
The Rare Selection of FOREIGN WINES –
The ALPS OF ICE and MOUNTAINS OF PINES,
The punch in OCEANS and sugary shrines,
The TEMPLE OF TASTE from GUNTER'S
　　　　DESIGNS –
In short, all that WEALTH with A FEAST combines,
　In a SPLENDID FAMILY MANSION.

Suffice it each mask'd outlandish guest
1210　Ate and drank of the very best,
　　According to critical conners –
And then they pledged the Hostess and Host,
But the Golden Leg was the standing toast,
　　　And as somebody swore,
　　　Walk'd off with more
　　Than its share of the 'Hips!' and honours!

　　　　'Miss Kilmansegg! –
　　　　Full glasses I beg! –
　　Miss Kilmansegg and her Precious Leg!'

1220   And away went the bottle careering!
       Wine in bumpers! and shouts in peals!
       Till the Clown didn't know his head from his heels,
       The Mussulman's eyes danced two-some reels,
           And the Quaker was hoarse with cheering!

HER DREAM

       Miss Kilmansegg took off her leg,
       And laid it down like a cribbage-peg,
           For the Rout was done and the riot:
       The Square was hush'd; not a sound was heard;
       The sky was gray, and no creature stirr'd,
1230   Except one little precocious bird,
           That chirp'd – and then was quiet.

       So still without, – so still within; –
               It had been a sin
               To drop a pin –
       So intense is silence after a din,
           It seem'd like Death's rehearsal!
       To stir the air no eddy came;
       And the taper burnt with as still a flame,
       As to flicker had been a burning shame,
1240   In a calm so universal.

       The time for sleep had come at last;
       And there was the bed, so soft, so vast,
           Quite a field of Bedfordshire clover;
       Softer, cooler, and calmer, no doubt,
       From the piece of work just ravell'd out,
       For one of the pleasures of having a rout
           Is the pleasure of having it over.

       No sordid pallet, or truckle mean,
       Of straw, and rug, and tatters unclean;
1250   But a splendid, gilded, carved machine,

That was fit for a Royal Chamber.
On the top was a gorgeous golden wreath;
And the damask curtains hung beneath,
　　Like clouds of crimson and amber.

Curtains, held up by two little plump things,
With golden bodies and golden wings, –
　　Mere fins for such solidities –
　　　　Two Cupids, in short,
　　　　Of the regular sort,
1260　　But the housemaid call'd them 'Cupidities'.

No patchwork quilt, all seams and scars,
But velvet, powder'd with golden stars,
　　A fit mantle for *Night*-Commanders!
And the pillow, as white as snow undimm'd,
And as cool as the pool that the breeze has skimm'd,
Was cased in the finest cambric, and trimm'd
　　With the costliest lace of Flanders.

And the bed – of the Eider's softest down,
'Twas a place to revel, to smother, to drown
1270　　In a bliss inferr'd by the Poet;
For if Ignorance be indeed a bliss,
What blessed ignorance equals this,
　　To sleep – and not to know it?

Oh, bed! oh, bed! delicious bed!
That heaven upon earth to the weary head;
But a place that to name would be ill-bred,
　　To the head with a wakeful trouble –
'Tis held by such a different lease!
To one, a place of comfort and peace,
1280　All stuff'd with the down of stubble geese,
　　To another with only the stubble!

To one, a perfect Halcyon nest,
All calm, and balm, and quiet, and rest,
    And soft as the fur of the cony –
To another, so restless for body and head,
That the bed seems borrow'd from Nettlebed,
    And the pillow from Stratford the Stony!

To the happy, a first-class carriage of ease,
To the Land of Nod, or where you please;
1290   But alas! for the watchers and weepers,
Who turn, and turn, and turn again,
But turn, and turn, and turn in vain,
        With an anxious brain,
        And thoughts in a train
    That does not run upon *sleepers!*

Wide awake as the mousing owl,
Night-hawk, or other nocturnal fowl, –
    But more profitless vigils keeping, –
Wide awake in the dark they stare,
1300 Filling with phantoms the vacant air,
As if that Crook-Back'd Tyrant Care
    Had plotted to kill them sleeping.

And oh! when the blessed diurnal light
Is quench'd by the providential night,
    To render our slumber more certain,
Pity, pity the wretches that weep,
For they must be wretched who cannot sleep
    When God himself draws the curtain!

The careful Betty the pillow beats,
1310 And airs the blankets, and smoothes the sheets,
    And gives the mattress a shaking –
But vainly Betty performs her part,
If a ruffled head and a rumpled heart
    As well as the couch want making.

There's Morbid, all bile, and verjuice, and nerves,
Where other people would make preserves,
   He turns his fruits into pickles:
Jealous, envious, and fretful by day,
At night, to his own sharp fancies a prey,
1320 He lies like a hedgehog rolled up the wrong way,
   Tormenting himself with his prickles.

But a child – that bids the world good night,
In downright earnest and cuts it quite –
   A Cherub no Art can copy, –
'Tis a perfect picture to see him lie
As if he had supp'd on dormouse pie,
(An ancient classical dish by the by)
   With a sauce of syrup of poppy.

Oh, bed! bed! bed! delicious bed!
1330 That heav'n upon earth to the weary head,
   Whether lofty or low its condition!
But instead of putting our plagues on shelves,
In our blankets how often we toss ourselves,
Or are toss'd by such allegorical elves
   As Pride, Hate, Greed, and Ambition!

The independent Miss Kilmansegg
Took off her independent Leg
   And laid it beneath her pillow,
And then on the bed her frame she cast,
1340 The time for repose had come at last,
But long, long, after the storm is past
   Rolls the turbid, turbulent billow.

No part she had in vulgar cares
That belong to common household affairs –
Nocturnal annoyances such as theirs
   Who lie with a shrewd surmising
That while they are couchant (a bitter cup!)
Their bread and butter are getting up,
   And the coals – confound them! – are rising.

1350 No fear she had her sleep to postpone,
Like the crippled Widow who weeps alone,
And cannot make a doze her own,
 For the dread that mayhap on the morrow,
The true and Christian reading to balk,
A broker will take up her bed and walk,
 By way of curing her sorrow.

No cause like these she had to bewail:
But the breath of applause had blown a gale,
And winds from that quarter seldom fail
1360 To cause some human commotion;
But whenever such breezes coincide
  With the very spring-tide
  Of human pride,
 There's no such swell on the ocean!

Peace, and ease, and slumber lost,
She turn'd, and roll'd, and tumbled, and toss'd,
 With a tumult that would not settle:
A common case, indeed, with such
As have too little, or think too much,
1370 Of the precious and glittering metal.

Gold! – she saw at her golden foot
The Peer whose tree had an olden root,
The Proud, the Great, the Learned to boot,
 The handsome, the gay, and the witty –
The Man of Science – of Arms – of Art,
The man who deals but at Pleasure's mart,
 And the man who deals in the City.

Gold, still gold – and true to the mould!
In the very scheme of her dream it told;
1380 For, by magical transmutation,
From her Leg through her body it seem'd to go,
Till, gold above, and gold below,
She was gold, all gold, from her little gold toe
 To her organ of Veneration!

And still she retain'd, through Fancy's art,
The Golden Bow, and the Golden Dart,
With which she had played a Goddess's part
   In her recent glorification.
And still, like one of the self-same brood,
1390 On a Plinth of the selfsame metal she stood
   For the whole world's adoration.

And hymns and incense around her roll'd,
From Golden Harps and Censers of Gold, –
For Fancy in dreams is as uncontroll'd
   As a horse without a bridle:
What wonder, then, from all checks exempt,
If, inspired by the Golden Leg, she dreamt
   She was turn'd to a Golden Idol?

HER COURTSHIP

When leaving Eden's happy land
1400 The grieving Angel led by the hand
   Our banish'd Father and Mother,
Forgotten amid their awful doom,
The tears, the fears, and the future's gloom,
On each brow was a wreath of Paradise bloom,
   That our Parents had twined for each other.

It was only while sitting like figures of stone,
For the grieving Angel had skyward flown,
As they sat, those Two, in the world alone,
   With disconsolate hearts nigh cloven,
1410 That scenting the gust of happier hours,
They look'd around for the precious flow'rs,
And lo! – a last relic of Eden's dear bow'rs –
   The chaplet that Love had woven!

And still, when a pair of Lovers meet,
There's a sweetness in air, unearthly sweet,
That savours still of that happy retreat

Where Eve by Adam was courted:
Whilst the joyous Thrush, and the gentle Dove,
Woo'd their mates in the boughs above,
1420   And the Serpent, as yet, only sported.

Who hath not felt that breath in the air,
A perfume and freshness strange and rare,
A warmth in the light, and a bliss every where,
    When young hearts yearn together?
All sweets below, and all sunny above,
Oh! there's nothing in life like making love,
    Save making hay in fine weather!

Who hath not found amongst his flow'rs
A blossom too bright for this world of ours,
1430   Like a rose among snows of Sweden?
But to turn again to Miss Kilmansegg,
Where must Love have gone to beg,
If such a thing as a Golden Leg
    Had put its foot in Eden!

And yet – to tell the rigid truth –
Her favour was sought by Age and Youth –
    For the prey will find a prowler!
She was follow'd, flatter'd, courted, address'd,
Woo'd, and coo'd, and wheedled, and press'd,
1440   By suitors from North, South, East, and West,
    Like the Heiress, in song, Tibbie Fowler!

But, alas! alas! for the Woman's fate,
Who has from a mob to choose a mate!
    'Tis a strange and painful mystery!
But the more the eggs, the worse the hatch;
The more the fish, the worse the catch;
The more the sparks, the worse the match;
    Is a fact in Woman's history.

Give her between a brace to pick,
1450 And, mayhap, with luck to help the trick,
She will take the Faustus, and leave the Old Nick –
    But her future bliss to baffle,
Amongst a score let her have a voice,
And she'll have as little cause to rejoice,
As if she had won the 'Man of her choice'
    In a matrimonial raffle!

Thus, even thus, with the Heiress and Hope,
Fulfilling the adage of too much rope,
    With so ample a competition,
1460 She chose the least worthy of all the group,
Just as the vulture makes a stoop,
And singles out from the herd or troop
    The beast of the worst condition.

A Foreign Count – who came incog.,
Not under a cloud, but under a fog,
    In a Calais packet's fore-cabin,
To charm some lady British-born,
With his eyes as black as the fruit of the thorn,
And his hooky nose, and his beard half-shorn,
1470   Like a half-converted Rabbin.

And because the Sex confess a charm
In the man who has slash'd a head or arm,
    Or has been a throat's undoing,
He was dress'd like one of the glorious trade,
At least when Glory is off parade,
With a stock, and a frock, well trimm'd with braid,
    And frogs – that went a-wooing.

Moreover, as Counts are apt to do,
On the left-hand side of his dark surtout,
1480 At one of those holes that buttons go through,
    (To be a precise recorder)

A ribbon he wore, or rather a scrap,
About an inch of ribbon mayhap,
That one of his rivals, a whimsical chap,
   Described as his 'Retail Order'.

And then – and much it help'd his chance –
He could sing, and play first fiddle, and dance,
Perform charades, and Proverbs of France –
   Act the tender, and do the cruel;
1490 For amongst his other killing parts,
He had broken a brace of female hearts,
   And murder'd three men in duel!

Savage at heart, and false of tongue,
Subtle with age, and smooth to the young,
   Like a snake in his coiling and curling –
Such was the Count – to give him a niche –
Who came to court that Heiress rich,
And knelt at her foot – one needn't say which –
   Besieging her Castle of *Sterling*.

1500 With pray'rs and vows he open'd his trench,
And plied her with English, Spanish, and French,
   In phrases the most sentimental:
And quoted poems in High and Low Dutch,
With now and then an Italian touch,
Till she yielded, without resisting much,
   To homage so continental.

And then the sordid bargain to close,
With a miniature sketch of his hooky nose,
And his dear dark eyes, as black as sloes,
1510 And his beard and whiskers as black as those,
   The lady's consent he requited –
And instead of the lock that lovers beg,
The Count received from Miss Kilmansegg
A model, in small, of her Precious Leg –
   And so the couple were plighted!

But, oh! the love that gold must crown!
Better – better, the love of the clown,
Who admires his lass in her Sunday gown,
     As if all the fairies had dress'd her!
1520   Whose brain to no crooked thought gives birth,
Except that he never will part on earth
     With his true love's crooked tester!

Alas! for the love that's link'd with gold!
Better – better a thousand times told –
     More honest, happy, and laudable,
The downright loving of pretty Cis,
Who wipes her lips, though there's nothing amiss,
And takes a kiss, and gives a kiss,
     In which her heart is audible!

1530   Pretty Cis, so smiling and bright,
Who loves as she labours, with all her might,
     And without any sordid leaven!
Who blushes as red as haws and hips,
Down to her very finger-tips,
For Roger's blue ribbons – to her, like strips
     Cut out of the azure of Heaven!

HER MARRIAGE

'Twas morn – a more auspicious one!
From the Golden East, the Golden Sun
Came forth his glorious race to run,
1540   Through clouds of most splendid tinges;
Clouds that lately slept in shade,
          But now seem'd made
          Of gold brocade,
     With magnificent golden fringes.

Gold above, and gold below,
The earth reflected the golden glow,
    From river, and hill, and valley;
Gilt by the golden light of morn,
The Thames – it look'd like the Golden Horn,
1550 And the Barge, that carried coal or corn,
    Like Cleopatra's Galley!

Bright as clusters of Golden-rod,
Suburban poplars began to nod,
    With extempore splendour furnish'd;
While London was bright with glittering clocks,
Golden dragons, and Golden cocks,
        And above them all,
        The dome of St Paul,
With its Golden Cross and its Golden ball,
1560   Shone out as if newly burnish'd!

And lo! for Golden Hours and Joys,
Troops of glittering Golden Boys
Danced along with a jocund noise,
    And their gilded emblems carried!
In short, 'twas the year's most Golden Day,
By mortals call'd the First of May,
        When Miss Kilmansegg,
        Of the Golden Leg,
    With a Golden Ring was married!

1570 And thousands of children, women, and men,
Counted the clock from eight till ten,
    From St James's sonorous steeple;
For next to that interesting job,
The hanging of Jack, or Bill, or Bob,
There's nothing so draws a London mob
    As the noosing of very rich people.

And a treat it was for a mob to behold
The Bridal Carriage that blazed with gold!
And the Footmen tall, and the Coachman bold,
1580   In liveries so resplendent –
Coats you wonder'd to see in place,
They seem'd so rich with golden lace,
    That they might have been independent.

Coats that made those menials proud
Gaze with scorn on the dingy crowd,
    From their gilded elevations;
Not to forget that saucy lad
(Ostentation's favourite cad),
The Page, who look'd, so splendidly clad,
1590   Like a Page of the 'Wealth of Nations'.

But the Coachman carried off the state,
With what was a Lancashire body of late
    Turn'd into a Dresden Figure;
With a bridal Nosegay of early bloom,
About the size of a birchen broom,
And so huge a White Favour, had Gog been Groom
    He need not have worn a bigger.

And then to see the Groom! the Count!
With Foreign Orders to such an amount,
1600   And whiskers so wild – nay, bestial;
He seem'd to have borrow'd the shaggy hair
As well as the Stars of the Polar Bear,
    To make him look celestial!

And then – Great Jove! – the struggle, the crush,
The screams, the heaving, the awful rush,
    The swearing, the tearing, and fighting,
The hats and bonnets smash'd like an egg –
To catch a glimpse of the Golden Leg,
Which, between the steps and Miss Kilmansegg,
1610   Was fully display'd in alighting!

From the Golden Ankle up to the Knee
There it was for the mob to see!
A shocking act had it chanced to be
   A crooked leg or a skinny:
But although a magnificent veil she wore,
Such as never was seen before,
In case of blushes, she blush'd no more
   Than George the First on a guinea!

Another step, and lo! she was launch'd!
1620   All in white, as Brides are *blanch'd*,
   With a wreath of most wonderful splendour –
Diamonds, and pearls, so rich in device,
That, according to calculation nice,
Her head was worth as royal a price
   As the head of the Young Pretender.

Bravely she shone – and shone the more
As she sail'd through the crowd of squalid and poor,
   Thief, beggar, and tatterdemalion –
Led by the Count, with his sloe-black eyes
1630   Bright with triumph, and some surprise,
Like Anson on making sure of his prize
   The famous Mexican Galleon!

Anon came Lady K., with her face
Quite made up to act with grace,
   But she cut the performance shorter;
For instead of pacing stately and stiff,
At the stare of the vulgar she took a miff,
And ran, full speed, into Church, as if
   To get married before her daughter.

1640   But Sir Jacob walk'd more slowly, and bow'd
Right and left to the gaping crowd,
   Wherever a glance was seizable;

For Sir Jacob thought he bow'd like a Guelph,
And therefore bow'd to imp and elf,
And would gladly have made a bow to himself,
    Had such a bow been feasible.

And last – and not the least of the sight,
Six 'Handsome Fortunes', all in white,
Came to help in the marriage rite, –
1650   And rehearse their own hymeneals;
And then the bright procession to close,
They were followed by just as many Beaux
    Quite fine enough for Ideals.

Glittering men, and splendid dames,
Thus they enter'd the porch of St James',
    Pursued by a thunder of laughter:
For the Beadle was forced to intervene,
For Jim the Crow, and his Mayday Queen,
With her gilded ladle, and Jack i' the Green,
1660   Would fain have follow'd after!

Beadle-like he hush'd the shout;
But the temple was full 'inside and out',
And a buzz kept buzzing all round about
    Like bees when the day is sunny –
A buzz universal that interfered
With the rite that ought to have been revered,
As if the couple already were smear'd
    With Wedlock's treacle and honey!

Yet Wedlock's a very awful thing!
1670   'Tis something like that feat in the ring
    Which requires good nerve to do it –
When one of a 'Grand Equestrian Troop'
Makes a jump at a gilded hoop,
            Not certain at all
            Of what may befall
    After his getting through it!

But the Count he felt the nervous work
No more than any polygamous Turk,
   Or bold piratical schipper,
1680 Who, during his buccaneering search,
Would as soon engage 'a hand' in church
   As a hand on board his clipper!

And how did the Bride perform her part?
Like any Bride who is cold at heart,
   Mere snow with the ice's glitter;
What but a life of winter for her!
Bright but chilly, alive without stir,
So splendidly comfortless, – just like a Fir
   When the frost is severe and bitter.

1690 Such were the future man and wife!
Whose bale or bliss to the end of life
   A few short words were to settle –
     Wilt thou have this woman?
      I will – and then,
     Wilt thou have this man?
      I will, and Amen –
And those Two were one Flesh, in the Angels' ken,
   Except one Leg – that was metal.

Then the names were sign'd – and kiss'd the kiss:
1700 And the Bride, who came from her coach a Miss,
   As a Countess walk'd to her carriage –
Whilst Hymen preen'd his plumes like a dove,
And Cupid flutter'd his wings above,
In the shape of a fly – as little a Love
   As ever look'd in at a marriage!

Another crash – and away they dash'd,
And the gilded carriage and footmen flash'd
   From the eyes of the gaping people –

Who turn'd to gaze at the toe-and-heel
1710 Of the Golden Boys beginning a reel,
To the merry sound of a wedding-peal
    From St James's musical steeple.

Those wedding-bells! those wedding-bells!
How sweetly they sound in pastoral dells
    From a tow'r in an ivy-green jacket!
But town-made joys how dearly they cost;
And after all are tumbled and tost,
Like a peal from a London steeple, and lost
    In town-made riot and racket.

1720 The wedding-peal, how sweetly it peals
With grass or heather beneath our heels, –
    For bells are Music's laughter! –
But a London peal, well mingled, be sure,
With vulgar noises and voices impure,
What a harsh and discordant overture
    To the Harmony meant to come after!

But hence with Discord – perchance, too soon
To cloud the face of the honeymoon
    With a dismal occultation! –
1730 Whatever Fate's concerted trick,
The Countess and Count, at the present nick,
Have a chicken and not a crow to pick
    At a sumptuous Cold Collation.

A Breakfast – no unsubstantial mess,
But one in the style of Good Queen Bess,
    Who, – hearty as hippocampus, –
Broke her fast with ale and beef,
Instead of toast and the Chinese leaf,
    And in lieu of anchovy – grampus!

1740 A breakfast of fowl, and fish, and flesh,
Whatever was sweet, or salt, or fresh;
    With wines the most rare and curious –

Wines, of the richest flavour and hue;
With fruits from the worlds both Old and New;
And fruits obtain'd before they were due
　　At a discount most usurious.

For wealthy palates there be, that scout
What is *in* season, for what is *out*,
　　And prefer all precocious savour:
1750　For instance, early green peas, of the sort
That costs some four or five guineas a quart;
　　Where the *Mint* is the principal flavour.

And many a wealthy man was there,
Such as the wealthy City could spare,
　　To put in a portly appearance –
Men whom their fathers had help'd to gild:
And men who had had their fortunes to build
And – much to their credit – had richly fill'd
　　Their purses by *pursy-verance*.

1760　Men, by popular rumour at least,
Not the last to enjoy a feast!
　　And truly they were not idle!
Luckier far than the chestnut tits,
Which, down at the door, stood champing their bitts,
　　At a different sort of bridle.

For the time was come – and the whisker'd Count
Help'd his Bride in the carriage to mount,
　　And fain would the Muse deny it,
But the crowd, including two butchers in blue,
1770　(The regular killing Whitechapel hue,)
Of her Precious Calf had as ample a view,
　　As if they had come to buy it!

Then away! away! with all the speed
That golden spurs can give to the steed, –
Both Yellow Boys and Guineas, indeed,

Concurr'd to urge the cattle –
Away they went, with favours white,
Yellow jackets, and pannels bright,
And left the mob, like a mob at night,
1780   Agape at the sound of a rattle.

Away! away! they rattled and roll'd,
The Count, and his Bride, and her Leg of Gold –
      That fated charm to the charmer!
Away, – through Old Brentford rang the din,
Of wheels and heels, on their way to win
That hill, named after one of her kin,
      The Hill of the Golden Farmer!

Gold, still gold – it flew like dust!
It tipp'd the post-boy, and paid the trust;
1790   In each open palm it was freely thrust;
      There was nothing but giving and taking!
And if gold could ensure the future hour,
What hopes attended that Bride to her bow'r,
But alas! even hearts with a four-horse pow'r
      Of opulence end in breaking!

HER HONEYMOON

The moon – the moon, so silver and cold,
Her fickle temper has oft been told,
      Now shady – now bright and sunny –
But of all the lunar things that change,
1800   The one that shews most fickle and strange,
And takes the most eccentric range
      Is the moon – so called – of honey!

To some a full-grown orb reveal'd,
As big and as round as Norval's shield,
      And as bright as a burner Bude-lighted;

To others as dull, and dingy, and damp,
As any oleaginous lamp,
Of the regular old parochial stamp,
   In a London fog benighted.

1810   To the loving, a bright and constant sphere,
That makes earth's commonest scenes appear
   All poetic, romantic, and tender:
Hanging with jewels a cabbage-stump,
And investing a common post, or a pump,
A currant-bush, or a gooseberry-clump,
   With a halo of dreamlike splendour.

A sphere such as shone from Italian skies,
In Juliet's dear, dark, liquid eyes,
   Tipping trees with its argent braveries –
1820   And to couples not favour'd with Fortune's boons,
One of the most delightful of moons,
For it brightens their pewter platters and spoons
   Like a silver service of Savory's!

For all is bright, and beauteous, and clear,
And the meanest thing most precious and dear,
   When the magic of love is present:
Love, that lends a sweetness of grace
To the humblest spot and the plainest face –
That turns Wilderness Row into Paradise Place,
1830   And Garlick Hill to Mount Pleasant!

Love that sweetens sugarless tea,
And makes contentment and joy agree
   With the coarsest boarding and bedding:
Love that no golden ties can attach,
But nestles under the humblest thatch,
And will fly away from an Emperor's match
   To dance at a Penny Wedding!

Oh, happy, happy, thrice happy state,
When such a bright Planet governs the fate
1840   Of a pair of united lovers!
'Tis theirs, in spite of the Serpent's hiss,
To enjoy the pure primeval kiss,
With as much of the old original bliss
     As mortality ever recovers!

There's strength in double joints, no doubt,
In double X Ale, and Dublin Stout,
That the single sorts know nothing about –
     And a fist is strongest when doubled –
And double aqua-fortis, of course,
1850   And double soda-water, perforce,
     Are the strongest that ever bubbled!

There's double beauty whenever a Swan
Swims on a Lake, with her double thereon;
And ask the gardener, Luke or John,
     Of the beauty of double-blowing –
A double dahlia delights the eye;
And it's far the loveliest sight in the sky
     When a double rainbow is glowing!

There's warmth in a pair of double soles;
1860   As well as a double allowance of coals –
     In a coat that is double-breasted –
In double windows and double doors;
And a double U wind is blest by scores
     For its warmth to the tender-chested.

There's a twofold sweetness in double pipes;
And a double barrel and double snipes
     Give the sportsman a duplicate pleasure:
There's double safety in double locks;
And double letters bring cash for the box;
1870   And all the world knows that double knocks
     Are gentility's double measure.

There's a double sweetness in double rhymes,
And a double at Whist and a double Times
    In profit are certainly double –
By doubling, the Hare contrives to escape:
And all seamen delight in a doubled Cape,
    And a double-reef'd topsail in trouble.

There's a double chuck at a double chin,
And of course there's a double pleasure therein,
1880   If the parties were brought to telling:
And however our Dennises take offence,
A double meaning shews double sense;
        And if proverbs tell truth,
            A double tooth
    Is Wisdom's adopted dwelling!

But double wisdom, and pleasure, and sense,
Beauty, respect, strength, comfort, and thence
    Through whatever the list discovers,
They are all in the double blessedness summ'd,
1890 Of what was formerly double-drumm'd,
    The Marriage of two true Lovers!

Now the Kilmansegg Moon – it must be told –
Though instead of silver it tipp'd with gold –
Shone rather wan, and distant, and cold,
    And before its days were at thirty,
Such gloomy clouds began to collect,
With an ominous ring of ill effect,
As gave but too much cause to expect
    Such weather as seamen call dirty!

1900 And yet the moon was the 'Young May Moon',
And the scented hawthorn had blossom'd soon,
    And the thrush and the blackbird were singing –
The snow-white lambs were skipping in play,
And the bee was humming a tune all day
To flowers as welcome as flowers in May,
    And the trout in the stream was springing!

But what were the hues of the blooming earth,
Its scents – its sounds – or the music and mirth
   Of its furr'd or its feather'd creatures,
1910 To a Pair in the world's last sordid stage,
Who had never look'd into Nature's page,
And had strange ideas of a Golden Age,
    Without any Arcadian features?

And what were joys of the pastoral kind
To a Bride – town-made – with a heart and mind
   With simplicity ever at battle?
A bride of an ostentatious race,
Who, thrown in the Golden Farmer's place,
Would have trimm'd her shepherds with golden lace,
1920   And gilt the horns of her cattle.

She could not please the pigs with her whim,
And the sheep wouldn't cast their eyes at a limb
   For which she had been such a martyr:
The deer in the park, and the colts at grass,
And the cows unheeded let it pass;
And the ass on the common was such an ass,
    That he wouldn't have swapp'd
    The thistle he cropp'd
   For her Leg, including the Garter!

1930 She hated lanes, and she hated fields –
She hated all that the country yields –
   And barely knew turnips from clover;
She hated walking in any shape,
And a country stile was an awkward scrape,
Without the bribe of a mob to gape
   At the Leg in clambering over!

O blessed nature, 'O rus! O rus!'
Who cannot sigh for the country thus,
   Absorbed in a worldly torpor –

1940   Who does not yearn for its meadow-sweet breath,
Untainted by care, and crime, and death,
And to stand sometimes upon grass or heath –
    That soul, spite of gold, is a pauper!

But to hail the pearly advent of morn,
And relish the odour fresh from the thorn,
    She was far too pamper'd a madam –
Or to joy in the daylight waxing strong,
While, after ages of sorrow and wrong,
The scorn of the proud, the misrule of the strong,
1950   And all the woes that to man belong,
The lark still carols the self-same song
    That he did to the uncurst Adam!

The Lark! she had given all Leipsic's flocks
For a Vauxhall tune in a musical box;
    And as for the birds in the thicket,
Thrush or ousel in leafy niche,
The linnet or finch, she was far too rich
To care for a Morning Concert to which
    She was welcome without any ticket.

1960   Gold, still gold, her standard of old,
All pastoral joys were tried by gold,
    Or by fancies golden and crural –
Till ere she had pass'd one week unblest,
As her agricultural Uncle's guest,
Her mind was made up and fully imprest
    That felicity could not be rural!

And the Count? – to the snow-white lambs at play,
And all the scents and the sights of May,
    And the birds that warbled their passion,
1970   His ears, and dark eyes, and decided nose,
Were as deaf and as blind and as dull as those

That overlook the Bouquet de Rose,
       The Huile Antique,
       And Parfum Unique,
   In a Barber's Temple of Fashion.

To tell, indeed, the true extent
Of his rural bias so far it went
       As to covet estates in ring fences –
And for rural lore he had learn'd in town
1980   That the country was green, turn'd up with brown,
And garnish'd with trees that a man might cut down
       Instead of his own expenses.

And yet had that fault been his only one,
The Pair might have had few quarrels or none,
       For their tastes thus far were in common;
But faults he had that a haughty bride
With a Golden Leg could hardly abide –
Faults that would even have roused the pride
       Of a far less metalsome woman!

1990   It was early days indeed for a wife,
In the very spring of her married life,
       To be chill'd by its wintry weather –
But instead of sitting as Love-Birds do,
Or Hymen's turtles that bill and coo –
Enjoying their 'moon and honey for two'
       They were scarcely seen together!

In vain she sat with her Precious Leg
A little exposed, *à la* Kilmansegg,
       And roll'd her eyes in their sockets!
2000   He left her in spite of her tender regards,
And those loving murmurs described by bards,
For the rattling of dice and the shuffling of cards,
       And the poking of balls into pockets!

Moreover he loved the deepest stake
And the heaviest bets the players would make;
   And he drank – the reverse of sparely, –
And he used strange curses that made her fret;
And when he play'd with herself at piquet,
     She found, to her cost,
2010   For she always lost,
   That the Count did not count quite fairly.

And then came dark mistrust and doubt,
Gather'd by worming his secrets out,
   And slips in his conversations –
Fears, which all her peace destroy'd,
That his title was null – his coffers were void –
And his French Château was in Spain, or enjoy'd
   The most airy of situations.

But still his heart – if he had such a part –
2020 She – only she – might possess his heart,
   And hold his affections in fetters –
Alas! that hope, like a crazy ship,
Was forced its anchor and cable to slip
When, seduced by her fears, she took a dip
   In his private papers and letters.

Letters that told of dangerous leagues;
And notes that hinted as many intrigues
   As the Count's in the 'Barber of Seville' –
In short such mysteries came to light,
2030 That the Countess-Bride, on the thirtieth night,
Woke and started up in affright,
And kick'd and scream'd with all her might,
And finally fainted away outright,
   For she dreamt she had married the Devil!

HER MISERY

Who hath not met with home-made bread,
A heavy compound of putty and lead –
And home-made wines that rack the head,
   And home-made liqueurs and waters?
Home-made pop that will not foam,
2040 And home-made dishes that drive one from home,
       Not to name each mess,
       For the face or dress,
   Home-made by the homely daughters?

Home-made physic, that sickens the sick;
Thick for thin and thin for thick; –
In short each homogeneous trick
   For poisoning domesticity?
And since our Parents, called the First,
A little family squabble nurst,
2050 Of all our evils the worst of the worst
     Is home-made infelicity.

There's a Golden Bird that claps its wings,
And dances for joy on its perch, and sings
   With a Persian exaltation:
For the Sun is shining into the room,
And brightens up the carpet-bloom,
As if it were new, bran new from the loom,
   Or the lone Nun's fabrication.

And thence the glorious radiance flames
2060 On pictures in massy gilded frames –
Enshrining, however, no painted Dames,
   But portraits of colts and fillies –
Pictures hanging on walls which shine,
In spite of the bard's familiar line,
   With clusters of 'gilded lilies'.

And still the flooding sunlight shares
Its lustre with gilded sofas and chairs,
    That shine as if freshly burnish'd –
And gilded tables, with glittering stocks
2070 Of gilded china, and golden clocks,
Toy, and trinket, and musical box,
    That Peace and Paris have furnish'd.

And lo! with the brightest gleam of all
The glowing sunbeam is seen to fall
    On an object as rare as splendid –
The golden foot of the Golden Leg
Of the Countess – once Miss Kilmansegg –
    But there all sunshine is ended.

Her cheek is pale, and her eye is dim,
2080 And downward cast, yet not at the limb,
    Once the centre of all speculation;
But downward drooping in comfort's dearth,
As gloomy thoughts are drawn to the earth –
Whence human sorrows derive their birth –
    By a moral gravitation.

Her golden hair is out of its braids,
And her sighs betray the gloomy shades
    That her evil planet revolves in –
And tears are falling that catch a gleam
2090 So bright as they drop in the sunny beam,
That tears of *aqua regia* they seem,
    The water that gold dissolves in!

Yet, not in filial grief were shed
    Those tears for a mother's insanity;
Nor yet because her father was dead,
For the bowing Sir Jacob had bow'd his head
    To Death – with his usual urbanity;
The waters that down her visage rill'd
Were drops of unrectified spirit distill'd
2100   From the limbeck of Pride and Vanity.

Tears that fell alone and uncheckt,
Without relief, and without respect,
Like the fabled pearls that the pigs neglect,
    When pigs have that opportunity –
And of all the griefs that mortals share,
The one that seems the hardest to bear
    Is the grief without community.

How bless'd the heart that has a friend
A sympathising ear to lend
2110   To troubles too great to smother!
For as ale and porter, when flat, are restored
Till a sparkling bubbling head they afford,
So sorrow is cheer'd by being pour'd
    From one vessel into another.

But friend or gossip she had not one
To hear the vile deeds that the Count had done,
    How night after night he rambled;
And how she had learn'd by sad degrees
That he drank, and smoked, and worse than these,
2120   That he 'swindled, intrigued, and gambled'.

How he kiss'd the maids, and sparr'd with John;
And came to bed with his garments on;
    With other offences as heinous –
And brought *strange* gentlemen home to dine,
That he said were in the Fancy Line,
And they fancied spirits instead of wine,
    And call'd her lap-dog 'Wenus'.

Of 'making a book' how he made a stir,
But never had written a line to her,
2130   Once his idol and Cara Sposa:
And how he had storm'd, and treated her ill,
Because she refused to go down to a mill,
She didn't know where, but remember'd still
    That the Miller's name was Mendoza.

How often he waked her up at night,
And oftener still by the morning light,
   Reeling home from his haunts unlawful;
Singing songs that shouldn't be sung,
Except by beggars and thieves unhung –
2140 Or volleying oaths, that a foreign tongue
   Made still more horrid and awful!

How oft, instead of otto of rose,
With vulgar smells he offended her nose,
   From gin, tobacco, and onion!
And then how wildly he used to stare!
And shake his fist at nothing, and swear, –
And pluck by the handful his shaggy hair,
Till he look'd like a study of Giant Despair
   For a new Edition of Bunyan!

2150 For dice will run the contrary way,
As well is known to all who play,
   And cards will conspire as in treason:
And what with keeping a hunting-box,
         Following fox –
         Friends in flocks,
         Burgundies, Hocks,
         From London Docks;
         Stultz's frocks,
         Manton and Nock's
2160   Barrels and locks,
         Shooting blue rocks,
         Trainers and jocks,
         Buskins and socks,
         Pugilistical knocks,
         And fighting-cocks,
If he found himself short in funds and stocks,
   These rhymes will furnish the reason!

His friends, indeed, were falling away –
Friends who insist on play or pay –
2170 And he fear'd at no very distant day

To be cut by Lord and by cadger,
As one who was gone or going to smash,
For his checks no longer drew the cash,
Because, as his comrades explain'd in flash,
    'He had overdrawn his badger'.

Gold, gold – alas! for the gold
Spent where souls are bought and sold,
    In Vice's Walpurgis revel!
Alas! for muffles, and bulldogs, and guns,
2180   The leg that walks, and the leg that runs,
All real evils, though Fancy ones,
When they lead to debt, dishonour, and duns,
    Nay, to death, and perchance the devil!

Alas! for the last of a Golden race!
Had she cried her wrongs in the market-place,
    She had warrant for all her clamour –
For the worst of rogues, and brutes, and rakes,
Was breaking her heart by constant aches,
With as little remorse as the Pauper who breaks
2190   A flint with a parish hammer!

HER LAST WILL

Now the Precious Leg while cash was flush,
Or the Count's acceptance worth a rush,
    Had never excited dissension;
But no sooner the stocks began to fall,
Than, without any ossification at all,
The limb became what people call
    A perfect bone of contention.

For alter'd days brought alter'd ways,
And instead of the complimentary phrase,
2200   So current before her bridal –

The Countess heard, in language low,
That her Precious Leg was precious slow,
A good 'un to look at but bad to go,
   And kept quite a sum lying idle.

That instead of playing musical airs,
Like Colin's foot in going up-stairs –
As the wife in the Scotish ballad declares –
   It made an infernal stumping.
Whereas a member of cork, or wood,
2210 Would be lighter and cheaper and quite as good,
   Without the unbearable thumping.

P'rhaps she thought it a decent thing
To shew her calf to cobbler and king,
   But nothing could be absurder –
While none but the crazy would advertise
Their gold before their servants' eyes,
Who of course some night would make it a prize,
   By a Shocking and Barbarous Murder.

But spite of hint, and threat, and scoff,
2220   The Leg kept its situation:
For legs are not to be taken off
   By a verbal amputation.

And mortals when they take a whim,
The greater the folly the stiffer the limb
   That stands upon it or by it –
So the Countess, then Miss Kilmansegg,
At her marriage refused to stir a peg,
Till the Lawyers had fastened on her Leg,
   As fast as the Law could tie it.

2230   Firmly then – and more firmly yet –
With scorn for scorn, and with threat for threat,
    The Proud One confronted the Cruel:
And loud and bitter the quarrel arose,
Fierce and merciless – one of those,
With spoken daggers, and looks like blows,
    In all but the bloodshed a duel!

Rash, and wild, and wretched, and wrong,
Were the words that came from Weak and Strong,
    Till madden'd for desperate matters,
2240   Fierce as tigress escaped from her den,
She flew to her desk – 'twas open'd – and then,
In the time it takes to try a pen,
Or the clerk to utter his slow Amen,
    Her Will was in fifty tatters!

But the Count, instead of curses wild,
Only nodded his head and smiled,
As if at the spleen of an angry child;
    But the calm was deceitful and sinister!
A lull like the lull of the treacherous sea –
2250   For Hate in that moment had sworn to be
The Golden Leg's sole Legatee,
    And that very night to administer!

HER DEATH

'Tis a stern and startling thing to think
How often mortality stands on the brink
    Of its grave without any misgiving:
And yet in this slippery world of strife,
In the stir of human bustle so rife,
There are daily sounds to tell us that Life
    Is dying, and Death is living!

2260   Ay, Beauty the Girl, and Love the Boy,
Bright as they are with hope and joy,
    How their souls would sadden instanter,

To remember that one of those wedding bells,
Which ring so merrily through the dells,
    Is the same that knells
    Our last farewells,
    Only broken into a canter!

But breath and blood set doom at nought –
How little the wretched Countess thought,
2270   When at night she unloosed her sandal,
That the Fates had woven her burial-cloth,
And that Death, in the shape of a Death's Head Moth,
    Was fluttering round her candle!

As she look'd at her clock of or-molu,
For the hours she had gone so wearily through
    At the end of a day of trial –
How little she saw in her pride of prime
The Dart of Death in the Hand of Time –
    That hand which moved on the dial!

2280 As she went with her taper up the stair,
How little her swollen eye was aware
    That the Shadow which follow'd was double!
Or when she closed her chamber door,
It was shutting out, and for evermore,
    The world – and its worldly trouble.

Little she dreamt, as she laid aside
Her jewels – after one glance of pride –
    They were solemn bequests to Vanity –
Or when her robes she began to doff,
2290 That she stood so near to the putting off
    Of the flesh that clothes humanity.

And when she quench'd the taper's light,
How little she thought as the smoke took flight,
That her day was done – and merged in a night

Of dreams and duration uncertain –
   Or, along with her own,
   That a Hand of Bone
Was closing mortality's curtain!

But life is sweet, and mortality blind,
2300   And youth is hopeful, and Fate is kind
      In concealing the day of sorrow;
And enough is the present tense of toil –
For this world is, to all, a stiffish soil –
And the mind flies back with a glad recoil
      From the debts not due till to-morrow.

Wherefore else does the Spirit fly
And bid its daily cares good-bye,
      Along with its daily clothing?
Just as the felon condemned to die –
2310   With a very natural loathing –
Leaving the Sheriff to dream of ropes,
From his gloomy cell in a vision elopes,
To caper on sunny greens and slopes,
      Instead of the dance upon nothing.

Thus, even thus, the Countess slept,
While Death still nearer and nearer crept,
      Like the Thane who smote the sleeping –
But her mind was busy with early joys,
Her golden treasures and golden toys,
2320   That flash'd a bright
      And golden light
Under lids still red with weeping.

The golden doll that she used to hug!
Her coral of gold, and the golden mug!
      Her godfather's golden presents!
The golden service she had at her meals,
The golden watch, and chain, and seals,
Her golden scissors, and thread, and reels,
      And her golden fishes and pheasants!

2330   The golden guineas in silken purse –
  And the Golden Legends she heard from her nurse,
   Of the Mayor in his gilded carriage –
  And London streets that were paved with gold –
  And the Golden Eggs that were laid of old –
    With each golden thing
    To the golden ring
   At her own auriferous Marriage!

  And still the golden light of the sun
  Through her golden dream appear'd to run,
2340 Though the night that roar'd without was one
   To terrify seamen or gipsies –
  While the moon, as if in malicious mirth,
  Kept peeping down at the ruffled earth,
  As though she enjoyed the tempest's birth,
   In revenge of her old eclipses.

  But vainly, vainly, the thunder fell,
  For the soul of the Sleeper was under a spell
   That time had lately embitter'd –
  The Count, as once at her foot he knelt –
2350 That Foot which now he wanted to melt!
  But – hush! – 'twas a stir at her pillow she felt –
   And some object before her glitter'd.

  'Twas the Golden Leg! – she knew its gleam!
  And up she started, and tried to scream, –
   But ev'n in the moment she started –
  Down came the limb with a frightful smash,
  And, lost in the universal flash
  That her eyeballs made at so mortal a crash,
   The Spark, called Vital, departed!

   *   *   *   *

2360 Gold, still gold! hard, yellow, and cold,
For gold she had lived, and she died for gold –
By a golden weapon – not oaken;
In the morning they found her all alone –
Stiff, and bloody, and cold as stone –
But her Leg, the Golden Leg was gone,
    And the 'Golden Bowl was broken'!

Gold – still gold! it haunted her yet –
At the Golden Lion the Inquest met –
    Its foreman, a carver and gilder –
2370 And the Jury debated from twelve till three
What the Verdict ought to be,
And they brought it in as Felo de Se,
    'Because her own Leg had killed her!'

HER MORAL

Gold! Gold! Gold! Gold!
Bright and yellow, hard and cold,
Molten, graven, hammer'd, and roll'd;
Heavy to get, and light to hold;
Hoarded, barter'd, bought, and sold,
Stolen, borrow'd, squander'd, doled:
2380 Spurn'd by the young, but hugg'd by the old
To the very verge of the churchyard mould;
Price of many a crime untold;
Gold! Gold! Gold! Gold:
Good or bad a thousand-fold!
    How widely its agencies vary –
To save – to ruin – to curse – to bless –
As even its minted coins express,
Now stamp'd with the image of Good Queen Bess,
    And now of a Bloody Mary!

Lear

A poor old king, with sorrow for my crown,
Thron'd upon straw, and mantled with the wind –
For pity, my own tears have made me blind
That I might never see my children's frown;
And may be, madness, like a friend, has thrown
A folded fillet over my dark mind,
So that unkindly speech may sound for kind, –
Albeit I know not. – I am childish grown –
And have not gold to purchase wit withal –
10 I that have once maintain'd most royal state –
A very bankrupt now that may not call
My child, my child – all-beggar'd save in tears,
Wherewith I daily weep an old man's fate,
Foolish – and blind – and overcome with years!

The Song of the Shirt

With fingers weary and worn,
    With eyelids heavy and red,
A Woman sat, in unwomanly rags,
    Plying her needle and thread –
        Stitch! stitch! stitch!
In poverty, hunger, and dirt,
    And still with a voice of dolorous pitch
She sang the 'Song of the Shirt'!

    'Work! work! work!
10 While the cock is crowing aloof!
        And work – work – work,
Till the stars shine through the roof!
It's O! to be a slave
    Along with the barbarous Turk,
Where woman has never a soul to save,
    If this is Christian work!

Work – work – work
Till the brain begins to swim;
Work – work – work
20   Till the eyes are heavy and dim!
Seam, and gusset, and band,
    Band, and gusset, and seam,
       Till over the buttons I fall asleep,
    And sew them on in a dream!

O! Men, with Sisters dear!
    O! Men! with Mothers and Wives!
It is not linen you're wearing out,
    But human creatures' lives!
       Stitch – stitch – stitch,
30   In poverty, hunger and dirt,
Sewing at once, with a double thread,
    A Shroud as well as a Shirt.

But why do I talk of Death?
    That Phantom of grisly bone,
I hardly fear its terrible shape,
    It seems so like my own –
    It seems so like my own,
    Because of the fasts I keep,
Oh! God! that bread should be so dear,
40   And flesh and blood so cheap!

Work – work – work!
    My labour never flags;
And what are its wages? A bed of straw,
    A crust of bread – and rags.
That shatter'd roof – and this naked floor –
    A table – a broken chair –
And a wall so blank, my shadow I thank
    For sometimes falling there!

Work – work – work!
50   From weary chime to chime,
    Work – work – work –
As prisoners work for crime!
    Band, and gusset, and seam,
    Seam, and gusset, and band,
Till the heart is sick, and the brain benumb'd,
    As well as the weary hand.

    Work – work – work,
In the dull December light,
    And work – work – work,
60   When the weather is warm and bright!
While underneath the eaves
    The brooding swallows cling
As if to show me their sunny backs
    And twit me with the spring.

    Oh! but to breathe the breath
Of the cowslip and primrose sweet –
    With the sky above my head,
And the grass beneath my feet,
For only one short hour
70   To feel as I used to feel,
Before I knew the woes of want
    And the walk that costs a meal!

    Oh! but for one short hour!
    A respite however brief!
No blessed leisure for Love or Hope,
    But only time for Grief!
A little weeping would ease my heart,
    But in their briny bed
My tears must stop, for every drop
80   Hinders needle and thread!'

With fingers weary and worn,
  With eyelids heavy and red,
A Woman sate in unwomanly rags,
  Plying her needle and thread –
    Stitch! stitch! stitch!
  In poverty, hunger, and dirt,
And still with a voice of dolorous pitch,
Would that its tone could reach the Rich!
  She sang this 'Song of the Shirt'!

The Workhouse Clock

An Allegory

There's a murmur in the air,
And noise in every street –
The murmur of many tongues,
The noise of numerous feet –
While round the Workhouse door
The Labouring Classes flock,
For why? the Overseer of the Poor
Is setting the Workhouse Clock.

Who does not hear the tramp
10   Of thousands speeding along
Of either sex and various stamp,
Sickly, crippled, or strong,
Walking, limping, creeping
From court, and alley, and lane,
But all in one direction sweeping
Like rivers that seek the main?

Who does not see them sally
From mill, and garret, and room,
In lane, and court and alley,
20   From homes in poverty's lowest valley,
Furnished with shuttle and loom –

Poor slaves of Civilization's galley –
And in the road and footways rally,
As if for the Day of Doom?
Some, of hardly human form,
Stunted, crooked, and crippled by toil;
Dingy with smoke and dust and oil,
And smirch'd besides with vicious soil,
Clustering, mustering, all in a swarm.
30   Father, mother, and careful child,
Looking as if it had never smiled –
The Sempstress, lean, and weary, and wan,
With only the ghosts of garments on –
The Weaver, her sallow neighbour,
The grim and sooty Artisan;
Every soul – child, woman, or man,
Who lives – or dies – by labour.

Stirred by an overwhelming zeal,
And social impulse, a terrible throng!
40   Leaving shuttle, and needle, and wheel,
Furnace, and grindstone, spindle, and reel,
Thread, and yarn, and iron, and steel –
Yea, rest and the yet untasted meal –
Gushing, rushing, crushing along,
A very torrent of Man!
Urged by the sighs of sorrow and wrong,
Grown at last to a hurricane strong,
Stop its course who can!
Stop who can its onward course
50   And irresistible moral force;
O! vain and idle dream!
For surely as men are all akin,
Whether of fair or sable skin,
According to Nature's scheme,
That Human Movement contains within
A Blood-Power stronger than Steam.

Onward, onward, with hasty feet,
They swarm – and westward still –
Masses born to drink and eat,
60   But starving amidst Whitechapel's meat,
And famishing down Cornhill!
Through the Poultry – but still unfed –
Christian Charity, hang your head!
Hungry – passing the Street of Bread;
Thirsty – the street of Milk;
Ragged – beside the Ludgate Mart,
So gorgeous, through Mechanic-Art,
With cotton, and wool, and silk!

At last, before that door
70   That bears so many a knock
Ere ever it opens to Sick or Poor,
Like sheep they huddle and flock –
And would that all the Good and Wise
Could see the Million of hollow eyes,
With a gleam deriv'd from Hope and the skies,
Upturn'd to the Workhouse Clock!

Oh! that the Parish Powers,
Who regulate Labour's hours,
The daily amount of human trial,
80   Weariness, pain, and self-denial
Would turn from the artificial dial
That striketh ten or eleven,
And go, for once, by that older one
That stands in the light of Nature's sun,
And takes its time from Heaven!

The Bridge of Sighs

'Drown'd! drowned' – *Hamlet*

One more Unfortunate,
Weary of breath,
Rashly importunate,
Gone to her death!

Take her up tenderly,
Lift her with care;
Fashion'd so slenderly,
Young, and so fair!

Look at her garments
10   Clinging like cerements;
Whilst the wave constantly
Drips from her clothing;
Take her up instantly,
Loving, not loathing. –

Touch her not scornfully;
Think of her mournfully,
Gently and humanly;
Not of the stains of her,
All that remains of her
20   Now is pure womanly.

Make no deep scrutiny
Into her mutiny
Rash and undutiful:
Past all dishonour,
Death has left on her
Only the beautiful.

Still, for all slips of hers,
One of Eve's family –
Wipe those poor lips of hers
30   Oozing so clammily.

Loop up her tresses
Escaped from the comb,
Her fair auburn tresses;
Whilst wonderment guesses
Where was her home?

Who was her father?
Who was her mother?
Had she a sister?
Had she a brother?
40   Or was there a dearer one
Still, and a nearer one
Yet, than all other?

Alas! for the rarity
Of Christian charity
Under the sun!
Oh! it was pitiful!
Near a whole city full,
Home she had none.

Sisterly, brotherly,
50   Fatherly, motherly,
Feelings had changed:
Love, by harsh evidence,
Thrown from its eminence;
Even God's providence
Seeming estranged.

Where the lamps quiver
So far in the river,
With many a light

From window and casement,
60   From garret to basement,
She stood, with amazement,
Houseless by night.

The bleak wind of March
Made her tremble and shiver;
But not the dark arch,
Or the black flowing river:
Mad from life's history,
Glad to death's mystery,
Swift to be hurl'd –
70   Any where, any where
Out of the world!

In she plunged boldly,
No matter how coldly
The rough river ran, –
Over the brink of it,
Picture it – think of it,
Dissolute Man!
Lave in it, drink of it,
Then, if you can!

80   Take her up tenderly,
Lift her with care;
Fashion'd so slenderly,
Young, and so fair!

Ere her limbs frigidly
Stiffen too rigidly,
Decently, – kindly, –
Smoothe, and compose them;
And her eyes, close them,
Staring so blindly!

90   Dreadfully staring
Thro' muddy impurity,
As when with the daring
Last look of despairing
Fix'd on futurity.

Perishing gloomily,
Spurr'd by contumely,
Cold inhumanity,
Burning insanity,
Into her rest. –
100 Cross her hands humbly,
As if praying dumbly,
Over her breast!

Owning her weakness,
Her evil behaviour,
And leaving, with meekness,
Her sins to her Saviour!

Stanzas (Farewell, Life!)

Farewell, Life! My senses swim;
And the world is growing dim;
Thronging shadows cloud the light,
Like the advent of the night, –
Colder, colder, colder still
Upward steals a vapour chill –
Strong the earthy odour grows –
I smell the Mould above the Rose!

Welcome, Life! the Spirit strives!
10 Strength returns, and hope revives;
Cloudy fears and shapes forlorn
Fly like shadows at the morn, –

O'er the earth there comes a bloom –
Sunny light for sullen gloom,
Warm perfume for vapour cold –
I smell the Rose above the Mould!

WINTHROP MACKWORTH PRAED

1802–39

Winthrop Mackworth Praed was born in London. He began his education at Langley Broom School, near Colnbrook, in 1810, and left in 1814 for Eton, which he attended until 1821. His first published writing appeared in school periodicals, and in 1820 he founded and coedited *The Etonian,* to which he contributed poems. In 1821 he matriculated at Trinity College, Cambridge, where, as in his school-days, he won prizes for his poetry; he also helped to launch and contributed to *Knight's Quarterly Magazine,* and published his poem *Australasia.* On graduating in 1825 he became a tutor at Eton, where he remained until 1827 when he was elected as a fellow of Trinity College. Having read law, Praed was called to the Bar in 1829. In 1830 he entered Parliament as a Conservative, but was defeated in the Reform redistricting of 1832; he returned to Parliament in 1834. After falling ill at the end of 1836, his health began to worsen; in 1838 he contracted tuberculosis and he died the year after.

His poetic output was characterized by its deftness of wit and lyricism, and consisted largely of *vers-de-société* and political satire, though he also wrote some romantic verse. His work usually appeared in magazines, newspapers and gift-book annuals, including *New Monthly Magazine, London Magazine* and *Literary Souvenir.*

PREFACE

'Having been favoured by Nature with a long face, a short purse, and two elder Brothers, I find no way of making myself popular in the circle in which she has placed me, except versifying,' Praed wrote to his school friend and future editor, Derwent Coleridge.[1] This generously self-deprecating wit was taken by nineteenth-century readers as the hallmark of Praed's style. Looking back a half century after his death, George Saintsbury proposed that 'playing with literature and with life, not frivolously or without heart, but with no very deep cares and no very passionate feeling, is Praed's attitude whenever he is at his best. And he does not play at playing as many writers do: it is all perfectly genuine.'[2] Echoing this judgement, Kenneth Allott remarks, 'Plainly his world fitted him like a glove, but it is equally plain that he looked on its proceedings – from Parliamentary divisions to flirtations, from the Duke of Wellington's friendly salutes to the confidences of match-making dowagers – as an immensely complicated and highly pleasurable game.'[3]

Like Hood, Praed was consumptive, but like Hood, too, he was determined not to give in to weak health, even when its exhaustions were apparent to his colleagues in Parliament in his last years. Throughout his life he revelled in the fun of what his son-in-law George Young describes as his 'sparkling versification'.[4] In their earlier days together at Cambridge, classmate Bulwer-Lytton noticed 'a face pale, long, worn, with large eyes and hollow cheeks, but not without a certain kind of beauty' – 'a restless exuberance of energy and life, all the more striking from its contrast with a frame and countenance painfully delicate'.[5]

This restless exuberance marked Praed's remarkable precocity as a student, his striking aptitude for languages and verse writing, his elegant wit and skilled debating. Here is Bulwer-Lytton again:

> What's the last news? – the medal Praed has won;
> What's the last joke? – Praed's epigram or pun;

> And every week, that club-room, famous then,
> Where striplings settled questions spoilt by men,
> When grand MACAULAY sate triumphant down,
> Heard PRAED'S reply, and long'd to halve the crown.[6]

Praed's rapid wit follows the tone of Prior's poems, of Pope's satires and of eighteenth-century *vers de société*, a genre in which he is routinely classed, even self-classed – calling himself a 'rhymer' rather than a poet.[7]

The society to which the verse is turned and the rhymes are tuned may seem a world whose nuances are too faint for full modern comprehension. Writing in the 1820s and early 30s – during the post-Regency/pre-Reform reigns of George IV and William IV, when he was studying law and entering political life – Praed found his sharpest inspirations in the élite circles of Eton (he founded and coedited *The Etonian* in 1820) and Cambridge, in the suburban society resorts and watering places, in urban ballrooms, and in the whirl of Whig and then of conservative Parliamentary politics. Looking back from only a half century or so later, in 1872, H. G. Hewlett, writing for the *Contemporary Review*, confessed to finding these scenes somewhat remote, evoking a time 'when terms for which we have now to consult a dictionary – Spadille, Loo, Quadrille, Vole, – and others fast becoming archaic, buck, exquisite, blue – were in common use – when ladies played the harp, kept "albums", and ordered dresses of a "mantuamaker"; and gentlemen wore pumps, buckles, stays, and cravats' (p. 256). 'I have sometimes believed it useful to think of Praed's verses as being produced by a composite character out of *Mansfield Park*, two-thirds Henry Crawford and one-third Edmund Bertram,' Kenneth Allott suggests helpfully, with a similar sense of historical distance, in his Introduction (*Selected Poems*, p. xxxvii).

But if Jane Austen's grammar is never truly opaque, whatever its specific syntax and vocabulary (to the contrary, it has proved resiliently current), neither is Praed's. Without a dictionary, Hewlett could delight in the sharp social observation, especially of the ballroom and watering-place poems, which 'might belong to our own day'. The superstructure may need a gloss, but its basis – social and political ambitions, rituals and balls, matchmaking and lovemaking, flirtations and seriously superficial calculations, self-

confessed triviality and political sparring, and, occasionally, some
quiet desperation – is legible enough and thoroughly enjoyable in
all its sharp wit and light-hearted fun:

> Good-night to the Season! – the rages
>   Led off by the chiefs of the throng,
> The Lady Matilda's new pages,
>   The Lady Eliza's new song;
> Miss Fennel's Macaw, which at Boodle's
>   Was held to have something to say;
> Mrs Splenetic's musical Poodles,
>   Which bark 'Batti, Batti!' all day.

Praed liked this patter form. It has a modern tone all its own, even
as it depends for its effect on a certain kind of familiar inevitability.
The rhymes delight in part by the general sense of expectation, the
momentum of rhythm and alliteration, but the lines that bear them
are also typically surprising in Praed's turns and flourishes, the
flashes of puns, the deft shifts from romance to bathos.

Ranging from the early *Etonian* verses to the periodical publications
of the 1820s and 30s, our selection includes tales, lyrics, social satires
and political verses. Praed published chiefly in newspapers, weekly
and monthly magazines and the gift-book annuals, and did not think
of poetry either as his vocation or as his profession. He did not
devote his attention to the sort of self-presentation entailed in
collecting his verses and supervising a career of publication. Except
for a privately printed and coterie-circulated collection of Tory
Political Poems in 1835, the editions are all posthumous. The 'author-
ized' nineteenth-century edition, a quarter of a century after Praed's
death, is Derwent Coleridge's two-volume *Poems* (1864), a collection
almost devoid of the political poetry. This partiality was remedied
in 1888 by George Young's edition of *Political and Occasional Poems*,
more scrupulous than Coleridge's, moreover, in giving a source for
each of its selections. Yet because both Coleridge and Young apply
numerous silent emendations to both accidental and substantive
matters (altered titles; dropped stanzas, notes and epigraphs; errors
of transcription and misprints) – even Allott has silently emended
to some degree – we have used these volumes chiefly for reference,

and for our texts have sought the original sources in the periodicals and annuals, with the added value of presenting the versions that delighted Praed's contemporaries. Our only silent interventions are modernizing certain conventions of punctuation and correcting obvious printers' errata. Unlike Coleridge and Allott, who arrange their contents by genre or tone ('verse-tales', 'poems of love and fancy', 'poems of life and manners', 'political poems'), we favour a chronological arrangement in order to display the arc of Praed's career of writing and its various commitments at any given phase, and we have found it both convenient and informative in this arrangement to group poems under the site of their original publication. Our notes give the source for each poem – this information, as well as more than a few of our glosses, indebted to the editions of Young and Allott.

Notes

1. Quoted by Derek Hudson, *A Poet in Parliament*, p. 78.
2. George Saintsbury, *Macmillan's Magazine*, 1888; reprinted in *Essays in English Literature*, p. 401.
3. Kenneth Allott, *Selected Poems*, p. xvii.
4. George Young, *Political and Occasional Poems*, p. xi.
5. Quoted by Hudson, pp. 67–9.
6. *St Stephen's* (anon. 1860); quoted by Hudson (p. 79) and Allott (pp. lxii–lxiii).
7. Letter to his sister Susan Praed, quoted by Allott (p. xxxii).

from *THE ETONIAN*

Laura

'For she in shape and beauty did excel
All other idols that the heathen do adore'

'And all about her altar scatter'd lay
Great sorts of lovers piteously complaining' – Spenser

A look as blithe, a step as light,
As fabled nymph, or fairy sprite;
A voice, whose every word and tone,
Might make a thousand hearts its own;
A brow of fervour, and a mien
Bright with the hopes of gay fifteen;
These, lov'd and lost one! – these were thine,
When first I bowed at beauty's shrine;
But I have torn my wavering soul
From woman's proud and weak control;
The fane where I so often knelt,
The flame of my heart so truly felt,
Are visions of another time,
Themes for my laughter, – and my rhyme.

She saw, and conquered; in her eye
There was a careless cruelty
That shone destruction, while it seem'd
Unconscious of the fire it beam'd.
And oh! that negligence of dress,
That wild infantine playfulness,
That archness of the trifling brow
That could command – we know not how –
Were links of gold, that held me then,
In bonds I may not bear again;
For dearer to an honest heart
Is childhood's mirth than woman's art.

Already many an aged dame,
Skilful in scandalizing fame,
Foresaw the reign of Laura's face,
30   Her sway, her folly, and disgrace.
Minding the beauty of the day
More than her partner, or her play: –
'Laura a beauty? – flippant chit!
I vow I hate her forward wit!'
('I lead a club') – 'why, Ma'am, between us,
Her mother thinks her quite a Venus;
But every parent loves, you know,
To make a pigeon of her crow.'
'Some folks are apt to look too high –
40   She has a dukedom in her eye.'
'The girl is straight,' ('we call the ace',)
'But that's the merit of her stays.'
'I'm sure I loath malicious hints –
But – only look, how Laura squints.'
'Yet Miss, forsooth,' – ('who play'd the ten?')
'Is quite perfection with the men;
The flattering fools – they make me sick,'
('Well – four by honours, and the trick.')

While thus the crones hold high debate,
50   On Laura's charms, and Laura's fate;
A few short years have roll'd along,
And – first in pleasure's idle throng,
Laura, in ripen'd beauty proud,
Smiles haughty on the flattering crowd;
Her sex's envy – fashion's boast,
An heiress – and a reigning toast.

The circling waltz and gay quadrille
Are in, or out, at Laura's will;
The tragic bard, and comic wit,
60   Heed not the critic in the pit,
If Laura's undisputed sway
Ordains full houses to the play;

And fair ones, of a humbler fate,
That envy, while they imitate,
From Laura's whisper strive to guess
The changes of inconstant dress.
Where'er her step in beauty moves,
Around her fly a thousand loves;
A thousand graces go before,
70   While striplings wonder and adore:
And some are wounded by a sigh,
Some by the lustre of her eye;
And these her studied smiles ensnare,
And those the ringlets of her hair.

The first his fluttering heart to lose,
Was Captain Piercy, of the Blues;
He squeez'd her hand, — he gaz'd and swore
He never was in love before;
He entertain'd his charmer's ear,
80   With tales of wonder and of fear;
Talk'd much, and long, of siege and fight,
Marches by day, alarms by night;
And Laura listen'd to the story,
Whether it spoke of love or glory;
For many an anecdote had he,
Of combat, and of gallantry;
Of long blockades, and sharp attacks,
Of bullets, and of bivouacks;
Of towns o'ercome – and ladies too –
90   Of billet – and of billet-doux;
Of nunneries, and escalades,
And damsels – and Damascus blades.

Alas! too soon the Captain found
How swiftly Fortune's wheel goes round;
Laura at last began to doze,
E'en in the midst of Badajoz;
And hurried to a game at loo,
From Wellington and Waterloo.

The hero, – in heroics left, –
100   Of fortune – and a wife – bereft;
With nought to cheer his close of day,
But celibacy – and half-pay;
Since Laura – and his stars were cruel,
Sought his quietus in a duel.

He fought, and perish'd; Laura sigh'd,
To hear how hapless Piercy died;
And wip'd her eyes, and thus express'd
The feelings of her tender breast: –
'What? dead! – poor fellow – what a pity!
110   He was *so* handsome and *so* witty;
Shot in a duel too – good gracious!
– How I did hate that man's mustachios!!'

Next came the interesting beau,
The trifling youth – Frivolio;
He came to see – and to be seen,
Grace and good breeding in his mien;
Shone all Delcroix upon his head,
The West-end spoke in all he said;
And in his neckcloth's studied fold,
120   Sat Fashion, on a throne of gold.
He came, impatient to resign
What heart he had, at Laura's shrine;
Though deep in self-conceit encas'd,
He learned to bow to Laura's taste;
Consulted her on new quadrilles,
Spot waistcoats, lavender, and gills;
As will'd the proud and fickle fair,
He tied his cloth, and curl'd his hair;
Varied his manners – or his clothes,
130   And chang'd his tailor or his oaths.

Oh! how did Laura love to vex
The fair one of the other sex!
For him she practised every art
That captivates and plagues the heart.
Did he bring tickets for the play?
No – Laura had the spleen to-day.
Did he escort her to the ball?
No – Laura would not dance at all.
Did he look grave? – 'the fool was sad';
140 Was he jocose? – 'the man was mad'.
E'en when he knelt before her feet,
And there, in accent soft and sweet,
Laid rank and fortune, heart and hand,
At Laura's absolute command,
Instead of blushing her consent,
She 'wonder'd what the blockhead meant'.

Yet still the fashionable fool
Was proud of Laura's ridicule;
Though still despised, he still pursued,
150 In ostentatious servitude,
Seeming, like lady's lap-dog, vain
Of being led by beauty's chain.
He knelt, he gaz'd, he sigh'd, and swore,
While 'twas the fashion to adore;
When years had passed, and Laura's frown
Had ceas'd to terrify the town,
He hurried from the fallen grace,
To idolize a newer face:
Constant to nothing was the ass,
160 Save to his follies – and his glass.

The next to gain the beauty's ear
Was William Lisle, the sonneteer,
Well deem'd the prince of rhyme and blank;
For long and deeply had he drank

Of Helicon's poetic tide,
Where nonsense flows, and numbers glide;
And slumber'd on the herbage green,
That decks the banks of Hippocrene.
In short – his very footmen know it –
170   William is mad – or else a poet.*

He came – and rhym'd – he talked of fountains,
Of Pindus, and Pierian mountains;
Of wandering lambs, of gurgling rills,
And roses, and Castalian hills;
He thought a lover's vow grew sweeter,
When it meander'd into metre;
And planted every speech with flowers,
Fresh blooming from Aonian bowers.

'Laura – I perish for your sake,' –
180   (Here he digress'd, about a lake);
'The charms thy features all disclose,' –
(A simile about a rose);
'Have set my very soul on fire,' –
(An episode about his lyre);
'Though you despise – I still must love,' –
(Something about a turtle dove);
'Alas! in death's unstartled sleep,' –
(Just here he did his best to weep);
'Laura, the willow soon shall wave,
190   Over thy lover's lowly grave.'
Then he began, with pathos due,
To speak of cypress and of rue:
But Fortune's unforeseen award
Parted the beauty from the bard;
For Laura, in that evil hour
When unpropitious stars had power,
Unmindful of the thanks she owed,
Lighted her taper with an ode.

*'Aut insanit homo, – aut versus facit.' – Horace [WMP]
  'All Bedlam – or Parnassus is let out.' – Pope [WMP]

Poor William all his vows forgot,
200 And hurried from the fatal spot,
In all the bitterness of quarrel,
To write lampoons – and dream of laurel.

Years fleeted by, and every grace
Began to fade from Laura's face;
Through every circle whispers ran,
And aged dowagers began
To gratify their secret spite: –
'How shocking Laura looks to-night!
We know her waiting-maid is clever,
210 But rouge won't make one young for ever;
Laura should think of being sage,
You know – she's of a *certain* age.'

Her wonted wit began to fail,
Her eyes grew dim, her features pale;
Her fame was past, – her race was done,
Her lovers left her one by one;
Her slaves diminish'd by degrees,
They ceas'd to fawn – as she to please.
Last of the gay deceitful crew,
220 Chremes, the usurer, withdrew;
By many an art he strove to net
The guineas of the rich coquette;
But (so the adverse fates decreed),
Chremes and Laura disagreed;
For Chremes talked too much of stocks,
And Laura of her opera box.

Unhappy Laura! sadness marr'd
What tints of beauty time had spared;
For all her wide-extended sway
230 Had faded, like a dream, away;
And they that lov'd her pass'd her by,
With alter'd or averted eye.

That silent scorn, that chilling air
The fallen tyrant could not bear;
She could not live, when none admir'd,
And perish'd, as her reign expir'd.

I gaz'd upon that lifeless form,
So late with Hope and Fancy warm;
That pallid brow – that eye of jet,
240   Where lustre seem'd to linger yet;
Where sparkled through an auburn tress
The last dim light of loveliness,
Whose trembling ray was only seen,
To bid us sigh for what had been.
Alas! I said, my wavering soul
Was torn from woman's weak control;
But when, amid the evening's gloom,
I look'd on Laura's early tomb;
And thought on her, so bright and fair,
250   That slumber'd in oblivion there;
That calm resolve I could not keep,
And then I wept, – as now I weep.

To Julia,

Preparing for her First Season in Town

Julia, while London's fancied bliss
Bids you despise a life like this,
While —— and its joys you leave,
For hopes, that flatter to deceive,
You will not scornfully refuse,
(Though dull the theme, and weak the Muse),
To look upon my line, and hear
What Friendship sends to Beauty's ear.

Four miles from Town, a neat abode
10   O'erlooks a rose-bush, and a road;
A paling, clean'd with constant care,
Surrounds ten yards of neat parterre,
Where dusty ivy strives to crawl
Five inches up the whiten'd wall.
The open window, thickly set
With myrtle, and with mignonette,
Behind whose cultivated row
A brace of globes peep out for show,
The avenue – the burnish'd plate,
20   That decks the would-be rustic gate,
Denote the fane where Fashion dwells,
– 'Lyce's Academy for Belles'.

'T was here, in earlier, happier days,
Retired from Pleasure's weary maze,
You found, unknown to care or pain,
The peace you will not find again.
Here Friendships, far too fond to last,
A bright, but fleeting radiance cast,
On every sport that Mirth devised,
30   And every scene that Childhood prized,
And every bliss, that bids you yet
Recall those moments with regret.

Those friends have mingled in the strife
That fills the busy scene of life,
And Pride and Folly – Cares and Fears,
Look dark upon their future years:
But by their wrecks may Julia learn,
Whither her fragile bark to turn;
And, o'er the troubled sea of fate,
40   Avoid the rocks they found too late.

You know Camilla – o'er the plain
She guides the fiery hunter's rein;
First in the chase she sounds the horn,
Trampling to earth the farmer's corn,

That hardly deign'd to bend its head,
Beneath her namesake's lighter tread.
With Bob the Squire, her polish'd lover,
She wields the gun, or beats the cover;
And then her steed! – why! every clown
50   Tells how she rubs Smolensko down,
And combs the mane, and cleans the hoof,
While wondering hostlers stand aloof.

At night, before the Christmas fire
She plays backgammon with the Squire;
Shares in his laugh, and in his liquor,
Mimics her father and the Vicar;
Swears at the grooms – without a blush
Dips in her ale the captured brush,
Until – her father duly tired –
60   The parson's wig as duly fired –
The dogs all still – the Squire asleep,
And dreaming of his usual leap, –
She leaves the dregs of white and red,
And lounges languidly to bed;
And still in nightly visions borne,
She gallops o'er the rustic's corn;
Still wields the lash – still shakes the box,
Dreaming of 'sixes' – and the fox.

And this is bliss! – the story runs,
70   Camilla never wept – save once;
Yes! once indeed Camilla cried –
'T was when her dear Blue-stockings died.

Pretty Cordelia thinks she's ill –
She seeks her med'cine at Quadrille;
With hope, and fear, and envy sick,
She gazes on the dubious trick,
As if Eternity were laid
Upon a diamond, or a spade.
And I have seen a transient pique
80   Wake, o'er that soft and girlish cheek,

A chilly and a feverish hue,
Blighting the soil where Beauty grew,
And bidding Hate and Malice rove
In eyes that ought to beam with love.

Turn we to Fannia – she was fair
As the soft fleeting forms of air,
Shaped by the fancy, – fitting theme
For youthful bard's enamour'd dream.
The neck, on whose transparent glow
90 The auburn ringlets sweetly flow,
The eye that swims in liquid fire,
The brow that frowns in playful ire;
All these, when Fannia's early youth
Look'd lovely in its native truth,
Diffused a bright, unconscious grace,
Almost divine, o'er form and face.

Her lip has lost its fragrant dew,
Her cheek has lost its rosy hue,
Her eye the glad enlivening rays
100 That glitter'd there in happier days,
Her heart the ignorance of woe
Which Fashion's votaries may not know.

The city's smoke – the noxious air –
The constant crowd – the torch's glare –
The morning sleep – the noonday call –
The late repast – the midnight ball,
Bid Faith and Beauty die, and taint
Her heart with fraud, her face with paint.

And what the boon, the prize enjoy'd,
110 For fame defaced, and peace destroy'd!
Why ask we this? With conscious grace
She criticises silk and lace;
Queen of the modes, she reigns alike
O'er sarcenet, bobbin, net, vandyke;

O'er rouge and ribbons, combs and curls,
Perfumes and patches, pins and pearls;
Feelings and faintings, songs and sighs,
Small-talk and scandal, love and lies.

Circled by beaux behold her sit,
While Dandies tremble at her wit;
The Captain hates 'a woman's gab';
'A devil!' cries the shy Cantab;
The young Etonian strives to fly
The glance of her sarcastic eye,
For well he knows she looks him o'er,
To stamp him 'buck', or dub him 'bore'.

Such is her life – a life of waste,
A life of wretchedness – and *taste,*
And all the glory Fannia boasts,
And all the price that glory costs,
At once are reckon'd up, in one –
One word of bliss and folly – *Ton.*

Not these the thoughts that could perplex
The fancies of our fickle sex,
When England's favourite, good Queen Bess,
Was Queen alike o'er war and dress.
Then ladies gay play'd *chesse* – and ballads,
And learnt to dress their hair – and salads;
Sweets – and sweet looks were studied then,
And both were pleasing to the men;
For cookery was allied to taste,
And girls were taught to blush, – and baste.
Dishes were bright – and so were eyes,
And lords made love, – and ladies, pies.

Then Valour won the wavering field,
By dint of hauberk, and of shield;
And Beauty won the wavering heart,
By dint of pickle, and of tart.

The minuet was the favourite dance,
150 Girls loved the needle – boys the lance;
And Cupid took his constant post
At dinner, by the boil'd and roast,
Or secretly was wont to lurk,
In tournament, or needle-work.
Oh! 't was a reign of all delights,
Of hot *Sir*-loins, – and hot *Sir* knights;
Feasting and fighting, hand in hand,
Fatten'd, and glorified the land;
And noble chiefs had noble cheer,
160 And knights grew strong upon strong beer;
Honour and oxen both were nourish'd,
And chivalry – and pudding flourish'd.

I'd rather see that magic face,
That look of love, that form of grace,
Circled by whalebone, and by ruffs,
Intent on puddings, and on puffs,
I'd rather view thee thus, than see
'A Fashionable' rise in thee.
If Life is dark, 't is not for you,
170 (If partial Friendship's voice is true)
To cure its griefs, and drown its cares,
By leaping gates, and murdering hares,
Nor to confine that feeling soul,
To winning lovers, – or the vole.

If these, and such pursuits are thine,
Julia! thou art no friend of mine!
I love plain dress, – I eat plain joints,
I cannot play ten guinea points,
I make no study of a pin,
180 And hate a female whipper-in.

The Bachelor

T. Quince, Esq., to the Rev. Matthew Pringle

You wonder that your ancient friend
Has come so near his journey's end,
And borne his heavy load of ill
O'er Sorrow's slough, and Labour's hill,
Without a partner to beguile
The toilsome way with constant smile,
To share in happiness and pain,
To guide, to comfort, to sustain,
And cheer the last, long, weary stage,
10   That leads to Death, through gloomy Age!
To drop these metaphoric jokes,
And speak like reasonable folks,
It seems you wonder, Mr Pringle,
That old Tom Quince is living single!

Since my old crony and myself
Laid crabbed Euclid on the shelf,
And made our Congé to the Cam,
Long years have pass'd; and here I am
With nerves and gout, but yet alive,
20   A Bachelor, and fifty-five.
Sir, I'm a Bachelor, and mean,
Until the closing of the scene,
Or be it right, or be it wrong,
To play the part I've play'd so long,
Nor be the rat that others are,
Caught by a ribbon or a star.

'As years increase,' your worship cries,
'All troubles and anxieties
Come swiftly on: you feel vexation
30   About your neighbours, or the nation;
The gout in fingers or in toes
Awakes you from your first repose;

You'll want a clever nurse, when life
Begins to fail you! – take a wife;
Believe me, from the mind's disease
Her soothing voice might give you ease,
And when the twinge comes shooting through you,
Her care might be of service to you!'

   Sir, I'm not dying, though I know
40 You charitably think me so;
Not dying yet, though you, and others,
In augury your learned brothers,
Take pains to prophesy events,
Which lie some twenty winters hence.
Some twenty? – look! you shake your head,
As if I were insane or dead,
And tell your children and your wife, –
'Old men grow *very* fond of life!'
Alas! your prescience never ends
50 As long as it concerns your friends;
But your own fifty-third December
Is what you never can remember!
And when I talk about my health,
And future hopes of weal or wealth,
With something 'twixt a grunt and groan,
You mutter, in an under-tone,
'Hark, how the dotard chatters still!*
He'll not believe he's old or ill!
He goes on forming great designs, –
60 Has just laid in a stock of wines, –
And promises his niece a ball,
As if gray hairs would never fall!

*I must confess that Dr Swift
  Has lent me here a little lift:
  For when *I* steal some trifling hits
  From older and from brighter wits,
  I have some touch of conscience left,
  And seldom like to *hide* the theft.
  This is *my* plan! – I name no name,
  But wish *all* others did the same. – *Author's note*

I really think he's all but mad.'
Then, with a wink and sigh, you add,
'Tom is a friend I dearly prize,
But – never thought him *over* wise!'

You – who are clever to foretel
Where ignorance might be as well,
Would marvel how my health has stood:
70 My pulse is firm, digestion good,
I walk to see my turnips grow,
Manage to ride a mile or so,
Get to the village church to pray,
And drink my pint of wine a day;
And often, in an idle mood,
Emerging from my solitude,
Look at my sheep, and geese, and fowls,
And scare the sparrows and the owls,
Or talk with Dick about my crops,
80 And learn the price of malt and hops.

You say, that, when you saw me last,
My appetite was going fast,
My eye was dim, my cheek was pale,
My bread – and stories – both were stale,
My wine and wit were growing worse,
And all things else, – except my purse;
In short, the very blind might see
I was not what I used to be.

My glass (which I believe before ye)
90 Will teach me quite another story;
My wrinkles are not many yet, –
My hair is still as black as jet,
My legs are full – my cheeks are ruddy –
My eyes, though somewhat sunk by study,
Retain a most vivacious ray,
And tell no stories of decay;

And then my waist, unvex'd, unstay'd,
By fetters of the tailor's trade,
Tells you, as plain as waist can tell,
100   I'm most unfashionably well.

And yet *you* think I'm growing thinner! —
You'd stare to see me eat my dinner!
You know that I was held by all
The greatest epicure in Hall,
And that the voice of Granta's sons
Styled me the Gourmand of St John's,
I have not yet been found unable
To do my duty to my table,
Though at its head no Lady gay
110   Hath driven British food away,
And made her hapless husband bear
Alike her fury and her fare.
If some kind-hearted chum calls in,
An extra dish, and older bin,
And John in all his finery drest,
Do honour to the welcome guest;
And then we talk of other times,
Of parted friends, and distant climes,
And lengthen'd converse, tale, and jest,
120   Lull every anxious care to rest,
And when unwillingly I rise,
With newly-waken'd sympathies,
From conversation — and the bowl,
The feast of stomach — and of soul,
I lay me down and seem to leap
O'er forty summers in my sleep;
And youth, with all its joy and pain,
Comes rushing on my soul again.
I rove where'er my boyhood roved —
130   I love whate'er my boyhood loved —
And rocks, and vales, and woods, and streams,
Fleet o'er my pillow in my dreams,
'Tis true some ugly foes arise
E'en in this earthly paradise,

Which you, good Pringle, may beguile
By Mrs P's unceasing smile.
I am an independent elf,
And keep my comforts in myself.
If my best sheep have got the rot –
140　Or if the Parson hits a blot –
Or if young Witless prates of laurel –
Or if my tithe produces quarrel –
Or if my roofing wants repairs –
Or if I'm angry with my heirs –
Or if I've nothing else to do –
I grumble for an hour or two;
Riots, or rumours, unrepress'd,
My niece, or knuckle, over-dress'd,
The lateness of a wish'd-for post,
150　Miss Mackrell's story of the ghost,
New wine, new fashions, or new faces,
New bills, new taxes, or new places,
Or Mr Hume's enumeration
Of all the troubles of the nation,
Will sometimes wear my patience out!
Then, as I said before, the gout –
Well, well, my heart was never faint!
And yet it might provoke a saint.
A rise of bread, or fall of rain,
160　Sometimes unite to give me pain,
And oft my lawyer's bag of papers
Gives me a taste of spleen and vapours.
Angry or sad, alone or ill,
I have my senses with me still;
Although my eyes are somewhat weak,
Yet can I dissipate my pique
By Poem, Paper, or Review;
And though I'm dozy in my pew,
At Dr Poundtext's second leaf,
170　I am not yet so very deaf
As to require the rousing noise
Of screaming girls and roaring boys.

Thrice – thrice accursed be the day
When I shall fling my bliss away,
And, to disturb my quiet life,
Take Discord in the shape of wife!
Time, in his endless muster-roll,
Shall mark the hour with blackest coal,
When old Tom Quince shall cease to see
180   The *Chronicle* with toast and tea,
Confine his rambles to his park,
And never dine till after dark,
And change his comfort and his crony,
For crowd and conversazione.

If every aiding thought is vain,
And momentary grief and pain
Urge the old man to frown and fret,
He has another comfort yet:
This earth has thorns, as poets sing,
190   But not for ever can they sting:
Our sand from out its narrow glass
Rapidly passes! – let it pass!
I seek not – I – to check or stay
The progress of a single day,
But rather cheer my hours of pain
Because so few of them remain.
Care circles every mortal head, –
The dust will be a calmer bed!
From Life's alloy no Life is free,
200   But – Life is not eternity!

When that unerring day shall come
To call me from my wandering, home,
The dark, and still, and painful day,
When breath shall fleet in groans away,
When comfort shall be vainly sought,
And doubt shall be in every thought,
When words shall fail th' unutter'd vow,
And fever heat the burning brow,

When the dim eye shall gaze, and fear
210   To close the glance that lingers here,
Snatching the faint departing light,
That seems to flicker in its flight,
When the lone heart, in that long strife,
Shall cling unconsciously to life,
I'll have no shrieking female by
To shed her drops of sympathy;
To listen to each smother'd throe,
To feel, or feign, officious woe;
To bring me every useless cup,
220   And beg 'dear Tom' to drink it up;
To turn my oldest servants off,
E'en as she hears my gurgling cough;
And then expectantly to stand,
And chafe my temples with her hand;
And pull a cleaner nightcap o'er 'em,
That I may die with due decorum;
And watch the while my ebbing breath,
And count the tardy steps of death;
Grudging the Leech his growing bill,
230   And wrapt in dreams about the will.
I'll have no Furies round my bed! –
They shall not plague me – till I'm dead!

Believe me! ill my dust would rest,
If the plain marble o'er my breast,
That tells, in letters large and clear,
'The Bones of Thomas Quince lie here!'
Should add a talisman of strife,
'Also the Bones of Jane, his Wife!'

No, while beneath this simple stone
240   Old Quince shall sleep, and sleep alone,
Some Village Oracle, who well
Knows how to speak, and read, and spell,
Shall slowly construe, bit by bit,
My '*Natus*' and my '*Obiit*',
And then, with sage discourse and long,
Recite my virtues to the throng.

'The Gentleman came straight from College!
A most prodigious man for knowledge!
He used to pay all men their due,
250   Hated a miser, – and a Jew,
But always open'd wide his door
To the first knocking of the poor.
None, as the grateful Parish knows,
Save the Churchwardens, were his foes;
They could not bear the virtuous pride
Which gave the sixpence *they* denied.
If neighbours had a mind to quarrel,
He used to treat them to a barrel;
And that, I think, was sounder law
260   Than any book I ever saw.
The Ladies never used to flout him;
But this was rather strange about him,
That, gay or thoughtful, young or old,
He took no wife for love or gold;
Woman he call'd "a pretty thing", –
But never could abide a ring!'

Good Mr Pringle! – you must see
Your arguments are light with me;
They buzz like feeble flies around me,
270   But leave me firm, as first they found me:
Silence your logic! burn your pen!
The poet says 'we are all men';
And all 'condemn'd alike to groan'!
You with a wife, and I with none.
Well! – yours may be a happier lot,
But it is one I envy not;
And you'll allow me, Sir, to pray,
That, at some near-approaching day,
You may not have to wince and whine,
280   And find some cause to envy mine!

*   *   *

from *THE BRAZEN HEAD*

Chaunt I

And do you, brazen companion of my solitary hours, pronounce
while I recline, a prologue to those sentiments of wisdom and virtue,
which hereafter are to be the oracles of statesmen, and the guides of
philosophers. Wiser Hierophants shall be yours than ever Trophon-
ius entranced, or Apollo received. Give me to-night a proem of our
essay, an opening of our case, a division of our subject. Speak!
    Slow music. The Friar falls asleep. The Head chaunts as follows: –

I think, whatever mortals crave,
    With impotent endeavour,
A wreath, – a rank, – a throne, – a grave, –
    The world goes round for ever;
I think that life is not too long,
    And therefore I determine
That many people read a song,
    Who will not read a sermon.

I think you've look'd through many hearts,
    And mused on many actions,
And studied man's component parts,
    And nature's compound fractions;
I think you've pick'd up truth by bits
    From foreigner and neighbour,
I think the world has lost its wits,
    And you have lost your labour.

I think the studies of the wise,
    The hero's noisy quarrel,
The majesty of woman's eyes,
    The poet's cherish'd laurel;

And all that makes us lean or fat,
  And all that charms or troubles, –
This bubble is more bright than that,
  But still they all are bubbles.

I think the thing you call Renown,
  This unsubstantial vapour
For which a soldier burns a town,
  The sonneteer a taper,
Is like the mist which, as he flies,
30 The horseman leaves behind him;
He cannot mark its wreaths arise,
  Or, if he does, they blind him.

I think one nod of mistress Chance
  Makes creditors of debtors,
And shifts the funeral for the dance,
  The sceptre for the fetters;
I think that Fortune's favoured guest
  May live to gnaw the platters;
And he that wears the purple vest
40 May wear the rags and tatters.

I think the Tories love to buy
  'Your Lordships' and 'Your Graces',
By loathing common honesty,
  And lauding common places;
I think that some are very wise,
  And some are very funny,
And some grow rich by telling lies,
  And some by telling money.

I think the Whigs are wicked knaves,
50 And very like the Tories,
Who doubt that Britain rules the waves,
  And ask the price of glories;

I think that many fret and fume
    At what their friends are planning,
And Mr Hume hates Mr Brougham
    As much as Mr Canning.

I think that friars and their hoods,
    Their doctrines and their maggots,
Have lighted up too many feuds,
60   And far too many faggots;
I think while zealots fast and frown,
    And fight for two or seven,
That there are fifty roads to town,
    And rather more to Heaven.

I think that, thanks to Paget's lance,
    And thanks to Chester's learning,
The hearts that burn'd for fame in France,
    At home are safe from burning;
I think the Pope is on his back,
70   And, though 'tis fun to shake him,
I think the Devil not so black,
    As many people make him.

I think that Love is like a play
    Where tears and smiles are blended,
Or like a faithless April day,
    Whose shine with shower is ended;
Like Colnbrook pavement, rather rough,
    Like trade, exposed to losses,
And like a Highland plaid, all stuff,
80   And very full of crosses.

I think the world, though dark it be,
    Has aye one rapturous pleasure,
Conceal'd in life's monotony,
    For those who seek the treasure;

One planet in a starless night, –
    One blossom on a briar, –
One friend not quite a hypocrite, –
    One woman not a liar!

I think poor beggars court St Giles,
90   Rich beggars court St Stephen;
And Death looks down with nods and smiles,
    And makes the odds all even;
I think some die upon the field,
    And some upon the billow,
And some are laid beneath a shield,
    And some beneath a willow.

I think that very few have sigh'd,
    When Fate at last has found them,
Though bitter foes were by their side,
100   And barren moss around them;
I think that some have died of drought,
    And some have died of drinking; –
I think that nought is worth a thought,
    And I'm a fool for thinking!

Chaunt II

As for me, I am growing sick of all things: every day there is the
same routine of pleasure or of weariness; the same loungers at the
Club, the same fashionables in the Park; the same criticisms on the
last Opera, the same anticipations of the next; the same speeches in
Parliament, the same advertisements in the Newspaper. There is
nothing new beneath the sun.

The Head

The world pursues the very track
    Which it pursued at its creation;
And mortals shrink in horror back
    From any hint of innovation:

From year to year the children do
    Exactly what their sires have done;
Time is! time was! – there's nothing new, –
    There's nothing new beneath the sun!

Still lovers hope to be believed,
10   Still clients hope to win their causes;
Still plays and farces are received
    With most encouraging applauses;
Still dancers have fantastic toes;
    Still dandies shudder at a dun;
Still dinners have their fricandeaus, –
    There's nothing new beneath the sun!

Still cooks torment the hapless eels,
    Still boys torment the dumb cockchafers;
Lord Eldon still adores the seals,
20   Lord Clifford still adores the wafers;
Still asses have enormous ears,
    Still gambling bets are lost and won;
Still opera-dancers marry peers, –
    There's nothing new beneath the sun!

Still women are absurdly weak,
    Still infants dote upon a rattle;
Still Mr Martin cannot speak
    Of any thing but beaten cattle;
Still brokers swear the shares will rise,
30   Still cockneys boast of Manton's gun;
Still listeners swallow monstrous lies, –
    There's nothing new beneath the sun!

Still genius is a jest to earls,
    Still honesty is down to zero;
Still heroines have spontaneous curls,
    Still novels have a handsome hero;

Still Madame Vestris plays a man,
　　Still fools adore her, I for one;
Still youths write sonnets to a fan, –
40　　　There's nothing new beneath the sun!

Still people make a plaguy fuss,
　　About all things that don't concern them,
As if it matters aught to us,
　　What happens to our grandsons, burn them!
Still life is nothing to the dead,
　　Still Folly's toil is Wisdom's fun;
And still, except the Brazen Head, –
　　There's nothing new beneath the sun!

*　*　*

from *THE NEW MONTHLY MAGAZINE*

Time's Song

O'er the level plains, where mountains greet me as I go,
O'er the desert waste where fountains at my bidding flow,
On the boundless beam by day, on the cloud by night,
I am rushing hence away! Who will chain my flight?

War his weary watch was keeping; – I have crush'd his
    spear:
Grief within her bower was weeping; – I have dried her
    tear:
Pleasure caught a minute's hold; – then I hurried by,
Leaving all her banquet cold, and her goblet dry.

Power had won a throne of glory; – where is now his fame?
Genius said, – 'I live in story'; – who hath heard his name?
Love, beneath a myrtle bough, whisper'd, – 'Why so fast?'
And the roses on his brow wither'd as I past.

I have heard the heifer lowing o'er the wild wave's bed;
I have seen the billow flowing where the cattle fed;
Where began my wanderings? – Memory will not say!
Where will rest my weary wings? – Science turns away!

Good-Night to the Season

'Thus runs the world away' – *Hamlet*

Good-night to the Season! 'tis over!
    Gay dwellings no longer are gay;
The courtier, the gambler, the lover,
    Are scatter'd like swallows away:

There's nobody left to invite one,
    Except my good uncle and spouse;
My mistress is bathing at Brighton,
    My patron is sailing at Cowes:
For want of a better employment,
    Till Ponto and Don can get out,
I'll cultivate rural enjoyment,
    And angle immensely for trout.

Good-night to the Season! – the lobbies,
    Their changes, and rumours of change,
Which startled the rustic Sir Bobbies,
    And made all the Bishops look strange:
The breaches, and battles, and blunders,
    Perform'd by the Commons and Peers;
The Marquis's eloquent thunders,
    The Baronet's eloquent ears:
Denouncings of Papists and treasons
    Of foreign dominion and oats;
Misrepresentations of reasons,
    And misunderstandings of notes.

Good-night to the Season! – the buildings
    Enough to make Inigo sick;
The paintings, and plasterings, and gildings,
    Of stucco, and marble, and brick;
The orders deliciously blended,
    From love of effect, into one;
The club-houses only intended,
    The palaces only begun;
The hell where the fiend, in his glory,
    Sits staring at putty and stones,
And scrambles from story to story,
    To rattle at midnight his bones.

Good-night to the Season! – the dances,
    The fillings of hot little rooms,
The glancings of rapturous glances,
    The fancyings of fancy costumes;

The pleasures which Fashion makes duties,
    The praisings of fiddles and flutes,
The luxury of looking at beauties,
    The tedium of talking to mutes;
The female diplomatists, planners
    Of matches for Laura and Jane,
The ice of her Ladyship's manners,
    The ice of his Lordship's champagne.

Good-night to the Season! – the rages
50   Led off by the chiefs of the throng,
The Lady Matilda's new pages,
    The Lady Eliza's new song;
Miss Fennel's Macaw, which at Boodle's
    Was held to have something to say;
Mrs Splenetic's musical Poodles,
    Which bark 'Batti, Batti!' all day;
The pony Sir Araby sported,
    As hot and as black as a coal,
And the Lion his mother imported,
60   In bearskins and grease, from the Pole.

Good-night to the Season! – the Toso,
    So very majestic and tall;
Miss Ayton, whose singing was so so,
    And Pasta, divinest of all;
The labour in vain of the Ballet,
    So sadly deficient in stars;
The foreigners thronging the Alley,
    Exhaling the breath of cigars;
The 'loge' where some heiress, how killing
70   Environ'd with Exquisites sits,
The lovely one out of her drilling,
    The silly ones out of their wits.

Good-night to the Season! – the splendour
    That beam'd in the Spanish Bazaar;
Where I purchased – my heart was so tender –
    A card-case, – a pasteboard guitar, –

A bottle of perfume, – a girdle, –
  A lithograph'd Riego full-grown,
Whom Bigotry drew on a hurdle,
80   That artists might draw him on stone, –
A small panorama of Seville, –
  A trap for demolishing flies, –
A caricature of the Devil, –
  And a look from Miss Sheridan's eyes.

Good-night to the Season! – the flowers
  Of the grand horticultural fête,
When boudoirs were quitted for bowers,
  And the fashion was not to be late;
When all who had money and leisure
90   Grew rural o'er ices and wines,
All pleasantly toiling for pleasure,
  All hungrily pining for pines,
And making of beautiful speeches,
  And marring of beautiful shows,
And feeding on delicate peaches,
  And treading on delicate toes.

Good-night to the Season! – another
  Will come with its trifles and toys,
And hurry away, like its brother,
100   In sunshine, and odour, and noise.
Will it come with a rose or a briar?
  Will it come with a blessing or curse?
Will its bonnets be lower or higher?
  Will its morals be better or worse?
Will it find me grown thinner or fatter,
  Or fonder of wrong or of right,
Or married, or buried? – no matter,
  Good-night to the Season, Good-night!

My Partner

'There is, perhaps, no subject of more universal interest in the whole
range of natural knowledge, than that of the unceasing fluctuations
which take place in the atmosphere in which we are immersed.' –
British Almanack

At Cheltenham, where one drinks one's fill
   Of folly and cold water,
I danced, last year, my first quadrille,
   With old Sir Geoffrey's daughter.
Her cheek with Summer's rose might vie,
   When Summer's rose is newest;
Her eyes were blue as Autumn's sky,
   When Autumn's sky is bluest:
And well my heart might deem her one
10   Of Life's most precious flowers,
For half her thoughts were of its Sun,
   And half were of its Showers.

I spoke of Novels: – 'Vivian Grey'
   Was positively charming,
And 'Almack's' infinitely gay,
   And 'Frankenstein' alarming;
I said 'De Vere' was chastely told,
   Thought well of 'Herbert Lacy',
Called Mr Banim's sketches 'bold',
20   And Lady Morgan's 'racy':
I vowed that last new thing of Hook's
   Was vastly entertaining;
And Laura said – 'I doat on books,
   Because it's always raining!'

I talk'd of Music's gorgeous fane;
   I raved about Rossini,
Hoped Ronzi would come back again,
   And criticised Pacini;

I wish'd the chorus-singers dumb,
30   The trumpets more pacific,
And eulogised Brocard's *à plomb*,
   And voted Paul 'terrific'.
What cared she for Medea's pride,
   Or Desdemona's sorrow?
'Alas!' my beauteous listener sigh'd,
   'We *must* have rain to-morrow!'

I told her tales of other lands;
   Of ever-boiling fountains,
Of poisonous lakes, and barren sands,
40   Vast forests, trackless mountains:
I painted bright Italian skies,
   I lauded Persian roses,
Coin'd similes for Spanish eyes,
   And jests for Indian noses:
I laugh'd at Lisbon's love of Mass,
   Vienna's dread of treason;
And Laura ask'd me where the glass
   Stood at Madrid last season.

I broach'd whate'er had gone its rounds,
50   The week before, of scandal:
What made Sir Luke lay down his hounds,
   And Jane take up her Handel;
Why Julia walk'd upon the heath,
   With the pale Moon above her;
Where Flora lost her false front teeth,
   And Anne her falser lover;
How Lord de B. and Mrs L.
   Had crossed the sea together;
My shuddering partner cried – 'O Ciel!
60   How *could* they – in such weather?'

Was she a Blue? – I put my trust
   In strata, petals, gases;
A Boudoir-pedant? – I discuss'd
   The Toga and the Fasces;

A Cockney-Muse? – I mouth'd a deal
    Of folly from Endymion;
A Saint? – I praised the pious zeal
    Of Messrs Way and Simeon;
A Politician? – it was vain,
70   To quote the Morning Paper;
The horrid phantoms came again,
    Rain, Hail, and Snow, and Vapour.

Flat Flattery was my only chance:
    I acted deep devotion,
Found magic in her every glance,
    Grace in her every motion;
I wasted all a Stripling's lore,
    Prayer, passion, folly, feeling;
And wildly look'd upon the floor,
80   And wildly on the ceiling;
I envied gloves upon her arm,
    And shawls upon her shoulder;
And when my worship was most warm,
    She 'never found it colder'.

I don't object to wealth or land:
    And she will have the giving
Of an extremely pretty hand,
    Some thousands, and a living.
She makes silk purses, broiders stools,
90   Sings sweetly, dances finely,
Paints screens, subscribes to Sunday schools,
    And sits a horse divinely.
But to be linked for life to her! –
    The desperate man who tried it,
Might marry a Barometer,
    And hang himself beside it!

The Fancy Ball

'A visor for a visor! what care I
What curious eye doth quote deformities?' – Shakspeare

'You used to talk,' said Miss Mac Call,
   'Of flowers, and flames, and Cupid;
But now you never talk at all,
   You're getting vastly stupid.
You'd better burn your Blackstone, Sir,
   You never will get through it;
There's a Fancy Ball at Winchester, –
   Do let us take you to it.'

I made that night a solemn vow,
10   To startle all beholders;
I wore white muslin on my brow,
   Green velvet on my shoulders;
My trousers were supremely wide,
   I learn'd to swear 'by Allah';
I stuck a poniard by my side,
   And called myself 'Abdallah'.

Oh! a Fancy Ball's a strange affair,
   Made up of silks and leathers,
Light heads, light heels, false hearts, false hair,
20   Pins, paint, and ostrich feathers;
The dullest Duke in all the town,
   To-night may shine a droll one;
And rakes, who have not half-a-crown,
   Look royal in a whole one.

[Go, call the lawyer from his pleas,
   The school-boy from his Latin;
Be stoics here in ecstasies,
   And savages in satin;

Let young and old forego – forget
30   Their labour and their sorrow,
And none – except the Cabinet –
        Take counsel for the morrow.

Begone, dull care! This life of ours
        Is very dark and chilly;
We'll sleep through all its serious hours,
        And laugh through all its silly.
Be mine such motley scene as this,
        Where, by established usance,
Miss Gravity is quite amiss,
40   And Madam Sense a nuisance!]

Hail, blest Confusion! here are met
        All tongues, and times, and faces,
The Lancers flirt with Juliet,
        The Brahmin talks of races;
And where's your genius, bright Corinne?
        And where your brogue, Sir Lucius?
And, Chinca Ti, you have not seen
        One chapter of Confucius.

Lo! dandies from Kamschatka flirt
50   With beauties from the Wrekin;
And belles from Berne look very pert
        On Mandarins from Pekin;
The Cardinal is here from Rome,
        The Commandant from Seville,
And Hamlet's father from the tomb,
        And Faustus from the Devil.

[O sweet Anne Page! – those dancing eyes
        Have peril in their splendour!
'O sweet Anne Page!' – so Slender sighs,
60   And what am I, but slender?

Alas! when next your spells engage
    So fond and starved a sinner,
My pretty Page, be Shakspeare's Page,
    And ask the fool to dinner!]

What mean those laughing Nuns, I pray,
    What mean they, Nun or Fairy?
I guess they told no beads to-day,
    And sang no Ave Mary;
From Mass and Matins, Priest and Pix,
70   Barred door, and window grated,
I wish all pretty Catholics
    Were thus emancipated.

Four Seasons come to dance quadrilles,
    With four well-seasoned sailors;
And Raleigh talks of rail-road bills
    With Timon, prince of railers;
I find Sir Charles of Aubyn Park,
    Equipp'd for a walk to Mecca;
And I run away from Joan of Arc,
80   To romp with sad Rebecca.

Fair Cleopatra's very plain,
    Puck halts, and Ariel swaggers;
And Cæsar's murder'd o'er again,
    Though not by Roman daggers:
Great Charlemagne is four feet high,
    Sad stuff has Bacon spoken;
Queen Mary's waist is all awry,
    And Psyche's nose is broken.

Our happiest bride, how very odd!
90   Is the mourning Isabella;
And the heaviest foot that ever trod
    Is the foot of Cinderella;

Here sad Calista laughs outright,
   There Yorick looks most grave, Sir,
And a Templar waves the cross to-night,
   Who never cross'd the wave, Sir.

And what a Babel is the talk!
   'The Giraffe' – 'plays the fiddle' –
'Macadam's roads' – 'I hate this chalk' –
100   'Sweet girl' – 'a charming riddle' –
'I'm nearly drunk with' – 'Epsom salts' –
   'Yes, separate beds' – 'such cronies!' –
'Good Heaven! who taught that man to valtz?' –
   'A pair of Shetland ponies.'

'Lord D——' – 'an enchanting shape' –
   'Will move for' – 'Maraschino' –
'Pray, Julia, how's your mother's ape?' –
   'He died at Navarino!' –
'The gout by Jove is' – 'apple pie' –
110   'Don Miguel' – 'Tom the tinker' –
'His Lordship's pedigree's as high
   As –' – 'Whipcord, dam by Clinker.'

'Love's shafts are weak' – 'my chesnut kicks' –
   'Heart broken' – 'broke the traces' –
'What say you now of politics?' –
   'Change sides and to your places,' –
'A five barred-gate' – 'a precious pearl' –
   'Grave things may all be punn'd on!' –
'The Whigs, thank God, are' – 'out of curl!' –
120   'Her age is' – 'four by London!'

Thus run the giddy hours away,
   Till morning's light is beaming,
And we must go to dream by day
   All we to-night are dreaming;

To smile and sigh, to love and change;
  Oh! in our heart's recesses,
We dress in fancies quite as strange
  As these our fancy-dresses.

A Letter of Advice

From Miss Medora Trevilian, at Padua,
to Miss Araminta Vavasour, in London

'Enfin Monsieur, un homme aimable;
Voila pourquoi je ne saurais l'aimer.' – Scribe

You tell me you're promised a lover,
  My own Araminta, next week;
Why cannot my fancy discover
  The hue of his coat and his cheek?
Alas! if he look like another,
  A vicar, a banker, a beau,
Be deaf to your father and mother,
  My own Araminta, say 'No!'

Miss Lane, at her Temple of Fashion,
10   Taught us both how to sing and to speak,
And we loved one another with passion,
  Before we had been there a week:
You gave me a ring for a token,
  I wear it wherever I go;
I gave you a chain, – is it broken?
  My own Araminta, say 'No!'

O think of our favourite cottage,
  And think of our dear Lalla Rookh;
How we shared with the milkmaids their pottage,
20   And drank of the stream from the brook:

How fondly our loving lips falter'd,
   'What further can grandeur bestow?'
My heart is the same, – is yours alter'd?
   My own Araminta, say 'No!'

Remember the thrilling Romances
   We read on the bank in the glen;
Remember the suitors our fancies
   Would picture for both of us then:
They wore the red cross on their shoulder,
30   They had vanquish'd and pardon'd their foe –
Sweet friend, are you wiser or colder? –
   My own Araminta, say 'No!'

You know, when Lord Rigmarole's carriage
   Drove off with your Cousin Justine,
You wept, dearest girl, at the marriage,
   And whisper'd, 'How base she has been!'
You said you were sure it would kill you
   If ever your husband look'd so;
And you will not apostatize, – will you? –
40   My own Araminta, say 'No!'

When I heard I was going abroad, Love,
   I thought I was going to die;
We walk'd arm-in-arm to the road, Love,
   We look'd arm-in-arm to the sky;
And I said, 'When a foreign postilion
   Has hurried me off to the Po,
Forget not Medora Trevilian; –
   My own Araminta, say "No!"'

We parted! but sympathy's fetters
50   Reach far over valley and hill;
I muse o'er your exquisite letters,
   And feel that your heart is mine still.

And he who would share it with me, Love,
    The richest of treasures below, –
If he's not what Orlando should be, Love,
    My own Araminta, say 'No!'

If he wears a top-boot in his wooing,
    If he comes to you riding a cob,
If he talks of his baking or brewing,
60   If he puts up his feet on the hob,
If he ever drinks port after dinner,
    If his brow or his breeding is low,
If he calls himself 'Thompson', or 'Skinner',
    My dear Araminta, say 'No!'

If he studies the news in the papers,
    While you are preparing the tea,
If he talks of the damps and the vapours,
    While moonlight lies soft on the sea,
If he's sleepy while you are capricious,
70   If he has not a musical 'Oh!'
If he does not call Werter delicious, –
    My own Araminta, say 'No!'

If he ever sets foot in the city,
    Among the stockbrokers and Jews,
If he has not a heart full of pity,
    If he don't stand six feet in his shoes,
If his lips are not redder than roses,
    If his hands are not whiter than snow,
If he has not the model of noses, –
80   My own Araminta, say 'No!'

If he speaks of a tax or a duty,
    If he does not look grand on his knees,
If he's blind to a landscape of beauty,
    Hills, valleys, rocks, waters, and trees,

If he dotes not on desolate towers,
    If he likes not to hear the blast blow,
If he knows not the language of flowers, –
    My own Araminta, say 'No!'

He must walk like a God of old story,
90   Come down from the home of his rest;
He must smile, like the sun in his glory,
    On the buds he loves ever the best;
And oh, from its ivory portal
    Like music his soft speech must flow! –
If he speak, smile, or walk like a mortal, –
    My own Araminta, say 'No!'

Don't listen to tales of his bounty,
    Don't hear what they tell of his birth,
Don't look at his seat in the county,
100   Don't calculate what he is worth;
But give him a theme to write verse on,
    And see if he turns out his toe; –
If he's only an excellent person, –
    My own Araminta, say 'No!'

*   *   *

Twenty-eight and Twenty-nine

'Rien n'est changé, mes amis!'* – Charles Dix

I heard a sick man's dying sigh,
  And an infant's idle laughter;
The old Year went with mourning by,
  The new came dancing after:
Let Sorrow shed her lonely tear,
  Let Revelry hold her ladle;
Bring boughs of cypress for the bier,
  Fling roses on the cradle:
Mutes to wait on the funeral state!
  Pages to pour the wine!
A requiem for Twenty-eight, –
  And a health to Twenty-nine!

Alas! for human happiness,
  Alas! for human sorrow;
Our Yesterday is nothingness,
  What else will be our Morrow?
Still Beauty must be stealing hearts,
  And Knavery stealing purses;
Still Cooks must live by making tarts,
  And Wits by making verses;
While Sages prate, and Courts debate,
  The same Stars set and shine;
And the World, as it roll'd through Twenty-eight,
  Must roll through Twenty-nine.

*I have taken these words for my motto because they enable me to tell a
story. When the present King of France received his first address on the
return from the emigration, his answer was, 'Rien n'est changé, mes amis; il
n'y a qu'un Français de plus.' When the Giraffe arrived in the Jardin des
Plantes, the Parisians had a caricature, in which the ass, and the hog, and
the monkey were presenting an address to the stranger, while the elephant
and the lion stalked angrily away. Of course, the portraits were recognizable;
and the animal was responding graciously, 'Rien n'est changé, mes amis; il
n'y a qu'un bête de plus!'

Some King will come, in Heaven's good time,
  To the tomb his Father came to;
Some Thief will wade through blood and crime
  To a crown he has no claim to:
Some suffering Land will rend in twain
30   The manacles that bound her,
And gather the links of the broken chain
  To fasten them proudly round her:
The grand and great will love, and hate,
  And combat, and combine;
And much where we were in Twenty-eight,
  We shall be in Twenty-nine.

O'Connell will toil to raise the Rent,
  And Kenyon to sink the Nation;
And Sheil will abuse the Parliament,
40   And Peel the Association:
And the thought of bayonets and swords
  Will make ex-Chancellors merry;
And jokes will be cut in the House of Lords,
  And throats in the county Kerry:
And writers of weight will speculate
  On the Cabinet's design;
And just what it did in Twenty-eight,
  It will do in Twenty-nine.

Mathews will be extremely gay,
50   And Hook extremely dirty;
And brick and mortar still will say
  'Try Warren, No. 30':
And 'General Sauce' will have its puff,
  And so will General Jackson;
And peasants will drink up heavy stuff,
  Which they pay a heavy tax on:
And long and late, at many a fête,
  Gooseberry champagne will shine;
And as old as it was in Twenty-eight,
60   It will be in Twenty-nine.

And the Goddess of Love will keep her smiles,
   And the God of Cups his orgies;
And there'll be riots in St Giles,
   And weddings in St George's:
And Mendicants will sup like Kings,
   And Lords will swear like Lacqueys;
And black eyes oft will lead to rings,
   And rings will lead to black eyes:
And pretty Kate will scold her mate,
70   In a dialect all divine;
Alas! they married in Twenty-eight, –
   They will part in Twenty-nine!

John Thomas Mugg, on a lonely hill,
   Will do a deed of mystery;
The Morning Chronicle will fill
   Five columns with the history:
The Jury will be all surprise,
   The Prisoner quite collected;
And Justice Park will wipe his eyes,
80   And be very much affected:
And folks will relate poor Corder's fate,
   As they hurry home to dine,
Comparing the hangings of Twenty-eight
   With the hangings of Twenty-nine.

A Curate will go from the house of prayer
   To wrong his worthy neighbour,
By dint of quoting the texts of Blair,
   And singing the songs of Weber:
Sir Harry will leave the Craven hounds,
90   To trace the guilty parties;
And ask of the Court five thousand pounds,
   To prove how rack'd his heart is:
An Advocate will execrate
   The spoiler of Hymen's shrine;
And the speech that did for Twenty-eight
   Will do for Twenty-nine.

My Uncle will swathe his gouty limbs,
   And tell of his oils and blubbers;
My Aunt, Miss Dobbs, will play longer hymns,
100   And rather longer rubbers:
My Cousin in Parliament will prove
   How utterly ruin'd trade is;
My Brother at Eton will fall in love
   With half a hundred ladies:
My Patron will sate his pride from plate,
   And his thirst from the Bordeaux vine;
His nose was red in Twenty-eight, –
   'Twill be redder in Twenty-nine!

And oh! I shall find, how, day by day,
110   All thoughts and things look older;
How the laugh of Pleasure grows less gay,
   And the heart of Friendship colder;
But still I shall be what I have been,
   Sworn foe to Lady Reason,
And seldom troubled with the spleen,
   And fond of talking treason:
I shall buckle my skait, and leap my gate,
   And throw, and write, my line;
And the woman I worshipped in Twenty-eight,
120   I shall worship in Twenty-nine!

* * *

from *LONDON MAGAZINE*

Arrivals at a Watering-Place

SCENE – A Conversazione at Lady Crumpton's. – Whist and weariness, Caricatures and Chinese Puzzle. – Young Ladies making tea, and Young Gentlemen making the agreeable. – The Stable-Boy handing rout-cakes. – Music expressive of there being nothing to do.

I play a spade: – such strange new faces
    Are flocking in from near and far:
Such frights – Miss Dobbs holds all the aces, –
    One can't imagine who they are!
The Lodgings at enormous prices,
    New Donkeys, and another fly;
And Madame Bonbon out of ices,
    Although we're scarcely in July:
We're quite as sociable as any,
10   But our old horse can scarcely crawl;
And really where there are so many,
    We can't tell where we ought to call.

Pray who has seen the odd old fellow
    Who took the Doctor's house last week? –
A pretty chariot, – livery yellow,
    Almost as yellow as his cheek:
A widower, sixty-five, and surly,
    And stiffer than a poplar-tree;
Drinks rum and water, gets up early
20   To dip his carcass in the sea:
He's always in a monstrous hurry,
    And always talking of Bengal;
They say his cook makes noble curry; –
    I think, Louisa, we should call.

And so Miss Jones, the mantua-maker,
    Has let her cottage on the hill? –
The drollest man, a sugar-baker, –
    Last year imported from the till:
Prates of his *orses* and his *oney*,
30   Is quite in love with fields and farms;
A horrid Vandal, – but his money
    Will buy a glorious coat of arms:
Old Clyster makes him take the waters;
    Some say he means to give a ball;
And, after all, with thirteen daughters,
    I think, Sir Thomas, you might call.

That poor young man! – I'm sure and certain
    Despair is making up his shroud:
He walks all night beneath the curtain
40   Of the dim sky and mirky cloud:
Draws landscapes, – throws such mournful glances! –
    Writes verses, – has such splendid eyes;
An ugly name, – but Laura fancies
    He's some great person in disguise! –
And since his dress is all the fashion,
    And since he's very dark and tall,
I think that, out of pure compassion,
    I'll get Papa to go and call.

So Lord St Ives is occupying
50   The whole of Mr Ford's Hotel;
Last Saturday his man was trying
    A little nag I want to sell.
He brought a lady in the carriage;
    Blue eyes, – eighteen, or thereabouts; –
Of course, you know, we *hope* it's marriage!
    But yet the *femme de chambre* doubts.
She look'd so pensive when we met her;
    Poor thing! and such a charming shawl! –
Well! till we understand it better,
60   It's quite impossible to call!

Old Mr Fund, the London banker,
   Arrived to-day at Premium Court;
I would not, for the world, cast anchor
   In such a horrid dangerous port;
Such dust and rubbish, lath and plaster, –
   (Contractors play the meanest tricks) –
The roof's as crazy as its master,
   And he was born in fifty-six:
Stairs creaking – cracks in every landing, –
70   The colonnade is sure to fall; –
We sha'n't find post or pillar standing,
   Unless we make great haste to call.

Who was that sweetest of sweet creatures,
   Last Sunday, in the Rector's seat?
The finest shape, – the loveliest features, –
   I never saw such tiny feet.
My brother, – (this is quite between us)
   Poor Arthur, – 'twas a sad affair!
Love at first sight, – She's quite a Venus, –
80   But then she's poorer far than fair:
And so my father and my mother
   Agreed it would not do at all;
And so, – I'm sorry for my brother! –
   It's settled that we're not to call.

And there's an Author, full of knowledge;
   And there's a Captain on half-pay;
And there's a Baronet from college,
   Who keeps a boy, and rides a bay;
And sweet Sir Marcus from the Shannon,
90   Fine specimen of brogue and bone;
And Doctor Calipee, the canon,
   Who weighs, I fancy, twenty stone:
A maiden Lady is adorning
   The faded front of Lily Hall: –
Upon my word, the first fine morning,
   We'll make a round, my dear, and call.

Alas! disturb not, maid and matron,
  The swallow in my humble thatch;
Your son may find a better patron,
100   Your niece may meet a richer match:
I can't afford to give a dinner,
  I never was on Almack's list;
And since I seldom rise a winner,
  I never like to play at whist:
Unknown to me the stocks are falling;
  Unwatch'd by me the glass may fall;
Let all the world pursue its calling, –
  I'm not at home if people call.

You'll Come to Our Ball (Our Ball)

'Comment! c'est lui? – que je le regarde encore! – c'est que vraiment
il est bien changé; n'est [ce] pas, mon papa?' – *Les Premiers Amours*

You'll come to our Ball; – since we parted,
  I've thought of you, more than I'll say;
Indeed, I was half broken-hearted,
  For a week, when they took you away.
Fond Fancy brought back to my slumbers
  Our walks on the Ness and the Den,
And echoed the musical numbers
  Which you used to sing to me then.
I know the romance, since it's over,
10   'Twere idle, or worse, to recall: –
I know you're a terrible rover;
  But, Clarence, – you'll come to our Ball!

It's only a year since, at College,
  You put on your cap and your gown;
But, Clarence, you're grown out of knowledge,
  And changed from the spur to the crown:

The voice that was best when it faltered
   Is fuller and firmer in tone;
And the smile that should never have altered, –
20   Dear Clarence, – it is not your own:
Your cravat was badly selected,
   Your coat don't become you at all;
And why is your hair so neglected?
   You *must* have it curled for our Ball.

I've often been out upon Haldon,
   To look for a covey with Pup;
I've often been over to Shaldon,
   To see how your boat is laid up:
In spite of the terrors of Aunty,
30   I've ridden the filly you broke;
And I've studied your sweet little Dante,
   In the shade of your favourite oak:
When I sat in July to Sir Lawrence,
   I sat in your love of a shawl;
And I'll wear what you brought me from Florence,
   Perhaps, if you'll come to our Ball.

You'll find us all changed since you vanished:
   We've set up a National School;
And waltzing is utterly banished;
40   And Ellen has married a fool;
The Major is going to travel;
   Miss Hyacinth threatens a rout;
The walk is laid down with fresh gravel;
   Papa is laid up with the gout:
And Jane has gone on with her easels,
   And Anne has gone off with Sir Paul;
And Fanny is sick with the measles, –
   And I'll tell you the rest at the Ball.

You'll meet all your Beauties; – the Lily,
50   And the Fairy of Willowbrook Farm,
And Lucy, who made me so silly
   At Dawlish, by taking your arm;

Miss Manners, who always abused you,
    For talking so much about Hock;
And her sister who often amused you,
    By raving of rebels and Rock;
And something which surely would answer,
    An heiress, quite fresh from Bengal; –
So, though you were seldom a dancer,
60   You'll dance, just for once, at our Ball.

But out on the world! – from the flowers
    It shuts out the sunshine of truth;
It blights the green leaves in the bowers,
    It makes an old age of our youth:
And the flow of our feeling, once in it,
    Like a streamlet beginning to freeze,
Though it cannot turn ice in a minute,
    Grows harder by sudden degrees.
Time treads o'er the grave of Affection;
70   Sweet honey is turned into gall: –
Perhaps you have no recollection
    That ever you danced at our Ball.

You once could be pleased with our ballads; –
    To-day you have critical ears:
You once could be charmed with our salads; –
    Alas! you've been dining with Peers:
You trifled and flirted with many;
    You've forgotten the when and the how:
There was *one* you liked better than any; –
80   Perhaps you've forgotten *her* now.
But of those you remember most newly,
    Of those who delight or enthrall,
None love you a quarter so truly
    As some you will find at our Ball.

They tell me you've many who flatter,
    Because of your wit and your song;
They tell me (and what does it matter?)
    You like to be praised by the throng:

They tell me you're shadowed with laurel,
90   They tell me you're loved by a Blue;
They tell me you're sadly immoral, –
      Dear Clarence, *that* cannot be true!
But to me you are still what I found you
      Before you grew clever and tall;
And you'll think of the spell that once bound you;
      And you'll come – *won't* you come? – to our Ball!

School and Schoolfellows

'Floreat Etona'

Twelve years ago I made a mock
      Of filthy trades and traffics;
I wonder'd what they meant by stock,
      I wrote delightful sapphics;
I knew the streets of Rome and Troy,
      I supp'd with Fates and Furies; –
Twelve years ago I was a boy,
      A happy boy, at Drury's.

Twelve years ago! – how many a thought
10   Of faded pains and pleasures
Those whisper'd syllables have brought
      From Memory's hoarded treasures;
The fields, the farms, the bats, the books,
      The glories, and disgraces,
The voices of dear friends, the looks
      Of old familiar faces.

Kind Mater smiles again to me,
      As bright as when we parted;
I seem again the frank, the free,
20   Stout-limb'd, and simple-hearted;

Pursuing ev'ry idle dream,
    And shunning every warning;
With no hard work but Bovney Stream,
    No chill except Long Morning:

Now stopping Harry Vernon's ball,
    That rattled like a rocket;
Now hearing Wentworth's 'fourteen all',
    And striking for the pocket:
Now feasting on a cheese and flitch,
30   Now drinking from the pewter;
Now leaping over Chalvey ditch,
    Now laughing at my tutor.

Where are my friends? I am alone,
    No playmate shares my beaker;
Some lie beneath the churchyard stone,
    And some before the Speaker
And some compose a tragedy,
    And some compose a rondo;
And some draw sword for liberty,
40   And some draw pleas for John Doe.

Tom Mill was used to blacken eyes,
    Without the fear of sessions;
Charles Medlar loath'd false quantities,
    As much as false professions:
Now Mill keeps order in the land,
    A magistrate pedantic;
And Medlar's feet repose, unscann'd,
    Beneath the wide Atlantic.

Wild Nick, whose oaths made such a din,
50   Does Dr Martext's duty;
And Mullion, with that monstrous chin,
    Is married to a beauty;
And Darrell studies, week by week,
    His Mant, and not his Manton;
And Ball, who was but poor at Greek,
    Is very rich at Canton.

And I am eight-and-twenty now;
   The world's cold chains have bound me;
And darker shades are on my brow,
60   And sadder scenes around me:
In Parliament I fill my seat,
   With many other noodles;
And lay my head in Jermyn-street,
   And sip my hock at Boodle's.

But often, when the cares of life
   Have set my temples aching,
When visions haunt me of a wife,
   When duns await my waking;
When Lady Jane is in a pet,
70   Or Hoby in a hurry,
When Captain Hazard wins a bet,
   Or Beaulieu spoils a curry;

For hours and hours I think and talk
   Of each remember'd hobby;
I long to lounge in Poets' Walk,
   To shiver in the lobby;
I wish that I could run away
   From House, and court, and levee,
Where bearded men appear to-day,
80   Just Eton boys, grown heavy;

That I could bask in childhood's sun,
   And dance o'er childhood's roses;
And find huge wealth in one pound one,
   Vast wit in broken noses;
And play Sir Giles at Datchet Lane,
   And call the milk-maids Houris; –
That I could be a boy again,
   A happy boy, at Drury's!

*   *   *

from *THE CASKET*

Childhood and His Visitors

Once on a time, when sunny May
    Was kissing up the April showers,
I saw fair Childhood hard at play
    Upon a bank of blushing flowers;
Happy, – he knew not whence or how;
    And smiling, – who could choose but love him?
For not more glad than Childhood's brow,
    Was the blue heaven that beamed above him.

Old Time, in most appalling wrath,
10   That valley's green repose invaded;
The brooks grew dry upon his path,
    The birds were mute, the lilies faded;
But Time so swiftly winged his flight,
    In haste a Grecian tomb to batter,
That Childhood watched his paper kite,
    And knew just nothing of the matter.

With curling lip, and glancing eye,
    Guilt gazed upon the scene a minute,
But Childhood's glance of purity
20   Had such a holy spell within it,
That the dark demon to the air
    Spread forth again his baffled pinion,
And hid his envy and despair,
    Self-tortured, in his own dominion.

Then stepped a gloomy phantom up,
    Pale, cypress-crowned, night's awful daughter,
And proffered him a fearful cup,
    Full to the brim of bitter water:

Poor Childhood bade her tell her name,
30   And when the beldame muttered 'Sorrow',
He said, – 'don't interrupt my game,
    I'll taste it, if I must, to-morrow.'

The Muse of Pindus thither came,
    And wooed him with the softest numbers
That ever scattered wealth and fame
    Upon a youthful poet's slumbers;
Though sweet the music of the lay,
    To Childhood it was all a riddle,
And 'Oh,' he cried, 'do send away
40   That noisy woman with the fiddle.'

Then Wisdom stole his bat and ball,
    And taught him, with most sage endeavour,
Why bubbles rise, and acorns fall,
    And why no toy may last for ever:
She talked of all the wondrous laws
    Which Nature's open book discloses,
And Childhood, ere she made a pause,
    Was fast asleep among the roses.

Sleep on, sleep on! – Oh! Manhood's dreams
50   Are all of earthly pain, or pleasure,
Of Glory's toils, Ambition's schemes,
    Of cherished love, or hoarded treasure:
But to the couch where Childhood lies
    A more delicious trance is given,
Lit up by rays from Seraph eyes,
    And glimpses of remembered heaven!

Beauty and Her Vistors

I looked for Beauty: – on a throne,
    A dazzling throne of light, I found her;
And music poured its softest tone,
    And flowers their sweetest breath, around her.
A score or two of idle gods,
    Some dressed as Peers, and some as Peasants,
Were watching all her smiles and nods,
    And making compliments, and presents.

And first young Love, the rosy boy,
10   Exhibited his bow and arrows,
And gave her many a pretty toy,
    Torches, and bleeding hearts, and sparrows:
She told him, as he passed, she knew
    Her court would scarcely do without him;
But yet – she hoped they were not true –
    There *were* some awkward tales about him.

Wealth deemed that magic had no charm
    More mighty than the gifts he brought her,
And linked around her radiant arm
20   Bright diamonds of the purest water:
The Goddess, with a scornful touch,
    Unclasped the gaudy, galling fetter;
And said, – she thanked him very much, –
    She liked a wreath of roses better.

Then Genius snatched his golden lute,
    And told a tale of love and glory;
The crowd around were hushed and mute,
    To hear so sad and sweet a story:
And Beauty marked the minstrel's cheek,
30   So very pale – no bust was paler; –
Vowed she could listen for a week;
    But really – he *should* change his tailor!

As died the echo of the strings,
  A shadowy Phantom kneeled before her,
Looked all unutterable things,
  And swore to see was to adore her:
He called her veil a cruel cloud,
  Her cheek a rose, her smile a battery;
She fancied it was Wit that bowed, –
40 I'm almost certain it was Flattery.

There was a Beldame finding fault
  With every person's every feature,
And by the sneer, and by the halt,
  I knew at once the odious creature;
'You see,' quoth Envy, 'I am come
  To bow – as is my bounden duty; –
They tell me Beauty is at Home; –
  Impossible! that *can't* be Beauty!'

I heard a murmur far and wide
50 Of – 'Lord! how quick the dotard passes!'
As Time threw down at Beauty's side
  The prettiest of his clocks and glasses:
But it was noticed in the throng,
  How Beauty marred the maker's cunning;
For, when she talked, the hands went wrong,
  And, when she smiled, the sands stopped running.

Death, in a Doctor's wig and gown,
  Came, arm in arm with Lethe, thither,
And crowned her with a withered crown,
60 And hinted, Beauty too must wither!
'Avaunt!' she cried; 'how came he here?
  The frightful fiend – he's my abhorrence!' –
I went and whispered in her ear,
  'He shall not hurt you; – sit to Lawrence.'

*   *   *

Anticipation

'Oh, yes! he is in Parliament;
   He's been returning thanks;
You can't conceive the time he's spent
   Already on his franks.
He'll think of nothing, night and day,
   But place, and the gazette':
No matter what the people say, –
   You won't believe them yet.

'He filled an album, long ago,
10   With such delicious rhymes;
Now we shall only see, you know,
   His speeches in the "Times";
And liquid tone and beaming brow,
   Bright eyes and locks of jet,
He'll care for no such nonsense now': –
   Oh! don't believe them yet!

'I vow he's turned a Goth, a Hun,
   By that disgusting Bill;
He'll never make another pun;
20   He's danced his last quadrille.
We shall not see him flirt again
   With any fair coquette;
He'll never laugh at Drury Lane.' –
   Psha! – don't believe them yet.

'Last week I heard his uncle boast
   He's sure to have the seals;
I read it in the "Morning Post"
   That he has dined at Peel's;
You'll never see him any more,
30   He's in a different set;
He cannot eat at half-past four': –
   No? – don't believe them yet.

'In short, he'll soon be false and cold,
  And infinitely wise;
He'll grow next year extremely old,
  He'll tell enormous lies;
He'll learn to flatter and forsake,
  To feign and to forget': –
Oh, whisper – or my heart will break –
40   You won't believe them yet!

Lines

Written for a Blank Page of 'The Keepsake'

Lady, there's fragrance in your sighs,
  And sunlight in your glances;
I never saw such lips and eyes
  In pictures or romances;
And Love will readily suppose,
  To make you quite enslaving,
That you have taste for verse and prose,
  Hot pressed, and line engraving.

And then, you waltz so like a Fay,
10   That round you envy rankles;
Your partner's head is turned, they say
  As surely as his ankles;
And I was taught, in days far gone,
  By a most prudent mother,
That in this world of sorrow, one
  Good turn deserves another.

I may not win you! – that's a bore!
  But yet 'tis sweet to woo you;
And for this cause, – and twenty more,
20   I send this gay book to you.

If its songs please you, – by this light!
    I will not hold it treason
To bid you dream of me to-night,
    And dance with me next season.

*   *   *

from *THE LITERARY SOUVENIR*

The Legend of the Haunted Tree

'Deep is the bliss of the belted knight,
   When he kisses at dawn the silken glove,
And rides, in his glittering armour dight,
   To shiver a lance for his Lady-love!

Lightly he couches the beaming spear;
   His mistress sits with her maidens by,
Watching the speed of his swift career,
   With a whispered prayer and a murmured sigh.

Far from me is the gazing throng,
   The blazoned shield, and the nodding plume;
Nothing is mine but a worthless song,
   A joyless life, and a nameless tomb.'

'Nay, dearest Wilfrid, lay like this
On such an eve is much amiss:
Our mirth beneath the new May Moon
Should be echoed by livelier tune.
What need to thee of mail and crest,
Of foot in stirrup, spear in rest?
Over far mountains and deep seas,
Earth hath no fairer fields than these;
And who, in Beauty's gaudiest bowers,
Can love thee with more love than ours?'

The minstrel turned with a moody look
   From that sweet scene of guiltless glee;
From the old who talked beside the brook,
   And the young who danced beneath the tree:

222 WINTHROP MACKWORTH PRAED

Coldly he shrank from the gentle maid,
　From the chiding look and the pleading tone;
And he passed from the old elm's hoary shade,
30　　And followed the forest path alone.
One little sigh, one pettish glance,
　And the girl comes back to her playmates now,
And takes her place in the merry dance,
　With a slower step and a sadder brow.

'My soul is sick,' saith the wayward boy,
'Of the peasant's grief, and the peasant's joy;
I cannot breathe on from day to day,
Like the insects, which our wise men say
In the crevice of the cold rock dwell,
40　Till their shape is the shape of their dungeon's cell;
In the dull repose of our changeless life,
I long for passion, I long for strife,
As in the calm the mariner sighs
For rushing waves and groaning skies.
Oh for the lists, the lists of fame,
Oh for the herald's glad acclaim;
For floating pennon and prancing steed,
And Beauty's wonder at manhood's deed!'

Beneath an ancient oak he lay: –
50　More years than man can count, they say,
On the verge of the dim and solemn wood,
Through sunshine and storm, that oak had stood.
[Yet were it hard to trace a sign
On trunk or bough of that oak's decline:]
Many a loving, laughing sprite,
Tended the branches by day and by night;
[Fettered the winds that would invade
The quiet of its sacred shade,
And drove in a serried phalanx back
60　The red-eyed lightning's fierce attack:]
And the leaves of its age were as fresh and green
As the leaves of its early youth had been.

[Fretful brain and turbid breast
Under its canopy ill would rest;
For she that ruled the revels therein
Loved not the taint of human sin:
Moody brow with an evil eye
Would the Queen of the Fairy people spy;
Sullen tone with an angry ear
70　　Would the Queen of the Fairy people hear.
Oft would she mock the worldling's care
E'en in the grant of his unwise prayer,
Scattering wealth that was not gain,
Lavishing joy that turned to pain.]
Pure of thought should the mortal be
Who sleeps beneath the Haunted Tree.
That night the minstrel laid him down,
Ere his brow relaxed its sullen frown;
And slumber had bound his eyelids fast,
80　　Ere the evil wish from his soul had passed.

And a song on the sleeper's ear descended,
　　A song it was pain to hear, and pleasure;
So strangely wrath and love were blended
　　In every note of the mystic measure.

　　　　'I know thee, child of earth. —
　　　　The morning of thy birth
In through the lattice did my chariot glide;
　　　　I saw thy father weep
　　　　Over thy first wild sleep,
90　　I rocked thy cradle when thy mother died.

　　　　And I have seen thee gaze
　　　　Upon these birks and braes,
Which are my kingdoms, with irreverent scorn;
　　　　And heard thee pour reproof
　　　　Upon the vine–clad roof,
Beneath whose peaceful shelter thou wast born.

I bind thee in the snare
Of thine unholy prayer;
I seal thy forehead with a viewless seal:
100   I give into thine hand
The buckler and the brand,
And clasp the golden spur upon thy heel.

When thou hast made thee wise
In the sad lore of sighs,
When the world's visions fail thee and forsake,
Return, return to me,
And to my Haunted Tree; –
The charm hath bound thee now: Sir knight, awake!'

Sir Isumbras, in doubt and dread,
110   From his feverish sleep awoke;
And started up from his grassy bed
Under the ancient oak.
And he called the page who held his spear,
And, 'tell me, boy,' quoth he,
'How long have I been slumbering here,
Beneath the greenwood tree?' –
'Ere thou didst sleep, I chanced to throw
A stone into the rill;
And the ripple that disturbed its flow
120   Is on its surface still:
Ere thou didst sleep, thou bad'st me sing
King Arthur's favourite lay;
And the first echo of the string
Has hardly died away.'

'How strange is sleep!' the young knight said,
As he clasped the helm upon his head,
And mounting again his courser black,
To his gloomy tower rode slowly back;
'How strange is sleep! when his dark spell lies
130   On the drowsy lids of human eyes,
The years of a life will float along
In the compass of a page's song.

Methought I lived in a pleasant vale,
The haunt of the lark and the nightingale,
Where the summer rose had a brighter hue,
And the noonday sky a clearer blue,
And the spirit of man in age and youth
A fonder love, and a firmer truth.
And I lived on, a fair-haired boy,
140   In that sweet vale of tranquil joy;
Until at last my vain caprice
Grew weary of its bliss and peace.
And one there was, most dear and fair,
Of all that smiled around me there,
A gentle maid, with a cloudless face,
And a form so full of fairy grace;
Who, when I turned with scornful spleen
From the feast in the bower, or the dance on the green,
Would humour all my wayward will,
150   And love me, and forgive me, still.
Even now, methinks, her smile of light
Is there before me, mild and bright;
And I hear her voice of fond reproof,
Between the beats of my palfrey's hoof.
'T is idle all; – but I could weep; –
Alas!' said the knight, 'how strange is sleep!'

He struck with his spear the brazen plate
That hung before the castle gate;
The torch threw high its waves of flame
160   As forth the watchful menials came;
They lighted the way to the banquet hall,
They hung the shield upon the wall,
They spread the board, and they filled the bowl,
And the phantoms passed from his troubled soul.

[For all the ailments which infest
A solitary Briton's breast,
The peccant humours which defile
The thoughts in this fog-haunted isle,

Whatever name or style they bear –
170   Reflection, study, nerves, or care,
There's naught of such Lethean power
As dinner at the dinner-hour.
Sefton! the Premier, o'er thy plate,
Thinks little of last night's debate;
Cowan! the merchant, in thy hall,
Grows careless what may rise or fall;
The wit who feeds can puff away
His unsold tale, his unheard play;
And Mr Wellesley Pole forgets,
180   At eight o'clock, his duns and debts.
The Knight approved the roasted boar,
And mused upon his dream no more:
The Knight enjoyed the bright champagne,
And deemed himself himself again.]

Sir Isumbras was ever found
    Where blows were struck for glory;
There sate not at the Table Round
    A knight more famed in story:
The king on his throne would turn about
190   To see his courser prancing;
And, when Sir Launcelot was out, [had gout,]
    The queen would praise his dancing:
He quite wore out his father's spurs,
    Performing valour's duties;
Destroying mighty sorcerers,
    Avenging injured beauties,
And crossing many a trackless sand,
    And rescuing people's daughters
From dragons that infest the land,
200   And whales that walk the waters.
He throttled lions by the score,
    And giants by the dozen;
And, for his skill in lettered lore,
    They called him 'Merlin's Cousin'.

A score of steeds, with bit and rein,
   Stood ready in his stable;
An ox was every morning slain,
   And roasted for his table.
And he had friends, all brave and tall,
210   And crowned with praise and laurel,
Who kindly feasted in his hall,
   And tilted in his quarrel;
And minstrels came and sang his fame
   In very rugged verses;
And they were paid with wine and game,
   And rings, and cups, and purses.

And he loved a Lady of high degree,
   Faith's fortress, Beauty's flower;
A countess for her maid had she,
220   And a kingdom for her dower;
And a brow whose frowns were vastly grand,
   And an eye of sunlit brightness,
And a swan-like neck, and an arm and hand
   Of most bewitching whiteness;
And a voice of music, whose sweet tones
   Could most divinely prattle
Of battered casques, and broken bones,
   And all the bliss of battle.
He wore her scarf in many a fray,
230   He trained her hawks and ponies,
And filled her kitchen every day
   With leverets and conies;
He loved, and he was loved again; –
   I won't waste time in proving,
There is no pleasure like the pain
   Of being loved, and loving.

Dame Fortune is a fickle gipsy,
And always blind, and often tipsy;
Sometimes, for years and years together,
240 She'll bless you with the sunniest weather,

Bestowing honour, pudding, pence,
You can't imagine why, or whence; –
Then in a moment – Presto, pass! –
Your joys are withered like the grass;
You find your constitution vanish,
Almost as quickly as the Spanish;
The murrain spoils your flocks and fleeces;
The dry-rot pulls your house to pieces;
Your garden raises only weeds;
250   Your agent steals your title deeds;
Your banker's failure stuns the city;
Your father's will makes Sugden witty;
Your daughter, in her beauty's bloom,
Goes off to Gretna with the groom;
And you, good man, are left alone,
To battle with the gout and stone.

Ere long, Sir Isumbras began
To be a sad and thoughtful man:
They said the glance of an evil eye
260   Had been on the knight's prosperity:
Less swift on the quarry his falcon went,
Less true was his hound on the wild deer's scent,
And thrice in the list he came to the earth,
By the luckless chance of a broken girth.
And Poverty soon in her rags was seen
At the board where Plenty erst had been;
And the guests smiled not as they smiled before,
And the song of the minstrel was heard no more.
And a base ingrate, who was his foe,
270   Because, a little month ago,
He had cut him down, with friendly ardour,
From a rusty hook in an Ogre's larder,
Invented an atrocious fable,
And libelled his fame at the Royal Table:
And she at last, the worshipped one,
For whom his valorous deeds were done,
[The star of all his soul's reflections,
The rose of all his heart's affections,]

Who had heard his vows, and worn his jewels,
280   And made him fight so many duels, –
She, too, when Fate's relentless wheel
Deprived him of the Privy Seal,
Bestowed her smiles upon another,
And gave his letters to her mother.

['Tis the last drop, as all men know,
That makes the bucket overflow,
And the last parcel of the pack
That bends in two the camel's back.]
Fortune and fame, – he had seen them depart,
290   With a silent pride of a valiant heart:
Traitorous friends, – he had passed them by,
With a haughty brow, and a stifled sigh.
Boundless and black might roll the sea,
O'er which the course of his bark must be;
But he saw, through the storm that frowned above,
One guiding light, and the light was Love.
Now all was dark; the doom was spoken!
His wealth all spent, and his heart half-broken,
Poor youth, he had no earthly hope,
300   Except in laudanum, or a rope.

[If e'er you happened, by a twist,
Of Destiny's provoking wrist,
To find yourself one morning hurled
From all you had in all the world, –
Seeing your pretty limes and beeches
Supply the auction-mart with speeches, –
By base ingratitude disgusted
In him you most esteemed and trusted,
And cut, without the slightest reason,
310   By her who was so kind last season, –
You know how often meditation
Assures you, for your consolation,
That, if you had but been contented
To rent the house your father rented,

If, in Sir Paul you'd been inclined to
Suspect what no one else was blind to,
If, for that false girl, you had chosen
Either her sister or her cousin,
If any thing you had been doing
320   But just the very thing you're ruing,
You might have lived your day in clover,
Gay, rich, prized friend, and favored lover.
Thus was it with my Knight of knights;
While vanished all his vain delights,
The thought of being dupe and ass
Most galled the sick Sir Isumbras.]

He ordered out his horse, and tried,
As the Leech advised, a gentle ride.
    A pleasant path he took,
330   Where the turf, all bright with the April showers,
Was spangled with a hundred flowers,
    Beside a murmuring brook.
Never before had he roved that way;
And now, on a sunny first of May,
He chose the turning, you may guess,
Not for the laughing loveliness
Of turf, or flower, or stream; but only
Because it looked extremely lonely.

[Yet but that Megrim hovering here
340   Had dimmed the eye and dulled the ear,
Jocund and joyous all around
Were every sight and every sound.
The ancient forest, whose calm rest
No axe did ever yet molest,
    Stretched far upon the right;
Here, deepening into trackless shades,
There, opening long and verdant glades,
    Unto the cheerful light:

Wide on the left, whene'er the screen
350   Of hedgerows left a space between
        To stand and gaze awhile,
O'er varied scenes the eye might rove,
Orchard and garden, mead and grove,
        Spread out for many a mile.
Around, in all the joy of spring,
The sinless birds were carolling;
        Low hummed the studious bees;
And softly, sadly, rose and fell
The echo of the ocean-swell,
360   In the capricious breeze.
But truly Sir Isumbras cared as much
For all that a happier heart might touch,
As Cottenham cares for a Highland reel,
When counsel opens a Scotch Appeal,
Or Hume for Pasta's glorious scenes,
When the House is voting the Ways and Means.]

He had wandered, musing, scarce a mile,
        In his melancholy mood,
When, peeping o'er a rustic stile,
370   He saw a little village smile,
        Embowered in thick wood.
There were small cottages, arrayed
In the delicate jasmine's fragrant shade;
And gardens, whence the rose's bloom
Loaded the gale with rich perfume;
And there were happy hearts; for all
In that bright nook kept festival,
And welcomed in the merry May
With banquet and with roundelay.
380   Sir Isumbras sate gazing there,
With folded arms, and mournful air;
He fancied, – 't was an idle whim, –
That the village looked like a home to him.

And now a gentle maiden came,
Leaving her sisters and their game,
    And wandered up the vale;
Sir Isumbras had never seen
A thing so fair, – except the Queen, –
But out on passion's doubts and fears!
390   Her beautiful eyes were full of tears,
    And her cheeks were wan and pale.
None courted her stay of the joyous throng,
    As she passed from the group alone;
And he listened, which was very wrong,
And heard her singing a lively song,
    In a very dismal tone.

'Deep is the bliss of the belted knight,
    When he kisses at dawn the silken glove,
And goes, in his glittering armour dight,
400   To shiver a lance for his Lady-love!' –

That thrilling voice, – so soft and clear,
Was it familiar to his ear?
And those delicious drooping eyes,
As blue and as pure as the summer skies,
Had he, indeed, in other days,
Been blessed in the light of their holy rays?

He knew not; but his knee he bent
    Before her in most knightly fashion,
And grew superbly eloquent
410   About her beauty, and his passion.
He said that she was very fair,
    And that she warbled like a linnet;
And that he loved her, though he ne'er
    Had looked upon her till that minute.
[He said, that all the Court possessed
    Of gay or grave, of fat or slender,
Poor things! were only fit, at best,
    To hold a candle to her splendour.

He vowed that when she once should take
420   A little proper state upon her,
All lutes for her delight would wake,
     All lances shiver in her honour:]
He grieved to mention, that a Jew
     Had seized for debt his grand pavilion;
And he had little now, 't was true,
     To offer, but a heart and pillion:
But what was wealth? – In many a fight, –
     Though he, who should n't say it, said it, –
He still had borne him like a knight,
430   And had his share of blows and credit;
And, if she would but condescend
     To meet him at the Priest's to-morrow,
And be henceforth his guide, his friend,
     In every toil, in every sorrow, –
They'd sail instanter from the Downs;
     His hands just now were quite at leisure;
And, if she fancied foreign crowns,
     He'd win them with the greatest pleasure.

'A year is gone,' – the damsel sighed,
440 But blushed not, as she so replied, –
'Since one I loved, – alas! how well
He knew not, knows not, – left our dell.
Time brings to his deserted cot
No tidings of his after lot;
But his weal or woe is still the theme
Of my daily thought, and my nightly dream.
Poor Alice is not proud or coy;
But her heart is with her minstrel boy.'

Away from his arms the damsel bounded,
450 And left him more and more confounded.
He mused of the present, he mused of the past,
And he felt that a spell was o'er him cast;
He shed hot tears, he knew not why,
And talked to himself and made reply;

Till a calm o'er his troubled senses crept,
And, as the daylight waned, he slept.
Poor gentleman! – I need not say,
Beneath an ancient oak he lay.

     'He is welcome,' – o'er his bed,
460   Thus the bounteous Fairy said;

     'He has conned the lesson now;
       He has read the book of pain;
     There are furrows on his brow,
       I must make it smooth again.

    Lo, I knock the spurs away;
      Lo, I loosen belt and brand;
    Hark! I hear the courser neigh
      For his stall in Fairy-land.

    Bring the cap, and bring the vest;
470   Buckle on his sandal shoon;
    Fetch his memory from the chest
      In the treasury of the Moon.

    I have taught him to be wise,
      For a little maiden's sake; –
    Look, he opens his bright eyes,
      Softly, slowly; – minstrel, wake!'

The sun has risen, and Wilfrid is come
To his early friends and his cottage home.
His hazel eyes and his locks of gold
480 Are just as they were in the time of old;
But a blessing has been on the soul within,
For that is won from its secret sin;
More loving now, and worthier love
Of men below and of Saints above.
He reins a steed with a lordly air,
Which makes his country cousins stare;

And he speaks in a strange and courtly phrase,
Though his voice is the voice of other days.
But where he has learned to talk and ride,
490   He will tell to none but his bonny bride.

Waterloo

It was here that the French cavalry charged, and cut to pieces the
English squares. – *Narrative of a French Tourist*

Is it true, think you? – *Winter's Tale*

Ay, here such valorous deeds were done
    As ne'er were done before;
Ay, here the reddest wreath was won
    That ever Gallia wore:
Since Ariosto's wondrous knight
    Made all the Pagans dance,
There never dawned a day so bright
    As Waterloo's on France.

The trumpet poured its deafening sound –
10   Flags fluttered on the gale;
And cannon roared, and heads flew round
    As fast as summer hail:
The sabres flashed; with rage and fear
    The steeds began to prance;
The English quaked from front to rear, –
    They never quake in France!

The cuirassiers rode in and out,
    As fierce as wolves and bears;
'T was grand to see them slash about
20   Among the English squares!

And then the Polish lancer came,
    Careering with his lance; –
No wonder Britain blushed for shame,
    And ran away from France.

The Duke of York was killed that day –
    The King was sadly scarred; –
Lord Eldon, as he ran away,
    Was taken by the Guard.
Poor Wellington, with fifty Blues,
30   Escaped by some strange chance;
Henceforth, I think he'll hardly choose
    To shew himself in France.

So Buonaparte pitched his tent
    That day in Grosvenor Place;
And Ney rode straight to Parliament,
    And broke the Speaker's mace.
'Vive L'Empereur' was said and sung,
    From Peebles to Penzance;
The Mayor and Aldermen were hung,
40   Which made folks laugh in France.

They pulled the Tower of London down;
    They burned our wooden walls;
They brought his Holiness to Town,
    And lodged him in St Paul's.
And Gog and Magog rubbed their eyes,
    Awaking from a trance;
And grumbled out, in great surprise,
    'O mercy! we're in France!'

They sent a Regent to our Isle, –
50   The little King of Rome;
And squibs and crackers all the while
    Blazed in the Place Vendome.

And ever since, in arts and power
    They're making great advance;
They've had strong beer from that glad hour,
    And sea-coal fires in France.

My uncle, Captain Flanigan,
    Who lost a leg in Spain,
Tells stories of a little man,
60   Who died at St Helene.
But bless my heart! they can't be true,
    I'm sure they're all romance;
John Bull was beat at Waterloo –
    They'll swear to that in France!

The Belle of the Ball-Room, An Every-day Character

'Il faut juger des femmes depuis la chaussure jusqu'a la coiffure
exclusivement, à peu près comme on mesure le poisson entre queue
et tête.' – La Bruyère

Years, years ago, – ere yet my dreams
    Had been of being wise or witty; –
Ere I had done with writing themes,
    Or yawned o'er this infernal Chitty;
Years, years ago, – while all my joy
    Was in my fowling-piece and filly; –
In short, while I was yet a boy,
    I fell in love with Laura Lily.

I saw her at the Country-Ball:
10   There, when the sounds of flute and fiddle
Gave signal sweet in that old hall,
    Of hands across and down the middle,
Hers was the subtlest spell by far
    Of all that sets young hearts romancing;
She was our queen, our rose, our star;
    And then she danced – Oh heaven, her dancing!

Dark was her hair; her hand was white;
   Her voice was exquisitely tender;
Her eyes were full of liquid light;
20   I never saw a waist so slender!
Her every look, her every smile,
   Shot right and left a score of arrows;
I thought 't was Venus from her isle,
   And wondered where she'd left her sparrows.

She talked – of politics or prayers;
   Of Southey's prose, or Wordsworth's sonnets;
Of danglers, or of dancing bears,
   Of battles, or the last new bonnets:
By candlelight, at twelve o'clock,
30   To me it mattered not a tittle;
If those bright lips had quoted Locke,
   I might have thought they murmured Little.

Through sunny May, through sultry June,
   I loved her with a love eternal;
I spoke her praises to the moon,
   I wrote them to the Sunday Journal.
My mother laughed; – I soon found out
   That ancient ladies have no feeling:
My father frowned; – but how should gout
40   See any happiness in kneeling?

She was the daughter of a Dean,
   Rich, fat, and rather apoplectic;
She had one brother, just thirteen,
   Whose colour was extremely hectic;
Her grandmother for many a year
   Had fed the parish with her bounty;
Her second cousin was a peer,
   And Lord Lieutenant of the county.

But titles, and the three per cents,
50   And mortgages, and great relations,
And India bonds, and tithes, and rents,
   Oh, what are they to love's sensations!
Black eyes, fair forehead, clustering locks,
   Such wealth, such honours, Cupid chuses;
He cares as little for the Stocks,
   As Baron Rothschild for the Muses.

She sketched; – the vale, the wood, the beach
   Grew lovelier from her pencil's shading:
She botanized; – I envied each
60   Young blossom in her boudoir fading:
She warbled Handel; it was grand;
   She made the Catalini jealous:
She touched the organ; – I could stand
   For hours and hours to blow the bellows.

She kept an Album too at home,
   Well filled with all an Album's glories;
Paintings of butterflies, and Rome,
   Patterns for trimmings, Persian stories;
Soft songs to Julia's cockatoo,
70   Fierce odes to Famine and to Slaughter;
And autographs of Prince Leboo,
   And recipes of elder-water.

And she was flattered, worshipped, bored;
   Her steps were watched, her dress was noted;
Her poodle dog was quite adored,
   Her sayings were extremely quoted.
She laughed, and every heart was glad,
   As if the taxes were abolished;
She frowned, and every look was sad,
80   As if the Opera were demolished.

She smiled on many just for fun, –
　　I knew that there was nothing in it;
I was the first, – the only one,
　　Her heart had thought of for a minute.
I knew it; for she told me so,
　　In phrase which was divinely moulded;
She wrote a charming hand, – and oh!
　　How sweetly all her notes were folded!

Our love was like most other loves; –
90　　A little glow, a little shiver;
A rose-bud, and a pair of gloves,
　　And 'Fly not yet' upon the river;
Some jealousy of some one's heir,
　　Some hopes of dying broken-hearted;
A miniature, a lock of hair,
　　The usual vows, and then we parted.

We parted – months and years rolled by;
　　We met again four summers after;
Our parting was all sob and sigh;
100　　Our meeting was all mirth and laughter:
For in my heart's most secret cell
　　There had been many other lodgers;
And she was not the Ball-Room's Belle,
　　But only Mrs Something Rogers.

Stanzas

Written in Lady Myrtle's Boccaccio

In these gay pages there is food
For every mind, and every mood,
　　Fair Lady, if you dare to spell them:
Now merriment, now grief prevails;
But yet the best of all the tales
　　Is of the young group met to tell them.

Oh, was it not a pleasant thought,
To set the pestilence at nought,
  Chatting among sweet streams and flowers;
10   Of jealous husbands, fickle wives,
Of all the tricks which love contrives,
  To see through veils, and talk through towers?

Lady, they say the fearful guest,
Onward, still onward, to the west,
  Poised on his sulphurous wings, advances;
Who, on the frozen river's banks,
Has thinned the Russian despot's ranks,
  And marred the might of Warsaw's lances.

Another year – a brief, brief year!
20   And lo, the fell destroyer here,
  He comes with all his gloomy terrors;
Then guilt will read the properest books,
And folly wear the soberest looks,
  And virtue shudder at her errors.

And there'll be sermons in the street;
And every friend and foe we meet
  Will wear the dismal garb of sorrow;
And quacks will send their lies about,
And weary Halford will find out,
30   He must have four new bays to-morrow.

But you shall fly from these dark signs,
As did those happy Florentines,
  Ere from your cheek one rose is faded;
And hide your youth and loveliness
In some bright garden's green recess,
  By walls fenced round, by huge trees shaded:

There brooks shall dance in light along,
And birds shall trill their constant song
   Of pleasure, from their leafy dwelling;
40 You shall have music, novels, toys;
But still the chiefest of your joys
   Must be, fair Lady, story telling.

Be cautious how you choose your men:
Do n't look for people of the pen,
   Scholars who read, or write the papers;
Do n't think of wits, who talk to dine,
Who drink their patron's newest wine,
   And cure their patron's newest vapours.

Avoid all youths who toil for praise
50 By quoting Liston's last new phrase;
   Or sigh to leave high fame behind them;
For swallowing swords, or dancing jigs,
Or imitating ducks and pigs;
   Take men of sense, – if you can find them.

Live, laugh, tell stories; ere they're told,
New themes succeed upon the old;
   New follies come, new faults, new fashions;
An hour, a minute, will supply
To thought, a folio history
60   Of blighted hopes, and thwarted passions.

King Death, when he has snatched away
Drunkards from brandy, Dukes from play,
   And Common-councilmen from turtle;
Shall break his dart in Grosvenor Square,
And mutter in his fierce despair,
   'Why, what's become of Lady Myrtle?'

*   *   *

The Talented Man

A Letter from a Lady in London to a Lady at Lausanne

Dear Alice! you'll laugh when you know it, –
  Last week, at the Duchess's ball,
I danced with the clever new poet, –
  You've heard of him, – Tully St Paul.
Miss Jonquil was perfectly frantic;
  I wish you had seen Lady Anne!
It really was very romantic,
  He *is* such a talented man!

He came up from Brazen Nose College,
  Just caught, as they call it, this spring;
And his head, love, is stuffed full of knowledge
  Of every conceivable thing.
Of science and logic he chatters,
  As fine and as fast as he can;
Though *I* am no judge of such matters,
  I'm sure he's a talented man.

His stories and jests are delightful; –
  Not stories or jests, dear, for you;
The jests are exceedingly spiteful,
  The stories not always *quite* true.
Perhaps to be kind and veracious
  May do pretty well at Lausanne;
But it never would answer, – good gracious!
  Chez nous – in a talented man.

He sneers, – how my Alice would scold him! –
  At the bliss of a sigh or a tear;
He laughed – only think! – when I told him
  How we cried o'er Trevelyan last year;

I vow I was quite in a passion;
30   I broke all the sticks of my fan;
But sentiment's quite out of fashion,
        It seems, in a talented man.

Lady Bab, who is terribly moral,
        Has told me that Tully is vain,
And apt – which is silly – to quarrel,
        And fond – which is sad – of champagne.
I listened, and doubted, dear Alice,
        For I saw, when my lady began,
It was only the Dowager's malice; –
40   She *does* hate a talented man!

He's hideous, I own it. But fame, love,
        Is all that these eyes can adore;
He's lame, – but Lord Byron was lame, love,
        And dumpy, – but so is Tom Moore.
Then his voice, – *such* a voice! my sweet creature,
        It's like your Aunt Lucy's toucan:
But oh! what's a tone or a feature,
        When once one's a talented man?

My mother, you know, all the season,
50   Has talked of Sir Geoffrey's estate;
And truly, to do the fool reason,
        He *has* been less horrid of late.
But to-day, when we drive in the carriage,
        I'll tell her to lay down her plan; –
If ever I venture on marriage,
        It must be a talented man!

P. S. – I have found, on reflection,
        One fault in my friend, – *entre nous;*
Without it, he'd just be perfection; –
60   Poor fellow, he has not a *sou!*
And so, when he comes in September,
        To shoot with my uncle, Sir Dan,
I've promised mamma to remember
        He's *only* a talented man!

One More Quadrille (*The Last Quadrille*)

Not yet, not yet; it's hardly four;
   Not yet; we'll send the chair away;
Mirth still has many smiles in store,
   And love has fifty things to say.
Long leagues the weary Sun must drive,
   Ere pant his hot steeds o'er the hill;
The merry stars will dance till five;
   One more quadrille, – one more quadrille!

'Tis only thus, 'tis only here
10   That maids and minstrels may forget
The myriad ills they feel or fear,
   Ennui, taxation, cholera, debt;
With daylight busy cares and schemes
   Will come again to chafe or chill;
This is the fairy land of dreams;
   One more quadrille, – one more quadrille!

What tricks the French in Paris play,
   And what the Austrians are about,
And whether that tall knave, Lord Grey,
20   Is staying in, or going out;
And what the House of Lords will do,
   At last, with that eternal Bill,
I do not care a rush, – do you?
   One more quadrille, – one more quadrille!

My book don't sell, my play don't draw,
   My garden gives me only weeds;
And Mr Quirk has found a flaw –
   Deuce take him – in my title-deeds;
My Aunt has scratched her nephew's name
30   From that sweet corner in her will;
My dog is dead, my horse is lame;
   One more quadrille, – one more quadrille!

Not yet, not yet; it is not late;
  Don't whisper it to sister Jane;
Your brother, I am sure, will wait;
  Papa will go to cards again.
Not yet, not yet. Your eyes are bright,
  Your step is like a wood-nymph's still.
Oh no, you can't be tired, to-night!
40   One more quadrille, – one more quadrille!

*   *   *

from *THE MORNING POST*

Stanzas To the Speaker Asleep

Sleep, Mr SPEAKER; it's surely fair,
If you don't in your bed, that you should in your chair;
Louder and longer still they grow,
Tory and Radical, Aye and No;
Talking by night, and talking by day; –
Sleep, Mr SPEAKER; sleep, sleep, while you may!

Sleep, Mr SPEAKER; slumber lies
Light and brief on a SPEAKER's eyes.
FEILDEN or FINN, in a minute or two,
Some disorderly thing will do;
Riot will chase repose away; –
Sleep, Mr SPEAKER; sleep, sleep, while you may!

Sleep, Mr SPEAKER; COBBETT will soon
Move to abolish the Sun and Moon;
HUME, no doubt, will be taking the sense
Of the House on a saving of thirteen pence;
GRATTAN will growl, or BALDWIN bray; –
Sleep, Mr SPEAKER; sleep, sleep, while you may!

Sleep, Mr SPEAKER; dream of the time
When loyalty was not quite a crime,
When GRANT was a pupil in CANNING's school,
And PALMERSTON fancied WOOD a fool.
Lord, how principles pass away; –
Sleep, Mr SPEAKER; sleep, sleep, while you may!

Sleep, Mr SPEAKER; sweet to men
Is the sleep that comes but now and then;
Sweet to the sorrowful, sweet to the ill,
Sweet to the children that work in a mill;
You have more need of repose than they; –
30 Sleep, Mr SPEAKER; sleep, sleep, while you may!

THOMAS LOVELL BEDDOES

1803–49

Thomas Lovell Beddoes was born in Clifton, Bristol, the son of a dis-
tinguished physician. He was educated at Bath Grammar School and
Charterhouse, and, during 1820–23, attended college in Oxford. He
returned to Oxford briefly for exams in 1824 and again in May 1825
to complete his BA, but almost immediately decided on a change of
career and left for Göttingen University, Germany, to study medicine.
He never returned to England as a resident, living instead in Germany
and Switzerland, where he studied and then practised medicine. His
state of mind was volatile, given to and swayed by various passions,
from amorous to political. During the last years of his life he was ex-
pelled from various cities for political activism and spent long
stretches of time on aimless touring and travel. He first attempted
suicide in despair over his efforts to publish a drama that would claim
his attention for the rest of his life, the aptly titled *Death's Jest-Book,
or the Fool's Tragedy*. He tried again in 1848 after the end of his rela-
tionship with a young male actor and succeeded the next year.

A writer of morbid wit and powerful imagination, Beddoes pro-
duced both verse and dramatic works; his first published piece, *The
Comet*, appeared in 1819 in the *Morning Post*. While still in England
he published *The Improvisatore* (1821), *The Brides' Tragedy* (1822) and
The Romance of the Lilly (1823). His unfinished or fragmentary works
include *The Last Man, Torrismond* and *The Ivory Gate*. His most fa-
mous and widely admired work is the *Death's Jest-Book*, published in
1850.

PREFACE

'Mr Beddoes/(T.L.) prince of morticians' – so Pound dubbed him (*Canto LXXX*) – found his ultimate client in 1849. After an unsuccessful attempt at suicide the year before, using a razor to sever an artery in his leg (a mutilation that soon required amputation below the knee), Thomas Lovell Beddoes prevailed with poison, ending his life at the age of forty-five. Brilliant, solitary, eccentric, erratic, homosexual, politically radical, a poet of powerful, haunting imagination, Beddoes, like the other morbidly witty poets in this volume, is most characteristic for his defiance of easy characterization. He has been slotted, variously, as the last Elizabethan, a Jacobean scion, an eighteenth-century graveyard poet resurrected in the Romantic age, an original interpreter of the English–German vogue of 'Gothic' terror, the dark rearguard of second-generation Romanticism, a soul-mate of Baudelaire and Poe, the first modernist and, with his comic grotesqueries, a precursor of the twentieth-century theatre of the absurd. 'Death's Jest Book' is an apt enough genre for a career of scenes and songs devoted to ghoulishly comic effects, macabre turns of events, grotesque conjunctions and original interviews of the porous boundaries between life and death. But 'Beddoes is as good a poet as he is', Christopher Ricks suggests, 'because the romantic, lyrical, and assuaging things in him are as real in the best of his work as the antiromantic, harsh, and feverish things.'[1]

His mother was the sister of prodigious novelist Maria Edgeworth, his father, Dr Thomas Beddoes, a reader in chemistry at the University of Oxford until his liberal political opinions, including support of the French Revolution and opposition to the British government, created a scandal that forced him to resign the post. Beddoes père then became an eminent medical practitioner and scientific writer, a friend to many, including Coleridge and Southey. 'What a good Man, and good physician Dr Beddoes is!' wrote Dorothy Words-worth to her friend Mrs Thomas Clarkson (wife of the famous

abolitionist), who was under his care (1 June 1804); 'I have such a
faith in the eye of Dr Beddoes that I feel assured that you cannot
possibly do as well when he does not daily overlook you . . . I have
been quite well ever since I wrote to you, as if the very name of Dr
Beddoes had acted upon me like a charm' (24 June).[2] But charming
Dr Beddoes died when his son Thomas was quite young.

Thomas eventually entered Pembroke College, Oxford, where he
studied medicine and poetry. He published a volume of verse
and drama as a freshman, *The Improvisatore* (1821), a preliminary
exercise, but with some fine, lush moments. He then astonished
everyone the next year with *The Brides' Tragedy*, the reviews in
leading magazines heralding this self-described 'minor' as a worthy
heir of Shakespeare and Marlowe. In early 1825 Beddoes was fully
energized for this legacy, declaring, with patent self-reference, that

the man who is to awaken the drama must be a bold trampling fellow –
no creeper into worm-holes – no reviser even – however good. These
reanimations are vampire-cold – such ghosts as Marlowe – Webster &[c] are
better dramatists, better poets, I dare say, than any contemporary of ours
– but they are ghosts – the worm is in their pages – & we want to
see something that our great-grandsires did not know. With the greatest
reverence for all the antiquities of the drama, I still think that we had better
beget than revive – attempt to give the literature of this age an idiosyncrasy
& spirit of its own, & only raise a ghost to gaze on, not to live with – just
now the drama is a haunted ruin.[3]

Beddoes began four new plays almost immediately in the wake of
The Brides' Tragedy, but finished none; this play would be the last
lifetime volume. Almost as suddenly as he astonished the world
with the *Tragedy*, he left Oxford, left England, and matriculated as
a medical student in Göttingen, Germany.

By 1827 he declared his 'preference of Apollo's pill box to his
lyre', choosing 'Göttingen instead of Grub Street for [his] abode'.[4]
Even so, he could not let go of a play begun in 1825, his 'never-ending'
Death's Jest-Book, writing for and wrestling with it for the rest of
his life. If Wordsworth's *Prelude* is the preparatory poem that became
synonymous with his life and then his chief posthumous publication,
Beddoes's jest of death became the work of his life and then the
birth of his reputation with its posthumous publication in 1850, the

same year as *The Prelude*. Beddoes's allegiance to Apollo's pill box, moreover, was inconstant. He moved around Germany and Switzerland, enrolling in various universities, attending lectures on literature and history, reading German poetry and Elizabethan drama, getting involved in Republican politics and in trouble for revolutionary agitation, all the while enjoying the company of actors, journalists, politicians, and doctors.

'At the feast of the Muses,' wrote Edmund Gosse in the introduction to his edition of 1890, Beddoes 'appears bearing little except one small savoury dish, some cold preparation, we may say, of olives and anchovies, the strangeness of which has to make up for its lack of importance' (*Poetical Works*, I.xxxvi). Beddoes's suicide note, left folded on his bosom after he had ingested poison, is his final dish of epicurean, self-parodic poignancy: 'I am food for *what I am good* for – worms . . . Love . . . to Kelsall whom I beg to look at my MSS – and print or not as *he* thinks fit. I ought to have been among other things a good poet; Life was too great a bore on one peg & that a bad one. – Buy for Dr Ecklin above mentioned Reade's best stomach pump.' In addition to the final sarcasm, he could not resist the witty rhyme of 'I am food for/I am good for', nor what Ricks calls the 'retrospective contraction of "*f*or what I am g*ood*" into *food*',[5] nor a last rueful chime of 'beg' and 'peg'. Among other things, he was, to the end, a poet.

The textual situation of Beddoes's work is at once straightforward and for the most part heavily mediated. He did publish *The Improvisatore* but then went about suppressing it, destroying every copy he could find. He also published *The Brides' Tragedy*. Otherwise, except for a few pieces for which friends secured publication in his lifetime, almost everything he wrote after the mid 1820s appeared posthumously. Thomas Kelsall, Beddoes's lifelong friend and literary executor, assembled a text of *Death's Jest-Book* which appeared anonymously in 1850; for his complete edition of Beddoes (now named) the next year, he edited the poems and devised titles as he saw fit. His store of manuscripts was bequeathed to Robert Browning, who did nothing with them; at his death these materials devolved to his son Robert Barrett Browning, and then many of them were lost. Fortunately, meticulous transcriptions had been made by Dykes Campbell, and eventually received by Edmund Gosse, along with a box of correspondence from Robert Browning. From this store Gosse developed his important editions of the poems (1890 and 1928), with more fidelity to the manuscripts than Kelsall, and also produced editions of the letters. In 1935 H. W. Donner re-edited Beddoes's poems and letters from the best manuscript sources available.

We complement Donner's labour by presenting the versions that shaped the *fin de siècle* revival of interest in Beddoes a century ago, its readers on the verge of the modernist consciousness that would bring a fresh appreciation to Beddoes's strange and compelling sensibility. We use Gosse's landmark 1890 edition, with only a few exceptions: *The Brides' Tragedy*, for which we use the first edition of 1822 (adding only line numbers); the poem on P. B. Shelley that Kelsall placed in *The Athenaeum* in 1833; and a poem that appears only in Kelsall's memoir of 1851, not reprinted by Gosse ('Lines written in the album . . .'). Our selection spans Beddoes's career from his undergraduate poetry to his last revisions of *Death's Jest-Book*. Our order is generally chronological, except in a few cases where we honour the groups in the volumes that Beddoes planned (but did not publish): *Outidana*, *Death's Jest-Book* and *The Ivory Gate*. Within these groupings we observe chronology of composition when it can be determined.

Like previous editors, we present some manuscript 'fragments' as independent compositions; 'There is something fragmentary in the very mind and genius of Beddoes,' Donner remarks in his Introduction to the *Complete Works* (p. xxiii). This genius by fragments is perhaps what left Ian Jack closing a very qualified appraisal of Beddoes in *English Literature 1815–1832* with the remark that Beddoes was 'a man of genius who wrote nothing that is commonly remembered'.[6] We mean to improve and inspire memory with a selection that varies from previous ones in two chief ways. We present the songs for which Beddoes is most admired, not independently but in the dramatic contexts for which he intended them and by which they are (sometimes subversively, satirically) inflected. We also excerpt passages from the plays capable of standing independently, which we offer for their compelling conception, power of imagination and verbal artistry. In so doing, we recognize what the reviewer for *Blackwood's* expressed in 1856, with *Death's Jest-Book* in hand: 'In this mad and plotless play there are finer passages than any living dramatist has composed . . . grandeur, tenderness, and a power of description totally unequalled by the second-hand Elizabethans,' and 'it is in the short, brilliant, almost epigrammatic phrases with which the play is studded, that we find this writer's strength'.[7] 'Beddoes' genius was essentially lyrical', Arthur Symons put it more succinctly.[8] 'Now, as to the extracts which might be made,' Browning suggested to Kelsall, 'why, you might pick out scenes, passages, lyrics, fine as fine can be: the power of the man is immense & irresistible."[9]

Our notes give the dates of composition (when known) and the history of publication in the nineteenth century, as Beddoes's reputation emerged and was consolidated. We also include Beddoes's reflections (from his lively letters to his most sympathetic reader, Kelsall) on his work – both its local moments and its theoretical grounds – and we supply a sample of critical response, both from Beddoes's century and our own.

Notes

1. Christopher Ricks, 'Thomas Lovell Beddoes: "A dying start"', p. 146.
2. *The Letters of William and Dorothy Wordsworth: The Early Years, 1787–1805*, ed. Ernest de Selincourt (2nd edn revised by Chester L. Shaver, Oxford: Clarendon Press, 1967); pp. 479 and 485.
3. Letter to Thomas Forbes Kelsall, 11 January 1825, quoted from H. W. Donner, *Complete Works*, p. 595; first published in Kelsall's Memoir, *Poems* (1851), I.xxxviii.
4. Letter to Kelsall, October 1827; quoted from Donner, *Complete Works*, p. 636; first published in Memoir, *Poems*, I.lxxvii.
5. Ricks, p. 151; the note is quoted from Donner, *Complete Works*, p. 683.
6. Ian Jack, *English Literature 1815–1832* (Oxford: Oxford University Press, 1963), p. 144.
7. 'Mr Buttle's Review', *Blackwood's Edinburgh Magazine* 80 (October 1856), p. 448.
8. Arthur Symons, *Figures of Several Centuries*, p. 124.
9. Browning's remark is from a letter to Kelsall, 22 May 1868: Donner, *The Browning Box*, p. 105.

Alfarabi;

The World-Maker

A Rhapsodical Fragment

'Twas in those days
That never were, nor ever shall be, reader,
But on this paper; golden, glorious days,
Such as the sun, (poor fellow! by the way,
Where is he? I've not seen him all this winter,) –
Never could spin: days, as I said before,
Which shall be made as fine as ink can make them;
So, clouds, avaunt! and Boreas, hence! to blow
Old Ætna's porridge. We will make the sun
10   Rise, like a gentleman, at noon; clasped round
With the bright armour of his May-day beams;
The summer-garland on his beaming curls,
With buds of palest brightness; and one cloud –
Yes, (I'm an Englishman,) one snow-winged cloud,
To wander slowly down the trembling blue;
A wind that stops and pants along the grass,
Trembles and flies again, like thing pursued;
And indescribable, delightful sounds,
Which dart along the sky, we know not whence;
20   Bees we must have to hum, shrill-noted swallows
With their small, lightning wings, to fly about,
And tilt against the waters: – that will do.
And now, dear climate, only think what days
I'd make if you'd employ me: you should have
A necklace, every year, of such as this;
Each bead of the three hundred sixty five –
(Excuse me, puss, (&) I couldn't get you in,)
Made up of sunshine, moonshine, and blue skies:
Starlight I'd give you in: – but where are we?
30   I see: 'twas in those days that Alfarabi lived;
A man renowned in the newspapers:
He wrote in two reviews; raw pork at night
He ate, and opium; kept a bear at college:

A most extraordinary man was he.
But he was one not satisfied with man,
As man has made himself: he thought this life
Was something deeper than a jest, and sought
Into its roots: himself was his best science.
He touched the springs, the unheeded hieroglyphics
40   Deciphered; like an antiquary sage
Within an house of office, which he takes
For druid temple old, here he picked up
A tattered thought, and turned it o'er and o'er
'Till it was spelled; the names of all the tenants,
Pencilled upon the wall, he would unite;
Until he found the secret and the spell
Of life. 'Twas not by Logic, reader;
Her and her crabbed sister, Metaphysics,
Left he to wash Thought's shirt, the shirt bemired
50   On that proverbial morning. By his own mind,
The lamp that never fails us, dared we trust it,
He read the mystery; and it was one
To the dull sense of common man unknown,
Incomprehensible; a miracle
Of magic, yet as true and obvious,
For thoughtful ones to hit on, as the sun.
He knew the soul would free itself in sleep
From her dull sister, bear itself away,
Freer than air: to guide it with his will,
60   To bear his mortal sight and memory,
On these excursions, was the power he found.
He found it, and he used it. For, one night,
By the internal vision he saw Sleep,
Just after dinner, tapping at the door
Of his next neighbour, the old alderman.
Sleep rode a donkey with a pair of wings,
And, having fastened its ethereal bridle
Unto the rails, walked in. Now, Alfarabi!
Leap, Alfarabi! There! the saddle's won:
70   He kicks, he thwacks, he spurs, – the donkey flies.
On soared they, like the bright thought of an eye,
'Mid the infinity of elements.

First through the azure meads of night and day,
Among the rushing of the million flames,
They passed the bearded dragon-star, unchained
From Hell, (of old its sun,) yelling her way
Upon those wings, compact of mighty clouds
Bloodshot and black, or flaring devilish light,
Whose echo racks the shrieking universe,
80   Whose glimpse is tempest. O'er each silent star
Slept like a tomb that dark, marmoreal bird,
That spell-bound ocean, Night, – her breast o'erwrit
With golden secresies. All these he passed,
One after one: as he, who stalks by night,
With the ghost's step, the shaggy murderer
Leaves passed the dreamy city's sickly lamps.
Then through the horrid twilight did they plunge,
The universe's suburbs; dwelling dim
Of all that sin and suffer; midnight shrieks
90   Upon the water, when no help is near;
The blood-choked curse of him who dies in bed
By torch-light, with a dagger in his heart;
The parricidal and incestuous laugh;
And the last cries of those whom devils hale
Quick into hell; deepened the darkness.
And there were sounds of wings, broken and swift;
Blows of wrenched poniards, muffled in thick flesh;
Struggles and tramplings wild, splashes and falls,
And inarticulate yells from human breasts.
100 Nought was beheld: but Alfarabi's heart
Turned in his bosom, like a scorched leaf,
And his soul faded. When again he saw,
His steed had paused. It was within a space
Upon the very boundary and brim
Of the whole universe, the outer edge
Which seemed almost to end the infinite zone;
A chasm in the almighty thoughts, forgotten
By the omnipotent; a place apart,
Like some great, ruinous dream of broken worlds
110 Tumbling through heaven, or Tartarus' panting jaws
Open above the sun. Sky was there none,

Nor earth, nor water: but confusion strange;
Mountainous ribs and adamantine limbs
Of bursten worlds, and brazen pinions vast
Of planets ship-wrecked; many a wrinkled sun
Ate to the core by worms, with lightnings crushed;
And drossy bolts, melting like noonday snow.
Old towers of heaven were there, and fragments bright
Of the cerulean battlements, o'erthrown
120   When the gods struggled for the throne of light;
And 'mid them all a living mystery,
A shapeless image, or a vision wrapt
In clouds, and guessed at by its fearful shade;
Most like a ghost of the eternal flame,
An indistinct and unembodied horror
Which prophecies have told of; not wan Death,
Nor War the bacchanal of blood, nor Plague
The purple beast, but their great serpent-sire,
Destruction's patriarch, (dread name to speak!)
130   The End of all, the Universe's Death.
At that dread, ghostly thing, the atmosphere
And light of this, the world's, black charnel house,
Low bowed the Archimage, and thrice his life
Upraised its wing for passage; but the spell
Prevailed, and to his purposed task he rose.
He called unto the dead, and the swart powers,
That wander unconfined beyond the sight
Or thought of mortals; and, from the abyss
Of cavernous deep night, came forth the hands,
140   That dealt the mallet when this world of ours
Lay quivering on the anvil in its ore, –
Hands of eternal stone, which would unmesh
And fray this starry company of orbs,
As a young infant, on a dewy morn,
Rends into nought the tear-hung gossamer.
– To work they went, magician, hands, and Co,
With tongs and trowels, needles, scissors, paste,
Solder and glue, to make another world:
And, as a tinker, 'neath a highway hedge,
150   Turns, taps, and batters, rattles, bangs, and scrapes

A stew-pan ruinous, – or as, again,
The sibylline dame Gurton, ere she lost
Th' immortal bodkin, staunched the gaping wound
In Hodge's small-clothes famed, – so those great hands
Whisked round their monstrous loom, here stitching in
An island of green vallies, fitting there
A mountain extra with a hook and eye,
Caulking the sea, hemming the continents,
And lacing all behind to keep it tight.
160   'Tis done, – 'tis finished; and between the thumb
Depends, and the forefinger, – like a toy,
Button with pin impaled, in winter games
That dances on the board, – and now it flies
Into the abyssal blueness, spinning and bright,
Just at old Saturn's tail. The necromancer
Puffed from his pipe a British climate round,
And stars and moon, and angels beamed upon it.
Just as it joined the midnight choir of worlds,
It chanced a bearded sage espied its sweep,
170   And named it GEORGIUM SIDUS. Centuries
Danc'd o'er it, but . . . . .

*   *   *

from *THE IMPROVISATORE*, *in three Fyttes, with Other Poems*

To Night

So thou art come again, old black-winged Night,
    Like an huge bird, between us and the sun,
Hiding, with out-stretched form, the genial light;
    And still, beneath thine icy bosom's dun
And cloudy plumage, hatching fog-breathed blight,
    And embryo storms, and crabbèd frosts, that shun
Day's warm caress. The owls from ivied loop
    Are shrieking homage, as thou cowerest high,
Like sable crow pausing in eager stoop
10   On the dim world thou glutt'st thy clouded eye,
Silently waiting latest time's fell whoop,
        When thou shalt quit thine eyrie in the sky,
            To pounce upon the world with eager claw,
            And tomb time, death, and substance in thy maw.

To a Bunch of Grapes

Ripening in my Window

Cluster of pregnant berries, pressed
        In luscious warmth together,
Like golden eggs in glassy nest,
Hatched by the zephyr's dewy breast
        In sultry weather;
Or amber tears of those sad girls
        Who mourn their hapless brother;
Strung closely on the glossy curls
Of yon fair shrub, whose zigzag twirls
10   Clip one another;

Or silent swarm of golden bees
    Your velvet bosoms brushing,
Dropped odorous from the gummy breeze,
Lingering in sleep upon the trees,
    Whilst summer's blushing;
Or liquid sunbeams, swathed in net
    Spun by some vagrant fairy,
Like mimic lamps fresh trimmed and set
In thick festoons, with ripeness wet,
    Moonlight to carry;
Or drops of honey, lately stolen
    From the hive's treasury,
Bubbles of light, with sweetness swollen,
Balls of bright juice, by breezes rollen,
    And bandied high.
I watch with wondrous care each day
    Your little spotted blushes,
Dyed by the sun's rude staring ray;
And soon I hope you'll ooze away
    In sunny gushes.
Then shall ye, veiled in misty fume,
    In polished urn be flowing;
With blood of nectar, soul perfume,
Breathe on our cheeks a downy bloom
    With pleasure glowing.

*   *   *

THE BRIDES' TRAGEDY

FROM ACT I, SCENE I

Floribel 'Twas on a fragrant bank I laid me down,
Laced o'er and o'er with verdant tendrils, full
Of dark-red strawberries. Anon there came
On the wind's breast a thousand tiny noises,
Like flowers' voices, if they could but speak;
100   Then slowly did they blend in one sweet strain,
Melodiously divine; and buoyed the soul
Upon their undulations. Suddenly,
Methought, a cloud swam swanlike o'er the sky,
And gently kissed the earth, a fleecy nest,
With roses, rifled from the cheek of Morn,
Sportively strewn; upon the ethereal couch,
Her fair limbs blending with the enamoured mist,
Lovely above the portraiture of words,
In beauteous languor lay the Queen of Smiles:
110   In tangled garlands, like a golden haze,
Or fay-spun threads of light, her locks were floating,
And in their airy folds slumbered her eyes,
Dark as the nectar-grape that gems the vines
In the bright orchard of the Hesperides.
Within the ivory cradle of her breast
Gambolled the urchin god, with saucy hand
Dimpling her cheeks, or sipping eagerly
The rich ambrosia of her melting lips:
Beneath them swarmed a bustling mob of Loves,
120   Tending the sparrow stud, or with bees' wings
Imping their arrows. Here stood one alone
Blowing a pyre of blazing lovers' hearts
With bellows full of absence-caused sighs:
Near him his work-mate mended broken vows
With dangerous gold, or strung soft rhymes together
Upon a lady's tress. Some swelled their cheeks,
Like curling rose-leaves, or the red wine's bubbles,

In petulant debate, gallantly tilting
Astride their darts. And one there was alone,
130   Who with wet downcast eyelids threw aside
The remnants of a broken heart, and looked
Into my face and bid me 'ware of love,
Of fickleness, and woe, and mad despair.
    Hesperus Aye, so he said; and did my own dear girl
Deem me a false one for this foolish dream?
I wish I could be angry, hide, distrustful,
Those penitent blushes in my breast, while I
Sing you a silly song old nurses use
To hush their crying babes with. Tenderly
140   'Twill chide you.

    Song

    Poor old pilgrim Misery,
      Beneath the silent moon he sate,
    A-listening to the screech owl's cry,
      And the cold wind's goblin prate;
    Beside him lay his staff of yew
      With withered willow twined,
    His scant grey hair all wet with dew
      His cheeks with grief ybrined;
        And his cry it was ever, alack!
150   Alack, and woe is me.

    Anon a wanton imp astray
      His piteous moaning hears,
    And from his bosom steals away
      His rosary of tears:
    With his plunder fled that urchin elf,
      And hid it in your eyes,
    Then tell me back the stolen pelf,
      Give up the lawless prize;
        Or your cry shall be ever, alack!
160   Alack, and woe is me.

FROM ACT II, SCENE I

Boy (awaking) Dear master, didst thou call? I will not be
A second time so slothful.
    Orlando   Sleep, my boy,
Thy task is light and joyous, to be good.
    Boy Oh! if I must be good, then give me money,
I pray thee, give me some, and you shall find
I'll buy up every tear, and make them scarcer
Than diamonds.
20   *Orlando* Beautiful pity, thou shalt have enough;
But you must give me your last song.
    Boy   Nay, sir;
You're wont to say my rhymes are fit for girls,
And lovesick ideots; I have none you praise
Full of the heat of battle and the chase.
    Orlando Sing what you will, I'll like it.

Song

    A ho! A ho!
      Love's horn doth blow,
       And he will out a-hawking go.
    His shafts are light as beauty's sighs,
30   And bright as midnight's brightest eyes,
       And round his starry way
    The swan-winged horses of the skies,
    With summer's music in their manes,
    Curve their fair necks to zephyr's reins,
       And urge their graceful play.

    A ho! A ho!
      Love's horn doth blow,
       And he will out a-hawking go.
    The sparrows flutter round his wrist,
40   The feathery thieves that Venus kissed

And taught their morning song,
The linnets seek the airy list,
And swallows too, small pets of Spring,
Beat back the gale with swifter wing,
And dart and wheel along.

A ho! A ho!
Love's horn doth blow,
And he will out a-hawking go,
Now woe to every gnat that skips
50 To filch the fruit of ladies' lips,
His felon blood is shed;
And woe to flies whose airy ships
On beauty cast their anchoring bite,
And bandit wasp, that naughty wight,
Whose sting is slaughter-red.

Orlando Who is thy poet, boy?
Boy   I must not tell.
Orlando Then I will chide thee for him. Who first drew
Love as a blindfold imp, an earthen dwarf,
And armed him with blunt darts? His soul was kin
60 To the rough wind that dwells in the icy north,
The dead cold pedant, who thus dared confine
The universe's soul, for that is Love.
'Tis he that acts the nightingale, the thrush,
And all the living musics, he it is
That gives the lute, the harp and tabor speech,
That flutters on melodious wings and strikes
The mute and viewless lyres of sunny strings
Borne by the minstrel gales, mimicking vainly
The timid voice, that sent him to my breast,
70 That voice the wind hath treasured and doth use
When he bids roses open and be sweet.

FROM ACT III, SCENE II

FLORIBEL *alone*

And must I wake again? Oh come to me,
Thou that with dew-cold fingers softly closest
The wearied eye; thou sweet, thou gentle power,
Soother of woe, sole friend of the oppressed,
I long to lay me on thy peaceful breast.
But once I saw thee, beautiful as moonlight,
Upon a baby's lips, and thou didst kiss them,
Lingering and oft,
(As a wild bee doth kiss a rifled flower,
And clips its waist, and drops a little tear,
Remorsefully enamoured of his prey;)
Come so to me, sweet death, and I will wreath thee
An amorous chaplet for thy paly brows;
And on an odoured bank of wan white buds
In thy fair arms
I'll lie, and taste thy cool delicious breath,
And sleep, and sleep, and sleep.

*   *   *

from *THE ATHENAEUM*

LINES

Written by the Author of 'The Bride's [sic] *Tragedy', in the blank-leaf of the 'Prometheus Unbound'*

WRITE it in gold – a Spirit of the sun,
And Intellect ablaze with heavenly thoughts,
A Soul with all the dews of pathos shining,
Odorous with love, and sweet to silent woe
With the dark glories of concentrate song,
Was sphered in mortal earth. Angelic sounds,
Alive with panting thoughts, sunned the dim world:
The bright creations of a human heart
Wrought magic in the bosoms of mankind:
10   A flooding summer burst on Poetry,
Of which the crowning sun, the night of beauty,
The dancing showers, the birds, whose anthems wild,
Note after note, unbind the enchanted leaves
Of breaking buds, eve, and flow of dawn,
Were centred and condensed in his one name
As in a providence – and that was SHELLEY.

Oxford, 1822

*   *   *

fragments from *THE LAST MAN*

A Crocodile

Hard by the lilied Nile I saw
A duskish river-dragon stretched along,
The brown habergeon of his limbs enamelled
With sanguine almandines and rainy pearl:
And on his back there lay a young one sleeping,
No bigger than a mouse; with eyes like beads,
And a small fragment of its speckled egg
Remaining on its harmless, pulpy snout;
A thing to laugh at, as it gaped to catch
10   The baulking, merry flies. In the iron jaws
Of the great devil-beast, like a pale soul
Fluttering in rocky hell, lightsomely flew
A snowy troculus, with roseate beak
Tearing the hairy leeches from his throat.

Sweet to Die (*Death Sweet*)

Is it not sweet to die? for, what is death,
But sighing that we ne'er may sigh again,
Getting a length beyond our tedious selves;
But trampling the last tear from poisonous sorrow,
Spilling our woes, crushing our frozen hopes,
And passing like an incense out of man?
Then, if the body felt, what were its sense,
Turning to daisies gently in the grave,
If not the soul's most delicate delight
10   When it does filtrate, through the pores of thought
In love and the enamelled flowers of song?

Midnight Hymn

And many voices marshalled in one hymn
Wound through the night, whose still translucent moments
Lay on each side their breath; and the hymn passed
Its long, harmonious populace of words
Between the silvery silences, as when
The slaves of Egypt, like a wind between
The head and trunk of a dismembered king
On a strewn plank, with blood and footsteps sealed,
Vallied the unaccustomed sea.

A Lake

                              A lake
Is a river curled and asleep like a snake.

Dream of Dying

Shivering in fever, weak, and parched to sand,
My ears, those entrances of word-dressed thoughts,
My pictured eyes, and my assuring touch,
Fell from me, and my body turned me forth
From its beloved abode: then I was dead;
And in my grave beside my corpse I sat,
In vain attempting to return: meantime
There came the untimely spectres of two babes,
And played in my abandoned body's ruins;
They went away; and, one by one, by snakes
My limbs were swallowed; and, at last, I sat
With only one, blue-eyed, curled round my ribs,

Eating the last remainder of my heart,
And hissing to himself. O sleep, thou fiend!
Thou blackness of the night! how sad and frightful
Are these thy dreams!

*   *   *

from *OUTIDANA*, *or effusions, amorous, pathetic and fantastical*

Lines

Written at Geneva; July, 1824

The hour is starry, and the airs that stray,
Sad wanderers from their golden home of day,
On night's black mountain, melt and fade away
In sorrow that is music. Some there be
Make them blue pillows on Geneva's sea,
And sleep upon their best-loved planet's shade:
And every herb is sleeping in the glade; –
They have drunk sunshine and the linnet's song,
Till every leaf's soft sleep is dark and strong.
10   Or was there ever sound, or can what was
Now be so dead? Although no flowers or grass
Grow from the corpse of a deceased sound,
Somewhat, methinks, should mark the air around
Its dying place and tomb,
A gentle music, or a pale perfume:
For hath it not a body and a spirit,
A noise and meaning? and, when one doth hear it
Twice born, twice dying, doubly found and lost,
That second self, that echo, is its ghost.
20   But even the dead are all asleep this time,
And not a grave shakes with the dreams of crime: –
The earth is full of chambers for the dead,
And every soul is quiet in his bed;
Some who have seen their bodies moulder away,
Antediluvian minds, – most happy they,
Who have no body but the beauteous air,
No body but their minds. Some wretches are
Now lying with the last and only bone
Of their old selves, and that one worm alone

30   That ate their heart: some, buried just, behold
Their weary flesh, like an used mansion, sold
Unto a stranger, and see enter it
The earthquake winds and waters of the pit,
Or children's spirits in its holes to play.

A Dirge (To-day is a thought)

To-day is a thought, a fear is to-morrow,
And yesterday is our sin and our sorrow;
    And life is a death,
        Where the body's the tomb,
    And the pale sweet breath
        Is buried alive in its hideous gloom.
    Then waste no tear,
        For we are the dead; the living are here,
    In the stealing earth, and the heavy bier.
10   Death lives but an instant, and is but a sigh,
And his son is unnamed immortality,
Whose being is thine. Dear ghost, so to die
Is to live, – and life is a worthless lie. –
Then we weep for ourselves, and wish thee goodbye.

Sonnet:

To Tartar, a Terrier Beauty

Snow-drop of dogs, with ear of brownest dye,
Like the last orphan leaf of naked tree
Which shudders in bleak autumn; though by thee,
Of hearing careless and untutored eyes,
Not understood articulate speech of men,
Nor marked the artificial mind of books,
– The mortal's voice eternized by the pen, –
Yet hast thou thought and language all unknown

To Babel's scholars; oft intensest looks,
10   Long scrutiny o'er some dark-veined stone
Dost thou bestow, learning dead mysteries
Of the world's birth-day, oft in eager tone
With quick-tailed fellows bandiest prompt replies,
Solicitudes canine, four-footed amities.

Pygmalion,

or The Cyprian Statuary

There stood a city along Cyprus' side
Lavish of palaces, an arched tide
Of unrolled rocks; and, where the deities dwelled,
Their clustered domes pushed up the noon, and swelled
With the emotion of the god within, –
As doth earth's hemisphere, when showers begin
To tickle the still spirit at its core,
Till pastures tremble and the river-shore
Squeezes out buds at every dewy pore.
10   And there were pillars, from some mountain's heart,
Thronging beneath a wide, imperial floor
That bent with riches; and there stood apart
A palace, oft accompanied by trees,
That laid their shadows in the galleries
Under the coming of the endless light,
Net-like; – who trod the marble, night or day,
By moon, or lamp, or sunless day-shine white,
Would brush the shaking, ghostly leaves away,
Which might be tendrils or a knot of wine,
20   Burst from the depth of a faint window-vine,
With a bird pecking it: and round the hall
And wandering staircase, within every wall
Of sea-ward portico, and sleeping chamber,
Whose patient lamp distilled a day of amber,
There stood, and sate, or made rough steeds their throne,
Immortal generations wrung from stone,

Alike too beautiful for life and death,
And bodies that a soul of mortal breath
Would be the dross of.
               Such a house as this
30   Within a garden hard by Salamis,
(Cyprus's city-crown and capital
Ere Paphos was, and at whose ocean-wall
Beauty and love's paternal waves do beat
That sprouted Venus;) such a fair retreat
Lonely Pygmalion's self inhabited,
Whose fiery chisel with creation fed
The ship-wrecked rocks; who paid the heavens again
Diamonds for ice; who made gods who make men.
Lonely Pygmalion: you might see him go
40   Along the streets where markets thickest flow,
Doubling his gown across his thinking breast,
And the men fall aside; nor only pressed
Out of his elbows' way, but left a place,
A sun-room for him, that his mind had space
And none went near; none in his sweep would venture,
For you might feel that he was but the centre
Of an inspired round, the middle spark
Of a great moon, setting aside the dark
And cloudy people. As he went along
50   The chambered ladies silenced the half-song,
And let the wheel unheeded whirl and skim,
To get their eyes blest by the sight of him.
So locks were swept from every eye that drew
Sun for the soul through circles violet-blue,
Mild brown, or passionate black.
                    Still, discontent,
Over his sensual kind the sculptor went,
Walking his thoughts. Yet Cyprus' girls be fair;
Day-bright and evening-soft the maidens are,
And witching like the midnight, and their pleasure
60   Silent and deep as midnight's starry treasure.
Lovely and young, Pygmalion yet loved none.
His soul was bright and lovely as the sun,

Like which he could create; and in its might
There lived another Spirit wild and bright,
That came and went; and, when it came, its light
On these dim earthy things, turn where he will,
Its light, shape, beauty were reflected still.
Day-time and dark it came; like a dim mist
Shelt'ring a god, it rolled, and, ere he wist,
70   It fell aside, and dawned a shape of grace,
And an inspired and melancholy face,
Whose lips were smile-buds dewy: – into him
It rolled like sun-light till his sight was dim,
And it was in his heart and soul again,
Not seen but breathed.
     There was a grassy plain,
A pasture of the deer, – Olympus' mountain
Was the plain's night, the picture of its fountain:
Unto which unfrequented dell and wood
Unwittingly his solitary mood
80   Oft drew him. – In the water lay
A fragment of pale marble, which they say
Slipped from some fissure in the agued moon,
Which had caught earth-quake and a deadly swoon
When the sun touched her with his hilly shade.
Weeds grew upon it, and the streamlet made
A wanton music with its ragged side,
And birds had nests there. One still even-tide,
When they were perched and sleeping, passed this man,
Startling the air with thoughts which over-ran
90   The compass of his mind: writing the sand
Idly he paused, and laid unwitting hand
On the cold stone. How smooth the touch! It felt
Less porous than a lip which kisses melt,
And diamond-hard. That night his workmen wrought
With iron under it, and it was brought,
This dripping quarry, while the sky was starry,
Home to the weary, yearning statuary.
He saw no sky that day, no dark that night,
For through the hours his lamp was full of light,
100   Shadowing the pavement with his busy right.

Day after day they saw not in the street
The wondrous artist: some immortal feat
Absorbed him; and yet often in the noon,
When the town slept beneath the sweltering June,
– The rich within, the poor man on the stair, –
He stole unseen into the meadow's air,
And fed on sight of summer, till the life
Was too abundant in him; and so, rife
With light creative, he went in alone,
110   And poured it warm upon the growing stone.
The magic chisel thrust, and gashed, and swept,
Flying and manifold; no cloud e'er wept
So fast, so thick, so light upon the close
Of shapeless green it meant to make a rose: –
And as insensibly out of a stick,
Dead in the winter-time, the dew-drops quick,
And the thin sun-beams, and the airy shower
Raise and unwrap a many-leaved flower,
And then a fruit: so from the barren stock
120   Of the deer-shading, formless valley-rock,
This close stone-bud, he, quiet as the air,
Had shaped a lady wonderfully fair,
– Dear to the eyes, a delicate delight, –
For all her marble symmetry was white
As brow and bosom should be, save some azure
Which waited for a loving lip's erasure,
Upon her shoulder, to be turned to blush.
And she was smooth and full, as if one gush
Of life had washed her, or as if a sleep
130   Lay on her eye-lid, easier to sweep
Than bee from daisy. Who could help a sigh
At seeing a beauty stand so lifelessly,
But that it was too beautiful to die?
Dealer of immortality,
Greater than Jove himself, – for only he
Can such eternize as the grave has ta'en,
And open heaven by the gate of pain, –
What art thou now, divine Pygmalion?
Divine! gods counting human. Thou hast done

140 That glory, which has undone thee for ever.
For thou art weak, and tearful, and dost shiver
Wintrily sad; and thy life's healthy river,
With which thy body once was overflown,
Is dried and sunken to its banks of bone.
He carved it not; nor was the chisel's play,
That dashed the earthen hindrances away,
Driven and diverted by his muscle's sway.
The winged tool, as digging out a spell,
Followed a magnet wheresoe'er it fell,
150 That sucked and led it right: and for the rest,
The living form, with which the stone he blest,
Was the loved image stepping from his breast.
And therefore loves he it, and therefore stays
About the she-rock's feet, from hour to hour,
Anchored to her by his own heart: the power
Of the isle's Venus therefore thus he prays.
'Goddess, that made me, save thy son, and save
The man, that made thee goddess, from the grave.
Thou know'st it not; it is a fearful coop, –
160 Dark, cold, and horrible, – a blinded loop
In Pluto's madhouse'[s] green and wormy wall.
O save me from't! Let me not die, like all;
For I am but like one: not yet, not yet,
At least not yet; and why? My eyes are wet
With the thick dregs of immature despair;
With bitter blood out of my empty heart.
I breathe not aught but my own sighs for air,
And my life's strongest is a dying start.
No sour grief there is to me unwed;
170 I could not be more lifeless being dead.
Then let me die. . Ha! did she pity me?
Oh! she can never love. Did you not see,
How still she bears the music of my moan!
Her heart? Ah! touch it. Fool! I love the stone.
Inspire her, gods! oft ye have wasted life
On the deformed, the hideous, and the vile:
Oh! grant it my sweet rock, – my only wife.
I do not ask it long: a little while, –

A year, – a day, – an hour, – let it be!
180   For that I'll give you my eternity.
Or let it be a fiend, if ye will send
Something, yon form to humanize and bend,
Within those limbs, – and, when the new-poured blood
Flows in such veins, the worst must turn to good.
They will not hear. Thou, Jove, – or thou, Apollo –
Ay, thou! thou know'st, – O listen to my groan.
'Twas Niobe thou drov'st from flesh to stone:
Shew this the hole she broke, and let her follow
That mother's track of steps and eyelid rain,
190   Treading them backwards into life again.
Life, said I? Lives she not? Is there not gone
My life into her, which I pasture on;
Dead, where she is not? Live, thou statue fair,
Live, thou dear marble, – or I shall go wild.
I cover thee, my sweet; I leave thee there,
Behind this curtain, my delicious child,
That they may secretly begin to give
My prayer to thee: when I return, O live!
Oh! live, – or I live not.' And so he went,
200   Leaving the statue in its darksome tent.
       Morn after morn, sadder the artist came;
His prayer, his disappointment were the same.
But when he gazed she was more near to woman;
There was a fleshy pink, a dimple wrought
That trembled, and the cheek was growing human
With the flushed distance of a rising thought,
That still crept nearer: – yet no further sign!
And now, Pygmalion, that weak life of thine
Shakes like a dew-drop in a broken rose,
210   Or incense parting from the altar-glows.
'Tis the last look, – and he is mad no more:
By rule and figure he could prove at large
She never can be born, – and from the shore
His foot is stretching into Charon's barge.

Upon the pavement ghastly is he lying,
Cold with the last and stoniest embrace:
Elysium's light illumines all his face;
His eyes have a wild, starry grace
Of heaven, into whose depth of depths he's dying.
220   – A sound, with which the air doth shake,
Extinguishing the window of moonlight!
A pang of music dropping round delight,
As if sweet music's honiest heart did break!
Such a flash, and such a sound, the world
Is stung by, as if something was unfurled
That held great bliss within its inmost curled.
Roof after roof, the palace rends asunder;
And then – O sight of joy and placid wonder!
He lies, beside a fountain, on the knee
230   Of the sweet woman-statue, quietly
Weeping the tears of his felicity.

*   *   *

fragment from *LOVE'S ARROW POISONED*

Humble Beginnings

Why, Rome was naked once, a bastard smudge,
Tumbled on straw, the denfellow of whelps,
Fattened on roots, and, when a-thirst for milk,
He crept beneath and drank the swagging udder
Of Tyber's brave she-wolf; and Heaven's Judea
Was folded in a pannier.

*   *   *

from *TORRISMOND*

FROM ACT I, SCENE III

Veronica Come then, a song; a winding, gentle song,
To lead me into sleep. Let it be low
As zephyr, telling secrets to his rose,
For I would hear the murmuring of my thoughts;
And more of voice than of that other music
That grows around the strings of quivering lutes;
But most of thought; for with my mind I listen,
And when the leaves of sound are shed upon it,
If there's no seed remembrance grows not there.
10   So life, so death; a song, and then a dream!
Begin before another dewdrop fall
From the soft hold of these disturbed flowers,
For sleep is filling up my senses fast,
And from these words I sink.

Song

How many times do I love thee, dear?
    Tell me how many thoughts there be
        In the atmosphere
        Of a new-fall'n year,
Whose white and sable hours appear
20   The latest flake of Eternity: –
So many times do I love thee, dear.

How many times do I love again?
    Tell me how many beads there are
        In a silver chain
        Of evening rain,
Unravelled from the tumbling main,
    And threading the eye of a yellow star: –
So many times do I love again.

FROM ACT I, SCENE IV

    Torrismond O father, father! must I have no father,
To think how I shall please, to pray for him,
To spread his virtues out before my thought,
And set my soul in order after them?
To dream, and talk of in my dreaming sleep?
If I have children, and they question me
Of him who was to me as I to them
Who taught me love, and sports, and childish lore;
Placed smiles where tears had been; who bent his talk,
180   That it might enter my low apprehension,
And laughed when words were lost. – O father, father!
Must I give up the first word that my tongue,
The only one my heart has ever spoken?
Then take speech, thought, and knowledge quite away, –
Tear all my life out of the universe,
Take of my youth, unwrap me of my years,
And hunt me up the dark and broken past
Into my mother's womb: there unbeget me;
For 'till I'm in thy veins and unbegun,
190   Or to the food returned which makes the blood
That did make me, no possible lie can ever
Unroot my feet of thee. Canst thou make nothing?
Then do it here, for I would rather be
At home nowhere, than here nowhere at home.

    *   *   *

from *THE SECOND BROTHER*

FROM ACT I, SCENE I

Gentleman He's coming through this street,
Orazio, wrapt, like Bacchus, in the hide
Of a specked panther, with his dancing nymphs,
And torches bright and many, as his slaves
Had gathered up the fragments of the sun
That fell just now. Hark! here his music comes.

Enter ORAZIO, *between* ARMIDA *and* ROSAURA, *attended.*

Orazio Thrice to the moon, and thrice unto the sun,
80 And thrice unto the lesser stars of night,
From tower and hill, by trump and cannon's voice,
Have I proclaimed myself a deity's son:
Not Alexander's father, Ammon old,
But ivied Bacchus, do I call my sire.
Hymn it once more.

Song

Strew not earth with empty stars,
    Strew it not with roses,
Nor feathers from the crest of Mars,
    Nor summer's idle posies.
90 'Tis not the primrose-sandalled moon,
    Nor cold and silent morn,
Nor he that climbs the dusty noon,
Nor mower war with scythe that drops,
Stuck with helmed and turbaned tops
    Of enemies new shorn.

Ye cups, ye lyres, ye trumpets know,
Pour your music, let it flow,
'Tis Bacchus' son who walks below.

FROM ACT I, SCENE II

A saloon in ORAZIO'*s palace, brilliantly lighted: at the bottom of the stage open folding-doors, through which a banqueting-room is seen, with a table, at which* ORAZIO *and his guests, feasting, are partially visible.*

> Will you sleep these dark hours, maiden,
>   Beneath the vine that rested
> Its slender boughs, so purply-laden,
>   All the day around that elm
>   In the mead, nightingale-nested,
>   Which yon dark hill wears for an helm,
>   Pasture-robed and forest-crested?
>   There the night of lovely hue
>   Peeps the fearful branches through,
> And ends in those two eyes of blue.

10

FROM ACT II, SCENE I

> *Valeria*   Innocently thought,
> And worthy of thy youth! I should not say
> How thou art like the daisy in Noah's meadow,
> On which the foremost drop of rain fell warm
> And soft at evening; so the little flower
> Wrapped up its leaves, and shut the treacherous water
> Close to the golden welcome of its breast, –
> Delighting in the touch of that which led
> The shower of oceans, in whose billowy drops
> Tritons and lions of the sea were warring,
> And sometimes ships on fire sunk in the blood
> Of their own inmates; others were of ice,
> And some had islands rooted in their waves,
> Beasts on their rocks, and forest-powdering winds,
> And showers tumbling on their tumbling self, –
> And every sea of every ruined star
> Was but a drop in the world-melting flood. –

50

60

*   *   *

songs from *DEATH'S JEST-BOOK,*
or the Fool's Tragedy

OPENING OF ACT II, SCENE I

The interior of a church at Ancona. The DUKE, *in the garb of a*
pilgrim, SIBYLLA *and Knights, assembled round the corpse of*
WOLFRAM, *which is lying on a bier.*

>   *Dirge*

>   If thou wilt ease thine heart
>   Of love and all its smart,
>   Then sleep, dear, sleep;
>   And not a sorrow
>   Hang any tear on your eyelashes;
>   Lie still and deep,
>   Sad soul, until the sea-wave washes
>   The rim o' the sun to-morrow,
>   In eastern sky.

10   But wilt thou cure thine heart
>   Of love and all its smart,
>   Then die, dear, die;
>   'Tis deeper, sweeter,
>   Than on a rose bank to lie dreaming
>   With folded eye;
>   And then alone, amid the beaming
>   Of love's stars, thou'lt meet her
>   In eastern sky.

FROM ACT III, SCENE III

A church-yard with the ruins of a spacious gothic cathedral. On the cloister walls the DANCE OF DEATH *is painted. On one side the sepulchre of the Dukes with massy carved folding doors. Moonlight.*

*   *   *   *

    Duke   And what's your tune?
    Isbrand What is the night-bird's tune, wherewith she
        startles
The bee out of his dream, that turns and kisses
The inmost of his flower and sleeps again?
What is the lobster's tune when he is boiling?
I hate your ballads that are made to come
Round like a squirrel's cage, and round again.
We nightingales sing boldly from our hearts:
So listen to us.

    Song by Isbrand

    Squats on a toad-stool under a tree
        A bodiless childfull of life in the gloom,
    Crying with frog voice, 'What shall I be?
    Poor unborn ghost, for my mother killed me
        Scarcely alive in her wicked womb.
    What shall I be? shall I creep to the egg
        That's cracking asunder yonder by Nile,
           And with eighteen toes,
           And a snuff-taking nose,
        Make an Egyptian crocodile?
    Sing, "Catch a mummy by the leg
        And crunch him with an upper jaw,
        Wagging tail and clenching claw;
        Take a bill-full from my craw,
        Neighbour raven, caw, O caw,
        Grunt, my crocky, pretty maw!
           And give a paw."

290

300

Swine, shall I be you? Thou'rt a dear dog;
But for a smile, and kiss, and pout,
310   I much prefer *your* black-lipped snout,
        Little, gruntless, fairy hog,
        Godson of the hawthorn hedge.
    For, when Ringwood snuffs me out,
    And 'gins my tender paunch to grapple,
    Sing, " 'Twixt your ancles visage wedge,
        And roll up like an apple."

    Serpent Lucifer, how do you do?
    Of your worms and your snakes I'd be one or two;
        For in this dear planet of wool and of leather
320   'Tis pleasant to need no shirt, breeches, or shoe,
        And have arm, leg, and belly together.
        Then aches your head, or are you lazy?
        Sing, "Round your neck your belly wrap,
        Tail-a-top, and make your cap
            Any bee and daisy."

    I'll not be a fool, like the nightingale
    Who sits up all midnight without any ale,
        Making a noise with his nose;
    Nor a camel, although 'tis a beautiful back;
330   Nor a duck, notwithstanding the music of quack,
        And the webby, mud-patting toes.
    I'll be a new bird with the head of an ass,
        Two pigs' feet, two men's feet, and two of a hen;
    Devil-winged; dragon-bellied; grave-jawed, because
            grass
        Is a beard that's soon shaved, and grows seldom
            again
        Before it is summer; so cow all the rest;
        The new Dodo is finished. O! come to my nest.'

FROM ACT IV, SCENE III

Athulf   Dare I hope?

160 O no: methinks it is not so unlovely,
This calm unconscious state, this breathless peace,
Which all, but troublesome and riotous man,
Assume without resistance. Here I'll lay me,
And let life fall from off me tranquilly.

Enter singers and musicians led by SIEGFRIED; *they play under
the windows of Amala's apartment, and sing.*

Song

By female voices

We have bathed, where none have seen us,
  In the lake and in the fountain,
    Underneath the charmed statue
Of the timid, bending Venus,
  When the water-nymphs were counting
170 In the waves the stars of night,
    And those maidens started at you,
Your limbs shone through so soft and bright.
    But no secrets dare we tell,
      For thy slaves unlace thee,
      And he, who shall embrace thee,
    Waits to try thy beauty's spell.

By male voices

We have crowned thee queen of women,
  Since love's love, the rose, hath kept her
    Court within thy lips and blushes,
180 And thine eye, in beauty swimming,
    Kissing, we rendered up the sceptre,
At whose touch the startled soul
    Like an ocean bounds and gushes,
And spirits bend at thy controul.

But no secrets dare we tell,
 For thy slaves unlace thee,
 And he, who shall embrace thee,
Is at hand, and so farewell.

Athulf Shame on you! Do you sing their bridal song
190 Ere I have closed mine eyes? Who's there among you
That dare to be enamoured of a maid
So far above you, ye poor rhyming knaves?
Ha! there begins another.

Song by Siegfried

Lady, was it fair of thee
To seem so passing fair to me?
 Not every star to every eye
  Is fair; and why
Art thou another's share?
 Did thine eyes shed brighter glances,
200 Thine unkissed bosom heave more fair,
 To his than to my fancies?
  But I'll forgive thee still;
  Thou'rt fair without thy will.
  So be: but never know,
  That 'tis the hue of woe.

Lady, was it fair of thee
To be so gentle still to me?
 Not every lip to every eye
  Should let smiles fly.
210 Why didst thou never frown,
 To frighten from my pillow
Love's head, round which Hope wove a crown,
 And saw not 'twas of willow?
  But I'll forgive thee still;
  Thou knew'st not smiles could kill.
  Smile on: but never know,
  I die, nor of what woe.

Athulf Ha! Ha! That fellow moves my spleen;
A disappointed and contented lover.

220   Methinks he's above fifty by his voice:
If not, he should be whipped about the town,
For vending such tame doctrine in love-verses.
Up to the window, carry off the bride,
And away on horseback, squeaker!
    Siegfried Peace, thou bold drunken fellow that liest
        there! –
Leave him to sleep his folly out, good fellows.

                              [*Exit with musicians.*

    Athulf Well said: I do deserve it. I lie here
A thousand-fold fool, dying ridiculously
Because I could not have the girl I fancied.

230   Well, they are wedded; how long now will last
Affection or content? Besides 'twere possible
He might have quaffed a like draught. But 'tis done:
Villanous idiot that I am to think on't.
She willed it so. Then Amala, be fearless:
Wait but a little longer in thy chamber,
And he will be with thee whom thou hast chosen:
Or, if it make thee pastime, listen sweet one,
And I will sing to thee, here in the moonlight,
Thy bridal song and my own dirge in one.

    He sings.

240   A cypress-bough, and a rose-wreath sweet,
A wedding-robe, and a winding-sheet,
      A bridal-bed and a bier.
   Thine be the kisses, maid,
      And smiling Love's alarms;
   And thou, pale youth, be laid
      In the grave's cold arms.
   Each in his own charms,
      Death and Hymen both are here;
      So up with scythe and torch,
250   And to the old church porch,

While all the bells ring clear:
And rosy, rosy the bed shall bloom,
And earthy, earthy heap up the tomb.

Now tremble dimples on your cheek,
Sweet be your lips to taste and speak,
    For he who kisses is near:
        By her the bridegod fair,
            In youthful power and force;
        By him the grizard bare,
260   Pale knight on a pale horse,
                To woo him to a corse.
                    Death and Hymen both are here;
                        So up with scythe and torch,
                        And to the old church porch,
                    While all the bells ring clear:
                And rosy, rosy the bed shall bloom,
                And earthy, earthy heap up the tomb.

Athulf Now we'll lie down and wait for our two
        summoners;
Each patiently at least.

Enter AMALA.

                    O thou kind girl,
270   Are thou again there? Come and lay thine hand
In mine; and speak again thy soft way to me.
    Amala Thy voice is fainter, Athulf: why sang'st thou?
    Athulf It was my farewell: now I'll sing no more;
Nor speak a great deal after this. 'Tis well
You weep not. If you had esteemed me much,
It were a horrible mistake of mine.
Wilt close my eyes when I am dead, sweet maid?
    Amala O Athulf, thou might'st still have lived.

FROM ACT V, SCENE IV

Duke Now, having washed our hearts of love and
          sorrow,
50   And pledged the rosiness of many a cheek,
     And, with the name of many a lustrous maiden,
     Ennobled enough cups; feed, once again,
     Our hearing with another merry song.
         Isbrand 'Tis pity that the music of this dukedom,
     Under the former government, went wrong,
     Like all the rest: my ministers shall look to't.
     But sing again, my men.
         Siegfried   What shall it be,
     And of what turn? Shall battle's drum be heard?
     The chase's trumpet? Shall the noise of Bacchus
60   Swell in our cheeks, or lazy, sorrowing love
     Burthen with sighs our ballad?
         Isbrand   Try the piece,
     You sang me yesternight to sleep with best.
     It is for such most profitable ends
     We crownèd folks encourage all the arts.

        Song

     My goblet's golden lips are dry,
        And, as the rose doth pine
      For dew, so doth for wine
         My goblet's cup;
     Rain, O! rain, or it will die;
70   Rain, fill it up!

         Arise, and get thee wings to-night,
            Ætna! and let run o'er
          Thy wines, a hill no more,
             But darkly frown
       A cloud, where eagles dare not soar,
              Dropping rain down.

    Isbrand A very good and thirsty melody:
What say you to it, my court poet?
    Wolfram Good melody! If this be a good melody,
80 I have at home, fattening in my stye,
A sow that grunts above the nightingale.
Why this will serve for those who feed their veins
With crust, and cheese of dandelion's milk,
And the pure Rhine. When I am sick o' mornings,
With a horn-spoon tinkling my porridge-pot,
'Tis a brave ballad: but in Bacchanal night,
O'er wine, red, black, or purple-bubbling wine,
That takes a man by the brain and whirls him round,
By Bacchus' lip! I like a full-voiced fellow,
90 A craggy-throated, fat-cheeked trumpeter,
A barker, a moon-howler, who could sing
Thus, as I heard the snaky mermaids sing
In Phlegethon, that hydrophobic river,
One May-morning in Hell.

    Song

      Old Adam, the carrion crow,
        The old crow of Cairo;
      He sat in the shower, and let it flow
        Under his tail and over his crest;
          And through every feather
100   Leaked the wet weather;
      And the bough swung under his nest;
      For his beak it was heavy with marrow.
        Is that the wind dying? O no;
        It's only two devils, that blow
        Through a murderer's bones, to and fro,
          In the ghosts' moonshine.

      Ho! Eve, my grey carrion wife,
        When we have supped on king's marrow,
      Where shall we drink and make merry our life?

110   Our nest it is queen Cleopatra's skull,
                'Tis cloven and cracked,
                And battered and hacked,
            But with tears of blue eyes it is full:
            Let us drink then, my raven of Cairo.
                Is that the wind dying? O no;
                It's only two devils, that blow
                Through a murderer's bones, to and fro,
                In the ghosts' moonshine.

        Isbrand Pilgrim, it is with pleasure I acknowledge,
120   In this your friend, a man of genuine taste:
        He imitates my style in prose and verse:

                        *   *   *   *

            Dirge (for Sibylla)

            We do lie beneath the grass
                In the moonlight, in the shade
            Of the yew-tree. They that pass
                Hear us not. We are afraid
                    They would envy our delight,
                    In our graves by glow-worm night.
            Come follow us, and smile as we;
                We sail to the rock in the ancient waves,
230   Where the snow falls by thousands into the sea,
                And the drowned and the shipwrecked have
                        happy graves.

            *   *   *

Another Letter to the Same [Bryan Waller Procter]
From Göttingen; March 13, 1826

To-day a truant from the odd, old bones
And winds of flesh, which, as tamed rocks and stones
Piled cavernously make his body's dwelling,
Have housed man's soul: there, where time's billows
    swelling
Make a deep, ghostly, and invisible sea
Of melted worlds antediluvialy,
Upon the sand of ever-crumbling hours,
God-founded, stands the castle, all its towers
With veiny tendrils ivied: – this bright day
10 I leave its chambers, and with oars away
Seek some enchanted island, where to play.
And what do you that in the enchantment dwell,
And should be raving ever? a wild swell
Of passionate life rolling about the world,
Now sun-sucked to the clouds, dashed on the curled
Leaf-hidden daisies, an incarnate storm
Letting the sun through on the meadows yellow,
Or anything except that earthy fellow,
That wise dog's brother, man. O shame to tell!
20 Make tea in Circe's cup, boil the cool well,
The well Pierian, which no bird dare sip
But nightingales. There let kettles dip
Who write their simpering sonnets to its song,
And walk on Sundays in Parnassus' park: –
Take thy example from the sunny lark,
Throw off the mantle which conceals the soul,
The many-citied world, and seek thy goal
Straight as a star-beam falls. Creep not nor climb,
As they who place their topmost of sublime
30 On some peak of this planet pitifully,
Dart eagle-wise with open wings, and fly

Until you meet the gods. Thus counsel I
The men who can, but tremble to be great:
Cursed be the fool who taught to hesitate,
And to regret: time lost most bitterly!
And thus I write, and I dare write, to thee,
Fearing that still, as you were wont to do,
You feed and fear some asinine review.
Let Jaggernaut roll on; and we, whose sires
40   Blooded his wheels and prayed around his fires,
Laugh at the leaden ass in the god's skin.
Example follows precept. I have been
Giving some negro minutes of the night,
Freed from the slavery of my ruling spright
Anatomy the grim, to a new story,
In whose satiric pathos we will glory.
In it Despair has married wildest Mirth,
And, to their wedding-banquet, all the earth
Is bade to bring its enmities and loves,
50   Triumphs and horrors: you shall see the doves
Billing with quiet joy, and all the while
Their nest's the scull of some old king of Nile.
But he who fills the cups, and makes the jest,
Pipes to the dancers, is the fool o' th' feast, –
Who's he? I've dug him up and decked him trim,
And made a mock, a fool, a slave of him,
Who was the planet's tyrant: dotard Death;
Man's hate and dread. Not, with a stoical breath,
To meet him, like Augustus, standing up,
60   Nor with grave saws to season the cold cup,
Like the philosopher; nor yet to hail
His coming with a verse or jesting tale,
As Adrian did and More: – but of his night,
His moony ghostliness, and silent might
To rob him, to uncypress him i' the light,
To unmask all his secrets; make him play
Momus o'er wine by torch-light, – is the way
To conquer him, and kill; and from the day,
Spurn'd, hiss'd, and hooted, send him back again,
70   An unmask'd braggart to his bankrupt den.

For death is more 'a jest' than life; you see
Contempt grows quick from familiarity.
I owe this wisdom to Anatomy. –
Your Muse is younger in her soul than mine:
O feed her still on woman's smiles and wine,
And give the world a tender song once more;
For all the good can love and can adore
What's human, fair, and gentle. Few, I know,
Can bear to sit at my board, when I show
80 The wretchedness and folly of man's all,
And laugh myself right heartily. Your call
Is higher and more human: I will do
Unsociably my part, and still be true
To my own soul: but e'er admire you,
And own that you have nature's kindest trust,
Her weak and dear to nourish, – that I must.
Then fare, as you deserve it, well, and live
In the calm feelings you to others give.

The Ghosts' Moonshine

I.

It is midnight, my wedded;
    Let us lie under
The tempest bright undreaded,
    In the warm thunder:
(Tremble and weep not! What can you fear?)
    My heart's best wish is thine, –
That thou wert white, and bedded
    On the softest bier,
        In the ghosts' moonshine.
10   Is that the wind? No, no;
        Only two devils, that blow
    Through the murderer's ribs to and fro,
        In the ghosts' moonshine.

II.

Who is there, she said afraid, yet
        Stirring and awaking
The poor old dead? His spade, it
        Is only making, –
(Tremble and weep not! What do you crave?)
        Where yonder grasses twine,
20   A pleasant bed, my maid, that
        Children call a grave,
            In the cold moonshine.
        Is that the wind? No, no;
        Only two devils, that blow
        Through the murderer's ribs to and fro,
            In the ghosts' moonshine.

III.

What dost thou strain above her
        Lovely throat's whiteness?
A silken chain, to cover
        Her bosom's brightness?
30 (Tremble and weep not: what dost thou fear?)
        – My blood is spilt like wine,
        Thou hast strangled and slain me, lover,
        Thou hast stabbed me dear,
            In the ghosts' moonshine.
        Is that the wind? No, no;
        Only her goblin doth blow
        Through the murderer's ribs to and fro,
            In its own moonshine.

*Lines written in the album of one who had watched the
progress of the American and French revolutions*

Göttingen, April, 1827

My dear K——,

. . . I am now already so thoroughly penetrated with the conviction
of the absurdity and unsatisfactory nature of human life, that I
search with avidity for every shadow of a proof or probability of an
after-existence, both in the material and immaterial nature of man.
Those people, – perhaps they are few, – are greatly to be envied,
who believe, honestly and from conviction, in the christian doctrines:
but really in the New Testament it is difficult to scrape together
hints for a doctrine of immortality. Man appears to have found out
this secret for himself, and it is certainly the best part of all religion
and philosophy, – the only truth worth demonstrating: an anxious
question, full of hope and fear and promise, for which nature appears
to have appointed one solution, – Death. In times of revolution and
business, and even now the man, who can lay much value in the
society, praise, or glory of his fellows, may forget, and he, who is of
a callous, phlegmatic constitution, may never find, the dreadful
importance of the doubt. I am haunted for ever by it; and what but
an after life can satisfy the claims of the oppressed on nature, satiate
endless and admirable love and humanity, and quench the greediness
of the spirit for existence? but

As an almighty night doth pass away
From an old ruinous city in a desart,
And all its cloudy wrecks sink into day:
While every monstrous shape and ghostly wizard,
That dwelled within the cavernous old place,
Grows pale, and shrinks, and dies in its dismay:
And then the light comes in, and flowery grace
Covers the sand, and man doth come again
And live rejoicing in the new-born plain:
10   So you have seen great, gloomy centuries,

(The shadow of Rome's Death,) in which did dwell
The men of Europe, shudder and arise:
So you have seen break up that smoke of Hell,
Like a great superstitious snake, uncurled
From the pale temples of the awakening world.

These lines were written in the album of a man, who had busied himself during his pretty advanced life with political speculations, and watched the progress of the American and French revolutions with interest and expectation. No English person or English reader in Göttingen could, or would, understand them: for this reason I began to think they might be good, and have therefore rewritten them for you.

*   *   *

from *THE IVORY GATE*

Silenus in Proteus

Oh those were happy days, heaped up with wine-skins,
And ivy-wreathed and thyrsus-swinging days,
Swimming like streamy-tressed wanton Bacchantes,
When I was with thee, and sat kingly on thee,
My ass of asses. Then quite full of wine –
Morning, eve – and leaning on a fawn,
Still pretty steady, and on t'other side
Some vinous-lipped nymph of Ariadne,
Her bosom a soft cushion for my right:
10   Half dreaming and half waking, both in bliss,
I sat upon my ass and laughed at Jove.
But thou art dead, my dapple, and I too
Shall ride thee soon about the Elysian meadow,
Almost a skeleton as well as thou.
And why, oh dearest, couldst not keep thy legs
That sacred hair, sacred to sacred me?
Was this thy gratitude for pats and fondlings,
To die like any other mortal ass?
Was it for this, oh son of Semele,
20   I taught thee then, a little tumbling one,
To suck the goatskin oftener than the goat?

Lord Alcohol

'Before we proceed to the solemnity of the coronation,' said Norman who had now recovered some spirits out of a bottle of Madeira before him (thanks to the adulterators), after offering his congratulations to the conqueror – 'let me sing you a hymn of triumph, in which I defend my own opinions on the subject of this night's discussion . . .'

I.

Who tames the lion now?
Who smoothes Jove's wrinkles now?
Who is the reckless wight
   That in the horrid middle
Of the deserted night
Doth play upon man's brain,
   As on a wanton fiddle,
The mad and magic strain,
The reeling, tripping sound,
To which the world goes round?
   Sing heigh! ho! diddle!
        And then say –
Love, quotha, Love? nay, nay!
It is a spirit fine
Of ale or ancient wine,
     Lord Alcohol, the drunken fay,
      Lord Alcohol alway!

II.

Who maketh the pipe-clay man
Think all that nature can?
Who dares the gods to flout,
   Lay fate beneath the table,
And maketh him stammer out
   A thousand monstrous things,
   For history a fable,
   Dish-clouts for kings?

And sends the world along
Singing a ribald song
   Of heigho! Babel?
       Who, I pray –
30   Love, quotha, Love? nay, nay!
It is a spirit fine
Of ale or ancient wine,
    Lord Alcohol, the drunken fay,
      Lord Alcohol alway.

Dream-Pedlary

I.

If there were dreams to sell,
   What would you buy?
Some cost a passing bell;
   Some a light sigh,
That shakes from Life's fresh crown
Only a rose-leaf down.
If there were dreams to sell,
Merry and sad to tell,
And the crier rung the bell,
10   What would you buy?

II.

A cottage lone and still,
   With bowers nigh,
Shadowy, my woes to still,
   Until I die.
Such pearl from Life's fresh crown
Fain would I shake me down.
Were dreams to have at will,
This would best heal my ill,
   This would I buy.

III.

20 But there were dreams to sell
   Ill didst thou buy;
Life is a dream, they tell,
   Waking, to die.
Dreaming a dream to prize,
Is wishing ghosts to rise;
   And, if I had the spell
   To call the buried well,
     Which one would I?

IV.

If there are ghosts to raise,
30   What shall I call,
Out of hell's murky haze,
   Heaven's blue pall?
Raise my loved long-lost boy
To lead me to his joy. –
   There are no ghosts to raise;
   Out of death lead no ways;
     Vain is the call.

V.

Know'st thou not ghosts to sue
   No love thou hast.
40 Else lie, as I will do,
   And breathe thy last.
So out of Life's fresh crown
Fall like a rose-leaf down.
   Thus are the ghosts to woo;
   Thus are all dreams made true,
     Ever to last!

Love-in-Idleness

I.

'Shall I be your first love, lady, shall I be your first?
   Oh! then I'll fall before you, down on my velvet knee,
   And deeply bend my rosy head and press it upon thee,
And swear that there is nothing more, for which my heart
      doth thirst,
      But a downy kiss, and pink,
      Between your lips' soft chink.'

II.

'Yes, you shall be my first love, boy, and you shall be my
      first,
   And I will raise you up again unto my bosom's fold;
   And, when you kisses many one on lip and cheek have
      told,
I'll let you loose upon the grass, to leave me if you durst;
      And so we'll toy away
      The night besides the day.'

III.

'But let me be your second love, but let me be your second,
   For then I'll tap so gently, dear, upon your window
      pane,
   And creep between the curtains in, where never man has
      lain,
And never leave thy gentle side till the morning star hath
      beckoned,
      Within the silken lace
      Of thy young arms' embrace.'

IV.

'Well thou shalt be my second love, yes, gentle boy, my
      second,
   And I will wait at eve for thee within my lonely bower,
   And yield unto thy kisses, like a bud to April's shower,

From moon-set till the tower-clock the hour of dawn hath
    reckoned,
        And lock thee with my arms
        All silent up in charms.'

V.

'No, I will be thy third love, lady, ay I will be the third,
    And break upon thee, bathing, in woody place alone,
    And catch thee to my saddle and ride o'er stream and
        stone,
And press thee well, and kiss thee well, and never speak a
        word,
        'Till thou hast yielded up
30   The margin of love's cup.'

VI.

'Then thou shalt not be my first love, boy, nor my second,
        nor my third;
    If thou'rt the first, I'll laugh at thee, and pierce thy flesh
        with thorns;
    If the second, from my chamber pelt with jeering laugh
        and scorns;
And if thou darest be the third, I'll draw my dirk unheard
        And cut thy heart in two, –
        And then die, weeping you.'

Dirge (Let dew the flowers fill)

    Let dew the flowers fill;
        No need of fell despair,
        Though to the grave you bear
    One still of soul – but now too still,
        One fair – but now too fair.
    For, beneath your feet, the mound,
    And the waves, that play around,

Have meaning in their grassy, and their watery, smiles;
And, with a thousand sunny wiles,
10   Each says, as he reproves,
         Death's arrow oft is Love's.

An Unfinished Draft (A thousand buds are breaking)

A thousand buds are breaking
     Their prisons silently;
A thousand birds are making
     Their nests in leafy tree;
A thousand babes are waking
     On woman's breast to-day;
.   .   .   .

     Is born to man, to-day
     Beneath the sun of May:
Whence come ye, babes of flowers, and, Children, whence
         come ye?

10   The snow falls by thousands into the sea;
         A thousand blossoms covers
            The forsaken forest,
         And on its branches hovers
            The lark's song thousandfold;
         And maidens hear from lovers
            A thousand secrets guessed
         In June's abundant breast
            Before and yet are blessed –
Whence, blossoms rich, birds bold, beloved maidens,
            whence come ye?

20   The snow falls by thousands into the sea;
         A thousand flowers are shedding
            Their leaves all dead and dry;
         A thousand birds are threading
            Their passage through the sky;
         A thousand mourners treading

The tearful churchyard way
In funeral array:
Birds, whither fly ye? – whither, dead, pass ye?
The snow falls by thousands into the sea.

Song of the Stygian Naiades

'What do you think the mermaids of the Styx were singing as I
watched them bathing the other day' –

I.

Proserpine may pull her flowers,
   Wet with dew or wet with tears,
   Red with anger, pale with fears,
Is it any fault of ours,
If Pluto be an amorous king,
   And comes home nightly, laden,
Underneath his broad bat-wing,
   With a gentle, mortal maiden?
Is it so, Wind, is it so?
All that you and I do know
Is, that we saw fly and fix
'Mongst the reeds and flowers of Styx,
      Yesterday,
Where the Furies made their hay
For a bed of tiger cubs,
A great fly of Beelzebub's,
The bee of hearts, which mortals name
Cupid, Love, and Fie for shame.

II.

Proserpine may weep in rage,
   But, ere I and you have done
   Kissing, bathing in the sun,
What I have in yonder cage,
Bird or serpent, wild or tame,
   She shall guess and ask in vain;

But, if Pluto does't again,
It shall sing out loud his shame.
    What hast caught then? What hast caught?
    Nothing but a poet's thought,
    Which so light did fall and fix
30   'Mongst the reeds and flowers of Styx,
            Yesterday,
Where the Furies made their hay
For a bed of tiger cubs, –
A great fly of Beelzebub's,
The bee of hearts, which mortals name
Cupid, Love, and Fie for shame.

Thanatos to Kenelm

and the *Song* by THANATOS

'I have no feeling for the monuments of human labour,' she would say, 'the wood and the desert are more peopled with my household gods than the city or the cultivated country. Even with the living animals and the prevailing vegetation of the forests in this hemisphere, I have little sympathy. I know not the meaning of a daisy, nor what nature has symbolized by the light bird and the butterfly. But the sight of a palm with its lofty stem and tuft of long grassy leaves, high in the blue air, or even such a branch as this' (breaking off a large fern leaf) 'awake in me a feeling, a sort of nostalgy and longing for ages long past. When my ancient sire used to sit with me under the old dragon tree or Dracaena, I was as happy as the ephemeral fly balanced on his wing in the sun, whose setting will be his death-warrant. But why do I speak to you so? You cannot understand me.' – And then she would sing whisperingly to herself:

The mighty thoughts of an old world
Fan, like a dragon's wing unfurled,
    The surface of my yearnings deep;

And solemn shadows then awake,
Like the fish-lizard in the lake,
   Troubling a planet's morning sleep.

My waking is a Titan's dream,
Where a strange sun, long set, doth beam
   Through Montezuma's cypress bough:
10 Through the fern wilderness forlorn
Glisten the giant harts' great horn,
   And serpents vast with helmed brow.

The measureless from caverns rise
With steps of earthquake, thunderous cries,
   And graze upon the lofty wood;
The palmy grove, through which doth gleam
Such antediluvian ocean's stream,
   Haunts shadowy my domestic mood.

The Phantom-Wooer

I.

A ghost, that loved a lady fair,
Ever in the starry air
   Of midnight at her pillow stood;
And, with a sweetness skies above
The luring words of human love,
   Her soul the phantom wooed.
Sweet and sweet is their poisoned note,
The little snakes' of silver throat,
In mossy skulls that nest and lie,
10 Ever singing 'die, oh! die'.

II.

Young soul, put off your flesh, and come
With me into the quiet tomb,
   Our bed is lovely, dark, and sweet;
The earth will swing us, as she goes,

Beneath our coverlid of snows,
   And the warm leaden sheet.
Dear and dear is their poisoned note,
The little snakes' of silver throat,
In mossy skulls that nest and lie,
20 Ever singing 'die, oh! die'.

Threnody (Far away)

Far away,
   As we hear
The song of wild swans winging
   Through the day,
The thought of him, who is no more, comes ringing
   On my ear.

Gentle fear
   On the breast
Of my memory comes breaking,
10   Near and near,
As night winds' murmurous music waking
   Seas at rest.

As the blest
   Tearful eye
Sees the sun, behind the ocean,
   Red i' th' west,
Grow pale, and in changing hues and fading motion
   Wane and die:

So do I
20   Wake or dream
    *   *   *

  * * *

songs and fragments from the revisions of
DEATH'S JEST-BOOK

FROM ACT I, SCENE I

Song from the Ship

To sea, to sea! the calm is o'er;
   The wanton water leaps in sport,
And rattles down the pebbly shore;
   The dolphin wheels, the sea-cows snort.
And unseen Mermaids' pearly song
Comes bubbling up, the weeds among.
    Fling broad the sail, dip deep the oar:
    To sea, to sea! the calm is o'er.

To sea, to sea! our wide-winged bark
   Shall billowy cleave its sunny way,
And with its shadow, fleet and dark,
   Break the caved Tritons' azure ray,
Like mighty eagle soaring light
O'er antelopes on Alpine height.
    The anchor heaves, the ship swings free,
    The sails swell full. To sea, to sea!

Isbrand The idiot merriment of thoughtless men!
How the fish laugh at them, that swim and toy
About the ruined ship, wrecked deep below,
Whose pilot's skeleton, all full of sea weeds,
Leans on his anchor, grinning like their Hope.

FROM ACT I, SCENE II

A Beautiful Night

How lovely is the heaven of this night,
How deadly still its earth! The forest brute
Has crept into his cave, and laid himself
Where sleep has made him harmless like the lamb.
The horrid snake, his venom now forgot,
Is still and innocent as the honied flower
Under his head: and man, in whom are met
Leopard and snake, and all the gentleness
And beauty of the young lamb and the bud,
10   Has let his ghost out, put his thoughts aside
And lent his senses unto death himself.

FROM ACT I, SCENE IV

(SIBYLLA *throws herself on the body; the* DUKE *stands motionless;
the rest gather round in silence. The scene closes.*)

   A Voice from the waters

   The swallow leaves her nest,
   The soul my weary breast;
   But therefore let the rain
      On my grave
   Fall pure; for why complain?
   Since both will come again
      O'er the wave.

   The wind dead leaves and snow
   Doth hurry to and fro;
10   And, once, a day shall break
      O'er the wave,

When a storm of ghosts shall shake
The dead, until they wake
  In the grave.

A Subterranean City

I followed once a fleet and mighty serpent
Into a cavern in a mountain's side;
And, wading many lakes, descending gulphs,
At last I reached the ruins of a city,
Built not like ours but of another world,
As if the aged earth had loved in youth
The mightiest city of a perished planet,
And kept the image of it in her heart,
So dream-like, shadowy, and spectral was it.
Nought seemed alive there, and the bony dead
Were of another world the skeletons.
The mammoth, ribbed like to an arched cathedral,
Lay there, and ruins of great creatures else
More like a shipwrecked fleet, too great they seemed
For all the life that is to animate:
And vegetable rocks, tall sculptured palms,
Pines grown, not hewn, in stone; and giant ferns,
Whose earthquake-shaken leaves bore graves for nests.

10

FROM ACT V, SCENE I

The Slight and Degenerate Nature of Man

Antediluvianus loquitur

Pitiful post-diluvians! from whose hearts
The print of passions by the tide of hours
Is washed away for ever
As lions' footmark on the ocean sands;
While we, Adam's coevals, carry in us
The words indelible of buried feelings,
Like the millennial trees, whose hoary barks
Grow o'er the secrets cut into their core.

NOTES

See Further Reading for fuller information on works mentioned briefly in lists of abbreviations and notes below.

THOMAS HOOD

The following abbreviations have been used:

Blackwood's: *Blackwood's Edinburgh Magazine*

CA: *Comic Annual*, ed. Hood

CPW: *Complete Poetical Works of Thomas Hood*, ed. Walter Jerrold

HO: Hood, *Hood's Own, or Laughter from Year to Year: being former runnings of his comic vein, with an infusion of new blood for general circulation* (London: A. H. Baily, 1839; texts from 'new edition': London: E. Moxon, 1861)

LM: *London Magazine* (monthly)

Mem: *Memorials of Thomas Hood . . . Edited by his Daughter*

NMM: *New Monthly Magazine*, ed. Thomas Campbell, 1820–30, and Hood, August 1841 to January 1843

OED: *Oxford English Dictionary*

Plea: Hood, *The Plea of the Midsummer Fairies, Hero and Leander, Lycus the Centaur, and Other Poems* (London: Longman, Rees, Orme, Brown, and Green, 1827)

SP: *Selected Poems of Thomas Hood*, ed. John Clubbe

TLS: *Times Literary Supplement*

WO 1: Hood, *Whims and Oddities, in Prose and Verse, with Forty Original Designs*, first series 1826 (2nd edn, London: Lupton Relfe, 1827)

WO 2: *Whims and Oddities*, second series 1827 (2nd edn, London: Charles Tilt, 1829)

Works: *The Works of Thomas Hood*, edited by his son

The Ballad of 'Sally Brown, and Ben the Carpenter'
(*Faithless Sally Brown*)

First publication: *LM* 5 (March 1822) in 'The Lion's Head' (the reply column), pp. 202–4, unsigned; text: *WO 1* (I.33–7) but retaining a footnote in *LM*. *Whims and Oddities* (1826), Hood's first volume of comic verse, was quite popular. This ballad was set to the tune of 'Wapping Time' (*c.* 1829) by Jonathan Blewitt, as no. 2 of *The Ballad Singer* (*CPW*, p. 739). Reflecting his apprenticeship in the music-halls, Hood's comic ballads would inspire Lewis Carroll, Edward Lear and W. S. Gilbert. This one twists and turns with puns (faint/feint; beau, Ben/Benbow/woe began; tendership/ hardship; Wales/wails; birth/berth; told/tolled), sexual bawdy (19–20) and jaunty echoes of tragic voices (21 replays Medora's fainting farewell to Conrad in Byron's *Corsair*, I.481–2). A press-gang crew (6) kidnaps men for forced naval service; Eye-water (28) is slang for gin, cockney for 'high water'; old Benbow (30) is the legendary British naval hero, Admiral John Benbow (1653–1702); a tender (34) serves another vessel, bringing provisions and arms, conveying messages and intelligence. The virgin and the scales (42) are constellations Virgo and Libra, zodiac signs associated with love and justice; pipe his eye (60) means weep. *WO* nicely revises *LM*'s 'heav'd a bitter sigh' to 'heaved a heavy sigh' (58). *LM*'s footnote at 60 quotes from Catullus' *Poems* (3): 'To its mistress alone it [Lesbia's sparrow] would cheep continually'. *WO 1* has this Preface (the brackets enclose our glosses):

I have never been vainer of any verses than of my part in the following Ballad. Dr [Isaac] Watts, amongst evangelical nurses, has an enviable renown [*Divine Songs for Children*, 1715] – and [Thomas] Campbell's Ballads enjoy a snug genteel popularity. 'Sally Brown' has been favoured, perhaps, with as wide a patronage as the Moral Songs [Watts], though its circle may not have been of so select a class as the friends of 'Hohenlinden' [by Campbell (1802), on the fierce battle of December 1800 in which Napoleon vanquished the Austrians]. But I do not desire to see it amongst what are called Elegant Extracts [a popular anthology genre]. The lamented [John] Emery, – drest as Tom Tug [the hero of *The Waterman* (1774) by Charles Dibdin sen.], sang it at his last mortal Benefit at Covent Garden; – and, ever since, it has been a great favourite with the watermen of Thames, who time their oars to it, as the wherrymen of Venice time theirs to the lines of Tasso. With the watermen, it went naturally to Vauxhall [entertainment and recreation centre on the banks of the River Thames]: – and over land, to Sadler's Wells. The Guards – not the mail coach, but the Life Guards, – picked it out from a fluttering hundred of others – all going to one air – against the dead wall at Knightsbridge. Cheap Printers of Shoe Lane, and Cow-cross, (all pirates!) disputed about the Copyright, and published their own editions, – and, in the mean time, the Authors [?also John Hamilton Reynolds], to have made bread of their song, (it was poor old Homer's hard ancient case!) must have sung it about the streets. Such is the lot of Literature! the profits of 'Sally Brown' were divided by the Ballad Mongers: – it has cost, but has never brought me, a half-penny. (pp. 33–4)

'Thank you for Mr Hood,' Beddoes wrote to Kelsall about *Whims and Oddities*, October 1827; 'he seems to be pretty tolerable, & not at all in danger to be too deep for his readers. Apollo have mercy on him!' (Kelsall, Memoir in 1851 *Poems*, I.lxxviii; Donner, *Complete Works of Beddoes*, p. 638).

Fair Ines

First published in *LM* 7 (January 1823), pp. 96–7, signed 'H.', without the third stanza; our fuller text is from *Plea*, Hood's first and only purely serious volume, mostly in conscious imitation of and homage to Keats's favoured forms, themes and modes (the volume received mixed reviews and did not sell well). Poe admired this poem's 'inexpressible charm', quoting it entire and calling Hood 'one of the noblest – and . . . one of the most singularly fanciful of modern poets' in *The Poetic Principle* (1850), the lecture-essay that memorably begins with the declaration that 'a long poem' is 'simply a flat contradiction in terms' because the value of a poem is the degree to which it 'excites, by elevating the soul', an effect that 'cannot be sustained throughout a composition of any great length'; Poe also praised *The Bridge of Sighs*.

Ode: Autumn

First publication and text: *LM* 7 (February 1823), pp. 187–8, signed 'H.'; reprinted in *Plea*. Hood draws on a long literary tradition of Autumn odes, a genre typical of 'ubi sunt' nostalgia ('Where are the blooms of summer?') with sad awareness of coming winter-death. Keats's *To Autumn*, by contrast, celebrates the season's liminal beauties. Hood declines this approach for a more traditional melancholy, but his Keatsian echoes are so audible as to render a homage (*To Autumn*, *Ode to a Nightingale*, *La Belle Dame sans Merci*, *Ode on Melancholy*, the opening of *Hyperion*, even *When I have fears*, which Hood's sister-in-law Charlotte Reynolds had transcribed in MS); for details, see *SP*, p. 335. The most notable of the *Plea* variants are: 'Where are the songs of Summer? With the sun' (9); 'snatch'd from her flow'rs' (21); 'leaves all twinkling' (24); 'Whilst all the wither'd world looks drearily' (43); 'and a face of care' (51); 'and enough of gloom' (53); 'living bloom' (56); 'the earth' (59).

Sonnet. – Silence

First publication and text: *LM* 7 (February 1823), p. 215, where, signed 'T.', it led off 'The Miscellany'; reprinted in *Plea*. The sestet of this widely admired sonnet evokes Byron's 'And chiefless castles breathing stern farewells / From gray but leafy walls, where Ruin greenly dwells' (*Childe Harold's Pilgrimage*, Canto III.xlvi).

Sonnet Written in Keats's Endymion

First publication and text: *LM* 7 (May 1823), p. 541, signed 'T.'. *Endymion* (1818), Keats's only completed long poem (a romance epic of over 4000 lines), involved his aspirations for poetic fame with the tale of a shepherd prince in mythic Greece who dreams of erotic bliss with the moon goddess ('Dian') and after various adventures is united with her. The poem was harshly treated in the Tory press, infamously the *Quarterly Review* and *Blackwood's*; appearing in the oppositional *London Magazine*, Hood's sonnet implicitly addresses these attacks. The summary couplet (a Shakespearean form) echoes Shelley's elegy for Keats, *Adonais* (1821), also aimed at hostile reviews: 'He is made one with Nature: there is heard / His voice in all her music' (stanza xlii). Like Shelley, Hood confers a mythic identity on Keats, in his case, that of Keats's own visionary hero.

Sonnet: – Death

First publication and text: *LM* 7 (June 1823), p. 636, signed 'T.'; reprinted in *Plea* as *Sonnet*; other variants of note: 'these bright stars' (3); 'thought shall cease' (7); 'resurrection' (14). In both form and theme, Hood evokes Shakespeare's 'This thought is as a death' (Sonnet 64) and Keats's 'When I have fears that I may cease to be' (first published in 1848, but J. H. Reynolds had it in MS and Charlotte Reynolds in transcription), and in mood and diction, *Ode to a Nightingale*. Hood's single-sentence sonnet blends Shakespearean structure with a dramatic Petrarchan volta at line 9 and an overflowing (quasi-Spenserian) rhyme scheme in the quatrains (*ababbcbccdcd*), enriched with semantically tuned internal rhymes (death/breath; sunlight/night), assonance and alliteration ('lapp'd in alien clay and laid below') and phonic slides ('flesh shall').

The Death-Bed

First publication and text: *Englishman's Magazine*, August 1831, signed 'T. Hood'; reprinted in *Poems* (1846), II.3–4. In *Works* (V.102), the poet's son Tom dates the composition *c*. 1825 and quotes a Latin translation, by

Rev. H. Kynaston, published in *The London Times*, along with Hood's poem, 8 January 1846 (p. 7), eight months after Hood's death. J. M. Cohen suggests (*contra* Tom) that the occasion was the death of the poet's mother (*TLS*, 19 September 1952). Harriet Beecher Stowe incorporated the song, without attribution, in *Dred* (1866). The summary pun of 'mourn' in 'morn' is traditional, and the whole scene evokes the famous opening of Donne's *A Valediction: Forbidding Mourning* (1633):

> As virtuous men pass mildly away,
> And whisper to their souls to go,
> Whilst some of their sad friends do say
> The breath goes now, and some say, No . . .

A Friendly *Epistle to Mrs Fry* in *Newgate*

First publication and text: *Odes and Addresses to Great People*, '*Catching all the oddities, the whimsies, the absurdities, and the littlenesses of conscious greatness by the way*' (London: Baldwin, Cradock, and Joy, 1825), pp. 23–32; signed '*Citizen of the World*', co-authored with J. H. Reynolds. Framed in the manner of Horace and James Smith's overnight sensation of parodies, *Rejected Addresses* (1812), this volume was a success, quickly selling out three editions (2nd edn, Baldwin, Cradock and Joy, 1825; 3rd edn, Henry Colburn, 1826); after the first, the title became '*A Friendly Address . . .*'. Ottava-rima had satiric celebrity with Byron's *Beppo* (1818) and *Don Juan* (1819–24), and by force of this fame signalled the mode. Notoriously crowded, dark, and filthy Newgate prison was established in the twelfth century in the City of London, and until 1881 housed all manner of criminal, from debtor to murderer. Horrified by her visit in 1813, especially by the conditions of women and children, Quaker minister Elizabeth Fry (1780–1845) became a prison reformer. In 1817 she founded an association to improve conditions. She was famed for her devotion. Byron was wry about her at the end of *Don Juan* X (stanzas 84–7), and especially her campaign to clean up vile prison language (letter to John Murray, 4 December 1821); Hood mocks in this vein, his punning on 'Newgatory' (104), Coleridge exclaimed to Lamb (who, he thought, was responsible for the volume), 'transcendant!' (*Mem*, I.16–17). But Byron also found Fry's efforts an inspiration to his own commitments: 'Whoever goes into Greece at present [for the War of Independence] should do it as Mrs Fry went into Newgate – not in expectation of meeting with any especial indication of existing probity – but in the hope that time and better treatment will reclaim the present . . . tendencies' (Journal, 28 September 1823).

The epigraphs are from *As You Like It* (II.i.17; Duke Senior declares, 'Sweet are the uses of adversity' if one can find 'Sermons in stones, and good in everything') and *Macbeth* (V.i.38; Lady Macbeth's hallucinating the stain of her murder-victim's blood). The opening catalogue of 'I like' recalls the anaphora of Byron's encomium to England in *Beppo* (stanzas 42–3). Browne (4 et seq.) is Renaissance Puritan Robert Browne; Bernard Barton (7) is Fry's contemporary, 'the Quaker poet' (Beddoes detested his 'Bernardbartonizings': letter, 1824, Donner, *Complete Works*, p. 590). William Pitt, Tory Prime Minister 1783–1801, was opposed by Charles James Fox, a liberal Whig, whose party-colours were buff and blue. Line 52 puns Fry's name into the fear of eternal damnation that infuses a typical Methodist sermon. Anacreontic raisin (76) is wine, from ancient Greek poet Anacreon's many verses in praise of it (Hood himself would publish in this genre in the 1840s); the female prisoners' emblematic names (77–80) are from *The Beggar's Opera* (1728), an immensely popular 'Newgate' musical by John Gay. Baby-work (89) is basic sewing; Elizabeth Fry was related by marriage to the Quaker Fry family of chocolate (97) fame; *Pandeans* (100) are pipers (the instrument of Pan). Old Bailey (119) is either the street near, or an enclosure outside Newgate Prison; Charleys (127) are London nightwatchmen (*CPW*, p. 734); St Giles's (131) is the haunt of prostitutes, thieves and adventurers.

Stanzas (I remember, I remember)

First publication and text: *Friendship's Offering* for 1826, pp. 395–6, signed 'T. Hood, Esq.'; reprinted in *Plea*. Published by Smith and Elder, *Friendship's Offering* was one of the lavishly produced, affordably priced gift-book annuals. The fad was imported from Germany, introduced to England in 1823 by German-born London printer Rudolph Ackermann (1764–1834), with *Forget Me Not* (see *Ruth*, below), the first of a series 'expressly designed to serve as tokens of remembrance, friendship, or affection', replete with presentation plates. The market flourished in the 1820s and 30s, and held well into the century. The pay was handsome, attracting some of the most famous writers of the day, including Wordsworth, Scott, 'The Poet Laureate' (Southey), Lamb, L.E.L. (Landon), Hemans, Coleridge, et al. 'The world . . . seems mad about' these annuals, Scott exclaimed in 1828 when Charles Heath offered him £800 a year to edit *The Keepsake*. The general mood of Hood's poem is Wordsworthian nostalgia; Clubbe compares the first lines to those of J. H. Reynolds's *Stanzas on Revisiting Shrewsbury*: 'I remember well the time, – the sweet school-boy time' (*SP*, p. 332). Praed wrote a similarly toned poem titled *I remember, I remember*, with some anger at its close, in 1833 (*Poems*, ed. Derwent Coleridge, II.366–7).

Autumn

First publication and text: *Friendship's Offering*, 1826, signed 'T. Hood, Esq. Author of "Odes and Addresses to Great People" '; reprinted in *Plea*. This grimly jaunty ditty replays the trope of ageing voiced in Shakespeare's famous Sonnet 73 ('That time of year thou mayst in me behold'), with a stark refusal in its second stanza even of the grasshopper-and-ant moralism of Aesop's fable.

Faithless Nelly Gray

First publication and text: *WO 1* (I.139–42). The ballad form is punned by burthen (51), a term for the chorus. It was set to music by Blewitt, published *c*. 1829 as no. 4 of *The Ballad Singer* (*CPW*, p. 739). 'Pathetic' winks at the sentimental tradition of eighteenth-century balladry, the parody evident in the string of ghoulishly comic puns initiated by 'arms' at the end of stanza 1, and 'Foot' at the end of 2 (the 42nd Foot is a famous Scottish military unit). The pleasure of reading 'hinges not upon the unexpectedness of the puns, but on their ingenuity' (Henkle, p. 304). There is a sneer at Parliamentary representatives in lines 11–12; lines 15–16 pun on French *devoirs* (respects); take them off (20) is idiomatic for mimic or satirize. Badajoz (36) was a site in the Peninsular War (the British campaign in Iberia against Napoleon), a fortified city in south-west Spain, which Wellington besieged in 1811 and captured from the French in 1812, with notoriously outrageous acts of cruelty; *breaches* (punning on trousers) are gaps in a wall made by battering. Nell (48) puns on death-knell, line (56) on the military unit and (remotely) on the poetry at hand; nail (62) evokes the cliché 'dead as a doornail', and also denotes an 8-pound weight-measure and a scoundrel. Line 65 refers to a jury inquest; in folk-custom, suicides (denied consecrated burial) were interred at crossroads, with a stake through the heart (67–8).

The Last Man

First publication and text: *WO 1* (I.22–32). This popular theme in the wake of twenty-five years of European war was treated by many writers: in Jean-Baptiste Cousin de Grainville's *Le dernier homme*, translated as *The Last Man, or Omegarus and Syderia, A Romance in Futurity* (1806); then in Byron's poem *Darkness* (1816); Thomas Campbell's poem *The Last Man* (*NMM* 8 (1823), pp. 272–3); Mary Shelley's novel *The Last Man* (February 1826), John Edmund Reade's 'The Last Man', *Blackwood's* 19 (March 1826) – these last two preceding Hood; and later, George Dibdin Pitt's two-act drama, *The Last Man; or, The Miser of Eltham Green* (1833). In

1823 Beddoes began a verse play (unfinished) titled *The Last Man* (see below). For treatments of the theme, see A. J. Sambrook, 'A Romantic Theme: The Last Man', *Forum for Modern Language Studies* 2 (1966), pp. 25-33 and Fiona Stafford, *The Last of the Race* (Oxford: Oxford University Press, 1994). Depopulation by plague – the pest (5, 100) – was treated in Shelley's novel, Defoe's *Journal of the Plague Year* (1722) and John Wilson's *The City of the Plague* (1816). Wilson celebrated the great burlesque power of Hood's poem and quoted it entire in *Blackwood's* 21 (January 1827), pp. 54-7: 'Hood's Last Man is . . . worth fifty of Byron's "darkness", (a mere daub), a hundred and fifty of Campbell's Last Man, and five hundred of Mrs Shelly's abortion'. Newgate (17) was a London prison (see also *A Friendly Epistle*); workhouse sheds (108) were dismal places where dependants on public relief, including children, were forced to labour long hours at a pittance. Line 136 recalls Milton's famous description of Death: 'The likeness of a kingly crown had on' (*Paradise Lost*, II.673). Corals (152) are teething toys; blinded him in his bags (164) means blindfolded him in his clothing; the mid-sixteenth-century spelling 'decentlie' (182) invites punning attention to the grapheme 'lie'. Before the innovation of the long drop, friends of the convict were permitted to shorten the agony of strangulation by pulling the legs (222).

Mary's Ghost

First publication and text: *WO 2* (II.15-17); set to music *c.* 1829 by Blewitt and published as no. 1 of *The Ballad Singer* (*CPW*, p. 740). Hood parodies the old ballad theme of the lover's ghostly return – in, e.g., *Sweet William's Ghost*, *Fair Margaret and Sweet William*, Gottfried Bürger's *Lenore* and its adaptation by Scott as *William and Helen* (1796) – as well as recent treatments in Wordsworth's *Laodamia* (1815) and Keats's *Isabella, or the Pot of Basil* (1820). The punning dispersal of the female body literalizes with ghoulish comedy the Renaissance trope of the *blason* (the male lover's extravagant itemizing of his beloved's features); here the inventory of parts, motivated by the demands of (male) medical professionals, is described by the woman. In *WO 2* Hood's sketch of the grave-robbery renders a mordant visual pun on the epitaph 'Resurgam' (I will rise) with a related reference to the popular term for such robbers, 'Resurrection men'; the sketch is captioned 'Gin a body meet a body' (from Burns's ballad *Coming thro' the Rye*, where the meeting is sexual). Long home (11) is a phrase for the grave in Ecclesiastes 12:5; Mary-bone (19) is an irreverent name for the graveyard of Mary-le-Bone (London's church of St Mary-at-the-Bourne). Dr Vyse (22) may be medical writer and instrument-maker John Weiss (*SP*, p. 345); Weiss knew Sir Astley (44), the distinguished surgeon Sir Astley Cooper (1768-1841), whose lectures on anatomy at London's Guy's Hospital (24)

Keats attended as a medical student. Doctor Bell (27) may be medical researcher Sir Charles Bell (1774–1842); Dr Carpue (34) is Joseph Constantine Carpue (1764–1846), who kept a private anatomy school; Pickford's van (36) is from Pickford & Co. (Mr P., line 37), London's largest moving outfit (*SP*, p. 345). The cock-crow is a traditional signal for night-venturing ghosts to return: 'the morning cock crew loud, / And at the sound it shrunk in haste away / And vanished', Horatio reports of old Hamlet's ghost (I.ii.218–20). The final word 'anatomie' echoes 'an atom' with a punning slide into 'o' me'. The grim comedy seems to be repeated in Dickens's *Our Mutual Friend* (1864–5), when the wooden-legged Silas Wegg goes to visit his detached leg in the shop of the skeleton-assembler, Mr Venus.

Ruth

First publication and text: *Forget Me Not; A Christmas and New Year's Present* for 1827, p. 131, signed 'T. Hood, Esq.'; this was another popular gift-book annual. Reprinted in *Plea*, with revisions that tend to soften the suggestion of a dark lady/femme fatale: 'burning kiss' yields to 'glowing kiss' (4), 'darkest' to 'blackest' (10) and 'forehead darkly' to a 'tressy forehead' (14). The clearest echoes are of Keats's 'sad heart of Ruth, when, sick for home, / She stood in tears amid the alien corn' (*Ode to a Nightingale* (1820), 66–7, alluding to the gleaner of the Book of Ruth); Wordsworth's meditation on the solitary reaper in his poem of that title (1807); and, in the conclusion, Marlowe's *The Passionate Shepherd to His Love* (1600): 'Come live with me and be my love'. Stooks (15) are sheaves.

Song (The stars are with the voyager)

First publication and text: *Plea*, p. 197.

Death in the Kitchen

First publication and text: *Forget Me Not*, 1828, pp. 156–9. This volume had an all-star roster, leading off with Hemans, Campbell and Moore, and including Hogg, Bowles, L.E.L., Mitford and Cunningham, among names one might recognize today. Hood's credit in the Table of Contents was correspondingly pumped up: 'By Thomas Hood, Esq. Author of "*Whims and Oddities*", &c.' (p. viii); his poem was favoured with a full-page illustration (p. 156), captioned 'Corporal Trim / Moralizing in the kitchen'. His epigraph is from Sterne's mid-eighteenth-century comic novel, vol. V, ch. 7, the voice of Corporal Trim; Susannah and Jonathan are servants, and a scullery maid is scouring a fish-kettle when they receive news of the death of young Master Bobby (Tristram's brother). William Empson admires how

Hood's departure from his usual manner of punning yields an instrument of delicate humanity: 'Each verse moves about its pun as an axis, and yet the result is so lyrical and strong that one wonders if it can really be a matter of punning; whether the same effect could not be conveyed without any overt pun at all'; such 'associations' concern 'whole states of mind', referring to 'several universes of discourse, several modes of judgement or of feeling' (*Seven Types of Ambiguity*, ch. 3). The phrases in quotation in lines 34-6 are from Ophelia's lament over Hamlet's fall from his celebrity as the 'glass of fashion, and the mould of form' (*Hamlet* III.i.155) – i.e., mirror and pattern.

The Dream of Eugene Aram, the Murderer

First published as *The Dream of Eugene Aram* in 1829, in *The Gem*, a Christmas annual that Hood edited 1828-32, attracting such notable contributors as Lamb and Scott. He republished *The Dream* as a separate volume in 1831 (our text), with eight designs by W. Harvey (London: Charles Tilt) and a dedication to J. H. Reynolds including this sentence: 'you stand nearest to me in a stricter form of the brotherhood which the Dream is intended to enforce; I feel that I cannot inscribe it more appropriately or more willingly than to yourself'. Aram (1704–59) was a tutor (usher) at King's Lynn Grammar School for boys in Norfolk; Hood had heard the story of this uncommon criminal from a former pupil, James Burney (brother of Frances Burney), who had listened to Aram's anguished discourses and witnessed the scene described in the last stanza (*TLS*, 5 May 1945). Godwin alludes to this famous case in *Caleb Williams* (vol. III, ch. 3), citing the *Annual Register for 1759*: 'It signifies not what is the character of the individual at the hour of trial. How changed, how spotless and how useful avails him nothing. If they discover at the distance of fourteen ... years an action that ordains that his life shall be the forfeit.' Square brackets in the Preface are the editors'; in 1831 Hood followed the Preface with *The Defence of Eugene Aram* (pp. 11–17, slightly abridged from *Biographia Britannica*, reprinted in *Works*, VI.439–46), Aram's protest of innocence on the grounds of his character and of circumstantial evidence. The defence was unsuccessful and he was hanged at Newgate Prison. Inspired by Hood, Bulwer-Lytton published a three-decker novel on this story (1832).

Hood's ballad-like poem of a guilt-impelled narrative evokes Coleridge's *Rime of the Ancient Mariner* (1798). Keats's images of a world where 'youth grows pale, and spectre-thin' and where 'but to think is to be full of sorrow / And leaden-eyed despairs' (*Ode to a Nightingale*, 26–8) echo in lines 29–30. *The Death of Abel* (48), Mary Collyer's 1761 translation of Salomon Gessner's *Der Tod Abels* (1758), was immensely popular (twenty-seven editions by 1786 and at least nineteen more by 1845); the schoolboy, however, could not have read this translation in the moment of the poem's situation, which culminates in the arrest of Aram fourteen years after the date of the crime, 1745 (i.e., 1759). Milton's image of Sin (*Paradise Lost*, II.774-7) shapes lines 149-50. Thomas Cranmer, sixteenth-century English reformer and Protestant Divine, and Archbishop of Canterbury 1533-56, was tried for treason on the accession of Roman Catholic Queen Mary; convicted of heresy and condemned to death, he recanted, but the sentence was enforced; when asked to repeat his recantation at the stake, he refused, thrusting the hand (203-4) that had written it into the fire.

Domestic Asides; or, Truth in Parentheses

This double-voiced ditty was first published in *CA*, 1831, then in *HO*, pp. 72-4 (our text). Brussels (12) are carpets; dabby (16) means moist. *Comic Annual*, which Hood described in its preface as a 'Third Series of "Whims & Oddities"', was his sole means of support from 1830 to 1838.

Ode to Mr Malthus

First published in *CA*, 1832 (pp. 92-7); lightly revised for *HO* (our text), with *CA*'s 'King's/he' becoming 'Queen's/she' (25-6). In his treatise *On the Principle of Population As It Affects the Future Improvement of Society* (1798), a refutation of William Godwin's confidence in human progress towards happiness, Thomas Robert Malthus gave a dire statistical prophecy of intense competition over food supply as population increases, along with the deterioration in health and social values: 'Population, when unchecked, increases in a geometrical ratio. Subsistence increases only in an arithmetical ratio. A slight acquaintance with numbers will show the immensity of the first power in comparison of the second.' Hood was more inclined to Godwinian optimism than Malthusian pessimism, but the statistics were compelling: at the turn of the century, when the first census was taken, England's population was about 8 million; by 1831, Britain's was 14 million.

Pontypool (14) is a Welsh market-town; the steeple of St Mary's Church in Harrow (23) can be seen from quite far away. The nearby Humane Society watched the Serpentine (separating Hyde Park and Kensington Gardens) for potential drowners (45-9); Hood puns on the new financial institutions. Regent Square Church was founded by Scots clergyman Edward Irving, now lapsed from his initial popularity (65). Captain Swing is the icon of the farmworkers' riots of 1831 which attacked machinery and burnt the mills; the Foundling Hospital housed poor illegitimate cast-off children (75-8). On Easter Monday schoolboys received a glass of wine, two buns and a shilling from the Lord Mayor (79-81). Blue coats (81) identified students at charity-schools (Coleridge and Lamb attended Christ's

Hospital, the best known; others were in Islington, Wapping and Pall Mall, line 110). Marplot (83) is a character in Susanna Centlivre's popular comedy, *The Busie Body* (1709). The immensely domed St Paul's, the chief Anglican cathedral of London, hosted an annual service for the city's thousands of charity children (see Blake's *Holy Thursday* in *Songs of Innocence*). Richard Martin (105), MP for Galway (Ireland) 1801–26, supported humane treatment of animals and founded the RSPCA (known as 'Humanity Martin', he inspired one of Hood's *Odes and Addresses*, 1825; see *Mrs Fry*). The rich are compared to the fabled goose's golden egg (111); cajeput is medicinal oil (114); 'Orange Boven!' (118) is the cheer of the Orangemen, a political society formed in 1795 to defend Protestantism in Ireland; the pan-national cholera epidemic (122) reached England in October 1831 and raged in the British Isles from 1831 to 1833.

Sally Simpkin's Lament; or, John Jones's Kit-Cat-Astrophe

First publication and text: *CA*, 1834 (pp. 24–6); reprinted in *HO*. London's Kit-Cat Club, founded in 1700 by leading Whigs and including as members Addison, Steele and Congreve, met at the tavern of Christopher Cat, a cook famed for mutton-pies called kit-cats. A later meeting place in another home was so low-ceilinged that member-portraits had to be less than half-length; hence 'Kit-cat' described portraits of this kind. Astrophe parodically evokes Sidney's Astrophel, sonneteer-lover of Stella; it also puns 'a strophe' (stanza) and links into 'catastrophe'. A different version of the epigraph source, *Bryan and Pereene, A West-Indian Ballad*, appears in Percy's *Reliques*; John (Paul) Jones (3) is the name of the famous eighteenth-century naval adventurer, whose career involved slave-trading, smuggling and trading to the West Indies. A quarter's notice (32) is three-months' (a quarter-year) advance notice to vacate premises or resign a position.

A Waterloo Ballad

First published in *CA*, 1834 (our text); reprinted in *HO*. The celebrated victory of the Wellington alliance over Napoleon (June 1815) at Waterloo, a field near Brussels, with nearly 50,000 deaths (about half on each side), marked the end of nearly twenty-five years of continental warfare. The 92nd Regiment (8) heroically served Wellington here, and earlier in the Peninsular campaign against Napoleon (1808–14) (*SP*, p. 347). Peter Stone (4) is a jokey redundancy, the first name deriving from Latin for stone; the antecedent of 'mine' (12) is the pun 'beau'. Clubbe (*SP*, p. 347) credits the phrase 'March of Intellect' (19) to Southey's *Colloquies on the Progress and Prospects of Society* (2nd edn, London, 1831), but Hood probably knew the scepticism about 'a grand march of intellect' that Keats expressed in his letter to Reynolds, 3 May 1818. The *London Gazette* (39) carried official lists of battle casualties. A billet orders the compulsory lodging of military troops; 'every bullet has its billet' is an old saying attributed to King William (*OED*: 'only those are killed whose death Providence has ordained'); a crooked billet is a corrupt ballot (49–52). A cuirassier (53) is a heavily armoured cavalry man ('Cuirassiers all in steel for standing fight': *Paradise Regained*, III.328). Troops were paid four times a year, on Quarter-day (60). The Coldstream Guards (68) were a regiment first raised by Cromwell in 1650 for service in Scotland, the name taken from a border village where they lodged during a march to London in 1660; they served Wellington in the Peninsular campaign and Waterloo. The Hanoverian rulers (Georges I–IV, William IV, Victoria) descended from the Guelphs (74), the Papal faction in medieval Italy. Butcher (75) may recall Byron's reference to England as the country that 'butchered half the earth' (*Don Juan*, X.81); Clubbe (*SP*, p. 347) hears a near pun on Blücher, the Prussian general who was Wellington's Waterloo ally. New recruits got a shilling (12 old pence) to enlist (79); a tester (88) is a sixpence, a bed canopy and a piece of head armour; dress (90) means parade; mess (92) puns on military meals, with the corpse now the dish. To celebrate Napoleon's defeat and exile to Elba, in the summer of 1814 all of London's newly installed gas lamps were illuminated (96; cf. *Don Juan*, VII.44). The deft punning that begins at line 81 – 'shall' to 'shell' (with rhymes 'shall lie' with 'shell my') to 'Kernel' (colonel) – deploys words and wordplay that may tease at the regret B. W. Procter expressed about Hood's having 'given up serious poetry for the sake of cracking the shells of jokes which have not always a kernel' (letter to Kelsall, 25 March 1825, Donner, *Complete Works*, p. 597).

A Parental Ode to My Son, Aged Three Years and Five Months

First publication and text: *Blackwood's*, 41 (February 1837), pp. 172–3; reprinted in 'Domestic Poems', *CA*, 1837; Tom Hood was just over two at the first publication. The *CA* Preface has two epigraphs: 'It's hame, hame, hame' (from Allan Cunningham's version of an old Scots song, 'It's Hame, and It's Hame') and 'There's no place like home' (from 'Home, Sweet Home', a song frequently excerpted from John Howard Payne's opera, *Clari, the Maid of Milan*, which opened at Covent Garden, 8 May 1823). In this Preface Hood remarks that the English have few poems of such domestic nature:

The Muse does not sing like a cricket from our hearths; and with an abundance of home-made wines, we have scarcely a home-made song. This is a gap in our literature, a vacant shelf in our Family Library, that ought to be filled up. I cannot suppose that we are nationally deficient in the fireside feelings and homily [*sic*] affections which inspire a domestic ditty; – but take it for granted, that the vein exists, though it has not been worked. In the hope of drawing the attention of our Bards to the subject, I venture to offer a few specimens of Domestic Poems . . . (p. 155)

This account neglects women poets of this genre, especially Baillie and Hemans, though their poems are too serious to be termed 'ditties'. Other Romantic-era precedents for poems of parental affection and reflection on the very young (but without Hood's comedy) include Blake's *The Echoing Green*, *A Cradle Song* and *Nurse's Song* (*Songs of Innocence*, 1789); Baillie's *A Mother to Her Waking Infant* (1790; 1840); Coleridge's *Frost at Midnight* (1798 and after); Wordsworth's *To H.C.* (Hartley Coleridge) and 'Intimations' *Ode* (both 1807 and after). Puck (9) is the mischievous sprite of folklore; Hood's wife is named Jane; boys wore pinafores (frocks) until the age of five or so, when they donned breeches (14); Fays (20) are fairies.

I'm going to Bombay

Text: *HO*, pp. 169–70. The young woman, presumably jilted by Mr M. (60), is going to India (where many sought their fortunes) for another chance. Her special licence (79) is probably a general permission to marry without prior consent from her parents. Peter de Wint (11) was a renowned water-colourist (admired by Keats); ballet and dancing master James d'Egville (12) had studied with masters at the courts of Frederick the Great and Marie Antoinette, and choreographed ballets for the Royal Opera (he is alluded to in Praed's *My Partner*). Wilhelm Cramer (14) was a famous violinist and his son, Johann Baptist Cramer, a pianist and composer. Stanza 3 names various English resorts. Hyderapot (33) is probably Hyderabad, a city and former state in India famous for its diamonds. Stanza 6 suggests the impending culture-shock: rupees, doolies and bungalows are not edibles. Like doolies, palankeens (52) are palanquins, man-born litters.

Ode To the Advocates for the Removal of Smithfield Market

Text: *HO*, pp. 173–6. Smithfield, outside the City of London's north-west walls, was a horse-market and racing site in the fourteenth century, in the sixteenth century a site of cruel public executions during the reign of Bloody Queen Mary and a livestock market from 1614. The cause for removing cattle succeeded in 1855, but the market continued to thrive with dead meat and live poultry.

A band of fierce Barbarians, from the hills,
Rush'd like a torrent down upon the vale,
Sweeping our flocks and herds. The shepherds fled
For safety . . .

is the context of the epigraph from John Home's popular *Douglas, A Tragedy* (II.51–4), acted for decades after its first staging in 1756 (cf. the allusion to the same passage in *Miss Kilmansegg*, line 1804). Ovid's *Metamorphoses* (I.592 ff.) gives the story of Io, a maiden raped by Jupiter: to conceal her from discovery by Juno, he changed her into a heifer, a misery for her. Slaughter's (29) was a famous coffeehouse. Aries Taurus Virgo (33) are the constellations Ram, Bull, Virgin. Oxymuriate (44) is chlorine. *Night Thoughts* (1742–5) by Edward Young (64) was a long, immensely popular didactic poem. *OED* credits the punning *rump-us* (60) as the first use of this noun as a verb. George Wombwell's (67) itinerant wild animal menageries had one site at Hull's annual Wombwell Fair (on nearby Brown Cow Field); in 1825 he staged a controversial match between his prize lion Nero and six bull mastiffs; his 1830 show featured an elephant. In Psalm 22 David complains of being beset by the 'bulls of Bashan' (68), an ancient kingdom. In one of his adventures Tom Thumb (73) was swallowed by a cow; his was a common show-name for dwarfs and midgets. John Richardson (75, 92) famously staged performances at fairs, in particular Bartholomew Fair at Smithfield.

The Lament of Toby, the Learned Pig

Text: *HO*, pp. 539–40. With reputed abilities in spelling, reading, casting accounts, playing cards and even mind-reading, 'Toby, the Sapient Pig' was a famous exhibit in London, 1817; Wordsworth mentions seeing a prior prodigy at St Bartholomew's Fair in Smithfield, in 1804 (*The Prelude*, 1850: VII.708). Hood ventriloquizes Toby past his prime and facing ordinary pig-fate; his epigraph is ruefully recalled from Pope's *Essay on Criticism* (1711), Part 2.15. Blue (23) means not only sad but also educated (charity-school boys were termed 'blue-coats' after their uniforms, see also *Ode to Mr Malthus*) and haphazardly learned (learned women were derisively called 'blues'). Poignant puns ring in the surnames of Rev. Dr Dionysius Lardner (28), scientific writer and editor of *Cabinet Cyclopedia* and *Edinburgh Cabinet Library* (1830–44), Scots poet James Hogg (35), the Ettrick Shepherd (1770–1835), and scientist and essayist Francis Bacon (1561–1626) (36). Bunyan's allegorical *Pilgrim's Progress* (1678) ends in the world to come (42); the Seven Sages (43) of Greece are Thales of Miletus, Solon of Athens, Bias of Priene, Chilon of Sparta, Cleobulus of Lindus, Periander of Corinth, and Pittacus of Mitylene. Of the names in lines 53–4, Rev. Dr

Philip Bliss edited *Athenae Oxonienses* (1813–20), by Anthony à Wood; poet and church historian Henry Hart Milman (1791–1868) attended Oxford's Brasenose (61) College (and later as Poetry professor denounced Beddoes; see Beddoes to Kelsall, Donner, *Complete Works*, p. 604); Rev. Mr William Crowe (1745–1829) was associated with Oxford's New College (he, Bliss and Milman were all associated with *LM*: *Mem*, I.8); 'gown' (57) is academia. The influential Madras system (76) of late eighteenth-/early nineteenth-century education theorist Andrew Bell (1753–1832) used students as teaching assistants and monitors, and emphasized rote learning.

Miss Kilmansegg and Her Precious Leg

First published, serially, under 'Rhymes for the Times, and Reason for the Season', *NMM* 60 (September (pp. 83–99), October (pp. 255–63), November (pp. 392–403) 1840) and 61 (February 1841: pp. 261–72). Hood began to write for *NMM* in 1840, and in August 1841 he became editor at a salary of £300/annum, holding the post until January 1843. Text: *CA*, 1842, pp. 1–107 (there embellished with illustrations by John Leech); *SP* (p. 379) lists the few substantive variants. For this poem only, to prevent confusion with parenthetical line references, our notes enclose dates in [ ].

Hood's stanza is playfully innovative. The puns and wordplay of his title – Kill-man's egg, Leg-end – herald the ensuing symphony. While much of this play deploys wry allusions and topical references, most of the fun is deducible; for copious glosses, see *SP*, pp. 362–79. 'Kilmansegg' is probably not a direct reference to the Kielmannseggs, a German aristocratic family that came to London with the Hanoverian kings, but a name chosen for amenability to puns and rhymes – and to the anti-German sentiment that swirled around the 'vulgar' German aristocracy in Georgian England. This sentiment was partly reactivated by Queen Victoria's marriage to German Prince Albert in February 1840 (though Hood liked the couple) and fanned by Hood's personal dislike, developed during his recent German exile, 1835–7. William Caxton's *The Golden Legend* (cf. 2331) was a popular fifteenth-century collection of saints' lives, drawing on Jacobus de Voragine's thirteenth-century *Legenda Aurea*. The epigraph from Shakespeare (IV.iii.25–6) is uttered by Timon: in front of a cave where he has retreated in disgust from the parasites to his wealth, he discovers gold; he first reburies it in contempt of its worthlessness, then gives it to a banished Athenian general who uses it to finance an attack on Athens, conquering the city and wreaking vengeance on his and Timon's enemies.

HER PEDIGREE Among the many publications of biographer, historian and antiquarian Sir Nicholas Harris Nicolas (7) are ones on the English peerage, the history of knightly orders and genealogy. The exuberant auric catalogue includes the Golden Fleece that Jason found in Colchis (18); golden pippins, prized English apples (19); Hera's golden apples, guarded by the Hesperides (20); King Midas's golden touch, dissolved by his bath in the river Pactolus (34); the golden seals on Pope Gregory's Bulls (official proclamations) (40); *The Golden Ass* (47), Apuleius's (second-century AD) satirical romance; and the first chorus of Tasso's sixteenth-century romance *Aminta*, 'O bella eta del' oro!' (60), celebrating the mythic Golden Age. For Smithfield (39) see *Ode to the Advocates*, above. With trickery and deceit Jacob (65) increased the size of his cattle herd (Genesis 30:37–43). Muzio Clementi (73) [1752–1832] was a distinguished pianist, composer and conductor, as well as the founder of Clementi & Co., piano manufacturers and music publishers.

HER BIRTH Babbicome Bay (91) is a Devonshire resort, Natal Bay, an inlet of the Indian Ocean (91–2). George Henry Robins (104; cf. 1196–9) was a famous auctioneer; for a mess of pottage (105) Esau sells his birthright to younger brother Jacob (Genesis 25:29–34). Folklore hero Fòrtunatus (106) had a perpetual supply of gold; in Dekker's *Old Fortunatus* [1600], he is a beggar given a choice by Fortune between riches or wisdom, strength, beauty, health and long life; opting for riches, he has many adventures, but at their height Fortune ends his life. In Persian, Bulbul is a songbird, Gul (114–15) a rose. Plutus (136) is the Greek god of wealth, blind (indiscriminate), lame (slow to act), winged (fleeting). Expectant mothers take to bed, with straw mattresses (142); Otto (149) is attar (cf. 2142). In the Greek myth, Phaeton mismanaged his father Apollo's horses of the sun, scorching the earth and himself as a result (160–64); gildings (160) puns on geldings; a ship's cannon is usually a twenty-pounder (170). Marvellous portents accompanied the birth of Welsh magician Owen Glendower (175; cf. Shakespeare, *1 Henry IV*, III.i.12–42). Botargo is a relish of roe (189); the Rabelaisian babe (190) is the eponymous Gargantua [1534]. In *The Odyssey*, Book X, Circe (192) turns Ulysses's men into swine; the Naples Spider (197) is a tarantula, its bite linked to the tarantella, a lively dance. King John's scary night (199) is recounted in Shakespeare's *King John* (IV.ii.182–6); maroons (201) are fireworks. Croesus, the last king of Lydia and fabled to be the richest man on earth, had no dynastic issue (215). Gros de Naples (220) is heavy silk cloth; the drinks (223–4) are sweet liqueurs. The reign of Roman emperor Heliogabalus (priest of the sun) was infamously profligate, gluttonous, indecent, farcical (228–31); he was slain by his troops. Dalby's and gin (235) were used to dose children. Dantzic water (237) was also known as *goldwasser* (German: gold water), a liqueur originally made at Danzig. Cow-pox vaccination (242–3) started early in the nineteenth century; Viscount Althorp, the 3rd Earl Spencer (244) was a famous cattle-breeder.

HER CHRISTENING   The opening question is Juliet's lament over Romeo's surname (*Romeo and Juliet*, II.ii.43–4); Rev. William Dodd (248) came to the aid of penitent prostitutes and of imprisoned debtors; also a spendthrift and outlaw, he was hanged in 1777 for forging a bond for £4200, a celebrated case with many petitions in his behalf, one by Dr Johnson. Three Golden Balls (276) is the sign of a pawnbroker. In *Ali Baba and the Forty Thieves*, the brother's wife (287–8) is 'pozed' (puzzled) when a scale sent lent to Ali Baba's wife is returned with a gold coin stuck to the bushel-cup. William Combe's *The Devil Upon Two Sticks in England* (299) is a continuation [1790] of Le Sage's satirical novel, *Le Diable Boiteux* [The Lame Devil, 1707]; Samuel Foote's satire on physicians, *The Devil Upon Two Sticks*, was produced in 1768, two years after Foote's leg was amputated. 'N or M' (301) is the answer to the first question (name or names) asked in the Anglican catechism. The common phrase (322) is 'Cold of complexion, good of condition'. Dead-leaf satin (325) is very elegant. The Temple (334–5) is St Paul's Cathedral (cf. 1558–9). Elizabethan writer and explorer Sir Walter Ralegh (337) made several voyages to the Americas, his last an unsuccessful venture in search of gold (protests against his attack on Spanish settlements led to his arrest and execution on his return to England); the fabled South American city of gold 'El Dorado' (342) is mentioned in the lavish folio volumes of Alexander von Humboldt's *Voyage* [1805–34]. 'The dew of her youth' (358) echoes the Lord's description of David in Psalm 110:3. Rundell and Bridge's (375) were goldsmiths and diamond-jewellers to the Crown. *The Lass with the Golden Locks* (380) is an eighteenth-century poem by Christopher Smart. Lusting for Danaë (383), Zeus appeared to her as a shower of gold.

HER CHILDHOOD   In the game (423), invaders of a circled area cry, 'We're on Tom Tickler's ground, picking up gold and silver,' while trying to avoid capture by the player designated 'Tom Tickler'. 'Nix my Dolly' (430) (Never mind) is a thieves' phrase to call off a planned theft. French Protestants were slaughtered on the eve of St Bartholomew's Day (440), 24 August 1572, at the instigation of Catherine de Medici (namesake of the confection here). On top of the Fish Street Monument (451) commemorating the Great Fire of 1666 is a copper-gilt urn.

HER EDUCATION   Impressions (458) are proofs taken from an engraved plate before letters are inserted. L.S.D. (472) are pounds, shillings, pence. Novelist Maria Edgeworth (Beddoes's aunt) also wrote on education; poet Anna Barbauld also wrote didactic literature for children, as did Sarah Trimmer (478–80). Solon (501) is the renowned statesman, poet and lawmaker of Athens, *c.* 638–558 BC. The eighteenth-century volumes (523–

30) are Joseph Butler's *Sermons*, William Enfield's similar collection, John Entick's works, and Dr Johnson's *Dictionary*, the editions compared to lavishly produced gift-book annuals (so named); Johnson's rich attire (530–31), replete with gold-laced hat and waistcoat, at the première of *Irene* in 1749 is described by Boswell; Chambaud's *Fables* (532) was a famous primer for children; Lindley Murray's *English Grammar* (533) was a standard nineteenth-century school-text; Howell and James (537) sold expensive furniture. *I Promessi Sposi* (540) is Alessandro Manzoni's famous novel [1827], translated as *The Betrothed Lovers* [1828]; Coutts (542) is a major English bank; Golconda (544) is an old name for Hyderabad, an Indian district famed for diamonds (cf. *I'm going to Bombay*); Potosi in Peru is famed for silver mines (545). In 1520 Henry VIII met with Francis I of France in a gold-lamé draped pavilion on a field thence named Field of the Cloth of Gold (559).

HER ACCIDENT   In this mock-epic of Miss K.'s wild ride, Hood evokes horses rides, local and fabulous, and even John Higgins's wild ride in Hood's own *The Epping Hunt*. The fable (592) is one of Aesop's. Spinneys (598) are copses or thickets. Calmuck is Mongolian (613); to 'catch a Tartar' (a byword for savage) means 'to have an uncontrollable handful' (618). A tit (621) is a small horse or nag (cf. 1763); Tatt (621; the reading of *NMM* 60, p. 95; it is 'Tat' in *CA*) was the nickname of the eighteenth-century founder of Tattersall's, a principal market for riding and carriage horses. In German poet Gottfried Bürger's popular ballad, Lenore goes on a wild horse ride with her lover's ghost, terminating in his grave (631–2). Infamous eighteenth-century highwayman Dick Turpin made a great ride to York (634); Cossack leader Ivan Mazeppa, discovered in adultery, was tied naked to the back of a wild horse (637) and sent bounding across the plains – the ride a celebrated set piece in Byron's *Mazeppa* [1819] and a subsequent stage sensation. The Oaks (640) is a race for three-year-old fillies. Hood misremembers (643) Byron's phrase 'arrowy Rhone' (*Childe Harold*, III.lxxi). The Guelphs (649; cf. 1643), ancestors of the English Hanoverian rulers, were the Papal faction in medieval Italy, often at violent warfare with the Ghibellines, the aristocrats' party. By Hood's day, the gate at Hyde Park Corner (650–51) had been removed. The story of the Persian daughter (671) is in *The Arabian Nights*. Appointed surveyor-general of metropolitan roads in 1827, John McAdam gave his name to the even surface (684) he developed. Staffordshire is famed for porcelain (725); Singleton's was a popular eye ointment (727).

HER PRECIOUS LEG   This last chapter of the first *NMM* instalment opens with a quotation from Pope's *Epistle to Cobham* (150). St George's of Hanover Sq. (753) was favoured for fashionable weddings. Mexican gold was unalloyed (812); the Garter is English knighthood's highest order, its badge a garter buckled with gold (816). Scanderbeg (818) was the Turks' nickname for the fifteenth-century Albanian national hero Castriota, an opponent of Ottoman rule; Member (823) puns on MP.

HER FAME A Dead Weight (842) is that part of the national debt not connected to production or investment, including the half-pay and pensions of retired military officers. Slave-traders jettisoned diseased or frail Africans (851) in order to collect insurance on the lost cargo. William Burke was executed in 1829 for murders – usually by suffocation or strangulation (thus 'Burked') – to procure bodies to sell to medical schools; eighteenth-century political philosopher Edmund Burke's denunciation of the French Revolution in 1790, before the Terror, was famed for its prescience (862). To play the Turk (863) is to be violently treacherous; Goldsmith (865) is eighteenth-century writer Oliver Goldsmith. The Royal Exchange (for merchants) was located in Change Alley (869; it burned down in 1838 and would be rebuilt 1842–4); biblical chronology was controversially contested by recent fossil discoveries (870–72). Greenwich and Chelsea were charity hospitals for military pensioners (873). The terms in line 887 are from the game of rugby. Belles of Wapping, a tawdry dockside district, were prostitutes, who also frequented St Giles's (see *Mrs Fry* above), along with thieves and adventurers (899–900).

HER FIRST STEP Kerseymeres (912) are woollen trousers or hose. In 1835 the pro-removal faction of the Cherokees signed a treaty obligating the entire tribe to move west of the Mississippi, in exchange for payment from the US government; a cab is a carriage, a cob is a horse (932). Twenty-year-old Prince Leeboo (939) of the Pelew Islands died of smallpox on a visit to London in 1784; the scion (940) was not he, however, but King Liholiho of the Sandwich Islands (Kamehameha II), who visited London with his queen in May 1824; they both caught measles and died there in July; a lion (943) is a celebrity.

HER FANCY BALL This chapter ends the second *NMM* instalment. After Theobald Mathew (947) signed a pledge of temperance in April 1838, hundreds of thousands followed his example. With a pun, 'gutted' (993) means robbed; smalls (998) are knee-breeches. Shacabac (1017) is a beggar in *The Arabian Nights*; Tom, Jerry and Springheel'd Jack (1018) are characters in Pierce Egan's *Life in London* [1820–21]; a cover abets a pickpocket (1023). *Whang Fong; or, The Clown of China* [1812] is a pantomime by Charles Dibdin jun.; *Il Bondocani; or, The Caliph Robber* [1802] is a comic opera by T. J. Dibdin; at the end of Mozart's opera [1787] the Spectre drags Don Giovanni down to hell (1041–6). The Order (1066) is the Garter (cf. *Her Precious Leg*). In chess, a check (1077) is a threat to the king. The episode of the Hebrews' Golden Calf (1094, with a pun) is given in Exodus 32. Leg-bail (1099) means escape; Leg (1100) is short for Blackleg, a dishonest wagerer on horses. Troy weights (1117) are the standard system for precious metals and gemstones. Thomas Moore wrote the popular song cited in lines 1133–4, based on an Irish legend of a maid, adorned in jewels and costly dress and bearing a wand topped by an exquisite ring, who crossed the country unmolested, Erin's sons too honourable 'to be tempted by woman or gold'; Hood illustrated it (1135) in travesty in *WO 1*. Tom Tug (1144) is the honest young hero who wins the gardener's daughter in *The Waterman* [1774] by Charles Dibdin Sen.; a Bonze (1146) is a Buddhist monk; a *Figuranté* is a member of the *corps de ballet* (1156); bread (1165) is coins. Hopper (1176) puns on a brewer's vat. The forlorn (1177) were the starving Irish; 'Money Musk' (1182) is a country dance tune. *The Castle of Otranto* (1187) is Horace Walpole's popular gothic novel [1764]; the Mint puns on a common garnish for leg of lamb (1191–2; cf. 1752). The Great Enchanter (1196 ff.) was renowned auctioneer, George Henry Robins. The feast (1203 ff.) includes sherberts and exotic pineapples, the luxury evoking *Gunter's Confectionary Oracle, containing receipts for desserts* [1830]; conners (1211) are critics.

HER DREAM Cupidities (1260) are not cupids but icons of Avarice and Greed. 'Where ignorance is bliss, / 'Tis folly to be wise,' wrote Gray (1270) in *Ode on a Distant Prospect of Eton College* (99–100). In the old myth, two drowned lovers were transformed into kingfishers (Halcyons), with the gods calming the seas for one month each year that they might nest (1282 ff.). Sleepers (1295) support the rails of a railway. Verjuice (1315) is an acid liquor made from unripe fruit. Organ of Veneration (1384) refers to the phraseology of German physician and phrenologist Franz Joseph Gall [1758–1828] for the top, reverential part of the brain.

HER COURTSHIP The first stanza jauntily elaborates the end of *Paradise Lost* (XII.637 ff.). 'Tibbie Fowler' (1441) is a Scottish folksong. Sparks (1447) are dandies; Faustus (1451), the legendary medieval conjurer who trades his soul to the devil (Old Nick) to gain extraordinary powers, is treated in Marlowe's late-sixteenth-century drama *Dr Faustus*, and Goethe's dramatic poem *Faust* [completed in 1832]. A packet's fore-cabin (1466) offers a cheap passage; the anti-Jew-German portrait is clinched by the simile of the Rabbin (1470), or Rabbi (*OED*); for Hood's contempt of 'Jew Germans, and German Jews', see *Mem*, I.156, 250. A stock (1476) is a sword; frogs (1477) are ornamental fastenings, the image evoking the old ballad *Froggy Went A-courting*. Retail (1485) means minor or petty. Proverbs of France (1488) are morally pointed plays. A crooked tester (1522) is a bent sixpence; Cis (1526) is a dairymaid; Rogers & Co. (1535) was an up-market haberdasher.

HER MARRIAGE This chapter ends the third *NMM* instalment. The Golden Horn (1549), an inlet of the Bosporus, is the harbour of Istanbul, port of rich trade; Cleopatra greets her soon-to-be lover and husband Antony, sitting on a 'barge . . . like a burnished throne', its deck of 'beaten gold' (Shakespeare, *Antony and Cleopatra*, II.ii.193-4, drawing on Plutarch's *Life of Antony*) (1550-51). A golden dragon and a golden cock (1556) graced, respectively, the weather-vanes on the church-spires of St Mary-le-Bow (Cheapside) and St Bartholomew the Great (West Smithfield), both ornaments refurbished in early 1800s. At the junction of the first and second storeys of the 125-foot steeple of St James Piccadilly (1572) is a clock (as well as a gilded figure of St James). Adam Smith's founding treatise of modern capitalism, *The Wealth of Nations* [1776], was held to advocate the pursuit of unfettered self-interest (1590). Dresden (1593) is a famed centre for porcelain; in Revelation (20:8), Gog (1596) and Magog represent enemies of God; in British legend, they are the sole survivors of a monstrous race, brought in chains to London and enslaved as porters at the royal palace, on the site of the Guildhall, where their 14-foot effigies flanked the doors of its council chamber. The Polar Bear (1602), with a pun, is Ursa Major. In 1745, £30,000 was set on the head of the Young Pretender (1624-5), Bonnie Prince Charlie (Stuart), a popular but unsuccessful claimant to the throne who fled to the continent and ended his years in Rome as a drunk, expatriate 'Count'. In 1743, on his famous voyage around the world, Admiral George Anson (1631-2) captured a treasure-laden Spanish galleon bound from Mexico to Manila. 'Beaux . . . Ideals'(1652-3) puns on the aesthetic of the beau ideal. Crow (1658), a thief's look-out, puns on crowbar (also called a jimmy or jemmy); in the May-day sports of chimney-sweeps, Jack i' the Green (1659) is enclosed in a leaf-covered wicker pyramid (*OED*). The buzz universal (1665) comically alludes to the convocation of fallen angels in *Paradise Lost* (I.767 ff.). The Hippocampi (1736) are Neptune's seahorses; grampus is whale (1739). Butchers, whose chief place of slaughter and sale was Whitechapel Market, wore blue aprons (1769-70). Yellow boys (1775) were gold coins. The Golden Farmer (1787) was a pub in Surrey.

HER HONEYMOON The 'moon . . . rose last night, round as my shield', says Norval (1804), a valiant warrior in John Home's *Douglas* (II.49); Bude (1805) was a new kind of gas-burner. Savory's (1823) was a famous dealer of gold- and silverware; other London locales are named in 1829-30. In *Remarks on the Rape of the Lock* [1714], neo-classical critic John Dennis takes offence (1881) at Pope's puns for 'frequently shock[ing] not only the dictates of *Good Sense*, and the Rules of *true Pleasantry*, but those of *Grammar* and *common English*'; they 'please weak Capacities with a momentary Glittering'. 'The young May Moon is beaming love' (1900), begins one of Thomas Moore's songs. 'O rus, O rus!' (1937; 'O, the countryside!') begins a song in Horace's *The Town Mouse and the Country Mouse* (*Satires*, II.6). Great flocks of sheep graze in the countryside of Leipzig (1953); Vauxhall is the London pleasure-garden and entertainment centre (1954). Piquet (2008) is a card-game. The French phrase 'faire des châteaux en Espagne' is analogous to 'build castles in air' (2017-18). The barber of Beaumarchais's comedy *The Barber of Seville* [1775] and Rossini's opera *Il Barbiere di Siviglia* [1816] schemes to assist Count Almaviva's courtship of Rosina (2027-8).

HER MISERY 'To gild refinèd gold, to paint the lily' is 'wasteful and ridiculous excess', Salisbury counsels King John, who was insisting on a second coronation (2064-5; Shakespeare, *King John*, IV.ii.11-16). Aqua regia (2091) is so called because its mixture of acids can dissolve the 'noble' metals, gold and platinum. In the Sermon on the Mount, Christ admonishes, do not 'cast . . . your pearls before swine' (Matthew 7:6) (2103). Fancy gentlemen are pimps (2125); in German, 'wenus' sounds like 'Venus' (2127). Making a book (2128) is placing bets; boxer (miller) Daniel Mendoza [1764-1836] (2134), the first Jewish champion, revolutionized the prize ring (mill); Byron admired him, and he later became a celebrated boxing instructor, his school widely patronized by the nobility (Nat Fleischer, *Ring Record Book and Boxing Encyclopedia*). In Bunyan's *Pilgrim's Progress* [1678], Giant Despair (2148) imprisons wayfarers Christian and Hopeful in Doubting Castle. In the Count's ledger, Stultz's was a fashionable tailor, Manton and Nock's were gunsmiths, blue rocks are pigeons, buskins and socks are theatrical footware (2158-63). Flash (2174) is slang (street language); a badger is a bank account (2175). On Walpurgis Night (30 April), just before English nun St Walpurgis (2178) converted the Germans to Christianity, fable has it that the devil and witches held a festival in the mountains, the subject of a scene in Goethe's *Faust*, Part I; muffles are boxing gloves; bulldogs were for bull-baiting, a sport outlawed in 1835 (2179).

HER LAST WILL In the Scots ballad *Are Ye Sure the News is True?* (2206-7), Colin's 'very foot has music in't / As he comes up the stair'. Taken off (2221) also means killed. Gertrude begs Hamlet, 'speak to me no more,' for his words are 'like daggers' (*Hamlet*, III.iv.95-6) (2235).

HER DEATH Keats's *Ode on Melancholy* mentions the death's-head moth (2272), with skull-like markings; 2280 ff. renders a sour parody of Madeline's preparations for an erotic dream-encounter in Keats's *Eve of St Agnes* (stanzas 22–7). The Thane (2317) is Macbeth, murderer of King Duncan in Shakespeare's play. Dick Whittington, thrice Lord Mayor of London between 1397 and 1420, known for his liberal spending on himself and his subjects, came to the city, according to legend, on hearing that its streets were paved with gold (2331–3). At death, 'the golden bowl [is] broken' (Ecclesiastes 12:6) (2366). Felo de Se (2372), medieval Latin for 'evildoer on self', is accidental or deliberate suicide; in English law, such a crime entails penalties against the estate of the deceased.

HER MORAL   Good Queen Bess (Elizabeth I) and Bloody Mary (2388–9) were both children of Henry VIII.

Lear

First publication and text, *Poems* (1846), II.37; Tom Hood thinks it was written before 1842 (*Works*, VIII.254). The eponym of Shakespeare's tragedy was often compared with George III.

The Song of the Shirt

Hood's most famous, most popular poem (Rossetti has a facsimile from Hood's MS as a stiff-page plate after his Preface) first appeared in *Punch, or the London Charivari* 5 (16 December 1843, the Christmas number), having been rejected by three other journals (*SP*, p. 390); the editor not only overruled his colleagues' protest that *Punch* should remain a comic magazine, but featured the poem on a separate page (p. 260). The immediate inspiration was a report in *The London Times* (26 October 1843, p. 7) that reverberated in that newspaper over the next two months. A 'wretched-looking woman named Biddell, with a squalid, half-starved infant at her breast', had been charged with 'unlawfully pawning several articles of wearing apparel which she had been intrusted to make', the distraught prisoner explaining that 'January last her husband was killed in the docks, having fallen down the hold of a vessel on board of which he had been employed, leaving her with a child of two years old and pregnant of the infant she then held in her arms. . . . she had endeavoured to support herself and two children by her needlework, but the remuneration . . . was so wretched that she could not do so, and had been actually obliged to pawn things to procure dry bread for herself and her children'. The judge was astonished to learn she was paid only 1¼ pence for a shirt and '7 [pence] a pair' for trousers, even as her foreman claimed that an 'honest and industrious' worker could make a good living, which he placed at 7 shillings (84 pence) a week. 'A gentleman present . . . remarked that many of the advertising tailors drove a large trade, and acquired good profits out of the very vitals of the poor by the wretched prices at which they got them to make up garments. 9 [pence] and 1 [shilling], he understood, were the prices for making up fashionable trousers and waistcoats, and the poor people, as in the last case, were obliged to find their own thread.' Refusing to send Biddell to prison, the judge decided instead to remand her and her children to a workhouse, where they might stay together. Text: *Punch*.

Lines 14–15 refer to the Mohammedan designation of women as creatures without souls. Clubbe compares lines 27–8 to Scott's 'It's not fish ye're buying. It's men's lives' (*The Antiquary*, ch. 11) and notes that details of lines 43–6 are drawn from a letter in *The Times*, 31 October 1843 (*SP*, p. 391). Twit (64) is one of Hood's most famous, bitter puns (reproach, taunt, twitter). *CPW* inserts the following stanza after (and as) the penultimate, with a note that it was omitted in *Punch* (p. 626); but the MS (facsimile in *Mem*, I, after p. xx) shows that it came before:

> Seam, & gusset, & band,
> Band & gusset & seam!
>   Work, work, work,
> Like the Engine that works by Steam!
> A mere machine of iron & wood
>   That toils for Mammon's sake –
>   Without a brain
> ~~And has not a head~~ to think, & craze
>   Or a heart to feel – & break!

The emerging Marxist theme of worker as machine was punningly voiced by Shelley's address to workers in *The Mask of Anarchy* (1832): 'ye for them [tyrants] are made / Loom, and plough, and sword, and spade' (st. xli). The appallingly cruel exploitation of milliners and seamstresses would soon be detailed by Friedrich Engels in *The Condition of the Working Class in England* (1845; trans. W. O. Henderson and W. H. Chaloner, Stanford CA, 1958), at the end of ch. 8, 'The Proletariat', with a lukewarm footnote on Hood's *Song*: 'a fine poem . . . which wrung many compassionate tears from the daughters of the bourgeoisie'. But the poem was more than a sentimental sensation; it 'ran through the land like wildfire', was widely reprinted, sung in the streets, read in churches, translated into foreign languages, printed on handkerchiefs (*Mem*, II.182–3; cf. p. 191), and it tripled the circulation of *Punch* (Hobman, p. 401). For the topicality of this and following poems, see Alvin Whitley, 'Thomas Hood and *The Times*' (*TLS*, 17 May 1957, p. 309). When a fund was raised for a monument at Kensal Green Cemetery – bearing a crest, designed by Hood, representing 'a heart pierced with a needle, threaded with silver tears' (an engraving appears on the title-page of *Memorials*) – donations included 'trifling sums from Manchester, Preston, Bideford, and Bristol – from a few poor needle-women – from seven dressmakers – from twelve poor men' (*Mem*, I.xvii). Hood's self-chosen epitaph was 'He sang the Song of the Shirt'.

The Workhouse Clock

First publication and text: *Hood's Magazine and Comic Miscellany* 1.4 (April 1844), pp. 313–15, the lead poem, 'By the Editor.' These houses, dozens in London, were dismal sites of required labour by those on public relief. The New Poor Laws of 1834 divided this class into those who lived and worked in the houses and those 'outdoor', i.e. able to live in their homes and work elsewhere (the Labouring Classes, line 6); the days were long, 16–18 hours. Clubbe (*SP*, p. 391) thinks the house in question is St Marylebone's, London's largest; an article in *The Times* titled 'Christmas-Day in the Workhouses' (26 December 1842, p. 6) reported 5781 outdoor poor, over double the previous Christmas's population. Whitechapel (60) was London's main meat market; Cornhill (61) is the former site of the Corn (grain) Exchange; Poultry (62) is a district in London (where Hood was born), formerly the site of a poultry market; Bread and Milk Streets (64–5) are in Cheapside, a market district from medieval times; Ludgate Mart (66) in London was home to up-market shops.

The Bridge of Sighs

First publication and text: *Hood's Magazine* 1.5 (May 1844), pp. 414–17. Hood hoped this poem would attract investors: 'I have done a poem for the Mag some say beats The "Shirt",' he wrote to J. T. J. Hewlett, adding, 'If the moneyd man, does take to it – we will have a capital campaign' (April 1844; *Letters*, ed. Morgan, p. 604); the wide admiration for this poem (by Browning and Thackeray among others) is reflected in Rossetti's decision to open his edition, *Poetical Works*, with it. The sin to which Hood refers is the woman's suicide, a mortal sin.

The covered Bridge of Sighs in Venice conveyed convicts from the court in the Doges' Palace to San Marco Prison and often to execution; 'I stood in Venice, on the Bridge of Sighs; / A palace and a prison on each hand', Byron memorably opens *Childe Harold's Pilgrimage*, Canto IV (1818). Though the fallen woman is a generic figure, Hood's immediate inspiration was the case of Mary Furley, recounted in *The Times* from late March to mid May 1844. Unable to support herself and her two children by making shirts at less than 2 pence each as an inmate of the Bethnal Green Workhouse, and fearing the parish would separate her children from her (one of them quite sick she was not allowed to care for), this middle-aged woman plunged with her youngest, an eighteen-month-old son, into the Regent's Canal. She was saved (at her hearing, she said that 'death would have been a happy release to her, and she very much regretted that she had been rescued from a situation which must in a few moments have terminated her earthly sufferings'), but her son died. Without defence counsel, she was tried for murder and attempted suicide, and sentenced to death; a public outcry postponed her execution and eventually the sentence was commuted to transportation for seven years. This poem is connected to *The Song of the Shirt* through the plight of seamstresses, who (Engels reports) 'must put down as a deposit part of the value of the materials entrusted to them. . . . they can do this only by pawning a portion of the goods . . . and the employer knows very well that this is what happens. When the material in pawn is redeemed it can only be done at a loss, which falls on the needle-women. If they cannot redeem the material, they have to appear before a Justice of the Peace. . . . [a] poor girl, who got herself into this plight, drowned herself in a canal in August 1844' (Engels in *The Condition of the Working Class in England*; Henderson and Chaloner also note the relevant newspaper reports, p. 239).

Hood romantically converts several details: the suicide is solitary (no infanticide) and it succeeds; its victim is not middle-aged but young; its locale is the Thames's Waterloo Bridge (in one of London's poorer districts, a favourite of suicides) rather than a canal (*The Times*, 26 March 1844, p. 8). The epigraph is from Gertrude's report of Ophelia's possibly suicidal drowning (*Hamlet*, IV.vii.184). Baudelaire translated the poem and titled a prose-poem in *Le Spleen de Paris* (1869), in English, 'Anywhere Out of This World' (70-71); Poe quoted it entire in *The Poetic Principle* (see *Fair Ines*, above), remarking, 'The vigour of this poem is no less remarkable than its pathos. The versification [chiefly dactylic dimeter], although carrying the fanciful to the very verge of the fantastic, is nevertheless admirably adapted to the wild insanity which is the thesis of the poem.' In an earlier essay, Poe declared that 'the death . . . of a beautiful woman is, unquestionably, the most poetical topic in the world', because it so closely allies 'melancholy' to 'Beauty' (*The Philosophy of Composition*, *Graham's Magazine*, April 1846).

Stanzas (Farewell, Life!)

Hood's last poem was written in January 1845; first publication and text: *Hood's Magazine* 3 (February 1845), p. 142, signed 'H.'. Hood died on 3 May, after nearly five months of confinement to his bed.

WINTHROP MACKWORTH PRAED

Abbreviations:
1824: *The Etonian*, 3 vols. (4th edn, London: Henry Colburn and Charles
    Knight, 1824)
LM: *London Magazine* (monthly)
LS: *The Literary Souvenir, or Cabinet of Poetry and Romance*, ed. Alaric
    Watts (annual)
NMM: *The New Monthly Magazine*, ed. Thomas Campbell, 1820–30
Poems: *The Poems of Winthrop Mackworth Praed*, ed. Derwent Coleridge
    (1885 edn)
SP: *Selected Poems of Winthrop Mackworth Praed*, ed. Kenneth Allott
Young: *Political and Occasional Poems*, ed. George Young

          *   *   *

from *THE ETONIAN*

Laura

First published in *The Etonian* 1 (1820); text: *1824*, I.64–71; reprinted in
Poems, II.65–74. The epigraphs are from Spenser's description of Venus
in her Temple (*Faerie Queene*, IV.x.40 and 43). In the tradition of Popean
satire, Praed shapes his couplets with tonal antitheses and zeugma-crafted
syntaxes. 'Laura' is a conventional name for a beloved, most famously in
Petrarch's *Rime*, which involves the homophones of 'lauro' (laurel, the
poet's badge), 'l'oro' (gold) and 'l'aura' (halo), 'l'ora' (the hour he met her)
with the name; Laura dies early in his sequence of poetry, after which she
matters (even more) as spiritual mediatrix. Praed refuses this tradition
(though he lightly pays tribute with the pun of 'laurel' at line 202), giving
his Laura instead the genealogy of the *femme fatale*, whose ageing, fall from
grace and death liberate the poet. The 'fane' of worship (11) involves
pointed puns on 'fain' and 'feign' (though there is a final romantic elegy).
Laura is also a social arbiter: Sway (30; cf. 61), meaning 'influence' and
'reign', obliquely refers to physical flirtation. Women's torsos were cramped
into desirable shape by whalebone stays (42). The captain (75 ff.) bores
Laura with tales of the famously bloody victories of Waterloo (1815) and
the siege of Badajoz (1811), both campaigns led by Arthur Wellesley, first
Duke of Wellington, whom Praed's poems tend to treat as a heroic military
victor and patriotic opponent of Parliamentary Reform (which Praed also
opposed). A billet (90) is a compulsory order for the lodging of troops; a
billet-doux a love-letter; the soldier who hides in a nunnery is a staple of

romance adventure; an escalade is a ladder-assisted assault on a walled structure (91). The sonneteering suitor William Lisle (162 ff.) winks at William Lisle Bowles, whose *Fourteen Sonnets* (1789) are often credited with the revival of the form in the Romantic era, praised by Coleridge in the first chapter of *Biographia Literaria* (1817), but loathed by Beddoes: 'throw Bowles into the fire', he wrote to Kelsall (Donner, *Complete Works of Beddoes*, p. 592). Bowles was also famous for an edition of Pope (1806) with a prefatory essay deprecating his poetical and moral character: the 'Bowles controversy' erupted in 1819 when Thomas Campbell attacked this representation, Bowles defended himself, Isaac D'Israeli re-attacked Bowles, the reviews weighed in, and Byron joined the fray (1821), along with many others. Praed's own notes to line 170 cite Horace, *Satires*, II.vii.117 ('Either the man is raving or he is composing poetry,' says Horace's slave) and Pope, *Epistle to Dr Arbuthnot* (1735), line 4. Cypress, willow and rue (189, 192) are emblems of mourning. The phrase 'evil hour' (195) glances at the 'evil hour' of Eve's fall (*Paradise Lost*, IX.780).

To Julia

First published in *The Etonian* 3 (1820); text: *1824*, I.242-7; reprinted in *Poems*, II.58-64. Praed's sister Susan made her début in 1822 at a ball in one of the public rooms at Teignmouth. Praed knew Henry Luttrell's light verse in octosyllabic couplets, *Advice to Julia, A Letter in Rhyme* ('excellent in gay poetry', Byron tells John Murray, 'very good indeed'), which appeared in 1820; a great wit, Luttrell (?1765–1851) was a popular companion for dinner and travel. Praed's comic cautionary epistle to Julia, about to make her début in London, adds to the old country-v.-city debate (rural peace/simplicity/tedium, versus urban strife/decadence/excitement) a 'paradise lost' – and elaborates both with a system of values that equates simplicity and good home-making with the truly feminine, and its false, decadent forms with social vanity. Lyce's Academy (22) travesties the Lyceum, the suburban gymnasium of ancient Athens where Aristotle taught young men philosophy. Camilla (41) is the devotee to Diana (goddess of the hunt) who, Virgil reports, could run over a field of corn without bending the blades (*Aeneid*, VII.808); another likely reference is Frances Burney's comic romance, *Camilla, or a Picture of Youth* (1796), a popular female coming-of-age novel. Blue-stockings (72) are doves, with a glance at the common term of contempt for women of learning and letters who (unlike Praed) could not attend universities. Quadrille (74 ff.), a popular eighteenth-century card game, was yielding to whist by the century's end. A Cantab (122) is a Cambridge student. *Ton* (132), a French-imported term, means prevailing fashion or vogue. For whalebone (165), see note on *Laura* line 42. Winning

the vole (174) is a triumph at cards. The whipper-in (180) is the assistant
huntsman who drives in the hounds.

The Bachelor

First published in *The Etonian* 7 (1821); text: *1824*, II.256–64; reprinted
in *Poems*, II.79–89. This sketch anticipates the portrait of Quince in *An
Every-day Character* (*NMM*, February 1829). Line 8 echoes Wordsworth's
praise of his wife in *She Was a Phantom of Delight* (1807): 'A perfect Woman,
nobly planned, / To warn, to comfort, and command' (27–8). A Congé is
a formal departure; the Cam flows though Cambridge (17). Praed's note to
line 57 probably alludes to the opening of the 'Poem' proper in Swift's
Verses on the Death of Dr S[wift] (1731), 72–91 (*SP*, p. 335), also in iambic
tetrameter couplets. Granta (105) is the name for the River Cam south of
Cambridge. 'The feast of stomach – and of soul' (124) parodies the descrip-
tion of his Grotto-pleasures that Pope renders in his imitation of *The First
Satire of the Second Book of Horace*:

> There my retreat the best companions grace,
> . . .
> There St John mingles with my friendly bowl
> The Feast of Reason and the Flow of soul. (125–8)

Joseph Hume (153) was a Radical in Parliament (a favourite target). The
epitaph-reading of 240 ff. glances at the unknown 'Village-Hampden' in
Gray's *Elegy Written in a Country Churchyard* (57). The 'poet' quoted in
272–3 is Gray, the last stanza of *Ode on a Distant Prospect of Eton College*
(Praed attended Eton, 1814–21).

* * *

from *THE BRAZEN HEAD*

In the spring of 1826, Praed helped Charles Knight launch *The Brazen
Head*, a weekly paper 'to amuse the Town, during the depression that
followed on the commercial crisis of 1826' (*Young*, p. 72, citing Knight's
Autobiography); it lasted for four issues. In Robert Greene's comedy, *The
Honourable History of Friar Bacon and Friar Bungay* (1594), Friar Bacon
of Brasenose College Oxford makes a brazen head to deliver lectures and
utter philosophy. When the Head finally speaks (IV.i/scene ix), it utters,
serially, three statements – 'Time is!', 'Time was!', 'Time is past!' – all of
which Bacon misses while asleep; after the third, a hand appears in a flash
of lightning and breaks the Head with a hammer. Greene's source, an
anonymous mid-sixteenth-century prose romance, *The Famous Historie of*

Fryer Bacon, was reprinted in 1815; 'Now, like Friar Bacon's brazen head, I've spoken / "Time is, Time was, Time's past", a chymic treasure,' muses the narrator of Byron's *Don Juan* (I.217). Three *Chaunts* are printed in *Young*, pp. 72–83 (the one we identify as II is there identified as III).

Chaunt I

First publication and text: *The Brazen Head*, 26 April 1826; reprinted with variants in *Poems*, II.164–8. 'This poem reflects the spirit, or the decline of spirit, which characterized party politics in the later days of Lord Liverpool's ministers, and of Tory domination' (*Young*, p. 72). The prologue is Praed's elaboration: treasure-robbing adventurer Trophonius was swallowed up by the earth, and after his death was consulted as an oracle in a cave; his suppliants were famously melancholy after their news. Bubble (23 ff.) is slang for hoax or cheat. Apollo's oracles were interpreted by his priests (hierophants). 'Rule, Britannia, rule the waves' (51) opens the chorus of James Thomson's popular ode. The politicians (55–6) are: Joseph Hume (1777–1855), a Tory when he entered Parliament in 1812 but from 1818 to 1855 a Radical (see also *The Bachelor* and *The Speaker Asleep*); Henry Peter Brougham (1778–1868), lawyer, and Whig MP (1810–12, 1816–30), an important force in reform legislation and abolition, advocate of London University, and founder in 1826 of the Society for the Diffusion of Useful Knowledge (SDUK), to promote adult education for the sake of improving national productivity (Beddoes called him 'the greatest of Englishmen . . . England's future . . . a bright hope for the whole of humanity' (Donner, *Complete Works*, p. 739); and George Canning (1770–1827), at various points from 1794, MP, Foreign Secretary, and Leader of the House of Commons (1822–7), and who, as a leader of progressive Tories, promoted liberal policies at home and non-intervention in liberalizing movements abroad (Praed admired him). A maggot (58) is a fantastic or eccentric idea. The Catholic and Eastern Orthodox churches recognize seven sacraments, Reformed churches two (62). The stanza that begins at line 65 refers to the Catholic Relief Bill in the House of Lords, which the Bishop of Chester (Dr Charles James Blomfield) and Paget (Marquis of Anglesey, Lord Lieutenant of Ireland) both opposed. Wellington and other heroes of the war against France who also opposed it would have been executed by burning in Queen Mary's day. Colnbrook (77), west of London, is where Praed spent his early school-days. Thieves, prostitutes and beggars haunted the district of St Giles (89); the House of Commons met at St Stephen's Chapel, Westminster (89–90).

Chaunt II

First publication and text: *The Brazen Head*, 10 May 1826 (the last issue). The first stanza concludes with a blending of Ecclesiastes 1:9 into the Head's utterances. Fricandeaus (15) are meats roasted and glazed in their own juices; cockchafers (18) are scarab-like beetles; extreme Tory John Scott, Earl of Eldon (19), was Lord Chancellor 1801-27; Lord Clifford (20) was a Roman Catholic. MP Richard 'Humanity' Martin (27) founded the RSPCA, for the protection of animals; John Manton & son (30) were gunmakers to the royal family. Singer and actress Mme Lucia Elizabeth Vestris (1797-1856) had recently played Ariel in *The Tempest*, Apollo in *Midas* and Rosalind, a part with a long transvestite phase, in *As You Like It* (37).

*   *   *

from *THE NEW MONTHLY MAGAZINE*

Time's Song

First publication and text: *NMM* 17 (October 1826), p. 415, signed 'Φ.'; reprinted in *Poems*, I.337-8, with 'riding' instead of 'rushing' (4), thus losing the chime with 'crush'd' (5). In a formal mimesis of the traditional figure of 'wingèd Time', Praed deploys an unusual iambic heptameter line. Organized by caesurae into tetrameter and trimeter units marked by internal rhymes, the line evokes the ballad stanza; Wordsworth would use it in 1842 for *The Poet's Dream* and *The Norman Boy*, and Scott used it for *The Noble Moringer*. When Praed's line does not break this way, it recalls the impressive 'fourteeners' of George Chapman's celebrated translation of Homer's *Iliad* (*c.* 1611). Praed's metrics deftly play to both these traditions. Myrtle (11) is the emblem of Venus.

Good-Night to the Season

First publication and text: *NMM* 20 (August 1827), pp. 119-20, signed 'Φ.'; reprinted in *Poems*, II.179-83. The epigraph paraphrases Hamlet's gloating after Claudius walks out of *The Murder of Gonzago*: 'For some must watch, while some must sleep; / Thus runs the world away' (III.ii.276-7). Brighton (7) is a seaside resort; Cowes (8) the setting for yacht races; Commons and Peers (18) are members of Parliament's House of Commons and House of Lords. Inigo Jones (26) is the Renaissance architect and theatrical designer. A hell (33) is a gambling club; bones (36) are probably dice. Boodle's (53) was a fashionable club; 'Batti, Batti' (56) is a song from the first act of Mozart's *Don Giovanni*. Frances Ayton and Guiditta Pasta (63–4) were opera singers of the day; Pasta, for whom Pacini and Bellini wrote prima donna parts, was especially celebrated ('a most extraordinary singer, with tones more like those of an organ than any human creature', Beddoes wrote to Procter in 1824; 'divine' said Mary Shelley, who confessed 'adoration': letters 27 May 1825, 28 January 1826). Colonel Rafael Riego (78–80) instigated the Spanish Revolution of 1820; when it failed he fled, was captured, and hanged in 1823. Caroline Sheridan (84), granddaughter of dramatist Richard Brinsley Sheridan, was famed for her talent and beauty (especially her eyes); she and her sisters were celebrities in the inner circle of fashionable London society. As Caroline Norton, her intimate friendship with Lord Melbourne (William Lamb, widower of Byron's former mistress Caroline Lamb), would subject her to a scandalous divorce action in 1836.

My Partner

First publication and text: *NMM* 22 (April 1828), pp. 353–4, signed 'Φ.'; reprinted in *Poems*, II.150–53. The source of the epigraph, *The British Almanack*, edited by Charles Knight for the SDUK (see *Chaunts of the Brazen Head I*), began publication in 1828. The conversation glistens with cultural references, including popular novels (13–19): Benjamin Disraeli's first, *Vivian Grey* (1826–7); *Almack's*, an anonymous *roman à clef* (1826, by Mrs Marianne [Spencer] Stanhope); Mary Shelley's *Frankenstein* (1818); Robert P. Ward's *De Vere; or, the Man of Independence* (1827); man 'of birth and fashion' (so *Blackwood's* called him in April 1830, p. 688) T. H. Lister's *Herbert Lacy* (1828); *Tales of the O'Hara Family* (1825) by brothers John and Michael Banim. Disraeli, Ward, Bulwer-Lytton and Lister were of the 'silver-fork school' (fiction depicting the intimate details of life in high society). The then most recent novel by Irish woman of letters Lady Morgan (20) was *The O'Briens and the O'Flahertys, A National Tale* (1827), for which her publisher had paid £1300; Theodore Hook (21) was a socialite and novelist, known for his humour; he also edited the Tory paper *John Bull* and later *NMM* (succeeded, at his death, by Hood in 1841). The gorgeous fane (25) is the Royal Italian Opera House, enlarged by 1818, with a colonnade added in 1820; Claudia Ronzi de Begnis (?1800–1853) was famed for comedy roles ('charming', said Mary Shelley in January 1826); Giovanni Pacini (1796–1867) composed in the manner of Rossini (26–8); Mlles Brocard and Paul (31–2) were principal dancers in D'Egville's ballets at the Opera; Brocard, who performed in 1826 and 1827, made her début in *La Naissance de Venus*. A Blue (61) is a bluestocking or learned woman. A series of biting essays for *Blackwood's Edinburgh Magazine* from 1817 to well into the 1820s attacked 'the Cockney School', chiefly the poets Leigh Hunt and Keats (seen as his protégé); Keats's *Endymion* was widely

ridiculed in Tory reviews (65–6). Rev. Charles Simeon (1759–1836), fellow
of King's College Cambridge, was an influential Evangelical leader; Rev.
Lewis Way (1777–1842) preached the imminence of the last days and urged
the immediate conversion of the Jews (67–8).

The Fancy Ball

An earlier version was published in the *Hampshire Chronicle and Southampton
Courier*, 11 February 1828; text: *NMM* 23 (December 1828), pp. 505–6,
signed 'Φ.'; stanzas 4, 5 and 8, in square brackets, were added some time
later, for which we follow *Poems*, II.187–92. Before the masked ball in
Romeo and Juliet, Mercutio utters the lines of Praed's epigraph (I.iv.30–
31); in a famously ambiguous declaration, he is either disdaining or donning
a mask, which either is or is not like his face. Most of the characters at the
ball are familiar; of some that may need a gloss: the character of stanza 2
is a staple of the vogue Eastern Tale; the heroine of de Staël's popular novel
Corinne (1807) is Corinne (45), a character de Staël herself impersonated at
such balls; Sir Lucius O'Trigger (46) is the fire-eating dupe in Sheridan's
The Rivals (1775); the Commandant (54) is from Mozart's *Don Giovanni*;
Anne Page (57) is in *The Merry Wives of Windsor*; sad Rebecca (80) is the
heroine of Scott's *Ivanhoe* (1819), her life in peril from a charge of sorcery;
Queen Mary and Psyche seem male-impersonated (87–8); Isabella (90) is
the heroine of Boccaccio's fable of the Pot of Basil, recently retold by Keats
(1820); sad Calista (93) is in Nicholas Rowe's popular tragedy *The Fair
Penitent* (1703). Sir William Blackstone (5) is known for *Commentaries on
the Laws of England* (4 vols., 1765–69). John McAdam (1756–1836), eponym
of the road surface (99), was appointed surveyor-general of metropolitan
roads in 1827. In the Greek War for Independence, the Allies (France, Britain,
Russia) destroyed the Turkish fleet at Navarino (108), 20 October 1827.

A Letter of Advice

First publication and text: *NMM* 23 (December 1828), pp. 543–5, signed
'Φ.'; reprinted in *Poems*, II.193–7. Epigraph: 'In short, sir, a man to be
loved; / Which is why I should never be able to love him'; popular and
prolific French playwright Augustin Eugène Scribe (1791–1861) was famed
for his comedies of manners, his most recently successful, *Le Mariage de
raison* (1826) and *Le Mariage d'argent* (1828). The names in the title are
deftly turned: 'Medora' is the name Byron gave the pirate-hero's faithful
wife in *The Corsair* (1814), his sensationally popular verse-tale; female
characters in comedies by Vanbrugh and Congreve are named Araminta; a
vavasour is a feudal lord. A young Kashmiri poet entertains Princess Lalla
Rookh (18) with four verse-tales in Thomas Moore's popular *Lalla Rookh*

(1817). Orlando (55) is the hero of *Orlando Innamorato*, Boiardo's late-fifteenth-century romance epic poem. Werter (71) is the suicidally disappointed lover in Goethe's popular eighteenth-century novel *The Sorrows of Young Werther* (1774). In social ritual, flirtations and courtships could be conducted by sending specific flowers (87).

*   *   *

Twenty-eight and Twenty-nine

First publication and text: *NMM* 25 (January 1829), pp. 9–11, signed 'Φ.'; reprinted in *Poems*, II.168–71, and *Young*, pp. 107–13. Epigraph: 'Nothing has changed, my friends!' In the footnote, the sentence continues, 'only there is one Frenchman more' (and in the parody, 'one beast more'). Charles Dix is Charles X, King of France 1824–30; leaving France at the outbreak of the Revolution (1789), he led the émigré party, living mostly in England until the Bourbon Restoration of 1814. As king he insisted on re-establishing the *ancien régime*, but his extreme measures forced his abdication in July 1830. In 1823 Daniel O'Connell (37; 1775–1847) started the Catholic Association in Ireland, with a levy on supporters of a penny a month for the cause of Emancipation, a 'Catholic Rent' that was netting about £1000 a week by 1825; George III expressed reservations about Pitt's proposals for Catholic civil rights in letters to Lord Kenyon's father, which Lord Kenyon (38) leaked to a pamphleteering clergyman (*Young*, p. 107); in a speech in June 1828, Lord Plunket censured this publication. O'Connell had strong support from Richard Lalor Sheil (39), politician and dramatist (*Bellamira* of 1818 and *Evadne* of 1819, which Beddoes despised); Robert Peel (40) was an opponent of Catholic claims. Comedian Charles Mathews Sen. (49; 1776–1835) was famous for his 'At Homes'; he was performing monodramas and regular roles during the recent season (*Young*, p. 107), and was much appreciated for his impressions and impersonations. Theodore Hook (50) edited the scathingly satirical *John Bull* in the 1820s (see *My Partner*); Robert Warren (52), maker of boot-blacking, innovated advertising on walls; his address was 30 Strand; General Jackson (54) would become seventh President of the US in 1829. For St Giles, see *Chaunts* I; for St George's (64), see *Miss Kilmansegg*, 'Her Precious Leg', note to line 753. Sir James Park (1763–1838) was a Justice (79) for the Common Pleas (*SP*, p. 327). William Corder (81) was executed in 1828 for murdering his sweetheart; the *Sermons* of Rev. Hugh Blair (87), also a professor of rhetoric, were published in 1777–1802, and a collection of the 'Sentimental Beauties' of his writing in 1809. Weber (88) is probably German composer Carl Maria Von Weber (1786–1826), best known for romantic operas.

*   *   *

from *LONDON MAGAZINE*

Arrivals at a Watering-Place

First publication and text: *LM* (January 1829), pp. 14–16, signed 'Ξ'; reprinted in *Poems*, II.183–7. Praed was familiar with the social milieu of the spas and seaside resorts from his many seasons at Teignmouth (see the next poem). A mantua-maker (25) is a seamstress, usually a dressmaker. Calipee (91) is turtle-jelly. Almack's list (102) set admissions to exclusive Assembly Rooms in London; Byron regularly attended, but invitations were strictly controlled by the patronesses, and admission could be refused to the improperly attired, as the Duke of Wellington, wearing trousers rather than knee-breeches, discovered. Henry Luttrell's *Advice to Julia* (see *To Julia*) sets out the social economy:

> All on that magic LIST depends;
> Fame, fortune, fashion, lovers, friends.
> . . .
> If once to Almack's you belong,
> Like monarchs, you can do no wrong;
> But banished thence on Wednesday night,
> By Jove you can do nothing right.

You'll Come to Our Ball (Our Ball)

First publication and text: *LM* (February 1829), pp. 133–4, unsigned; in *Poems* titled *Our Ball* as the first of two *Letters from Teignmouth* (II.200–3). In Teignmouth, a Devon seaport on the English Channel and fashionable watering-place, was the Praeds' country seat, 'Britton House', where they spent Easter and summer vacations. Epigraph: 'What! is it he? Let me look at him again! He is truly much changed, is he not, papa?' (*First Loves*). Haldon (25) is a range of hills in Devon; Shaldon (27) is a village on the Teign across from Teignmouth; Sir Lawrence (33) may be an inept familiar reference to leading portrait-painter Sir Thomas Lawrence (see *Beauty and Her Visitors*). National schools (38) were established for educating the poor for social productivity (in 1838–9 Praed became active in the movement for their establishment). Rout is slang for fashionable soirée (42). Hock (54) is a German wine; 'Captain Rock' (56) was the signature of the leader of the Irish insurgents of 1822. A Blue (90) is a Bluestocking, a learned woman.

School and Schoolfellows

First publication and text: *LM* (March 1829), pp. 227–8, signed 'Ξ' (misprinted sideways); reprinted in *Poems*, II.221–4. Allott (*SP*, p. 333) thinks Praed was inspired by Hood's *Ode on a Distant Prospect of Clapham Academy* (*NMM*, 1824); a more obvious reference, evoked by both Hood's title and Praed's epigraph ('May Eton flourish'), is Gray's *Ode on a Distant Prospect of Eton College* (1747). Benjamin Heath Drury (8) was a young, unconventional assistant master during Praed's time at Eton, popular with the boys because of his love of the theatre, but disliked by headmaster John Keate who removed him in 1823, six years before this poem was written. The refrain, therefore, has a tone of joyous remembrance of a past Eton where a few fortunate boys enjoyed a freedom unusual in a public school. 'Old familiar faces' (16) is the title of Charles Lamb's nostalgic lyric (1798) for 'days of childhood' and 'joyful school-days'. Praed's characteristic 'skill in walking the tight-rope between sentiment and a sense of its absurdity' (*SP*, p. xviii) is reflected in the jaunty puns that punctuate this elegy ('Some lie beneath the churchyard stone, / And some before the Speaker'; 'Mill ... A magistrate pedantic; / And Medlar's feet repose, unscann'd, / Beneath the wide Atlantic') – a mixture that evokes 'Hood's manner' (Saintsbury, *Essays*, p. 398); 'until I came across this verse by Praed', Auden confessed, 'I would have said that a pathetic pun was impossible' (*A Certain World: A Commonplace Book*, New York: Viking, 1970). Bovney Reach (23) is on the Thames upstream from Windsor; all boys were taught Early School before breakfast, the fourth form alone having Long Morning (24), which began at 6 a.m. (later rescinded to 7.30). The terms 'fourteen all' and 'striking for the pocket' (27–8) are references to Eton Fives, the latter not used today but probably referring to an unplayable shot when the ball is aimed at the bottom of the Pepper-Pot, known now as 'Dead Man's Hole'; Chalvey ditch (31) is a stream which marked the northern bounds of the school. John Doe (40), a plaintiff in an imaginary law-suit, was invented by Blackstone in the late eighteenth century to illustrate a point of law. Bishop Richard Mant (1776–1848) published on theology and history; Manton was a London gunmaker (54). Praed would enter Parliament (61) in 1830. Poet's Walk (*sic*; 75), named after Gray, was said to be Praed's favourite Eton walk. At Eton he participated in the illegal Datchet Lane Theatre, which met at a Windsor coal-merchant's and was suppressed by Dr Keate (*SP*, p. 333); Sir Giles Overreach (85) is the villain of Massinger's *A New Way to Pay Old Debts* (1633), a part played by a succession of Eton boys, following the success of Edmund Kean in the role in London.

*   *   *

from *THE CASKET*

Praed signed these pieces 'Winthrop Mackworth Praed, Esq.'. Other contributors to *The Casket: A Miscellany, consisting of unpublished poems* (London: John Murray, 1829) included Crabbe, the Ettrick Shepherd, Mitford, Bulwer, Moore, Byron, Opie, Hemans, L.E.L., Baillie and Wordsworth.

Childhood and His Visitors

First publication and text: *The Casket*, pp. 21–3; reprinted in *Poems*, I. 358–60. The standard wistful regard of childhood innocence draws on the grim chronology of Gray's *Ode on a Distant Prospect of Eton College*, but restages it through the idiom of social *faux pas*, with Time, Guilt, Sorrow, the Muse of Pindus (a mountain-range in northern Greece) and Wisdom as inept spoil-sports, disarmed by a Wordsworthian blessing (from the 'Intimations' *Ode*) in the last line, itself disarmed of its darkening.

Beauty and Her Visitors

First publication and text: *The Casket*, pp. 155–8; reprinted in *Poems*, I.364–6. Sir Thomas Lawrence (1769–1830) was England's leading painter of portraits (64), famed for their elegance and courtliness; he was knighted in 1815 and became president of the Royal Academy in 1820.

*   *   *

Anticipation

Written in 1830 (*Poems*, I.396); first publication and text: *Poems*, I.394–6. A likely self-reference to Praed's entry into Parliament suggests composition in December 1830; Young prints another MS version, pp. 168–70, with more topical references, titled *The Young Whig* (Praed was no longer a Whig by this time). Allott, reading this other MS (which he dates May 1832), extends the title to *The Young Whig, Being a Lady's Lamentation for the Political Propensities of Her Lover*, and notes that both versions parody Thomas Haynes Bayly's popular song, 'Oh no, we never mention her' (*SP*, pp. 290–92, 347). Allott comments on 'the slightness of the changes needed to transform the non-political "Anticipations" into the political "The Young Whig"' (the political poems 'are not of a separate kind: essentially they are "Poems of Life and Manners" with subject-matter widened to include the political field', *SP*, p. xxxix). But *Anticipation* is not all that 'non-political'; Praed writes a satire about his supposed change of character, from socialite to politician. The 'Whig' version gains an edge from all the references to the young MP's bid for fame in conservative/Tory circles. Franks (4) are perquisites of office, such as free postage; the *London Gazette* (6) listed public notices; government appointments and promotions, etc. An album (9) was a collection or miscellany usually kept by a young lady, in which autographs, or better, extempore squibs, from popular writers were prized acquisitions. The Bill is the emerging Reform Bill, passed in 1832, Goth and Hun referring to the German-descended William IV's reluctant support for it (17–18); Drury Lane (23) is a major London theatre. Robert Peel supported Catholic Emancipation and temperately opposed the Reform Bill. *The Morning Post* (27) was a conservative newspaper in which Praed frequently published political verse (Beddoes published his first poem in the *Post*, in 1819).

Lines Written for a Blank Page of 'The Keepsake'

First publication and text: *Poems*, I.393–94, dated 1830. The poem inscribes a gift of *The Keepsake*, one of the most popular annuals (for this vogue see the note to Hood's *I Remember, I Remember*), this one edited by Frederic Mansel Reynolds. Among the contents of *The Keepsake* for 1830 were three tales by Mary Shelley, Lord Byron's letters to friends, a tragedy by Scott and poems by Coleridge. Cherished as much for collecting and drawing-room display as for literary contents, the annuals were aimed chiefly at women, as purchasers or recipients, more particularly ladies of the middle class eager for a small luxury signifying taste and refinement. By 1832 there were more than sixty such annuals, with Praed among the happy contributors. In the Preface of 1829 Reynolds italicized his boast of having invested '*eleven thousand guineas*' in the volume, and in the Preface of 1830 he assured his public that this next volume was worthy of its predecessors. 'Hot pressed' is a mode of production to give a gloss to the paper; steel engraving enabled the reproduction of high art (8).

*   *   *

from *THE LITERARY SOUVENIR*

Alaric Watts founded *The Literary Souvenir* in 1824 and edited this gift-book annual from 1825 to 1835. Its first volume was a small octavo, in pastel boards, its pages gilt-edged and featuring engravings of the works of great painters; priced at 12 shillings, it sold 6000 copies. The 1827 Preface boasted such 'embellishments' as 'the most splendid series of prints ever introduced in any work of the same class, including an engraving of "The Last Portrait Painted of Byron".'

The Legend of the Haunted Tree

Written in 1830; published in *LS*, 1831, pp. 1–16, signed 'by the Author of "Lillian" ' ('A Fairy Tale' written at Cambridge 1822; published 1823); revised and expanded in 1837 (*Poems*, I.176–94). Text: *LS*, with later text (following *Poems*) in square brackets; other substantive variants involve a few local wordings. *The Legend* led off *LS*, 1831, in which Praed had four more pieces, including *Waterloo* and *The Belle of the Ball-Room*. The meditative languor of Wordsworth's *The Haunted Tree* (published 1820, under 'Poems of the Imagination') has a tone quite different from Praed's *Legend*, a semi-parody of the sort of verse-tale Scott popularized, with a tang of Byronic satire, for example, the rhyme of the hero 'Isumbras' with 'ass' (325–6). Saintsbury liked this burlesque 'far better' than the earlier romances and tales for showing 'in full swing that happy compound and contrast of sentiment and humour in which [Praed] excelled' (*Essays*, p. 390). 'The young May Moon is beaming love' (15–16), begins one of Thomas Moore's popular *Irish Melodies* (1807); his 'style is the best *false* one I know and glitters like broken glass,' Beddoes remarks; 'he . . . will show us a beautiful prospect in heav'n or earth, gives us a tube to look thro', which looks like a telescope and is a kaleidoscope' (Donner, *Complete Works*, p. 649). Leverets are hares and conies are rabbits (232). When Ferdinand VII of Spain, dethroned by Napoleon, was restored in 1814, he set aside the reform constitution of 1812 (245); but a revolution in 1820 compelled him to swear to a new, similarly modelled one; then, in 1823 French troops, supported by reactionary European regimes, entered Spain and helped re-establish a despotic monarchy. Edward Burtenshaw Sugden (252), Tory Solicitor-General 1829–30, bristled at Lord Chancellor Brougham's wit in court. Gretna Green (254), just across the border in Scotland, was a destination for eloping English couples. Laudanum (300) is tincture of opium. Scotland was on the verge of major reforms, realized after the Reform Bill, when popularly elected Municipalities were created for the first time since the fifteenth century; Charles Christopher Pepys Cottenham (363), KC, MP, was Solicitor General in 1834 and Lord Chancellor in 1836; Joseph Hume, radical MP for Aberdeen, was famed for his scrutiny of government expenditure; Pasta (see *Good-Night to the Season*) was a celebrated opera singer (365–6). The Downs (435) is off the Kent coast.

Waterloo

Written in February 1830 (*Young*, p. 113); first publication and text: *LS*, 1831, pp. 33–6 (the only piece by Praed in this volume he left unsigned); reprinted and credited to him by *Young*, pp. 113–16. 'At this time it was the fashion with French writers to assume that the English had already

been beaten at Waterloo, when somehow the French got "betrayed"'
(*Young*, p. 113). Wellington's celebrated victory over Bonaparte in June
1815 at once consolidated the restoration of the French monarchy and made
Waterloo a tourist mecca. The second epigraph is Shakespeare's credulous
shepherdess Mopsa (*The Winter's Tale*, IV.iv.266), hearing Autolycus
describe one of his ballads. The knight-hero of Ariosto's sixteenth-century
epic poem *Orlando Furioso* fights with Charlemagne against the Saracens
(Pagans) for the possession of Europe (5–6). The Duke of York (d. 1827),
second son of George III, was a scandalously incompetent and corrupt
field general (25); Eldon was Lord Chancellor 1801–27; the commander of
the Old Guard (28) at Waterloo was Napoleon's field marshal Ney (35),
executed for treason six months later. In British legend, Roman monsters
Gog and Magog (45) found their way to England, were eventually con-
quered, brought in chains to London, and forced to labour as porters at
the Royal Palace. Napoleon died in 1821, an exile on the Atlantic island of
St Helena (60).

The Belle of the Ball-Room, An Every-day Character

First publication and text: *LS*, 1831, pp. 111–15, 'by the Author of
"Lillian"'; reprinted in *Poems*, II.145–9. The epigraph is from Jean de La
Bruyère's satiric *Les Caractères* (1688), ch. 3, 'Des Femmes' ('One must
judge women exclusively from the footwear to the hairstyle, almost as one
measures a fish from the tail to the head'); *Les Caractères* combines sketches
of familiar social types with *pensées* and maxims. Joseph Chitty (4) published
various manuals on the law from 1797 to 1837. John Locke (31) is the
seventeenth-century philosopher; poet, songwriter and satirist Thomas
Moore wrote *Poems by the Late Thomas Little* (32). Nathan Mayer Rothschild
(1777–1836) is the powerful London banker (56). Soprano Angelica Catalani
(62) sang at the London and Paris operas, reigning as prima donna in
England from 1806 to 1813 and visiting again in 1828, the year she retired;
she died of cholera in Paris in 1830 (see *Stanzas*, below). The Album (65)
holds Coleridge's *Fire, Famine, and Slaughter* (*The Morning Post*, 1798;
collected 1828 and 1829), along with the signature of Prince Leboo (71) of
the Pelew islands, who died of smallpox on a visit to England in 1784. 'Fly
not yet, tis just the hour' (92) is another of Moore's *Irish Melodies* (1807).

Stanzas Written in Lady Myrtle's Boccaccio

First publication and text: *LS*, 1832, pp. 29–32, 'by the Author of "Lil-
lian"'; reprinted in *Poems*, I.396–9. The frame of Boccaccio's *Decameron*
is black-plague-ridden fourteenth-century Florence, from which several
young men and women retreat to a suburban estate and amuse themselves

with story-telling, an entertainment depicted in a full-page engraving accompanying Praed's poem (*LS*, p. 28). Praed involves this context with the cholera epidemic that was spreading from Russia and Eastern Europe into England in October 1831, raging in the British Isles over the next year. The physician, Sir Henry Halford (29), attended royalty (George IV, William IV and Princess Victoria). Celebrated comedian and Shakespearean comic actor John Liston (50; ?1776–1846) performed at the Olympic Theatre in 1832 (*SP*, p. 340) and at the Haymarket during most of the summer seasons from 1805 to 1830.

* * *

The Talented Man

The poem is undated; Allott conjectures 1831; text: *Poems*, II.197–9. Allott's title, based on the MS (see plate in *SP* facing p. 132), is the subtitle only; also following this MS, he has 'wrong' (not 'sad') in 36, and inserts the name 'Dora' after the penultimate stanza. Lausanne is a Swiss resort city. Brazen Nose (9) is an etymological recovery of Brasenose, a college at Oxford, the name derived from the nose-shaped brass knocker on one of the hall's doors. Trevelyan (28) may refer to Raleigh Trevelyan (1781–1865), whose poems and essays were published in 1819, or the novel *Trevelyan* (1831) 'by the author of *A Marriage in High Life*' (Caroline Lucy, Lady Scott). Byron's club-foot kept him from waltzing; 'dumpy' sneers back at his singular use of this adjective in *Don Juan* ('I hate a dumpy woman', I.488), a phrase Hood echoed in *John Trot, A Ballad* (1827): 'She was a dumpy woman / Tho' her family was high.' Thomas Moore was a beloved parlour-singer as well as poet (but a toucan is a tropical bird with an unlovely voice) (43–6).

One More Quadrille (The Last Quadrille)

Written 1832; not in *Poems*; text: *Select Poems of Winthrop Mackworth Praed*, edited by A. D. Godley (London, 1909). Allott's title, based on the MS, is *The Last Quadrille* (*SP*, p. 141). Bulwer-Lytton recalls that at Cambridge Praed was 'passionately fond of dancing; never missing a ball, though it were the night before an examination' (quoted by Hudson, *A Poet in Parliament*, pp. 67–9). At a Conservative ball celebrating his re-election to Parliament in 1835 Praed recalled that he 'kept dancing down long country-dances (fifty or sixty couples) from nine till four' (ibid., p. 210). Elder statesman Lord Grey was Prime Minister in the Whig administration that carried the Reform Bill in 1832 (19–22); Beddoes, who advocated reform, called him 'the Father of Reformers' (Donner, *Complete Works*, p. 736).

* * *

from *THE MORNING POST*

Stanzas To the Speaker Asleep

First publication and text: *The Morning Post*, 6 March 1833, p. 3e; reprinted in *Young*, pp. 214–16, retitled *Stanzas On seeing the Speaker asleep in his chair, during one of the debates of the First Reformed Parliament*. Saintsbury liked this poem so much that he quoted it in full (*Essays*, pp. 388–9). This Parliament met in 1833, the first year after the Reform Act. Charles Manners Sutton (1780–1845), a Tory, was for many years Speaker of the House of Commons. The defeat of the first Reform Bill in the Commons led to a dissolution of Parliament in April 1831; a second Bill passed by a new Parliament was rejected in the Lords. After another Bill was passed in the Commons by March 1832 but was defeated by a Lords committee, ministers resigned and William IV threatened to 'create peers' (i.e. enough Whig Lords to ensure passage); the Bill was passed in June. Macaulay supported it and Praed opposed it, not only with speeches in Parliament but also with political verses in the newspapers. Among the most important reforms legislated by the 1833 Parliament were the abolition of colonial slavery, restrictions on child labour (cf. 28), and funds for poor relief and national education. Named in the middle stanzas are: manufacturer John Fielden (not Feilden) (1784–1849), who stood for Parliament in Oldham on the condition that Cobbett stand with him (both were elected); Irish MP Finn, a supporter of O'Connell, along with Baldwin, MP 1833–5; Grattan may refer to one of the sons of Irish MP Grattan (d. 1820), both of whom were members of the first Reformed Parliament, William Cobbett (1763–1835), caustic political tract-writer, publisher of the widely read *Cobbett's Weekly Register* and, as an independent MP, truculent opponent of all manner of measures (he hated Radicals as much as Tories); Radical MP Joseph Hume (see *Chaunts* I); George Canning (see *Chaunts* I), Prime Minister in 1827; Charles Grant (1778–1866), a Tory who joined Canning's ministry as President of the Board of Trade but who gravitated towards the Whigs after Canning's death (1827), became president of the Board of Control in 1832, and championed abolition of slavery in the colonies; John Temple Palmerston (1784–1865), a Tory until Canning's death, then a champion of liberal causes; and Sir Matthew Wood (1768–1843), Whig MP for the City of London, municipal reformer (and, formerly, friend and adviser to Queen Caroline).

THOMAS LOVELL BEDDOES

Abbreviations:

BB: *Browning Box*, ed. Donner
D: *Complete Works of Thomas Lovell Beddoes*, ed. Donner
Donner: Donner, *Thomas Lovell Beddoes: The Making of a Poet*
G: *Poetical Works of Thomas Lovell Beddoes*, ed. Gosse
K: *The Poems, Posthumous and Collected, of Thomas Lovell Beddoes*, ed. Kelsall

We note the first publication and/or republication of texts in *K* and *G* in order to situate the texts in nineteenth-century reception, cross-referencing the letters with *D* (text of the letters follows *D*).

Alfarabi

Written in 1819; first published in *K*, I.133–9; text: *G*, I.3–8. Alfarabi, tenth-century Sufi mystic of Baghdad, was one of the most original Arab philosophers, noted for an epoch-making distinction between essence and existence, which provided a metaphysical basis both for the distinction between a necessary and a contingent being and for the concept of a universe created by and not merely emanating from God. Developing the notion of a single active intellect external to and illuminating individual minds with intelligible forms, Alfarabi argued that the mind receives these forms either by a process of abstraction from material being, or by a higher, intuitive, mystical knowledge, the end being a union with God, the external agent intellect (David Knowles, *The Evolution of Medieval Thought* (New York: Random House, 1962), pp. 196, 215). Byron kept a bear at Cambridge in 1807; Henry Fuseli was reported to sup on raw pork chops in order to have dreams to assist his painting of *The Nightmare* (32–3). Neither was an opium-eater, though others were: Coleridge, fellow Oxonian De Quincey, and Wilberforce – all of whom Beddoes would have been acquainted within his father's circle. Partly parodying Byron in the mood of *Manfred* (1817) (especially 35–62), Beddoes also indulges Shelleyan visionary imagination (100 ff.) in the tones of *Alastor* (1816) and at lines 125–9, of *Mont Blanc* (1817). The flying donkey (70) spoofs Silenus's ass and travesties Pegasus, the winged horse of myth and subsequently a symbol of poetic imagination. Archimage (133ff.) or Archimago is the enchanter of Spenser's *Faerie Queene*, a symbolic embodiment of Hypocrisy who, in the guise of the Red Cross Knight, deceives the maid Una (Book I). After he is exposed, he is confined to a deep dungeon, but reappears in Book II, seeking vengeance. In the mid-sixteenth-century verse-comedy, *Gammer Gurton's Needle*,

Gammer Gurton loses the needle needed to mend the breeches of her servant Hodge (152–4). GEORGIUM SIDUS (170) is nonce Latin for 'Georgian constellation', a sneer at the current English dynasty.

* * *

from *THE IMPROVISATORE*, in three Fyttes, with Other Poems

The début volume, a duodecimo of 128 pages, published in Oxford by J. Vincent, 1821, when Beddoes was a freshman at Oxford. He used as an epigraph for the volume, 'I have sung / With an unskilful, but a willing voice' (from Webster's *Appius and Virginia*, IV.i.332–4), but later wilfully tried to suppress the publication by destroying every copy he could find.

To Night

Written in 1818–19; not in *K*; text: *G*, I.248–9; one of several quatorzains, a 14-line form including but not restricted to the sonnet. Capel Lofft's five-volume *Laura; or an Anthology of sonnets . . . and Elegiac Quatorzains*, by divers hands, was published in London, 1814. Beddoes's meter and rhyme scheme evoke a Shakespearean sonnet, but the enjambments, both of lines and quatrains, press against the standard patterns of the 'uncouth animal with fourteen legs / And jingling feet' (so Beddoes mocked the sonnet in an early fragment, *D*, p. 171). Of personified Night in *The Brides' Tragedy* (III.iii.8–10), Douglas Bush remarks, 'While the Elizabethans and Jacobeans loved such large personifications, there is here a modern touch of conscious composition or aggregation' (*Mythology*, p. 193) – a comment that applies nicely to this earlier imagination.

To a Bunch of Grapes

Not in *K*; text: *G*, I.253–4. The concluding poem and 'glory' of the volume, 'an exquisite arabesque of playful imagination, where the central ideal, like the variations on a theme in music, strays away only to return, and returns repentant only to stray again' (*Donner*, p. 75). Beddoes's note to line 6 – 'The Sisters of Phaëton; see Ovid, *Met.* II.' – refers to the first story in *Metamorphoses*, Book II, of Phaeton's mismanagement of his father's horses, the chaos of the sun-chariot incinerating the earth and killing him; Phaeton's grieving sisters are transformed into trees, 'and from that bark there flowed tears which, hardened into amber by the sun, dropped from the new-made branches' (II.360–66, translation by Mary Innes, Penguin, 1955).

* * *

from *THE BRIDES' TRAGEDY*

Written in 1821–2; first publication and text: *The Brides' Tragedy* (London: Rivington, 1822), 'by Thomas Lovell Beddoes, of Pembroke College, Oxford'; reprinted in *K* and *G*; described in the dedicatory preface as 'a *Minor's Tragedy*'. The play is loosely based on actual events in early eighteenth-century Oxford.

The Manciple of one of the Colleges early in the last century had a very beautiful daughter, who was privately married to a student without the knowledge of the parents on either side.

During the long vacation subsequent to this union the husband was introduced to a young lady, who was at the same time proposed as his bride: absence, the fear of his father's displeasure, the presence of a lovely object, and, most likely, a natural fickleness of disposition overcame any regard he might have cherished for his ill-fated wife, and finally he became deeply enamoured of her unconscious rival. In the contest of duties and desires, which was the consequence of this passion, the worse part of man prevailed, and he formed and executed a design almost unparalleled in the annals of crime.

His second nuptials were at hand when he returned to Oxford, and to her who was now an obstacle to his happiness. Late at night he prevailed upon his victim to accompany him to a lone spot in the *Divinity Walk*, and there murdered and buried her. The wretch escaped detection, and the horrid deed remained unknown till he confessed it on his death-bed. The remains of the unfortunate girl were dug up in the place described, and the Divinity Walk was deserted and demolished, as haunted ground. (Preface, pp. vi–vii)

In the play, Hesperus is the undergraduate (his name is that of the evening star, the planet Venus), and Floribel is the Manciple's daughter. Orlando, a rival for Floribel, casts Hesperus's father in prison for debt, his release contingent on Hesperus renouncing Floribel and marrying Orlando's sister Olivia. Hesperus agrees, though in anguish, and murders Floribel in a fit of jealousy. When the murder is discovered, he is arrested and condemned; Floribel's mother (Leonora) spares him the disgrace of public execution by poisoning him with noxious flowers (no 'floribel'), and he dies in a Faustian exit, experiencing imminent damnation.

In the Preface, Beddoes says that his 'scenes were written . . . exclusively for the closet' – that is, for reading in one's private room (p. v). In recoil from the material forms of and the demands for action and sensation on the popular stage, the genre of closet drama emerged in the Romantic age, characterizing Baillie's *Plays on the Passions*, Shelley's *Prometheus Unbound*, Byron's *Manfred*, and theorized in Lamb's influential essay on the unsuitability of Shakespeare's plays for stage representation (1811). Beddoes later recanted his antipathy, telling Kelsall in 1829 that the stage 'is the highest aim of the dramatist, & I should be very desirous to get on it. To look down on it is a piece of impertinence as long as one chooses to write in the form of a play, and is generally the result of a consciousness of one's own inability to produce anything striking & affecting in that way. Shakspeare wrote only for it, Ld B. despised it, or rather affected this as well as every other passion, which is the secret of his style in poetry & life' (*D*, p. 640; cf. *K*, I.lxxix).

Late in 1825 Beddoes asked Kelsall to send a copy of the tragedy to Germany (*D*, p. 611), but by 1827 he judged it as 'a very sad boyish affair' (*D*, p. 637; cf. *K*, I.lxxviii). If the first reviews, in leading journals, were kinder, they were also prescient, praising poetic skill and imaginative power but noting weakness of dramatic structure. 'This Drama is undoubtedly one of the most promising performances of this "poetical" age. There are, indeed, few things which, *as mere poetry*, surpass it,' Procter opened a review in *London Magazine* 7 (February 1823, pp. 169–72); 'It has plenty of beauties too, – many delicacies, sometimes great power of expression, sometimes originality, and is seldom or never common place' (p. 169). He said as much again in *Edinburgh Review* 38 (February 1823), adding that the play 'betrays more promise (we ought to say, perhaps, more power) than that of almost any young poet, whose works have been before us for the first time' (p. 204). In *London Magazine* 8 (December 1823, pp. 646–8), 'John Lacy' (Darley, whom he praised in his preface) admired 'the energy of [the play's] language, the power of its sentiments, and the boldness of its imagery', 'the quality of its rhythm and metrical harmony', all yielding 'tragic power of the very highest order'; he heralded Beddoes as 'a scion worthy of the stock from which Shakspeare and Marlow sprung' – a review that Kelsall reprinted in the Appendix of *Poems* (I.223–7). In *Blackwood's Edinburgh Magazine* 14 (December 1823, pp. 723–9), 'Christopher North' (John Wilson) praised Beddoes for 'the luxuriance of his fancy', his 'tender and deep feeling, a wantoning sense of beauty, a sort of light, airy, and graceful delicacy of imagination, extremely delightful, and withal a power over the darker and more terrible passions' (724, 729).

ACT I.I.95–160 Floribel recounts a disturbing dream ('Twas on a fragrant bank I laid me down) – an early indication of what Lytton Strachey calls Beddoes's 'extraordinary eminence as a master of dramatic blank verse' (*Books and Characters*, p. 237). The Queen of Smiles (109) evokes Venus (also namesake of Hesperus, the planet Venus); the Hesperides were three sisters who guarded the golden apples that Hera received as a marriage gift; by transferral, the orchard is called the garden of the Hesperides (114) and the apples have been regarded as a symbol of immortality. Stud (120) means here a collection of domestic animals. Hesperus chides Floribel with a mocking *Song* (Poor old pilgrim Misery), which Beddoes later included in *Outidana* (*D*, p. x). (For *Outidana*, see below.)

ACT II.I.13−71 At the end of Act I, Orlando has imprisoned Hesperus's father, who begs Hesperus to marry Orlando's sister to secure his release; Hesperus agrees, feeling damned. Act II opens with a restless Orlando (like Brutus in *Julius Caesar*, II.i.230) envying his minstrel boy's ability to sleep. He asks for a song, and the boy obliges with 'A ho! A ho!', a song that Snow praises for 'the clearness of attack, the musical dexterity of the complicated stanza, the lightness of fancy . . . his control of metrics' (*Eccentric*, p. 133). It was included in *Outidana* (*D*, p. x).

ACT III.II.1−17 Floribel, in her parents' cottage, senses a change in Hesperus's affections (And must I wake again? Oh come to me); Hesperus murders her in the next scene. 'Throughout Beddoes' canon, women serve as pale victims, mere phantoms' (Wilner, *Gathering the Winds*, p. 77).

*   *   *

from *THE ATHENAEUM*

Lines Written by the Author of 'The Bride's [sic] *Tragedy', in the blank-leaf of the 'Prometheus Unbound'*

Written in 1822 before Shelley's death in July; first publication and text (with the title reading 'Bride's' rather than 'Brides' ') in *The Athenaeum* (18 May 1833), p. 313b; reprinted in *K*, I.163. Beddoes included it in *Outidana* (*D*, p. x). According to Donner (*D*, p. 796), Kelsall initiated the publication and supplied this preface to *The Athenaeum*:

When Mr Beddoes penned this fine extravaganza, the subject of its graceful idolatry was still living, and hopes, to be shortly after so ruthlessly destroyed, were indulged of that increasing luxuriance of his great genius, (season after season more prodigal than the last,) which, had life been granted, would certainly not have been wanting. Ten years have since elapsed, and in that long interval the author of the Bride's Tragedy has claimed no second 'award'. For aught, indeed, that our literature would have lost, he might have perished in the same fatal storm in the Gulf of Spezia. How much longer is he contented to be *un*-known as the author of the *Bride's Tragedy* − (that blossom of exquisite beauty − still but a blossom,) − and is expectation, in the few who know his really great and rare powers, to doze away at last into oblivion?

Prometheus Unbound was published in the summer of 1820. The obituaries of Shelley replayed the political controversies that marked the reception of his poetry throughout his life, his strongest praise coming from the progressive and radical press. But the general view that prevailed in the 1820s was

Tory, that of Shelley as atheistic opponent of Church and State. The posthumous idealizing was led in the 1820s by Mary Shelley, Leigh Hunt and Cambridge students (including Tennyson and Hallam); Thomas Medwin's somewhat equivocal 'Memoir of Shelley' and 'Shelley Papers' were being published serially in *The Athenaeum*, 1832–3. 'The disappearance of Shelley from the world seems, like the tropical setting of that luminary, (*aside*, I hate that word) to which his poetical genius can alone be compared with reference to the companions of his day, to have been followed by instant darkness and owl-season,' Beddoes wrote to Kelsall, 25 August 1824; 'whether the vociferous Darley is to be the comet, or tender, fullfaced L.E.L. the milk-and-watery moon of our darkness, are questions for the astrologers: if I were the literary weather-guesser for 1825 I would safely prognosticate fog, rain, blight in due succession for it's dullard months' (*D*, p. 589; cf. *G*, I.xvii; Kelsall published the letter with blanks for Darley and L.E.L. (Landon); *K*, I.xxxv). In addition to *Prometheus Unbound*, which he repeatedly asked Kelsall to send to him in Germany in December 1825 (*K*, I.liii; *D*, p. 611), Beddoes liked *The Cenci* ('admirably true': *K*, I.lxxxvi; *D*, p. 645; cf. *D*, p. 619), and many of the pieces in *Posthumous Poems* (*K*, I.xxxv; *D*, p. 590), the publication of which he assisted. Donner (*D*, p. 250) prints two lines from a manuscript (*c.* 1823–5), titled by Kelsall *A Shelleian Fancy*: 'From the dishevelled air / Torture wild shrieks and agonized fire.'

* * *

fragments from *THE LAST MAN*

Written in the summer of 1823 (*D*, p. 743), these pieces were identified by Gosse as intended for *The Last Man* (*G*, II.256). For the contemporary interest in this topic, see the note to Hood's *The Last Man*. Beddoes abandoned this play early in 1824 (letter, *D*, p. 580). On 1 April 1826 he tells Kelsall that he is glad that Mary Shelley had taken the subject 'from the New Monthly Fellow [editor, Thomas Campbell] – and am sure that in almost every respect, she will do much better than either of us: indeed she has no business to be a woman by her books' (*D*, p. 618); he was irritated by Campbell's claim to the subject (see Campbell's letter to *The Times*, 24 March 1825, reprinted in *D*, pp. 752–3, in which, hearing of Beddoes's plans, he insists that 'the conception of the *Last Man* had been mine fifteen years ago'). Beddoes assured Kelsall in 1825, 'I will do the Last Man before I die, but it is a subject I save up for a time when I have more knowledge, a freer pencil, a little menschen-lehre [study of humanity], a command of harmony, & an accumulation of picturesque ideas & dramatic characters fit for the theme' (*D*, p. 600; cf. *K*, I.xli). In October 1827 he tells Kelsall that he plans to use *The Last Man* materials for *Death's Jest-Book* (*K*, I.lxxvii; *D*, p. 636).

A Crocodile

This quatorzain was written in the *Outidana* notebook (*D*, p. 693); first published in *K*, I.108-9 (his title); text: *G*, II.261-2. Almandines (4) are garnet-like semi-precious minerals; the troculus (13) is the trochilus, a small Egyptian bird said by the ancients to pick the teeth of the crocodile and mentioned by several English writers with whom Beddoes would have been familiar (Lyly, Lodge, Sandys, Cleveland). Beddoes went to see 'a couple of live crocodiles' on exhibit in London in 1824 (*D*, p. 591). The poem 'possesses that enamelled and colourful morbidity (with a touch of shallowness) which, written seventy years later, would have been called *fin de siècle*', remarks Snow (*Eccentric*, p. 54); others find Beddoes's 'nightmares . . . far from insubstantial; they were powerfully realized in his poetry and gnawed on real flesh' (Wilner, *Gathering the Winds*, p. 74).

Sweet to Die (Death Sweet)

Written in the *Outidana* notebook (*D*, p. 694); first published and titled in *K*, I.113; text: *G*, II.265; titled *Death Sweet* in *D* (p. 243, after MS). 'In Beddoes's treatment of Death,' remarks Heath-Stubbs, 'there is, blended with the feeling of repulsion and horror, a softer emotion of sensual, we might well say sexual, tenderness' (*Darkling Plain*, p. 38). Ricks admires how line 8 ('turning to daisies') 'manages to incarnate so glidingly the life which it imagines even in the grave' with 'the gentle and delicate turn within the word *turning*', involving the sense of 'changing to' – 'a calm and peaceful metamorphosis so unlike the usual violences and violations of metamorphosis' – with 'something of an exquisite social attention, turning courteously to hear [the daisies'] thoughts' (*Force of Poetry*, p. 139).

Midnight Hymn

Written in the *Outidana* notebook (*D*, p. 693). First published and titled in *K*, I.110-11; text: *G*, II.263; in *D* titled *Hymn*. The simile refers to the escape of the enslaved children of Israel from Pharaoh's Egypt (Exodus 14:21-2).

A Lake

Written in the *Outidana* notebook (*D*, p. 694). In this 'perfectly rounded' fragment, observes Ricks, Beddoes's 'interlacing . . . does not just rhyme "lake" with "snake", but . . . rhymes "lake" with "*li*ke a sn*ake*", as if *lake* were the effortless curled contraction of those three words' (*Force of Poetry*, p. 147).

Dream of Dying

Written in the *Outidana* notebook (*D*, p. 694); first published in *K*, I.115–16; text: *G*, II.267–8. The dream of the corpse as playground is repeated at the end of *Lines Written at Geneva*. 'The fledgling adult ghost has as yet no voice with which to rebuke the ghost-children who are both younger and older than he' (Ricks, *Force of Poetry*, p. 160).

*   *   *

from *OUTIDANA*, or *effusions, amorous, pathetic and fantastical*

These pieces were written in 1821–5 in a notebook under this title (*D*, p. 692) and gathered for a possible publication (*G*, I.xxiv; *D*, p. x). For the list of notebook pieces, see *D*, pp. 693–4.

Lines Written at Geneva; July, 1824

Written in July 1824; first published in *K*, I.211–12; text: *G*, I.67–8. The fluid romance couplets (enjambed iambic pentameter) recall Keats's *Endymion* (1818) and Shelley's *Julian and Maddalo* (1824); the last line, apparently unrhymed, hooks back to the opening tercet. Donner prints 'a note at the end of the lines': 'N.B. To make use of this idea – in Herculaneum: a noise heard and the enquiry made what it is, an answer that it is a spirit &^{c}. getting away from its grave, and getting into a new body, – then enter Ziba' (*D*, p. 525). A draft of *Love's Arrow Poisoned* (*D*, pp. 522–3) sets this play in Herculaneum (buried like Pompeii in the eruption of Vesuvius and excavated in the eighteenth and nineteenth centuries); Ziba is an Arab with secret knowledge. The poem's final image anticipates Beddoes's remark to Kelsall in September 1825: the Germans 'treat their poets as the Romans did their emperors – alive they are golden heavenly fellows, for whom reviews ascend like triumphal arches; – they die, – a weeping willow & an elegy stick over their graves, and as the tree draws nourishment out of their decaying corporeal substance, a younger rival sets the roots of his fame in their literary remains, and flourishes as fast as these latter rot' (D, pp. 606–7; cf. K, I.xlviii).

A Dirge (To-day is a thought)

This quatorzain was written in the autumn of 1824 (D, p. xxviii); first published in K, I.179 and titled A Dirge (Written for a Drama); text: G, I.41. 'Here physical life is almost a disgrace, almost a sin against the ideal state' (Thompson, Beddoes, p. 106).

Sonnet: To Tartar, a Terrier Beauty

Written c. March 1825, Beddoes described it to Kelsall as an 'excellent sonnet' (K, I.xl; D, p. 599); first published, K, I.164; text: G, I.28. Ricks admires the imagination of its 'silent interlocutor, . . . the dog whom (not which) Beddoes addresses . . . in the knowledge that [it] cannot reply but is master of its own profound and daily language' (Force of Poetry, p. 150; cf. p. 156).

Pygmalion

Written in April 1825 (K, I.xli); Beddoes hoped that Oxford Quarterly would take it (K, I.xlix; D, p. 607) but it ceased publication; he then made it the last piece of Outidana; it did not appear until K (I.154–62), there titled Pygmalion; text: G, I.20–27. Following the MS, Donner deletes or from the title (D, p. 78 and facing plate). The story of Pygmalion, sculptor of Cyprus, is told in Ovid's Metamorphosis, Book X. Salamis was an ancient city on Cyprus (30–31); Paphos was the Cyprian birthplace of Venus (who granted Pygmalion's wish that the statue live); it is also the name Pygmalion and his bride gave their child (32–4). The initial portrait of Pygmalion (35–55) combines elements of Keats's otherworldly dreamer and potential dupe, Lycius (Lamia), and his female counterpart, 'hoodwink'd' Madeline in The Eve of St Agnes (both published 1820); Kelsall in fact sees this poem as 'the sole instance of a direct impress from another mind' (K, I.xxiii). For a subtle analysis of sound effects and tonal semantics in lines 94–7 see Ricks (Force of Poetry, pp. 147–8). Beddoes again deploys romance couplets, shaping a formal analogue for Pygmalion's overflowing imagination – for example, the semantically pointed enjambment of 'thoughts which over-ran / The compass of his mind' (89–90) or 'new-poured blood / Flows' (183–4). The story of Niobe (187 ff.) is told in Ovid's Metamorphoses, Book VI. Having borne six sons and six daughters, Niobe boasted of her superiority to Latona, mother of Apollo and Artemis; they slew her children in retribution. Her 'grief turned her to stone', and tears for ever 'trickled from her marble face'. 'Dissatisfaction is the lot of the poet, if it be that of

any being,' Beddoes wrote in October 1827; 'therefore the gushings of the
spirit, these pourings out of their innermost on imaginary topics, because
there was no altar in their home worthy of the libation . . . these involuntary
overflows of the soul, what it is that moves within us' (*D*, p. 635; cf. *K*,
I.lxxv–lxxvi). Despite this sympathy, Beddoes called the poem, perhaps
defensively, 'Pig stuff' in 1825 (*D*, p. 601; cf. *K*, I.xlii), and by 1837 regarded
it as 'considerable trash' (*K*, I.c; *D*, p. 662); but Bush finds nicely 'modern'
its rendering of the lonely artist 'of an age of idealism, frustration, and
Weltschmerz, whose life is apart from the world around him' (*Mythology*,
p. 194). The 'poem's painful irony', suggests Thompson, is that 'if art is
the full realization of the self, it may also displace the self and, symbolically,
destroy it' (*Beddoes*, p. 101), while Ricks enjoys the subtle wit by which
Beddoes brings the old story 'to an end by conceiving of the artistic creation
– the metamorphosis of the stone to the statue, and then of the statue to
the woman – as the artist's suicide. The poem ends with "the sweet
woman-statue" [230] clasping the dead body which had given her life, had
given her its life. Yet even here Beddoes has a last twist . . . Pygmalion has
joined the happier dead' (p. 138). Beddoes's syntax perhaps untwists this
reading of death: 'Weeping' could (as Bush, Thompson and Ricks assume)
be her weeping over him; but following from 'He' (229–31), it could also
be the sculptor's – a reading that accords with the Ovidian tale, in which
Pygmalion marries his statue-made-woman.

*   *   *

fragment from *LOVE'S ARROW POISONED*

Humble Beginnings

Written in 1823–5 (*D*, p. 254); published in *K*, I.117; Gosse identifies the
intention for *Love's Arrow Poisoned* (*G*, II.256); text: *G*, II.284. The central
allusion is the fable of Romulus, founder of Rome. He and his twin Remus
were sons of Mars and Rhea, a vestal virgin. When she gave birth, she was
murdered and the babies thrown into the Tiber river; they washed ashore,
were suckled by a she-wolf, then found by a herdsman and his wife who
brought them up. For a discussion of the 'sound effects that set the teeth
on edge', see Ricks, *Force of Poetry*, p. 144.

*   *   *

from *TORRISMOND*

ACT I.III 'Come then, a song; a winding, gentle song' and 'How many
times do I love thee, dear?' Written in 1824; first published in *K*, I.68–9;

text: *G*, II.237–8. In the one act completed, the profligate Torrismond, beloved by Veronica, is cast off for dissolute behaviour by his stern father, the Duke of Ferrara. Scene iii opens with a quatorzain in Veronica's voice, followed by the song, 'perhaps [Beddoes's] sweetest and most ingenious', Gosse suggests (*G*, I.xxxix); it was included in *Outidana* (*D*, p. x).

ACT I.IV 'O father, father! must I have no father'. Written in 1824; first published in *K*, I.84–5; text: *G*, II.251–2. In this last scene, Torrismond has been falsely accused of treason. Beddoes's father died when he was five.

*　*　*

from *THE SECOND BROTHER*

Begun in 1823 and abandoned in 1825, with a little more than three acts drafted. 'I really think it is very bad,' Beddoes told Kelsall (*D*, p. 601); first published in *K*, vol. I. The songs, composed late 1824–early 1825, were saved for *Outidana* (*D*, pp. x, xxviii). The play's fraternal antagonists are Orazio and Marcello, younger brothers of the Duke of Ferrara. The youngest, Orazio, is rich, handsome, popular, hedonistic; imagining himself a deity's son (82), he scorns the world, and believes himself next in line for the dukedom. When, after years of wandering abroad, Marcello, the 'second brother' and actual heir, returns disguised as a beggar, Orazio spurns him in the street.

ORAZIO'S ENTRANCE FROM ACT I.I Text: *G*, II.178–9. 'Here is one of those dim strange shadows of a coming evil fallen suddenly amid banquet lights, which make such wild music and take so powerful hold of the imagination in more than one of the old English dramatists,' remarked *The Athenaeum* 1247 (20 September 1851), p. 989.

OPENING OF ACT I.II 'Will you sleep these dark hours, maiden', in the banquet hall; text: *G*, II.185–6. Orazio is moody and weary of the festival.

SIMILE FROM ACT II.I Text: *G*, II.200. Orazio's neglected wife Valeria cannot sleep; when her maiden attendant tells her of her sensations of being in love, Valeria responds with 'Innocently thought'. Strachey admires the way Beddoes 'can pass in a moment from tiny sweetness to colossal turmoil' (*Books and Characters*, p. 260).

*　*　*

songs from *DEATH'S JEST-BOOK*

Written 1825–8; then revised and augmented, 1829–44; left incomplete
at Beddoes's death. First published, anonymously, by Kelsall: *Death's
Jest-Book, or The Fool's Tragedy* (London: William Pickering, 1850);
reprinted in *K*, vol. II. Kelsall and Gosse assimilate the post-1828 revisions;
in *D*, Donner sorts out the texts to distinguish the version Beddoes trans-
mitted to Procter and Kelsall in 1829, and in *Plays and Poems* (1950) he
presents the 1828 text.

Widely admired as Beddoes's major work and claim to fame, had *Death's
Jest-Book* been published in 1829, guesses Jonathan Wordsworth, 'the age
would have belonged to Beddoes' (Introduction to *The Brides' Tragedy*,
p. 9). 'I do not intend to finish that 2nd Brother,' Beddoes wrote from
Oxford to Kelsall, 8 June 1825, 'but am thinking of a very Gothic-styled
tragedy, for w^h I have a jewel of a name – DEATH'S JESTBOOK – of course
no one will ever read it' (*D*, p. 604; cf. *K*, I.xlii). Part drama, part anthology
of poetry, this work 'hangs tantalizingly beyond conventional literary boun-
daries: neither a stage-play nor the collection of lyrics anthologists have
made of it, relentlessly derivative in language and formidably original in
conception, Romantic in form and bitterly post-Romantic in sensibility'
(Richardson, *Mental Theater*, pp. 154–5).

Beddoes was experimenting with a bold and original combination of
poetic and medical semiotics. 'The studies . . . of the dramatist & physician
are closely, almost inseparably, allied; the application alone is different,' he
writes to Kelsall in December 1825, asking 'is it impossible for the same
man to combine these two professions, in some degree at least?' and stays
to answer, 'it still remains for some one to exhibit the sum of his experience
in mental pathology & therapeutics, not in a cold technical dead description,
but a living semiotical display, a series of anthropological experiments,
developed for the purpose of ascertaining some important psychical prin-
ciple – i.e. a tragedy . . . Death's Jest-book goes on like the tortoise – slow
& sure; I think it will be entertaining, very unamiable, & utterly unpopular'
(*D*, pp. 609–10; cf. *K*, I.li–lii; *G*, I.xxvi). A few months later he tells Kelsall,
'my thoughts all run on points very uninteresting to you – i.e. on entrails
and blood-vessels; except a few which every now and then assumed an
Iambic form towards the never-ending Jest-book . . . if my friend Death
lives long enough to finish his jest-book, it will come with its strangenesses
– it contains nothing else – like an electric shock among the small critics'
(1 April 1826; *D*, pp. 616–17; cf. *K*, I.lv; *G*, I.xxvii). In October 1826 he
wishes that Kelsall 'might look over my unhappy devil of a tragedy, which
is done and done for: its limbs being as scattered and unconnected as those
of the old gentleman whom Medea minced & boiled young. I have tried

20 times at least to copy it fair, but have given it up with disgust' (*D*, p. 620; cf. *K*, I.lviii; *G*, I.xxvii). It 'is finished in the rough', he tells Procter on the 9th; 'I will endeavour to write it out and send it to you before Easter' (*D*, p. 626; cf. *K*, I.lxv).

After receiving it early in 1829, Procter was unable to interest publishers, and urged substantial revisions. Beddoes was annoyed and discouraged (letters: 19 and 30 April 1829; *K*, I.lxxxii–lxxxvii; *D*, pp. 642–3, 645). Before this news he was full of glee with Kelsall (who always liked the play, but also, to Beddoes's disappointment, urged revisions; see *D*, pp. 644–45): 'Poor M^r professor Milman will really be quite horrified, if he should live to read the J. book, at the thought that a fellow of so villainous a school as its author should have been bred up at Oxford during his poetical dictatorship there. I hope he will review me' (27 Feb. 1829; *D*, p. 640; cf. *K*, I.lxxx; Beddoes reported earlier to Kelsall that Milman had denounced him 'as one of a "villainous school" '; *D*, p. 604). In July 1830 he informs Kelsall that he has put the play aside (*D*, p. 647; cf. *K*, I.lxxxviii) but by January 1831 it is clear that he is back at work on 'the never ending D's J. b.', reflecting carefully on various dramas as he begins 'to alter the ill-fitted play' (*D*, pp. 651–4; cf. *K*, I.xcii–xcvii); and in 1837 he conveys his hopes of publishing it, even as he images himself ruefully: 'And so I weave my Penelopean web and rip it up again: and so I roll my impudent Sisyphean stone' (*D*, pp. 662, 666; cf. *K*, I.ciii; a letter to Kelsall with new text shows that he is still fiddling with 'the endless J. B.' in 1844 (*D*, pp. 674–5; cf. *K*, I.cvi).

The 'historical nucleus', he tells Kelsall in October 1827, 'is an isolated and rather disputed fact, that Duke Boleslaus of Münsterberg in Silesia was killed by his court fool AD 1377, but that is the least important part of the whole fable. I have dead game in great quantities' (*D*, p. 636; cf. *K*, I.lxxvii, II.173). The genre is Elizabethan revenge tragedy / theatre of the absurd, set in fourteenth-century Egypt and Silesia. Isbrand and Wolfram, sons of the deposed Duke of Münsterberg, know that the usurper Duke Melveric has murdered him and their sister (Melveric's wife). Isbrand is angry with Wolfram for his affection for Melveric, whom Wolfram sets off to free from imprisonment by Moors in North Africa. With him in prison is Sibylla whom both he and Wolfram love. When the Duke discovers that Sibylla loves Wolfram, he plots his death, despite the fact that he has sworn himself Wolfram's brother-knight. After his first attempt fails, Wolfram not only forgives him but also saves his life. Then the Duke treacherously kills him. Later, when the Duke tries to summon the spirit of his late wife, with whom (it turns out) he is still in love, Wolfram's spirit appears instead – Isbrand having figured out how to exchange the corpses. Sibylla falls in love with Wolfram's spirit, then kills herself to join him. Isbrand, in the Duke's court in the guise of a fool, bides his time before attempting to

murder the Duke and his sons. He usurps the dukedom, turns tyrannical
and is assassinated by a political extremist. Wolfram's ghost drags the Duke,
still alive, into the world of the dead. 'There are more hideous apparitions
and revolting incidents in this drama than in the wildest imaginings of
superstition or romance' (*Blackwood's Edinburgh Magazine* 80 (October
1856), p. 447). 'This poem, or collection of poems – bizarre, grotesque,
often hauntingly lovely and certainly mordantly witty – demonstrates
that despite the frequently noted influence of the Jacobean playwrights,
[Beddoes's] true peers may actually be Poe and Baudelaire' (Thompson,
Beddoes, p. 9).

OPENING OF ACT II.1 *Dirge* (If thou wilt ease thine heart), written *c.* 1828
(*Donner*, p. 208); published in 1850 and *K*, II.38-9; text: *G*, II.38-9. In
D Donner inserts a new scene i and places this as the opening of II.ii.
Procter thought this dirge for Wolfram 'one of the most charming in the
English language' (*BB*, p. 50). 'This exquisitely worded dirge [is] as soft
and melodious as anything in Herrick or Ben Jonson's Masques,' said
Blackwood's 80 (October 1856, p. 449); 'he is really most successful in sweet
and graceful lyrics like this *Dirge*', suggests Symons (*Figures*, p. 127).
Reading these lines in *The Athenaeum*'s review of the play (26 October 1850),
Henry Beaufort Walmisley (organist of Holy Trinity Church, Westminster)
asked the publisher for permission to set it to music; it was sung by
Catherine Hayes in concert in 1851 and subsequently published (*BB*,
pp. 54, 151).

ACT III.III Lines 282-337, with *Song by Isbrand* (Squats on a toad-stool
under a tree); text: *G*, II.69, 80-82; line numbers keyed to *G*; cf. *D*,
pp. 432-3 (III.iii.310-67). *Song* was written in 1825-9. The nightingale's
song has various origins in pain and suffering: in the story in Ovid's
Metamorphoses, Philomela, her tongue cut out by her rapist Tereus to
prevent disclosure, is changed into a nightingale (Book VI); in another
fable, the nightingale's breast is pierced by a thorn. Charlotte Smith's
mournful *To a Nightingale*, its poet identifying with the bird, was one of
the best known of her *Elegiac Sonnets*. 'Procter has denounced the carrion
crows [Act V]: – I can spare them,' Beddoes wrote to Kelsall in April 1829,
'but he has also as "absolutely objectionable" anathematized Squats on a
toadstool, with its crocodile, – which I regard as almost necessary to the
vitality of the piece. What say you? . . . If you say it is nonsense – I and
Isbrand reply that we meant it to be so: and what were a Fool's Trag.
without a tolerable portion of nonsense? I thought it consistent with the
character and scene' (*D*, p. 645; cf. *K*, I.lxxxvii and letter to Procter, *D*,
p. 644). 'One of the most haunting songs in the play is actually about
reincarnation, in its grotesque form of rebirth into animals' (Frye, *English*

Romanticism, p. 64). Coxe gives a fine reading to the 'excess, conceit, and surrealism' that informs the song's parody of themes elsewhere stated 'with seriousness and full conviction': 'Man has no place in the world of this song, nor will Beddoes allow his "new Dodo" any of man's features save his feet – two out of six, on equal ground with a pig's and a hen's' ('Mask of Parody', pp. 259-61).

SONGS FROM ACT IV.III. 159-278 'We have bathed / We have crowned' was written in 1825-9, and 'A cypress-bough' *c*. 1828 (*Donner*, p. 208); 'Lady, was it fair of thee' (1829-1830) replaced another song, 'Maiden, thou sittest alone above' (see *D*, pp. 100, 459), 'wʰ was *very* commonplace and ought to have been abused by you', Beddoes chides Kelsall, July 1830 (*D*, p. 648, cf. *K*, I.xc). Our text is the revised one: *G*, II.113-18 (first published in *K*, II.124-8); for the first sequence, see Donner's *Plays and Poems* (1950), pp. 299-302. 'I put these three [songs] purposely together: one something Moorish [i.e., Thomas Moore] in rhythmus and expression, not equal to him (his song style is the best *false* one I know and glitters like broken glass . . .) but a tolerable watery imitation; – the 2ⁿᵈ a specimen of the bad but very popular sentimental if – oh! – and – why? lovesong; and the 3ʳᵈ in the style wʰ, to my conviction, is the right and genuine one in tone, feeling, and form, for a song of the tender and more poetic kind. No critic however will see what I meant' (to Kelsall, *D*, pp. 648-9; cf. *K*, I.xc). The scene is a garden, under the windows of Amala's apartment. Beloved by both of the Duke's sons, Athulf and Adalmar, she is plighted to Adalmar:

> brave, honourable is my bridegroom,
> But somewhat cold perhaps. If his wild brother
> Had but more constancy and less insolence
> In love, he were a man much to my heart. (III.ii.16 ff.)

Athulf has just taken poison in despair, and lies writhing, listening to the music of her bridal serenade, while Adalmar, having discovered him thus, seeks a magician to undo the poison. When Athulf is restored (later in IV.III), he kills Adalmar in order that 'Amala alone shall be my love'; Beddoes described this to Kelsall as 'the Cain & Abel scene' (*D*, p. 645; cf. *K*, I.lxxxvi).

ACT V.IV Lines 49-121 and 222-31, with songs 'My goblet's golden lips are dry', 'Old Adam, the carrion crow', *Dirge* (We do lie beneath the grass). Text: *G*, II.142-5, 149. 'Old Adam' was written late in 1824 (letter: *K*, I.xl; *D*, p. 598) and *Dirge c.* 1828 (*Donner*, p. 208). 'In the amazing final scene, where a *danse macabre* painted on the walls of the crypt comes to life, Athulf stabs himself, Isbrand is killed by a blind devotee of liberty . . . and Wolfram, who replaces Isbrand in the last scene, pulls the Duke down into his grave, "still alive, into the world of the dead", "dead" being

appropriately the last word in the play' (Frye, *English Romanticism*, p. 58).
Siegfried is Isbrand's confidant; Wolfram is a ghost by this point. Pound
was unusual in regretting the (still) prevalent practice of quoting 'Old
Adam' out of its context, whereby the song 'loses a deal of its force' (*Selected
Prose*, p. 382) – a context we restore. Phlegethon (93) is a 'blazing' river in
Hades, hence hydrophobic. 'The emptiness of the drama is redeemed only
in the self-parody of its songs, the best of which are triumphs of Romantic
irony,' says Bloom (*Visionary Company*, p. 443), citing 'Old Adam' as an
example. 'When Beddoes writes a dirge, it is sung by the dead, not the
living, but either way we are in the presence of something which is at once
a monologue and a dialogue' (Ricks, *Force of Poetry*, p. 161).

*   *   *

Another Letter to the Same [Bryan Waller Procter]

Undated; the envelope is postmarked 13 March 1826; the title in *G* (I.32)
reads 'March 13, 1836' but this must be a misprint (cf. *D*, pp. 86, 613);
text: *G*, I.32–4. Dramatist and poet Bryan Waller Procter ('Barry Cornwall';
1787–1874) was a close friend, second only to Kelsall; among other friends
Procter counted Coleridge, Wordsworth, Scott, Southey, Leigh Hunt,
Charles Lamb, Byron, Shelley, Keats, Hazlitt and Dickens. His *Poetical
Works* were collected in 1822, and he contributed to many of the periodicals,
including *The Literary Gazette*, *London Magazine*, *The New Monthly* and
The Athenaeum; in 1832 he became Metropolitan Commissioner of Lunacy,
a post he held until 1861 ('a high office in the government of the kingdom
of ye moon, upon which as a retired member of the company of poets he
was I suppose accustomed to draw liberally', Beddoes jested: *D*, p. 678).
The Pierides (21) are the Muses. The Juggernaut (39–40) is the Hindu
fire-god, whose image was borne on an enormous car; it was the custom of
worshippers to cast themselves in front of the wheels and be crushed. The
imagery of lines 43–4 is historically pertinent: slavery was still legal in
British colonies, and several European countries had yet to outlaw the
trade. The story of 'satiric pathos' (45–6) is *Death's Jest-Book*. Emperor
Hadrian (Adrian) spent his last hours composing a playfully melancholy
poem; Renaissance writer and churchman Thomas More famously jested
on the scaffold (60–63). Uncypress (65) is a verb of Beddoes's invention
('demystify'); Momus (67) is the god of mockery among the ancients. 'The
taunting triplet [71–3] depends not only on the nimbly blasé way in
which the familiar and contemptuous pun on "quick" is bred, but also on
Anatomy's being the subtle medical training as well as the unsubtle skeleton
itself' (Ricks, *Force of Poetry*, p. 137). 'How curiously different [*Death's
Jest-Book*] proves from that which is announced, and probably believed in,

by Beddoes in his letter of verse to Procter,' Browning remarks to Kelsall; 'he was to despoil Death of his terror, strip him of his dart, & so on, – make him the "fool of the feast" [54]: he does exactly the reverse, materializes and intensifies the horror, and frightens one to death at dying' (22 May 1868: *BB*, p. 104).

The Ghosts' Moonshine

Written in 1826–9; first published and titled in *K*, I.175–6; text: *G*, I.38–9. The title is from the refrain of 'Old Adam'. To 'the poetry of death' Beddoes 'adds the accent of persuasiveness . . . there is little finality to the grave and the frontiers between life and death are badly kept' (Snow, *Eccentric*, p. 137).

Lines written in the album of one who had watched the progress of the American and French revolutions

Written in 1825–7; text: *K*, I.lxv, lxix–lxx; Donner's title (*D*, p. 97). Beddoes mentions to Kelsall that he is attending 'most interesting' lectures 'by Saalfeld on the history of the French Revolution. This man is a real historian & no bad orator' (*D*, p. 612; cf. *K*, I.liv). Kelsall and Gosse do not include this poem in their contents proper; Donner does (*D*, p. 97), giving it the now conventional title, adapted from the sentence immediately after the poetry. Beddoes's father was an unembarrassed supporter of the Republican (anti-monarchal) principles of the French Revolution, an enthusiasm that forced him to resign his lectureship at Oxford.

* * *

from *THE IVORY GATE*

Collected in 1847; written *c.* 1830–39 (*D*, pp. xi–xii), with the exception of or disagreement about particular pieces, noted below. In Greek legend false dreams issue through the ivory gate of Sleep (*Odyssey*, XIX.562; *Aeneid*, end of Book VI). At the end of his visit to England in 1847 Beddoes gave Kelsall 'for consideration' a 'packet . . . comprising prose compositions, – tales, serious, playful, and grotesque, set in a framework of "imaginary conversations", and interspersed with lyrical poems, – the whole entitled . . . "*The Ivory-gate for* 18—, *containing conversations and criticisms on life and art*"' (*K*, I.cxx). This title is anticipated in a letter to Kelsall, 15 May 1837: 'the Ivory Gate or lesser Dionysiacs – (my new book –)' (*K*, I.ci; *D*, p. 663). In March Beddoes told Kelsall that he was preparing for press 'a volume of prosaic poetry and poetical prose. It will contain half a dozen

Tales, comic, tragic, and dithyrambic, satirical and semi-moral: perhaps half a hundred lyrical Jews-harpings in various styles and humours, and the stillborn D. J. B. with critical and cacochymical remarks on the European literature, in specie the hapless drama, of our day. I am not asinine enough to imagine that it will be any very great shakes' (*D*, p. 659; cf. *K*, I.xcviii). One title-page for *Death's Jest-Book* reads: '*The Ivory Gate* . . . A story including *Death's Jest Book or The Fool's Tragedy* . . . *A dramatic Keepsake without engravings for 1838*' (*D*, p. 323); *The Keepsake* was one of the most popular of the gift-book annuals (see the note to Praed's *Lines*). That these volumes were typically graced with engravings involves Beddoes's disclaimer with a sarcastic pun on the many ungraved ghosts of the play.

Silenus in Proteus

Snow (*Eccentric*, p. 194) thinks this was written in 1825; first publication and text: *G*, I.86; *D* has variants: 'ivy-crowned' (2); 'sacred pair' (16). Donner prints a prose note, by Beddoes, after the poem:

The fragments of which these lines are a free version are quoted, it is true, by Athenaius, Lucian, and Porson from the Myrmidones and have been placed by Wilkes and Droyssen to the second tragedy of the Achillean trilogy. I think, if the reader has no objection, that we can just as well leave them here, altho' Ernest might certainly have forgotten that they belong to another play of Aeschylus which he might also have seen during his residence at Athens. (*D*, p. 137)

Lucian was a second-century Greek satirical writer; Richard Porson (1759–1808) was a Greek scholar and translator at Cambridge. The characters named in this 'genial, robust, and grotesque' poem (Bush, *Mythology*, p. 193), are: Silenus, leader of the satyrs and foster-father of Bacchus, god of wine (he rode an ass because he was too drunk to walk); the shape-changing god Proteus (Silenus is 'in' Proteus, perhaps, because he contemplates the changing shapes of the physical body); Ariadne, princess of Crete who, having helped Theseus to escape death in the infamous labyrinth on the expectation of marrying him, was abandoned by him on the isle of Naxos, whence Bacchus rescued her and made her his mistress; and Semele, Bacchus's mortal mother.

Lord Alcohol

Snow (*Eccentric*, p. 194) thinks this was written in 1825; first publication and text, with title: *G*, I.83–4 (the epigraph is from *D*, pp. 137–8); Gosse calls the poem 'vivid and extraordinary' (*G*, I.xxxix). This 'fine and sober poem . . . describes all the effects of intoxication, but suffers from none . . . The prosody is a marvel of perfection' (*Donner*, p. 334).

Dream-Pedlary

Written in 1829–30; first published in *K*, I.184–6; text: *G*, I.46–8.
Saintsbury's *History of English Prosody* (London: Macmillan, 1910) accords
its prosody the highest praise (III.150); see also *Donner*, pp. 276–81. Gosse
calls this the 'most exquisite' of Beddoes's songs (*G*, I.xxxix); 'for once
Beddoes speaks with the voice of the living who yearn for the dead, rather
than that of the dead yearning toward life'; the poem is an 'admirable fusion
of wistfulness of spirit with the fragile and delicate touch of its workmanship'
(Snow, *Eccentric*, p. 145).

Love-in-Idleness

Kelsall's title; first published in *K*, I.189–91; text: *G*, I.50–52. Snow likes
the 'saucy sophistication' (*Eccentric*, p. 141). The central allusion is to the
agent of confusion in *A Midsummer Night's Dream* (II.i.165–72): plotting
against Titania, Oberon recalls having seen 'the bolt of Cupid' pierce

> a little western flower,
> Before milk-white, now purple with love's wound,
> And maidens call it love-in-idleness
>
> . . .
>
> The juice of it on sleeping eyelids laid
> Will make or man or woman madly dote
> Upon the next live creature that it sees.

The flower is Heartsease, *Viola tricolor*.

Dirge (Let dew the flowers fill)

Written in 1830–39 (*D*, p. 120), first published in *K*, I.203; text: *G*, I.62–
3. Donner's longer version (*D*, p. 134) inserts after line 4: 'Since the still
soul fled –'; after line 5: 'The lily being dead –'; and adds four lines to the
end:

> Aye, doubt'st thou of the reading there,
>   About all nature's movements seek:
> Thou'lt find Death has his dimples every where,
>   Love only on the lovely cheek.

An Unfinished Draft (A thousand buds are breaking)

Written in 1830-39 (*D*, p. 120); first published in *D*, p. 140. The refrain (10, 20 and 29) repeats the penultimate line from Sibylla's *Dirge* in *Death's Jest-Book*, V.iv (above).

Song of the Stygian Naiades

Written in 1837; first published *K*, I.199-201; text: *G*, I.59-60, with the prose epigraph from *D* (p. 136); 'the title seems to be Kelsall's' (ibid.). In this poem of 'romantic whimsy' (Bush, *Mythology*, p. 193), Beddoes is the first to place these nymphs in the Styx, the river encircling the classical underworld. Its god is Pluto, abductor of Proserpine, a goddess he makes his involuntary queen, even as (in Beddoes's imagination) he continues to indulge his desire for ever-new earthly maidens. The Furies are avengers; Beelzebub is a denizen of hell, and in Milton's *Paradise Lost* Satan's lieutenant. Gosse cites this and 'Old Adam' as instances 'of fancy combined with grisly humour, of a class in which Beddoes has no English competitor' (*G*, I.xxxix). Bloom thinks this 'the finest' of Beddoes's lyrics: 'The poem's content and its delicate, complex metrical form are deliberately inconsonant' (*Visionary Company*, p. 444).

Thanatos to Kenelm

Snow thinks song was written in 1837 (*Eccentric*, p. 195); first published in *K*, I.212-13; text: *G*, I.68 (titled in both, *Stanzas from The Ivory Gate*). The prologue was written in 1830-39 (*D*, pp. xi-xii), first published in *D*, pp. 141-2. 'Thanatos, the wonderful beautiful maiden . . . is Kenelm's companion in the woods of Madeira – hardly a mortal maiden' (Dykes Campbell's note: *D*, p. 700). After the Titan gods were ejected from heaven, they were imprisoned under the earth; cypress (9) is an emblem of death. Line 13 echoes Coleridge's *Kubla Khan*, 'the caverns measureless to man' (27).

The Phantom-Wooer

Written in 1844-8 (*D*, p. 153); first published in *K*, I.178-9; text: *G*, I.40-41. Donner deletes the apostrophe from 'snakes' (lines 8 and 18; *D*, p. 159), but it makes sense as an elision (snakes' poisoned note). A ghost's courtship of a living lover was the subject of Bürger's popular ballad *Lenore*, adapted by Scott as *William and Helen*; murdered Lorenzo also courts Isabella thus in Keats's *Isabella*. But where these poems dramatize a ghoulish return, in Beddoes's imagining the 'horrible is thrust into the background that it may be only the more effective, is disguised in a honey sweetness that it may carry the more suggestion . . . it gives one a cerebral chill' (Snow, *Eccentric*, p. 136). 'Here is the very essence of Beddoes's lyrical voice: delicate, intimate, slyly persuasive, sinister, insidious, and above all perversely seductive' in its 'hypnotic quality' (Thompson, *Beddoes*, p. 113).

Threnody (Far away)

Written in 1844–8 (*D*, p. 153); first published and titled in *K*, I.219–20; text: *G*, I.74.

* * *

songs and fragments from the revisions of *DEATH'S JEST-BOOK*

The additions to Act I were written between 1838 and 1844, the others at various dates between 1829 and 1844 (*D*).

Song from the Ship (To sea, to sea!) First published and text: *G*, II.14; added to the end of I.i. To Isbrand's disgust, Wolfram has departed with his knights to win the release of the Duke from prison. Isbrand's contemptuous response is a 'grotesque' that 'deforms the happy lyric' (Wilner, *Gathering the Winds*, p. 93).

A Beautiful Night First published and titled in *K*, I.117; text: *G*, II.161–2. Donner locates this as a revision for I.ii (*Plays and Poems*, p. 339) and adds these 7 lines to the end:

> Whereby the King and beggar all lie down
> On straw or purple-tissue, are but bones
> And air, and blood, equal to one another
> And to the unborn and buried: so we go
> Placing ourselves among the unconceived
> And the old ghosts, wantonly, smilingly,
> For sleep is fair and warm –. (p. 341; cf. *D*, p. 492)

A Voice from the waters (The swallow leaves her nest); written in 1844 (*G*, I.xxx; *D*, p. 675); first published in 1850; then in *K*, II.37; text: *G*, II.37–8. With professions of his love for Sibylla, Wolfram has just died from wounds received from the Duke. *D* shows no stage directions and the title is *Song from the Waters*. 'How suddenly Beddoes has shifted from the quiet of swallow and soul to the *storm* of ghosts' (Snow, *Eccentric*, p. 138).

A Subterranean City (I followed once a fleet and mighty serpent) First published and titled in *K*, I.119–20; text: *G*, II.163; Donner says the lines were intended for III.i, at line 40 (*D*, p. 421); but later (*Poems and Plays*, pp. 357–8) he suggests II.iv; here he titles the lines *Ziba's Origin* and in both adds a first line, 'I found him in a buried city I went by torchlight through –.' The Duke is describing where he found this Egyptian necromancer who will assist him in his attempt to raise his wife from the dead (and who restores Athulf from his near-fatal self-poisoning). 'What lies below the familiar earth, and seemingly within the mind's depths, is a natural power so vast and brute that it appears in a form that can only swallow human life and hope in the alien enormity of its evolutionary destruction' (Wilner, *Gathering the Winds*, p. 86).

The Slight and Degenerate Nature of Man (Pitiful post-diluvians) First published and titled in *K*, I.121; text: *G*, II.164–5; identified as intended for V.i by Donner (*Poems and Plays*, p. 365). The subtitle may be translated, 'An antediluvian speaks' (antediluvian: 'one living before the flood').

INDEX OF TITLES AND FIRST LINES
(Some poems are known by several titles.)

THOMAS HOOD

A poor old king, with sorrow for my crown 141
According to metaphysical creed 81
'As the twig is bent, the tree's inclined' 90
Autumn 23
The Ballad of 'Sally Brown, and Ben the Carpenter' (*Faithless Sally Brown*) 9
Ben Battle was a soldier bold 23
The Bridge of Sighs 147
Death in the Kitchen 36
The Death-Bed 16
Domestic Asides; or, Truth in Parentheses 47
The Dream of Eugene Aram, the Murderer 38
Fair Ines 11
Faithless Nelly Gray 23
Faithless Sally Brown (*The Ballad of 'Sally Brown, and Ben the Carpenter'*) 9
Farewell, Life! My sense swim 150
A Friendly *Epistle to Mrs Fry in Newgate* 17
Gold! Gold! Gold! Gold! 140
I like you, Mrs Fry! I like your name! 17
I really take it very kind 47
I remember, I remember 22
I saw old Autumn in the misty morn 13
I saw pale Dian, sitting by the brink 15
I'm going to Bombay 58
It is not death, that some time in a sigh 16
The Lament of Toby, the Learned Pig 64
The Last Man 26
Lear 141
Mary's Ghost 33
Miss Kilmansegg and Her Precious Leg 67
   Her Pedigree 67

Her Birth 69
Her Christening 75
Her Childhood 79
Her Education 81
Her Accident 85
Her Precious Leg 90
Her Fame 93
Her First Step 95
Her Fancy Ball 96
Her Dream 105
Her Courtship 110
Her Marriage 114
Her Honeymoon 122
Her Misery 130
Her Last Will 134
Her Death 136
Her Moral 140
Miss Kilmansegg took off her leg 105
My dear, do pull the bell 48
My hair is brown, my eyes are blue 58
Now the Precious Leg while cash was flush 134
O heavy day! oh day of woe! 64
O PHILANTHROPIC men! 61
O saw ye not fair Ines? 11
Ode: Autumn 13
Ode to Mr Malthus 48
Ode To the Advocates for the Removal of Smithfield Market 61
Of all the spirits of evil fame 96
Oh! what is that comes gliding in 52
One more Unfortunate 147
Our youth! our childhood! that spring of springs! 79
A Parental Ode to My Son, Aged Three Years and Five Months 56
Ruth 35
Sally Simpkin's Lament; or, John Jones's Kit-Cat-Astrophe 52
She stood breast high amid the corn 35
Song (The stars are with the voyager) 35
The Song of the Shirt 141
Sonnet: – Death 16
Sonnet. – Silence 15
Sonnet Written in Keats's Endymion 15
Stanzas (Farewell, Life!) 150
Stanzas (I remember, I remember) 22

Supposing the Trunk and Limbs of Man 95
The autumn is old 23
The horse that carried Miss Kilmansegg 85
The moon – the moon, so silver and cold 122
The stars are with the voyager 35
There is a silence where hath been no sound 15
There's a murmur in the air 144
Thou happy, happy elf! 56
Though Shakspeare asks us, 'What's in a name?' 75
'Tis a stern and startling thing to think 136
To gratify stern ambition's whims 93
To trace the Kilmansegg pedigree 67
To Waterloo, with sad ado 53
Trim, thou art right! – 'Tis sure that I 36
'Twas in the middle of the night 33
'Twas in the prime of summer time 40
'Twas in the year two thousand and one 26
'Twas morn – a more auspicious one! 114
A Waterloo Ballad 53
We watch'd her breathing thro' the night 16
What different dooms our birthdays bring! 69
When leaving Eden's happy land 110
Who hath not met with home-made bread 130
With fingers weary and worn 141
The Workhouse Clock 144
Young Ben he was a nice young man 9

WINTHROP MACKWORTH PRAED

A look as blithe, a step as light 159
Anticipation 218
Arrivals at a Watering-Place 204
At Cheltenham, where one drinks one's fill 190
Ay, here such valorous deeds were done 235
The Bachelor 172
Beauty and Her Visitors 216
The Belle of the Ball-Room, An Every-day Character 237
Chaunt I 180
Chaunt II 183
Childhood and His Visitors 214
Dear Alice! you'll laugh when you know it 243
Deep is the bliss of the belted knight 221

The Fancy Ball 193
Good-Night to the Season 186
Good-night to the Season! 'tis over! 186
I heard a sick man's dying sigh 200
I looked for Beauty: – on a throne 216
I play a spade: – such strange new faces 204
I think, whatever mortals crave 180
In these gay pages there is food 240
Julia, while London's fancied bliss 166
Lady, there's fragrance in your sighs 219
The Last Quadrille 245
Laura 159
The Legend of the Haunted Tree 221
A Letter from a Lady 245 *in London to a Lady at Lausanne (The Talented man)* 243
A Letter of Advice 197
Lines Written for a Blank Page of 'The Keepsake' 219
My Partner 190
Not yet, not yet; it's hardly four 245
O'er the level plains, where mountains greet me as I go 186
Oh, yes! he is in Parliament 218
Once on a time, when sunny May 214
One More Quadrille (The Last Quadrille) 245
Our Ball 208
School and Schoolfellows 211
Sleep, Mr SPEAKER; it's surely fair 247
Stanzas To the Speaker Asleep 247
Stanzas Written in Lady Myrtle's Boccaccio 240
The Talented Man 243
The world pursues the very track 183
Time's Song 186
To Julia 166
Twelve years ago I made a mock 211
Twenty-eight and Twenty-nine 200
Waterloo 235
Years, years ago, – ere yet my dreams 237
You tell me you're promised a lover 197
'You used to talk,' said Miss Mac Call 193
You wonder that your ancient friend 172
You'll Come to Our Ball (Our Ball) 208
You'll come to our Ball; – since we parted 208

THOMAS LOVELL BEDDOES

A cypress-bough, and a rose-wreath sweet (Athulf's song) 292
A ghost, that loved a lady fair 312
A ho! A ho! (*Song* from *The Brides' Tragedy*) 266
A lake 271
A thousand buds are breaking 309
Alfarabi 257
And many voices marshalled in one hymn 271
And must I wake again? (Floribel's soliloquy from *The Brides' Tragedy*) 268
Another Letter to the Same [Bryan Waller Procter] 297
As an almighty night doth pass away 301
Athulf's song (A cypress-bough, and a rose-wreath sweet) 292
A Beautiful Night 315
Cluster of pregnant berries, pressed 262
Come then, a song; a winding, gentle song (Veronica's quatorzain from *Torrismond*) 283
A Crocodile 270
Death Sweet (*Sweet to Die*) 270
Death's Jest-Book 287, 314
Dirge (*Dirge for Wolfram*) (If thou wilt ease thine heart) 287
Dirge (Let dew the flowers fill) 308
Dirge (*Sibylla's Dirge*) (We do lie beneath the grass) 296
A Dirge (To-day is a thought) 274
Dream of Dying 271
Dream-Pedlary 305
Far away 313
Floribel's soliloquy from *The Brides' Tragedy* (And must I wake again?) 268
The Ghosts' Moonshine 299
Hard by the lilied Nile I saw 270
How lovely is the heaven of this night (*A Beautiful Night*) 315
How many times do I love thee, dear? (from *Torrismond*) 283
Humble Beginnings 282
Hymn (*Midnight Hymn*) 271
I followed once a fleet and mighty serpent 316
If there were dreams to sell 305
If thou wilt ease thine heart 287
Innocently thought . . . thou are like the daisy in Noah's meadow 286
Is it not sweet to die? for, what is death 270
Isbrand's Song (*Song by Isbrand*) 288

It is midnight, my wedded 299

Lady, was it fair of thee (*Song by Siegfried*) 291

A Lake 271

The Last Man (fragments) 270

Let dew the flowers fill 308

Lines Written at Geneva; July, 1824 273

Lines Written by the Author of 'The Bride's [sic] *Tragedy', in the blank-leaf
    of the 'Prometheus Unbound'* 269

*Lines written in the album of one who had watched the progress of the
    American and French revolutions* 301

Lord Alcohol 304

Love-in-Idleness 307

Love's Arrow Poisoned (fragment) 282

Midnight Hymn 271

My goblet's golden lips are dry (from *Death's Jest-Book*) 294

O father, father! must I have no father? (from *Torrismond*) 284

Oh those were happy days, heaped up with wine-skins 303

Old Adam, the carrion crow (*The Song that Wolfram heard in Hell*) 295

Outidana or effusions, amorous, pathetic and fantastical 273

The Phantom-Wooer 312

Pitiful post-diluvians! from whose hearts 316

Poor old pilgrim Misery (song from *The Brides' Tragedy*) 265

Proserpine may pull her flowers 310

Pygmalion 275

The Second Brother 285

Shall I be your first love, lady, shall I be your first 307

Shivering in fever, weak, and parched to sand 271

Sibylla's Dirge (We do lie beneath the grass) 296

Silenus in Proteus 303

The Slight and Degenerate Nature of Man (Pitiful post-diluvians!) 316

Snow-drop of dogs, with ear of brownest dye 274

So thou art come again, old black-winged Night 262

Song by Isbrand (*Isbrand's Song*) (Squats on a toad-stool under a tree) 288

Song by Siegfried (Lady, was it fair of thee) 291

Song by Siegfried (My goblet's golden lips are dry) 294

Song by Thanatos (The mighty thoughts of an old world) 311

Song from *The Brides' Tragedy* (A ho! A ho!) 266

Song from *The Brides' Tragedy* (Poor old pilgrim Misery) 265

Song from *The Second Brother* (Strew not earth with empty stars) 285

Song from *Torrismond* (How many times do I love thee, dear?) 283

Song from the Ship (To sea, to sea!) 314

Song from the Waters (The swallow leaves her nest) 315

Song of the Stygian Naiades 310

Song that Wolfram heard in Hell (Old Adam, the carrion crow) 295

Songs in Amala's Garden (from *Death's Jest-Book*) (We have bathed, where none have seen us 290; We have crowned thee queen of women 290; Lady, was it fair of thee 291; A cypress-bough, and a rose-wreath sweet 292

Sonnet: To Tartar, a Terrier Beauty 274

Squats on a toad-stool under a tree (*Song by Isbrand*) 288

Stanzas (from *The Ivory Gate*) 303

Strew not earth with empty stars (*Song* from *The Second Brother*) 285

A Subterranean City (I followed once a fleet and mighty serpent) 316

Sweet to Die (*Death Sweet*) 270

Thanatos to Kenelm 311

The hour is starry, and the airs that stray 273

The mighty thoughts of an old world 311

The swallow leaves her nest 315

There stood a city along Cyprus' side 275

Threnody (*Far away*) 313

To a Bunch of Grapes 262

To Night 262

To sea, to sea! the calm is o'er 314

To Tartar, a Terrier Beauty (*Sonnet*) 274

To-day a truant from the odd, old bones 297

To-day is a thought, a fear is to-morrow 274

Torrismond 283

'Twas in those days 257

'Twas on a fragrant bank I laid me down 264

An Unfinished Draft (A thousand buds are breaking) 309

Valeria's simile from *The Second Brother* (Innocently thought) 286

A Voice from the waters (*Wolfram's Dirge*) (The swallow leaves her nest) 315

We do lie beneath the grass 296

We have bathed, where none have seen us (*Song* at Amala's wedding) 290

We have crowned thee queen of women (*Song* at Amala's wedding) 290

Who tames the lion now? 304

Why, Rome was naked once, a bastard smudge 282

Will you sleep these dark hours, maiden 286

Wolfram's Dirge (*A Voice from the waters*) 315

WRITE it in gold – a Spirit of the sun 269

Written in the album of one who had watched the progress of the American and French revolutions 301